'The author of this important book carefully and gently tries to conceive of a simultaneously anti-racist and feminist response to the phenomenon of gang rapes in France and in Australia. Aware of the extremely controversial nature of the events that she has chosen to analyze, she scrutinizes the sometimes self-contradictory ways in which national public discourses and the media have constructed the figures of the victims and of the perpetrators, imposing their definition of the kind of violence that rape constitutes in this case. This books helps us disentangle the disturbing and often hidden connections between the racialization of migrant and Muslim bodies, secularism and certain types of nationalism, feminism and postcolonization.'

Mireille Rosello, *University of Amsterdam, Netherlands*

'This book is critically important. Sexual violence is becoming the central strategy of anti-immigration arguments. So it is crucial for both anti-racist activists and anti-rape activists to think through the complex intersections of racism and sexism that occur both in the public discourses and in real world cases. Grewal provides a balanced analysis that takes each of these concerns seriously, criticizes both left and right responses, and charts a path for the difficult work of talking about both race and rape with clarity and courage.'

Linda Martín Alcoff, *City University of New York, USA*

Racialised Gang Rape and the Reinforcement of Dominant Order

This path-breaking book provides a comparative analysis of public discourses in France and Australia on a series of highly mediatised racialised gang rapes that occurred during the early to mid-2000s. These rapes led to intense public debate in both countries regarding an apparent 'gang rape phenomenon' associated with young men of Muslim background. By comparing the responses to similar instances of sexual violence in two very different Western liberal democracies, this book explores the relationship between constructions of national, gender and ethnic identity in modern, developed nations of the West. The impact of immigration and cultural diversity on communities has become an issue of central concern to Western liberal democracies in recent years. With greater movements of people than ever before, and large temporary migrant populations who have not 'gone home', the discourse of a 'crisis of national identity' is a feature of many democracies in the West. At the same time, in a supposedly 'post-feminist' age, the focus of debates around women's rights in these democracies has increasingly been the extent to which the cultural values of immigrant and ethnic minority populations are compatible with the espoused gender equality of the West. Through an analysis of these rapes, Kiran Kaur Grewal identifies certain commonalities as well as interesting points of divergence within the two nations' public discourses. In doing so she identifies the limitations of current debates and proposes alternative ways of understanding the tensions at play when trying to respond to acts of extreme sexism and violence committed by members of ethnic minority communities.

Kiran Kaur Grewal is a Senior Research Fellow at the Institute for Social Justice, Australian Catholic University. Her areas of research specialisation include post-colonial and feminist legal theory, sexual violence, human and women's rights and the relationship between law and subaltern struggles for justice. Prior to joining ACU, Kiran was a lecturer in human rights and socio-legal studies at the University of Sydney. She has also worked with Amnesty International and as a litigation lawyer in Sydney, specialising in administrative and immigration law. Kiran is also the author of the book, *The Socio-Political Practice of Human Rights: Between the Universal and the Particular.*

Studies in Migration and Diaspora
Series Editor
Anne J. Kershen
Queen Mary University of London, UK

Studies in Migration and Diaspora is a series designed to showcase the interdisciplinary and multidisciplinary nature of research in this important field. Volumes in the series cover local, national and global issues and engage with both historical and contemporary events. The books will appeal to scholars, students and all those engaged in the study of migration and diaspora. Amongst the topics covered are minority ethnic relations, transnational movements and the cultural, social and political implications of moving from 'over there', to 'over here'.

Polish Migration to the UK in the 'New' European Union
After 2004
Edited by Kathy Burrell

Gendering Migration
Masculinity, femininity and ethnicity in post-war Britain
Edited by Louise Ryan and Wendy Webster

Contemporary British Identity
English language, migrants and public discourse
Christina Julios

Migration and Domestic Work
A European perspective on a global theme
Edited by Helma Lutz

Negotiating Boundaries in the City
Migration, ethnicity, and gender in Britain
Joanna Herbert

The Cultures of Economic Migration
International perspectives
Edited by Suman Gupta and Tope Omoniyi

Racialised Gang Rape and the Reinforcement of Dominant Order

Discourses of Gender, Race and Nation

Kiran Kaur Grewal

LONDON AND NEW YORK

First published 2017 by Routledge

2 Park Square, Milton Park, Abingdon, Oxfordshire OX14 4RN
711 Third Avenue, New York, NY 10017

Routledge is an imprint of the Taylor & Francis Group, an informa business

First issued in paperback 2018

Copyright © 2017 Kiran Kaur Grewal

The right of Kiran Kaur Grewal to be identified as author of this work has
been asserted by her in accordance with sections 77 and 78 of the
Copyright, Designs and Patents Act 1988.

All rights reserved. No part of this book may be reprinted or reproduced
or utilised in any form or by any electronic, mechanical, or other
means, now known or hereafter invented, including photocopying and
recording, or in any information storage or retrieval system, without
permission in writing from the publishers.

Notice:
Product or corporate names may be trademarks or registered trademarks,
and are used only for identification and explanation without intent to
infringe.

British Library Cataloguing in Publication Data
A catalogue record for this book is available from the British Library

Library of Congress Cataloging in Publication Data
Names: Grewal, Kiran Kaur, author.
Title: Racialised gang rape and the reinforcement of dominant order :
    discourses of gender, race and nation / Kiran Kaur Grewal.
Description: Abingdon, Oxon ; New York, NY : Routledge, 2017. | Includes
    bibliographical references and index.
Identifiers: LCCN 2016029982 | ISBN 9781472414991 (hardback) |
    ISBN 9781315580548 (ebook)
Subjects: LCSH: Gang rape—Australia—Case studies. | Gang rape—
    France—Case studies. | Racism. | Feminism.
Classification: LCC HV6558 .G748 2017 | DDC 364.15/320944—dc23
LC record available at https://lccn.loc.gov/2016029982

ISBN: 978-1-4724-1499-1 (hbk)
ISBN: 978-1-138-36807-1 (pbk)

Typeset in Times New Roman
by Apex CoVantage, LLC

Contents

List of cases	viii
Series editor's preface	ix
Acknowledgements	xi

1	Introduction	1
2	The 'Sydney gang rape' trials	10
3	'White angels' and 'Muslim misogynists': Survivor and rapist discourses	33
4	'Talking race or racism'? Public responses to the rapes	60
5	'Girls like you'	84
6	*La Squale*: 'Feminising the *banlieue*'	105
7	The (sexually) lost *banlieues* of the Republic	117
8	The '*beurette*' and the Republic	137
9	*Ni Putes Ni Soumises*: The new 'voice of the *banlieue*'?	163
10	Conclusion	186

Bibliography	196
Index	215

List of cases

R v AEM (jnr) and AEM (snr) and KEM, unreported judgment, District Court of New South Wales, 23 August 2001.
R v Aem; R v Kem; R v MM [2002] NSWCCA 58 (13 March 2002).
R v Bilal Skaf; R v Mohammed Skaf [2004] NSWCCA 37 (6 May 2004).
R v Brown and Others [1993] 2 All ER 75.
R v Chami, M. Skaf, Ghanem, B. Skaf, unreported judgment, District Court of New South Wales, 15 August 2002.
R v Chami, M. Skaf, Ghanem, B. Skaf [2004] NSWCCA 36 (7 April 2004).
R v L (1992) 174 CLR 379.
R v MSK and Mak [2004] NSWCCA 308 (6 September 2004).
R v MAK; R v MSK [2004] NSWSC 319 (22 April 2004).
R v MAK; R v MSK [2006] NSWSC 237 (5 April 2006).
R v Mak; R v MSK [2006] NSWCCA 381 (30 November 2006).
Wilson [1996] 3 WLR 125.

Series editor's preface

As both a lawyer and an academic, the author of this book has worked in the fields of international human rights, criminal justice and social activism. Accordingly she is highly qualified to approach the underlying themes of this book, one which has as its spine gang rapes carried out in France and Australia in the early years of the twenty-first century. Kiran Kaur Grewal approaches her critical analysis of the media reporting and writings on the 'Sydney gang rapes' and the gang rapes in the *banlieue* of Paris through a lens which incorporates feminist and anti-racist writing and theory. She applies a number of tools to the deconstruction of the discourses on these attacks, including the in-depth analysis of autobiographies written by two victims of gang rape – one French and one Australian. In this, as elsewhere in the book, she highlights the differences in the political, social and media responses to the assaults, ones which demonstrate the very essence of the two countries' nationhood.

Grewal suggests that the reaction to the 'Sydney gang rapes' emphasises the nature of Australia's evolution and its colonial/postcolonial culture, which are manifest in the country's racialised patriarchal positioning of (White) women's bodies as 'symbols of the nation'. In contrast she considers that the French 'exclusion of discourses of race' places the emphasis on gender and sexuality, whilst race becomes a heavily underlined subtext. The contrasts continue in the highlighting of the whiteness of the victims in Australia, where the 'only female voices in the debate were White', and the non-White identity of the women in the *banlieue*. In France, the female voices to emerge were those of women of ethnic origin. One of whom, Samira Bellil, produced an autobiography, which Grewal claims was heavily influenced by the journalist Josée Stoquart, and consequently could not be read as an independent, unbiased 'self' version of her rape. In contrast, that of its counterpart in Sydney was solely the work of one of the victims, Tegan Wagner – an account which, Grewal argues, though having its limitations, was free from external influence. In her detailed analysis of the two books, Grewal again highlights the differences between these two victims, one an autonomous and independent White woman, the other, as Grewal describes her, 'a passive, voiceless entity', a casualty of ethnic origin. What comes through throughout this book is the positioning of the female victims, their whiteness or non-White otherness, and the concern

x *Series editor's preface*

of the author that commentaries on the rapes were unable to combine 'anti-racist and feminist responses'.

In both countries the perpetrators of the crimes were labelled 'Muslim' men. In Australia they became known as the 'nasty migrants', individuals that had rejected the morals and culture of their host – White – society. Whilst not categorising '*les tournantes*' as nasty migrants, the gang rapists from the *banlieue* were seen as personifying all the negative characteristics of the orientalist culture, and as such they were deemed outsiders – not citizens of the Republic. Both Australia and France have a colonial history, though of a different nature, but while muted in one and articulated in the other, skin colour and ethnicity have played their part in the stigmatisation and reporting of the violent crimes carried out in both countries against members of their female population.

Whilst this book focuses on events that took place more than a decade ago, the cultural and religious differences between Occident and Orient in the context of sexual mores were highlighted yet again when on New Year's Eve 2015 it was reported that 1,000 men of North African appearance sexually assaulted 'western women' in the German city of Cologne – it should be noted that no accusations of actual rape were made at the time. In other European countries Muslim males have been recorded as committing sexual crimes on White females; in Sweden it was reported that 77 percent of rapists were found to be Muslim immigrant men. In England, in 2012 and again in 2015, Pakistani men were charged with grooming and trafficking young White females. In the recording and reporting of these crimes there is a difficult path to tread, one which has to be negotiated with care in order to disconnect colonial racialisation and female subordination from the post-colonial environment. It is essential that the voices of female victims be heard and that those of the 'Muslim Other' are not ignored, in order that the demonisation of *all* young Muslim men is not allowed to take hold. In producing this book Kiran Grewal has provided a much needed framework within which these discourses can take place.

Anne J. Kershen
Queen Mary University of London

Acknowledgements

I would like to thank Professor Murray Pratt, Associate Professor Catriona Elder, Dr Christina Ho and Dr Lucy Fiske for their helpful comments on various drafts of this book. I would also like to thank Professor Mireille Rosello and Dr Maja Mikula for their positive feedback and encouragement.

Finally, I would like to dedicate this book to Ahmad Khavafipour, who reminds me every day why this project is so important.

1 Introduction

The starting point for this book is a series of gang rapes that provoked widespread public debate in both Australia and France in the early 2000s. On 29 July 2001 the headlines '70 Girls Attacked by Rape Gangs', 'Police warning on new race crime' and 'Caucasian women the targets' appeared on the front page of the Melbourne-based tabloid the *Sun-Herald* with details of rapes that had been committed approximately a year before in Sydney (hereafter referred to as the 'Sydney gang rapes'). What followed were a series of highly publicised criminal trials, intense media coverage and commentary, political debate, and law reform.

While one victim emerged to speak for herself, for the most part the commentary was provided by media figures who simultaneously critiqued the inadequacies of state responses to sexual violence *and* immigration and multicultural policies. This 'racial' element, it was argued, was relevant not only because of the identity of the accused rapists but also the alleged racist statements made to the victims during the rapes and one accused's attempt to run a cultural defence in court. Meanwhile certain journalists drew links between the 'Sydney gang rapes' and a phenomenon of gang rape in the *banlieues* – the poor housing estates on the outskirts of the major cities – in France, known as '*les tournantes*'. The term, a *banlieue* slang, literally translates as 'taking turns' or 'passing around' and is most frequently used to refer to the sharing of a marijuana joint.

In France '*les tournantes*' became the subject of media attention after the release of the film *La Squale* in November 2000. This film, set in a Parisian *banlieue*, portrayed a gang of young men (mainly, though not exclusively, from immigrant backgrounds) who lure and gang rape young women (also from immigrant backgrounds). The first reports of criminal trials involving '*les tournantes*' followed in 2001, and in 2002 a gang rape survivor Samira Bellil published her autobiography, *Dans l'enfer des tournantes* (*In the hell of the Tournantes*). Bellil's story alongside the murder of a young woman named Sohane Benziane, who was set alight by young men in a cellar in the *banlieue* in which she lived, provided the focus for the emergence of a new women's movement '*Ni Putes Ni Soumises*' ('Neither Sluts Nor Submissives') in February 2003. This movement, launched by a nation-wide march, has since established itself as a prominent voice on issues of gender and the *banlieue* within the French public sphere.

2 Introduction

As someone committed to both a feminist and anti-racist politics, I initially found it very difficult to respond to these rapes. On the one hand I was deeply suspicious of the newfound 'feminist' sensibility being expressed by many. It did not sit well with the depressing statistics that showed the continued high prevalence and simultaneous underreporting of rape (Willis 2006, p. 1; Fougeyrollas-Schwebel 2005) or the process of attrition that led to about 5 percent of rape allegations resulting in successful prosecution (Willis 2006; Kelly, Lovett and Regan 2005). These figures were both common across many industrialised nations (including the two in this book) and contrasted strikingly with the treatment of other violent crimes. I was also too familiar with the feminist literature on rape that highlighted both the continuum that existed between normative conceptions of heterosexuality and rape and the ways in which this was frequently masked in social and legal responses through the deployment of rape myths that set up ideal victims and perpetrators and 'normal' gender and sexual behaviour (Cossins 2000; Wood and Rennie 1994; MacKinnon 1987; Vance 1984; Brownmiller 1975). The image of violent gang rape committed by non-White/low class men seemed to conform too neatly to the type of rape that has traditionally caused public outcry.[1]

At the same time, I was unconvinced and in fact troubled by the dominant critique of the outrage the rapes had provoked. In both France and Australia, left-wing academic commentators drew on the concept of 'moral panic' to argue these rapes were being used as a tool to further demonise and marginalise young, socio-economically deprived ethnic minority men. While certainly this was an important component of the debate, it did not seem capable of distinguishing between the instrumentalist uses of these rapes by some commentators for other (nationalist or racist) agendas and the rightful anger and indignation expressed by others: in particular, the rape survivors themselves and anti-rape advocates. Legislation passed in New South Wales (hereafter 'NSW') in response to the rapes preventing accused rapists from personally cross-examining their victims was for many an important feminist victory. So too the establishment of a feminist association providing services specifically to women in the *banlieue* – however it was characterised within broader French society – was welcomed by some women as addressing a real need they had that had been ignored for too long. To simply label any condemnation of the rapes and the rapists as 'racist' or feeding a moral panic seemed an injustice to the victims and many other women.

Ultimately these rapes seemed to suggest an impasse. Why was it so difficult to conceive of a simultaneously anti-racist and feminist response? At the same time, the comments of one of the Australian judges in his sentencing remarks, comparing the 'Sydney gang rapes' to those committed in times of war (discussed further in Chapter 2), opened up another dimension. I began to wonder how these rapes sat alongside the emergent recognition of 'rape as a weapon of war'. Drawing on feminist analyses of the symbolic role that women's bodies in general and rape in particular have played in demarcating the boundaries of the community and the nation, what was the significance of these gang rapes to French and Australian articulations of national identity? This book is an attempt to answer these questions.

Introduction 3

On the use of the term 'discourse'

Before turning to the content of the book I want to first explain the ways in which I use the term 'discourse' throughout. On the one hand it is clearly informed by a Foucauldian understanding of the constitutive and power-inflected process of linguistic knowledge production. On the other I also draw on the notion of discourse as used by Pierre Bourdieu to describe a form of embodied social action/interaction. As he elaborates upon in detail in *Ce que parler veut dire* (1982), discourse is reliant on the ability of the individual speaker to properly utilise language, his or her perceived authority or legitimacy within the particular field (an aspect, which is influenced by both the embodiment of the appropriate rules of the field *and* the performance itself) and finally by the conditions of the market. While focused on the site of social action/interaction, this definition also points to the significance of relations of power. This, in the context of Bourdieu's work more generally, indicates an understanding of social action that is neither completely free of – nor completely regulated by – existing structures of domination.

In fact Bourdieu's conceptual framework is crucial to my analysis as I seek to explain the interaction between the structural forces of historical and contemporary institutions of power and the potential for agency of individual actors. As I will explain further a little later, Bourdieu's concept of habitus as a form of 'embodied history' or 'embodied social structure' (Collins 1998, p. 728) within which individuals simultaneously perform their agency and are constrained by a set of social structures is particularly useful. So too is his description of 'symbolic violence': a form of domination that relies on the unconscious complicity of the oppressed in the process of their own oppression[2] (Bourdieu 1998, 2003). I also draw on his notions of 'the field' as a site for the exercise of force and for struggle (Pileggi and Patton 2003, p. 317), 'cultural capital' or 'a general facility for interacting appropriately in various contexts, a knowledge of and an ability to use the rules of engagement in particular settings' (Lewis 2003, p. 170), and 'illusio': 'participants in a field's investment in the values of the field, even if they are perpetual "losers"' (Pileggi and Patton 2003, p. 320).

Analysing 'public discourses'

Using critical discourse analysis (CDA) as my methodology, in this book I explore the ways in which the gang rapes described above were represented and responded to across a range of public discourses in each country. I accept the argument of a number of leading CDA scholars that the role of the mass media is a crucial one in the production and reproduction of dominant discourses (Macdonald 2003, p. 1; Jaworski and Coupland 1999, p. 216; Fairclough 1995b, p. 3; Kuhn 1995, p. 1; Jakubowicz, Goodall, Martin, Mitchell and Seneviratne 1994), which is why I dedicate a chapter to each of the two nations' mainstream media debates on the rapes.[3] However I also consider public discourse to entail more than just the media, which is why I seek to draw on popular culture, political and legal responses as significant social texts.

4   *Introduction*

Through engaging with a wide array of texts from different genres I hope to present as rich a portrayal as possible of the complex questions of politics, identity and representation that emerged in response to these rapes. It has been convincingly shown that the public sphere is never simply homogenous or singular (Couldry and Dreher 2007). Rather multiple public discourses will generally compete, with some given more prominence. There will also be conflict and contradictions between these public discourses. It is to capture this complexity that I have sought to analyse a variety of socio-cultural texts. By drawing on an array of sources from media, popular culture, law and politics, I argue that the fullest picture of Australian and French society can emerge. This is important to do justice to the specificity of the two nations and the role these rapes played within them.

The value of in-depth comparative study

One of the problems with much of the existing literature on ethnic diversity in liberal democracies and ongoing problems of sexism and racism is that they tend to treat 'the West' and the 'Western liberal democracy' as a monolithic category.[4] This often obscures rather than illuminates what is at stake in particular debates and the assumptions they are built upon. It can also lead to flawed points of comparison.

For example, as I will show a little later, the French academy, political sphere and general public are often frustrated by what they see as an attempt by the Anglophone world to impose the latter's prejudices, assumptions and histories when discussing issues such as race relations in France. I agree that debates such as that over *laïcité* (secularism) in France cannot be understood using the dominant framework employed by those of us operating in an Anglophone postcolonial context (and the particular type of multicultural politics it has spawned). It requires a much better understanding of the particular place of the school and other civic institutions within the national mythology of the Republic.

It also requires engagement with the particular social and political investment in the language of 'Republican values'. This potentially better explains the ways in which debates about secularism become inextricably connected with feminist debates in ways that are not entirely disingenuous. By the same token, to properly understand the significance of debates over the place of Islam, the *hijab* and gender equality in French society requires much greater attention to the particular form that French imperialism took. So too the fact that the 'problem' of immigration is generally framed around the place within the Republic of people from former colonies, particularly Algeria, points to the unresolved legacies of both the colonial project and the process of decolonisation.

Equally, while Australia as a former British colony has adopted the language and policy of multiculturalism, it is important to understand how this concept operates differently in Australia to the United Kingdom. As various scholars have now demonstrated, the politics and logics of the settler colony require us to think differently about both the colonial and postcolonial experience (Veracini 2010; Wolfe 1999). As I will show, the settler identity has significant implications for both race and gender politics in the supposedly 'postcolonial'[5] Australian state. So too does Australia's position as an 'outpost of British civilisation' in Asia.

As former British settler colony turned multicultural immigrant state, Australia has long struggled to articulate a national identity, caught between the unresolved dispossession of Indigenous Australians and the shifting demographics resulting from migrant flows. This has produced intense anxiety around maintaining Australia as 'White' throughout much of the nation's history. While overtly racist policies of the past – such as the denial of citizenship to Indigenous Australians and the White Australia immigration policy designed to exclude Asian immigration – gave way from the late 1980s to a language of multiculturalism, cultural tolerance and celebration of diversity, the legacies of this past continue to be felt. On the one hand there are regular backlashes against any suggested change to an Australian identity built on 'Anglo-Celtic' origins: most vividly demonstrated in the rejection of the policy of multiculturalism in preference for an assertion of 'Australian values' by the Howard government in the early 2000s. On the other the essential 'whiteness' of Australia has been rearticulated as benevolent rather than racist: founded on principles of decency and equality (mateship and a 'fair go') that rationalise and legitimate the exclusion of some (who do not adhere to these values) (Elder 2007; Hage 2003, 1998; Rutherford 2000; Vasta and Castles 1996).

National specificities also impact on the particular sites and voices that emerge as significant in public discourses. This was clearly evident in responses to the rapes. Perhaps as a result of the impact of 1968 on the French national imaginary, or perhaps dating back earlier than that to the revolutionary tradition, there has been much more public space in France given to social movements. The public *manifestation* (demonstration/march) remains a common and powerful form of popular mobilisation, even taking into account the decline in faith in collective action being witnessed globally. By contrast, in Australia we see the channeling of important social policy questions through the framework of the law: a process which Ran Hirschl (2008) has described as 'the judicialization of politics'. Australia's common law tradition – the legacy of its British colonial past – may explain why courtroom trials played such a central role (Friedman 2004, p. 696). The reporting on sexual violence cases has also generally been less in France than in Anglo-Saxon countries as a result of a greater emphasis in the Republican tradition on keeping sexuality outside of the public sphere (Ticktin 2008; Duparc Portier 2006; Fassin 2006, 2003). Indeed, many of the trials in France involving *tournantes* were conducted in closed session (Robert-Diard 2002; Tourancheau 2002b; Chambon 2001a; de Langhe 2001; du Tanney 2001).

The particular place of politically engaged cinema (O'Shaughnessey 2007) and the acclaimed genre of *banlieue* cinema that has emerged since the 1980s (Orlando 2003) also provided the backdrop against which the film *La Squale* could gain prominence and credibility within French public debate. Meanwhile the figure of the 'ordinary Australian', so central to Australian articulations of national identity (Elder 2007; Galligan and Roberts 2004), has been capitalised on by social commentators who claim the right to speak precisely because of their *lack* of specific expertise. This is contrasted with the much greater space given to 'expert' or

6 *Introduction*

'professional' voices in the French context – school teachers, social workers, health professionals – all historically valuable contributors to the colonial 'civilising mission'. The role of the 'native informant' is also arguably a much more established one in the context of a European colonial project that sought to 'civilise' than the more overtly annihilatory logic of the settler colony.

By providing a comparative study of these two distinct examples of liberal democratic societies I want to highlight and explore the differences in the two nations' responses. This might help us better understand how particular histories continue to inform the present: for example, the prominence given to an overtly feminist response to the rapes in France (and this feminism's particular Republican form) or the much lower inhibition demonstrated in Australia to identifying 'race' as a feature of the rapes.[6] At the same time, by being attentive to detail I expose some interesting and perhaps surprising (or not?) points of convergence and commonality that emerge in both contexts. This is also important, as this might allow us to say something productive about the Western liberal democratic state more generally and the possibilities for intersectional emancipatory politics within it.

The particular problem of the 'Muslim man'

On the one hand I am inclined to say that many of the arguments I make in relation to how the 'young Muslim man' is constructed can equally apply to other marginalised and racialised groups. For example, in Australia we have repeatedly seen public outcry about the levels of violence against women and children in Indigenous communities that follow similar patterns of pitting anti-racist and feminist discourses against each other. Similarly, there are parallels to be drawn in the ways in which *banlieue* men are characterised within French popular imaginary and the images of Black men of the 'ghetto' in the US (a point I make in later chapters).

However, I think it is also important to maintain attention to the significance of the rapists being linked to some sort of 'Muslim' identity as it tells us something important about the particular contemporary moment. The particular dynamics of the debates in Australia and France point to the distinct forms that discourses of race, gender and the place of difference within the nation take. Nonetheless, they also point to a certain common construction of the Muslim man as a sexual predator and civilisational threat. This highlights a striking universality and longevity – at least across the West – of the orientalist imagery Edward Said so evocatively described back in 1978 as a product of imperialism. It also seems to support the argument made by Poynting and Morgan (2012) of a dangerous transnational character to Islamophobia that is fueled and facilitated by processes of globalisation and geopolitical power.

Although this book focuses on events that took place within a particular time period in the recent past (the early 2000s), the arguments I make in this book are in some ways more relevant than ever. In the wake of new incidents of 'Islamic terrorism' – notably the attacks in Paris in January and November 2015 and the rise of the extremist Islamic militant organisation ISIS – the construction of the Muslim as a violent threat to 'civilisation' has become a cemented feature of

Introduction   7

popular public discourse across much of the industrialised West. Moreover this threat is specifically gendered and sexualised, drawing on imagery that dates back much earlier than 2001 and the 9/11 attacks on the World Trade Centre.

A particularly crude representation was provided recently by right-wing Polish magazine *wSieci*, which carried a cover entitled, 'Islamic Rape of Europe' and featured an image of a White woman, draped in the EU flag, being grabbed at by tanned, black-haired male arms (www.news.com.au/finance/economy/world-economy/cologne-is-every-day-europes-rape-epidemic/news-story/e2e618e17ad-4400b5ed65045e65e141d). This linked to an ongoing furore in Germany regarding alleged correlations between the recent increased numbers of asylum seekers arriving from the Middle East and a rise in sexual violence. The debate was sparked in January 2016 when it was reported that groups of 'Arab looking' men had conducted coordinated sexual attacks on women across Cologne during the city's New Year's Eve celebrations (BBC 2016; McMah 2016; Miller 2016; Richards 2016). Since then there have been similarly ideologically charged battles to those I describe in this book between those seeking to refute the racially targeted, anti-immigrant reporting and protests of these rapes and those who assert the importance of responding seriously to sexism and sexual violence.

The German case is only the most recent in fairly constant public debate about the relationship between Muslim immigrants and the European/Western 'cultural values' of sexual equality and freedom.[7] By focusing on two particular sets of gang rapes and the discourses they provoked, I hope to offer a more general insight into both the construction and significance of the gendered and sexualised threat allegedly posed by Muslim communities in the West.

A note on terminology

At this point it is also important to say something about the terminology being used in this book. It will no doubt be already noted that the terms 'race', 'culture', 'ethnicity' and 'Muslim' seem to be deployed in ways that suggest a shared meaning. This is an intentional gesture designed to reflect the conflation of these concepts within much of the public discourse problematised and analysed later in the book. While it became fashionable from the 1980s on to prefer the term 'ethnicity' to 'race' as a means of distancing from the latter's dubious history of biologism, the reality is that the distinction between the two has been largely an artificial one. While ethnicity was supposed to reflect opportunity for choice and mobility, to provide individuals with greater control over their own identity construction, in fact this 'myth of choice' has largely been a fallacy.

Moreover new forms of racism have largely moved away from relying on biological explanations of difference and inferiority in favour of equally deterministic and hierarchical assertions based on culture. For this reason – in an effort to render visible the racism underlying many of the discussions of culture – I have generally chosen to use the language of 'race' rather than ethnicity. I also refer to the rapes as 'racialised' to convey the ways in which ideas and debates about race became inextricably linked to these rapes.

8   *Introduction*

It is also important to highlight the ways in which the marker of 'Muslim' has come to mean something other than simply a religious follower of Islam. In both France and Australia, as the later chapters will demonstrate, 'Muslim' was used as an ethnic/racial marker, often interchangeably with (in France) 'Arab' or 'Maghrébin' and (in Australia) 'Middle Eastern' or particular national identifiers (Moroccan, Pakistani, Lebanese, Algerian). It was also used to describe people born in France/Australia into families with Muslim backgrounds regardless of whether or not they in fact practised this faith, reflecting what Jim House has called the construction of 'hereditary Muslims' (1996, p. 224).

Structure of the book

Turning to an outline of the book, I will start by elaborating on how the issue of gang rape became one of intense public concern in Australia. As I have said above, much of the public attention on the 'Sydney gang rapes' centred around the criminal trials. Therefore, starting with a brief description of the rapes and their ensuing criminal trials in Chapter 2, I examine the judicial discourses through the judgments and sentencing remarks of the judges. This is followed in Chapter 3 by an analysis of the discourses of victims (namely Tegan Wagner, who as noted above wrote about her experience) and the rapists (as they presented themselves within the public arena). In Chapter 4 I move to analysing the responses to the rapes within political debate and the media. Finally, I dedicate a chapter to analysing the book on the final set of gang rapes by columnist and social commentator Paul Sheehan (Chapter 5).

I then turn to '*les tournantes*' in France. Starting with an analysis of the film that triggered public attention (*La Squale*) in Chapter 6, I then look at responses to the rapes as articulated through national print media (in Chapter 7). This includes perspectives ostensibly from both inside and outside of the *banlieue*. Finally, I turn to the voices of women from the *banlieue*: both the survivor account provided by Samira Bellil (Chapter 8) and the commentary of *Ni Putes Ni Soumises* founder and political figure Fadela Amara (Chapter 9).

The concluding chapter of the book seeks to draw out and contextualise the differences between the two countries' debates, as well as the interesting points of similarity. In particular I focus on the ways in which the two nations' specific colonial and national histories have served to shape their responses. At the same time, I point to the ways in which gender relations have become a key site for shoring up hegemonic articulations of the nation in many parts of the West. This is particularly the case with Muslim migrants through an identification of Islam as inherently antithetical to feminist values. Through the creation of this binary, I argue, patriarchal and civilisational hierarchies are reinforced. Finally, I return to my attempt at various stages of the book to explain how and why the performances and discourses of many of the non-White actors in the rapes reinforced rather than challenged this order even as this served to disempower them further. I do this through developing the concept of the postcolonial habitus which draws on both Bourdieu's work and that of literary scholar Vivek Dhareshwar (1989). What is revealed in the process is both a particular set of gender, sexual and racial constructions that give these rapes a meaning beyond simply horrific individual acts of violence and a striking conformity to these constructions to be found in *all* the actors' discourses.

Notes

1 Ian Law (2001), in his book analysing race in the media, dedicates an entire chapter to media reporting of rape. He concludes that those cases involving non-White rapists were over-represented in the UK media. He refers specifically to a gang rape case in the UK in 1997 that attracted extensive media attention, involving eight young men of various ethnicities accused of raping an Austrian tourist. Similarly to the 'Sydney gang rapes' the media justified the inclusion of race in the coverage on the basis that the accused were reported to have made racist remarks to the victim, including calling her a 'White bitch'. Other infamous gang rape cases are the US Central Park jogger rape case (Hancock 2003; hooks 1990) and more recently the 2012 and 2014 gang rape cases in the north of England identified as involving mainly '(South) Asian gangs' (see Tufail 2015 for a detailed discussion).

2 'ce sont des coups, en quelque sorte, qui s'exercent avec la complicité tacite de ceux qui la subissent et de ceux qui l'exercent, dans la mesure où les uns et les autres sont inconscients de subir cette violence'.

3 I have limited my discussion of media to print media for the sake of manageability. I also looked specifically at the major national newspapers, representing a cross-section of the political spectrum. In Australia the analysis looks at articles from the conservative broadsheet, *The Australian*; the more moderate broadsheet, *The Sydney Morning Herald* (and its sister newspaper in Melbourne, *The Age*); and the widely read tabloid *The Daily Telegraph*. In France I focused on centre-left broadsheet *Le Monde*, centre-right broadsheet *Le Figaro* and left-wing broadsheet *Libération*. There are of course limitations to focusing on only these select publications; however they hopefully provide an insight into the mainstream media discourse and, alongside the other public texts, can convey much of the dominant debate.

4 See for example, Charles Taylor (2011) writing in positive terms about liberal democracy; see also Sherene Razack (2008) for a much more critical analysis.

5 In fact I prefer the language of 'postcolonising' proposed by Aileen Moreton-Robinson (2003).

6 I remember upon arriving in France, when I would tell fellow academics the topic of my proposed research, receiving disapproving looks accompanied by a 'mais non Mademoiselle . . .' I was told that while it might be appropriate to speak about gang rape in racialised terms in Australia, it was most definitely not the case in France. This contrasted with the responses I received outside of the academy that saw immediate parallels. However see Fassin and Fassin (2006) highlighting the false divide often drawn in French debates between 'social' issues and 'racial' issues.

7 For more on the German case, see www.gatestoneinstitute.org/7557/germany-rape-migrants-crisis. Similar debates have raged in Sweden (www.news.com.au/finance/economy/world-economy/cologne-is-every-day-europes-rape-epidemic/news-story/e2e618e17ad4400b5ed65045e65e141d) and earlier in Norway (Steyn 2002). See also Grewal (2012a) for a discussion of debates in the Netherlands.

2 The 'Sydney gang rape' trials

Introduction

Although the apparent 'rape spree' by young Lebanese men in the south-west of Sydney was presented as involving one gang, in fact what have now come to be known as the 'Sydney gang rapes' involved three separate groups of men; the gang rape of two young women by three young men known as AEM Snr, AEM Jnr and KEM in 2001, the 'Skaf rapes' involving up to 14 men on different occasions and apparently orchestrated by a young man identified as Bilal Skaf during 2000, and a series of rapes perpetrated in 2003 by four Pakistani brothers known as the 'K brothers'. The five trials and 17 appeals that followed led to a period of intense public scrutiny of the criminal justice system in Australia. The legal proceedings were reported in minute detail over the next five years and instigated two major pieces of law reform.[1] Let me start with a brief description of each of the cases.

The first trials: R v AEM Snr, AEM Jnr and KEM 2001

The first of the 'Sydney gang rape' cases involved three young men convicted of raping two 16-year-old women after having lured them away from a train station back to the house of two of the men. Due to the accused entering pleas of guilty and an agreed set of facts being submitted by both the defence and prosecution, the trial took place in relative anonymity. A plea-bargaining arrangement was entered into, and the victims were not required to testify, although one of the victims chose to submit a victim impact statement. It was only following the sentencing judgment that this case sparked public controversy.

Prison sentences of six years, 18 months and five years seven months respectively were handed down on 23 August 2001. In sentencing the accused, District Court Judge Megan Latham remarked that based on the case law she did not consider the case to fall into the 'worst category' of sexual offence and referred to a number of mitigating factors including the accuseds' guilty pleas and their expressed contrition. Furthermore, while there were allegations of racial

The 'Sydney gang rape' trials   11

motivation made by one of the victims in her victim impact statement, Judge Latham commented:

> There is no evidence before me of any racial element in the commission of these offences; there is nothing said or done at any stage by any of the offenders which provides the slightest basis for imputing to them some discrimination in terms of the nationality of the victims. The circumstances giving rise to the offences have all the hallmarks of an opportunistic encounter . . .
>
> (*R v AEM (jnr) and AEM (snr) and KEM*, unreported judgment, District Court of New South Wales, 23 August 2001)

She equally dismissed the claim by KEM that he was not aware he had done anything criminally wrong because he was unfamiliar with the laws of Australia. Her Honour imputed this to be an attempt to excuse or minimise his behaviour.

What followed was intense media and political discussion, which centred around two issues; the first was the apparent trivialisation of the seriousness of gang rape reflected in Judge Latham's comments and the sentences handed down. The second was Judge Latham's insistence on erasing all racial/ethnic aspects, which contrasted with the various statements subsequently made by the victims to the media and with the apparent attempt to introduce a cultural defence by at least one of the rapists.

So intense was the media and public outcry that a NSW Parliamentary Library briefing paper specifically looking at the response to the AEMs and KEM case was issued in September 2001. In reviewing the debate, the conclusion reached by the authors of the briefing paper was that the case highlighted an ongoing divide between the judiciary and society in relation to sentencing procedures and lengths, but also that it further fuelled an area of increasing public concern: the relationship between ethnicity and crime (Johns, Griffith and Simpson 2001, p. 18). Unfortunately, the two issues became inextricably intertwined due in part to the fact that a new gang rape trial involving young men described as being of 'Lebanese origin' was about to begin: the 'Skaf trials'.

With this new trial due to start in late 2001, the AEMs and KEM case had the effect of pushing hastily drafted legislation through the NSW Parliament, which introduced a new offence: 'aggravated sexual assault in company' – commonly referred to in the media as gang or pack rape. With this new offence the available maximum sentence was increased from 20 years to life imprisonment. The Director of Public Prosecutions also appealed the sentences of both AEMs and KEM (as well as that of MM, the fourth perpetrator identified later). On appeal the Supreme Court stated that the sentences imposed by Justice Latham were 'manifestly inadequate given the high degree of criminality involved in the commission of the offences'. The Appeal Court increased the sentences to a total of 13 years, with a nine-year non-parole period for AEM Snr, 14 years with a ten-year non-parole period for KEM and 13 years with a non-parole period of ten years for AEM Jnr.

12   The 'Sydney gang rape' trials

The 'Skaf trials'

After the AEM and KEM case came the most notorious trials: those involving brothers Bilal (identified as the ringleader) and Mohammed Skaf. It was alleged that Bilal Skaf had orchestrated numerous gang rapes involving up to 14 men at a time. Through intercepting mobile phone messages and calls between the men, police were eventually able to link the rapes back to Bilal Skaf, and he was brought to trial for his involvement in three separate incidents on 10, 12 and 30 August 2000.

Ultimately Bilal Skaf made NSW and Australian history by being the first person convicted under the new legislation and sentenced to 55 years, the harshest sentence ever handed down for a crime other than murder. Through various appeals, this sentence was reduced to 31 years, but by this stage Bilal Skaf had become cemented in Australian public imaginary. As his own defence lawyer commented, he had become the 'brand name for a gang rapist' ('Skaf: "Brand Name" for gang rapist', *Sydney Morning Herald*, 22 June 2008).

He also remained a figure of public interest both during and after his criminal trial. In court it was alleged and widely reported that Skaf made threatening gestures to a co-accused (running his finger across his throat in a cutting action). His demeanour was also commented upon extensively by both the media and Justice Finnane in his sentencing remarks: the fact that he showed no remorse and seemed to be amused throughout the trial, 'conduct[ing] himself as if the proceedings were a joke' (ABC 2002c). Following his conviction Skaf remained in the news. In July 2003 the *Sun Herald* newspaper printed cartoons he allegedly drew depicting a gang rape scenario involving his ex-fiancée with the caption, 'Hurry up, man, there's 50 others waiting' (Mitchell and Sutton 2003).

Prior to this incident, in March 2002 he was charged with sending a threatening letter to Corrective Services Commissioner Ron Woodham, which was quoted in the media as stating, 'Don't take this as a threat but if all Muslims aren't released by January 2003 Australia and citizens will be in danger of bombing' (Gibbs 2003). His mother was banned from visiting him for two years following an attempt to smuggle letters to his fiancée out of the prison, and his father was accused of bribing prison officers $100 to speak to Skaf on the telephone. A further scandal emerged in September 2008 when it was reported in the *Sun Herald* that there had been an attempt to smuggle in a mobile phone to Mohammed Skaf, sparking a wave of measures to tighten security in NSW's jails (Carty 2008).

Alongside the various appeals and re-trials that ensued from the original convictions of Skaf and his co-rapists, these stories of the Skaf family's antics assured Bilal Skaf a permanent presence in the Australian media and even a profile in parliamentary debates. As the Melbourne newspaper, *The Age*, noted in 2003: 'If Skaf thought he would be left to rot quietly for the next four decades, he was wrong. Public scrutiny of his thoughts and actions have, if anything, increased . . .' The article went on: 'The Crown Prosecutor at his trials, Margaret Cunneen, said Skaf's crimes had left an indelible stain on the psyche of the citizens of NSW'. It was also reported in January 2007 that a film on the Skaf gang rapes was in pre-production stages and had received Federal and NSW funding, although whether the film should in fact be made was the source of renewed public and political debate (Chesterton 2007; Connolly and Moran 2007; 'Misgivings over gang rape film', *Sydney Morning Herald*, 29 January 2007; 'Be sensitive to rape victim filmmakers urged', *Sydney Morning Herald*, 28 January 2007), and ultimately it has not been released.

At the same time, it was also suggested that it was not only the horrific nature of Bilal Skaf's actions that led to his ongoing public profile: 'Eleven months [after his conviction] Skaf is still a useful political tool. His presence was felt during the March 22 [2003] NSW election campaign and he mentioned [sic] in any debate about sentencing and prisons' ('Rapist out of sight but not out of mind', *The Age*, 2 August 2003). The political responses to the 'Sydney gang rapes' will be discussed further shortly.

The 'K brothers'

In mid-2003 the trials began of four Pakistani brothers accused of having conducted three separate gang rapes involving four girls over the course of the previous year. This set of trials reflected the final in the 'Sydney gang rape' series but also gained its own notoriety due in part to the conduct of two of the brothers who refused legal representation in favour of representing themselves. The two brothers repeatedly argued that they were the victims of an 'anti-Muslim' conspiracy and utilised various well-publicised and often highly dramatic delay tactics including one of the brothers announcing to the jury that he had already been convicted of gang rape to force a mistrial, throwing fruit at the jury, attempting to physically attack the prosecution lawyers and two of the victims' mothers in court and seeking to assert a defence of mental incapacity by claiming Satan spoke to him. These incidents resulted in the trials taking three years to complete. Ultimately the brothers were convicted on various counts in a number of separate trials, receiving cumulative sentences of 26 years, 22 years, 22 years and 19 years. Their cases were the focus of two books: the first by media commentator Paul Sheehan entitled *Girls Like You*, in 2006a, and the second by one of their victims, Tegan Wagner, entitled *The Making of Me*, released in 2007 (both discussed in detail in later chapters).

Judgments as social texts

In their linguistic analysis of Canadian rape judgments, Coates et al. observe: 'The language used in legal judgments is not merely a reflection of individual thought; it is important in and of itself' (Coates et al. 1994, p. 189). Reading written legal judgments as discursive texts provides an opportunity to explore the common understandings drawn from both legal and broader societal discourses that serve to shape judges' comments and choice of language. Equally, various socio-legal researchers have demonstrated the symbolic value large public criminal trials have in *shaping* societal understandings of crime. This is true not only in relation to understanding what constitutes criminal activity but also what sorts of people

14 *The 'Sydney gang rape' trials*

properly constitute victims and perpetrators of crime (de Carvalho Figueiredo 2004; Ehrlich 2001; Lacey 2001; Bumiller 1998; Coates et al. 1994). In this section I propose a reading of the judgments in the three major 'Sydney gang rape' trials that explores both the assumptions on which the judges seem to rely in their reasoning and the ways their narratives in turn possibly contribute to creating/reinforcing these assumptions. In particular, I focus on the specific discourses of gender, sexuality, culture and nation that are drawn upon and (re)articulated.

Reinforcing normative gender identity

A key feature of many commentaries on the 'Sydney gang rapes' was their representation as reflecting an affront to notions of gender equality entrenched within Australian society. I will return to this argument in detail in Chapter 4. However, it is interesting in this light to consider how the Australian courts characterised the gender dimension of the crimes within their judicial comments.

Rape as 'opportunistic encounter': Justice Latham's remarks in AEMs/KEM

Of the three cases, the judicial remarks that produced the greatest public outcry were those of Justice Megan Latham in the AEMs/KEM case. This was due to Her Honour's comments – mentioned earlier – that the case did not fall into the most serious category of rape cases. This remark provoked not only a governmental response (the parliamentary briefing paper referred to previously) but also an amendment to the criminal law to include a new offence specifically directed towards gang rape.

While accusations of Her Honour's apparent trivialisation of the rapes became increasingly intertwined with her dismissal of the supposed 'racial' dimensions, what went completely unremarked upon was Her Honour's characterisation of the rapists' motivations. In trying to explain why she did not see the rapes as particularly egregious, Her Honour stated that this was in her view, 'an opportunistic encounter between a number of adolescent males, who had gone for a drive because they were bored . . . and two adolescent females, who found themselves stranded at night without transport home'.

The fact that Justice Latham puts the rapes down to acts of opportunism and boredom presents a troubling view of (heterosexual) masculinity. It seems to suggest that *all* young men, given the chance and with nothing better to do, could or would engage in sexual violence. Furthermore, Her Honour paints a typical scenario of feminine vulnerability (stranded young women) at the mercy of young men who retain the power to choose how they treat these women. Her Honour ultimately condemns the men for their behaviour noting that they 'indulged in a gross display of sexual misconduct, adopting a pack mentality whereby they exploited the victims' fear, vulnerability and isolation from each other' and also recognises the degree of humiliation encountered by the victims. However she concludes by stating, 'these young men placed their reputation for sexual conquest above the standards of ordinary human decency' (Unreported judgment, District Court of New South Wales, 23 August 2001). This presents a disturbing construction of normative male sexuality. The fact that Her Honour does not seem to question the legitimacy of what she terms 'a reputation for sexual conquest' – simply the men's decision to put this 'above decency' – leads to her potentially reinforcing an image of male sexuality as inherently predatory. Yet Her Honour is not alone in her presentation of the sexual interactions between men and women in this way.

Rape as miscommunication or deviance: Appeal court judgment in R v Aem; R v Kem; R v MM [2002] NSWCCA 58 (13 March 2002)

Overall Justice Latham provides a fairly matter-of-fact summary of the circumstances within which the rapes took place and provides little in the way of additional commentary. This can be contrasted with the remarks of the Appeal Court judges upon re-sentencing AEM Snr and KEM and the trial judges in both of the other 'Sydney gang rape' cases. A possible explanation for this was the intense media and public interest in the cases which required a clearer and stronger statement from the Courts. However, the way the Appeal judges chose to frame their discussion about the seriousness of the crimes raises problems of its own.

It is assumed that the decision by the Appeal Court to include further information regarding the circumstances of the rapes was considered necessary to justify the increased sentences.[2] However, the added detail is disturbing in its graphic nature. For example, not only are the sexual acts re-described, but the Appeal Court also quotes at length the remarks of the accused men to their victims:

- 'KEM made [victim] JH massage his shoulders saying, "You're good at that."'

(para. 16)

- 'MM entered the bathroom and he and KEM simultaneously forced their penises into JH's mouth whilst she was on her knees in the bath, saying to her "lick it" forcing her to perform fellatio on them at the same time. MM was berating her saying, "[y]ou're a sick bitch . . . enjoying this, see I told you, you would have fun."'

(para. 17)

The relevance of these descriptions is unclear. After all, they contribute little to assessing the violence or the victim's lack of consent necessary to establish the offence. The accuseds' subjective enjoyment or otherwise is not relevant to assessing their criminality. Furthermore, it is unlikely that in any other form of assault there would be reference to an accused's apparent pleasure in inflicting the injury (a point I will return to in a moment).

The only other possible effect of reproducing these comments is to demonstrate the level of deviance of the accused. Their words come to represent one of two

16 *The 'Sydney gang rape' trials*

versions of the classic rape scripts produced over and over again in social and legal discourse. The first is a form of communicative deficit in which the problem becomes a 'miscommunication' between the victim and accused in a consensual sexual encounter. The other version allows these statements to be seen as further evidence of the accuseds' depravity. This allows them to be classed as beyond the scope of any 'normal' man, reinforcing the belief that rape is an act reserved for perverts and sexual deviants. This would seem to fit with Wood and Rennie's suggestion that:

> [m]en want rape to stay in the realm of the reprehensible, a realm peopled by the deranged and the sick. This categorization is a useful accounting device. It effectively shifts attention away from the man; further *it denies the continuity between date and stranger rape, and between rape and acceptable sexual conventions.*
>
> (1994, p. 145, emphasis added)

The picture presented of the rapists in the Appeal Court judgment is certainly one of sexually depraved individuals. Their simultaneous performance of forced oral sex presents a particularly deviant image of their sexuality and, through the homoerotic undertones, calls into question their relationship with each other. Through this the reader is left with no doubt that these are not 'normal' men, which allows for the rapes to be classified as aberrations. In a manner similar to that identified by Michael Awkward's (1995) analysis of the responses to the Mike Tyson/Desiree Washington rape trial, the broader societal implications of the rapes are completely erased through the pathologisation of the individual rapists.

Rape as 'education': Justice Sully in R v MAK; R v MSK [2004] NSWSC 319 (22 April 2004)

However, of all of the 'Sydney gang rape' judgments, Justice Sully's closing suggestions are perhaps the most vivid example of the law's constitutive role in normative gender/sexual identity. In a section of his judgment entitled, 'Two matters collateral to sentence', aside from critiquing the legal reform, which removed the right of the accused to cross-examine their victims, Justice Sully also suggests an 'educational' initiative:

> The second matter which I wish now to raise concerns the triple O [emergency] call made by [victim] LS in the immediate aftermath of her dumping [by the 'K brothers' following the rape], in company with [victim] HG, at Campsie. The call was taped. . . .
>
> What can be heard on the tape is chilling in its depiction of what it really means to be a rape victim. From the moment when I first heard the tape, *I thought of it as an ideal educational aid warning young people, boys and girls alike, of the need to take care not to become in the one case a perpetrator, and in the other case a victim, of any form of sexual offence.* To that end I invited

The 'Sydney gang rape' trials   17

the learned Crown Prosecutor to take up that idea in the appropriate quarters.

(paras. 140 and 141, emphasis added)

His Honour goes on to note that this proposal was received favourably by the NSW Police force and as a result recommends that steps be taken as soon as possible to incorporate the tape into the existing child protection package sent out to schools. Aside from this seeming a rather extreme way of making a point (and one that excludes the possibility of male rape), the assumptions contained within Justice Sully's comments are significant. He goes on to explain how exactly he sees the tape being useful:

> In that connection, I venture the suggestion that the stark horror of what can be heard on the tape might be supplemented usefully by putting to an audience some simple propositions of fact.

For boys, the propositions might be to the following effect:

> [1] Forced sex of any kind with any woman or girl is not a game, or a prank, or a practical joke, or part of becoming or of being a man. It is, quite simply, a crime.
>
> [2] If you commit such a crime the high odds are that you will be found out, tracked down, and sent to gaol. Police experience and expertise, and scientific advances, are constantly making detection and punishment increasingly likely.
>
> [3] It is no excuse for a serious sexual crime that it was carried out by someone who was young; or weak-willed; or easily led; or drunk; or on drugs. Even in such cases a gaol sentence of some kind is practically certain.
>
> [4] If you do go to gaol for such a crime, then you will be as much at risk from others as your victim was at risk from you . . .

And then, perhaps, this simple question:

> How would you ever think, and how could you possibly think, that it was worth your while to take risks like those?

(paras. 144–146)

These suggestions provide a fascinating insight into how Justice Sully conceptualises the problem of rape. For a start, his first proposition is interesting for his failure to discuss how or why anyone could/would think forced sex was a 'game'/ 'prank'/'joke'/'rite of passage' in the first place. Implicit in this statement is that there is a pre-existing, albeit erroneous in His Honour's opinion, assumption that many men/boys (according to Justice Sully) are drawing upon that leads them to rape.

Justice Sully's choice of language in his final warning to boys is also intriguing. In asking the question, how young men could see it as 'worth their while' to take such risks, Justice Sully does not seem to ask the question of what the value of

18 *The 'Sydney gang rape' trials*

forced sex is in the first place. Instead, he takes it for granted that such sex could be pleasurable and desirable, were it not for the fact that it carries a risk of punishment. He does not ask, 'why would you possibly want to force a woman/girl to have sex?' Rather, he suggests it is simply not worth the risk involved. Does that mean if the man/boy evaluates the situation and decides the risk of detection is limited, it *could* be worthwhile? In light of the research, which demonstrates the majority of coerced sex is performed within relationships, this comment is troubling. After all, it is precisely these instances that feminists have demonstrated are infrequently prosecuted and convicted, suggesting that there is in fact little risk involved. We need only look to the fact that rape within marriage was only deemed capable of criminal prosecution in Australia in 1992[3] and the continued difficulty in successfully prosecuting intimate partner rape (Buddie and Miller 2001) to see why feminist critics remain sceptical of the law's ability to truly address the violence and violation experienced by women.

The normative heterosexuality/rape continuum

Finally, the 'logical' conclusion that His Honour draws – that to rape means to take the risk of punishment and the possibility of becoming a victim of rape oneself – articulates a logic also presented in *La Squale* (discussed in Chapter 6). In this discourse what dissuades someone from rape is the possible risk of rape against themselves. As it is only men who are seen as capable of rape, it remains for men to avenge violence committed against women (who will only ever emerge as passive victims). Just as in *La Squale*, Toussaint, the gang leader, is punished for his gang rape of Leila by her cousin in turn raping him, so too Justice Sully envisages a system within which rape is repaid with rape. Justice Sully does not envisage male rape as a 'fact of life' in the way he seems to envisage female rape. This is evident in the highly gendered warnings he provides to young men (not to rape) and young women (not to be raped). Instead, male rape is only possible for Justice Sully in a context where there are no women (i.e.prison). The act of rape becomes itself a feminising act with the act of submitting (or being forced to submit) and being penetrated the very nature of femininity (de Carvalho Figueiredo 2004, p. 223; Awkward 1995; MacKinnon 1989, p. 130).

This seems to highlight a continuum between normative heterosexuality and rape, with the latter simply an extreme manifestation of the former rather than an aberration. In the words of Anne Cossins: 'If, as many feminists argue, the social definition of sexuality involves the erotisation of male dominance and female submission, then the use of coercive means to achieve sexual conquest may represent a crude exaggeration of prevailing norms, but not a departure from them' (Cossins 2000, p. 43).

Justice Sully is not the only legal figure to legitimate this: then-NSW Director of Public Prosecutions, Nicholas Cowdery QC, made this extraordinary remark in a 2005 article: 'The sexual urge ensures the survival of the species and it is strong. The criminal law steps in when it is misdirected in certain ways – typically against the unwilling or the vulnerable: against those capable (at law) of consenting who

The 'Sydney gang rape' trials   19

do not consent and against those whom society has decreed must be protected from such abuse.' (Cowdery 2005, n.p.).

In this narrative, women remain sexually passive and objectified: the bodies upon which heterosexual masculinity is performed. At the same time, the risk of rape to men is not one that is ever-present but, when it does occur, it represents a simultaneously feminising and disempowering act. In this way, normative heterosexual gender identity is reinforced through the construction of masculine gender identity as that of action, aggression and sexual agency, whilst feminine gender identity remains passive and vulnerable. The legal system's incorporation of these dominant constructions of 'normal' male and female sexuality and behaviour also implicitly informs its understanding of what rape 'looks like'. In the words of Ngaire Naffine, 'the dominant tale of coercive heterosexuality-as-natural is a powerful one (1994, p. 103). Moreover, as Sharon Marcus (1992) points out, it is through the discourse of rape that women are in fact *made* inherently rapeable: through the socially constructed scripted interactions, which inscribe men with the power to rape and women the inherent vulnerability to rape. This script not only constructs particular gender identities, it also formulates a normative heterosexuality that is always linked to potential violence. This reality was exemplified in the judicial response to the injuries of one victim, 'Kelly'.

What 'real' rape looks like

In her expert report tendered by the prosecution, Dr Eva Jackson, a gynaecologist who had examined 'Kelly' following the rapes, commented that of the 1,700 clinical vaginal inspections she had conducted, 'Kelly's' injuries were, 'probably the worst I have seen'. This led to lengthy legal debate during which it was argued by the defence lawyers that these injuries could have been the consequence of consensual sexual intercourse (a scenario Dr Jackson stated was extremely unlikely). Paul Sheehan provides the following quoted passage from the interaction between Justice Sully and the Crown Prosecutor based on his trial observation and reference to the transcript:

Judge: What troubles me is that, as soon as she is permitted to say the type of injury is more commonly [in rape], a jury will say that is good enough for us, it must follow that those injuries are caused by non-consensual intercourse. But that is fallacious reasoning . . . In so far as consent is an issue, it has to be proved beyond reasonable doubt. That is one thing she can't do.

Crown [clearly exasperated]:   No, she can't but, surely in the Crown's submission, the girls are entitled to be supported by a doctor who says that, in cases of non-consent, injuries such as this are much more likely to occur . . . When a very severe injury is present, it must point more conclusively to a lack of consent because, surely, when pain begins to present itself, a person having sexual intercourse, if it is consensual, will stop.

Judge: I don't think that necessarily follows at all.

(Sheehan 2006a, p. 99)

20 *The 'Sydney gang rape' trials*

In light of the law's position on other forms of harm – that a person cannot consent to any form of injury that involves actual bodily harm or greater, a point which has resulted in the prosecution of various voluntary participants of sado-masochistic activities,[4] the refusal by the judge to allow evidence that might support the victim's claim that she was not consenting appears perverse. However, it also reinforces a version of female sexuality that has often been accepted by the law: a sexuality that is at best understood to be passive, at worst inherently masochistic and within which the line between pleasure and pain remains constantly ambiguous.

As my discussion of Sheehan's commentary in Chapter 5 will show, his book generally provides little in the way of feminist analysis. However, his reporting of this incident and his critique of the approach allowed by the Court in which it was suggested that the level of injury could also have been the result of sexual inexperience (which still does not explain why either party would have persisted in the sexual intercourse when it would have involved a great deal of pain) provides an excellent example of the ongoing failure of the law to revise traditional conceptions of female sexual identity and agency. Even though, in the eyes of the law, it is generally considered unreasonable for a person to consensually allow harm to be inflicted upon them, female sexuality is unproblematically constructed on just that principle. Rather than being sexual subjects in their own right, women are still understood as sexual objects upon which the acts of (heterosexual) sex are performed.

The failure even within many feminist critiques to challenge the conception of there being an inherent vulnerability associated with 'being a woman' results in little being done to challenge the underlying assumptions of what constitutes normative sexuality or gender identity.[5] As a result, the identity of 'woman' is constructed around this apparent vulnerability. Rape – and women as already raped or inherently rapeable – becomes a process of feminisation, another way for women to be recognised as women:

> The language of rape solicits women to position ourselves as endangered, violable, and fearful and invites men to position themselves as legitimately violent and entitled to women's sexual services. This language structures physical actions and responses as well as words, and forms, for example, the would-be rapist's feelings of powerfulness and our commonplace sense of paralysis when threatened with rape.
>
> (Marcus 1992, p. 390)

Marcus' words seem to absolutely capture the essence of the judges' reasoning in the 'Sydney gang rape' trials. This does little to challenge the 'taken for granted' nature of rape. A society in which rape does not occur is unimaginable and unrealistic. Instead the emphasis remains on dissuading/persuading/threatening men to resist the desire to rape. Even more remarkably, in Justice Sully's suggestion, this is done through the threat of feminisation (and thus, disempowerment) through the threat of potential rape. He and indeed all the judges in the 'Sydney gang rape'

The 'Sydney gang rape' trials 21

trials envisage no manner in which women could themselves disrupt the apparent male monopoly on power in rape situations.

This lack of agency imputed to women is perhaps even more evident in Justice Sully's suggested propositions to girls listening to his 'educational' tape:

> For girls, those propositions [accompanying the tape] might be to the following effect:
>
> [1] If you get into or onto any vehicle with any man whom you do not know, or whom you barely know, then without more you are at risk.
>
> [2] The risk is hugely increased if you join up in that way, not with one stranger but with a group of strangers.
>
> [3] The risk can take various forms. You might be robbed. You might find yourself the object of a sexual advance that is unwelcome and sleazy but at least non-violent. You might find yourself the victim of an indecent assault stopping short of forced sexual intercourse. You might find yourself, if things go badly wrong, the victim of forced sexual intercourse with one, or with more than one, attacker.
>
> [4] You should not think that a mobile phone is some kind of guaranteed protection against those risks. The two girls whom you can hear on the tape had mobile phones; and the phones did not protect them at all.
>
> [5] Do not let anyone tell you that there is anything glamorous, or exciting, or 'cool' in any other sense about risking sexual assault of any kind. Any kind of forced sex is dirty and degrading. It is frightening, as you can tell from the tape. It can easily cause physical damage and will certainly cause emotional damage.
>
> (para. 147)
>
> And then exactly the same question as that earlier suggested [to the boys].

Again, Justice Sully's comments suggest an interesting understanding of normative female sexuality; does His Honour really think that young women need to be told that forced sex is not pleasurable? His construction of female sexuality appears to conform to exactly that which feminist scholars have so long critiqued: a sexuality that takes pleasure from objectification. This seems to invoke the connection radical feminist legal scholar Catharine MacKinnon has controversially asserted between pornography and sexual and gendered violence. For MacKinnon the central question that pornography raises is, 'the question of social causation by which pornography *constructs* women and sex, defines what "woman" means and what sexuality is, in terms of each other' (1987, p. 161, emphasis in original).

MacKinnon's argument has been powerfully critiqued. She has been accused of over-essentialising the category of 'woman', reinforcing a denial of female agency and – through her calls for tighter censorship – assisting discourses of the conservative right that seek to link open sexuality with sexual violence (thus preserving the dichotomy between the innocent female victim and the promiscuous, sexually available woman who is 'asking for it'). Yet if we read MacKinnon's analysis less literally and rather focus on the discursive function of pornography, it would seem

22   *The 'Sydney gang rape' trials*

to hold some merit when considering Justice Sully's choice of language. His Honour's narrative shows a depressing currency to old feminist arguments on pornography: that it contributes to the sexualisation and eroticisation of female domination and objectification and that these images in turn come to represent women generally within everyday discourses, limiting their potential to that of sexual objects (Awkward 1995; MacKinnon 1989; Smart 1989).

In fact, all the judges in the various 'Sydney gang rape' hearings appear unable to articulate the severity of the damage done to the victims without resort to highly eroticised images of violation. Even Justice Latham's attempts at an unemotional description of the rapes cannot escape the need to detail the exact moment of ejaculation, a point that would seem to be irrelevant if the focus of the law was indeed punishing the experience of violation of the individual woman at losing the right to decide when and how she engages in sexual activity of any sort. It seems these judges – to draw on Carol Smart's (1989) analysis – remain trapped within a phallocentric (legal) culture that is unable to understand women's pleasure and thus either effaces its possibility completely or defines it according to what is pleasurable to (heterosexual) men.

While Justice Finnane and the Appeal Court judges in AEMs/KEM indulge in an extensive and graphic description of the rapes which seemingly unconsciously parallel scripts of some of the more violent and degrading pornographic tropes identified and condemned by feminists, Justice Sully and Justice Latham reassert the construction of a normative dominant and dominating male sexuality. At no stage do any of the judges envisage a world in which female sexuality does not require policing or protecting. Their comments seem to conform to what Carol Smart identifies as a central feature of rape trials: a celebration of the 'category of Man' (1989, p. 42) in which women cannot be seen as either citizens or sexual subjects (Heath and Naffine 1994, p. 34).

Creating rape victims

Furthermore, Justice Sully's comments also demonstrate not only the reflective but also the *constitutive* power of the law. While his assumptions regarding female sexual behaviour and sexuality appear on the one hand to be reflective of broader societal discourses, his suggestion that young women require further education to prevent them from 'taking risks' helps to reinforce and rearticulate a feminine identity based around sexual vulnerability. He also ignores the position adopted by experts in the area (such as rape crisis centres) who refuse to use rape horror stories in law reform and legal education campaigns for the very reason that they see the practice as treading a fine line between allowing the woman to tell her story and 'its use as a kind of pornography which is damaging to women' (Smart 1989, p. 48).

His statement that young women accepting lifts from strangers is immediately 'risk taking behaviour' is not only clearly gendered (while he notes robbery is one of the risks, he does not suggest that young men should also be wary, nor does he foresee any situation within which young men could place themselves in a

The 'Sydney gang rape' trials   23

situation of sexual vulnerability, except in jail), it also resorts to the common response of victim-blaming in rape cases. He does not question the logical and linguistic leap that remains unexplained between a woman accepting a lift from a stranger to her appearing to be consenting to sex. In fairness, His Honour does add:

> All relevant social institutions, the Courts not least among them, [should] make it crystal clear that any girl or woman who associates with any boy or man in circumstances which put her at risk of sexual assault, does not become thereby nothing more than an available sexual object. In our society, to force a woman, any woman, to have sexual intercourse is, always and every-where, at once a base act and a major crime. It is not, ever or anywhere, a defence that the woman was flighty, flirtatious or simply foolish.
>
> (para. 48)

Yet his absolute condemnation of rape is diluted by his acceptance that women cannot expect to exercise the same freedom of movement as men without it being the height of foolishness or, as he describes the actions of victims LS and HG, 'breathtaking imprudence'. For His Honour it is for men to benevolently refrain from raping, for the power ultimately resides with them. Once again this seems to highlight the need for there to be a fundamental shift in understandings of norma-tive and acceptable male and female behaviour, sexual and otherwise. That being alone with strangers is, in itself, accepting a degree of risk leaves open the possibil-ity for imputing a certain amount of responsibility to the victim, even as Justice Sully seeks to deny this. Arguably this would suggest that the legal response to rape has still not come far from the heavily criticised comment by Judge Bertrand Richards in 1982: 'It is the height of imprudence for any girl to hitch-hike at night. That is plain, it isn't really worth stating. She is in the true sense asking for it.' (Smart 1989, p. 35). The question Carol Smart posed back in 1989 remains unan-swered: 'how is it that for a woman to say yes to a lift means she is saying yes to something completely different (e.g. sex)?' (Smart 1989, p. 36).

Justice Sully's passing comment regarding why the victims chose to accept the lift from strangers in the first place is also suggestive: 'I observe parenthetically that the evidence does not explain why either or both of the girls could not have made a telephone call to home in order to get help' (para. 15). It would seem to conform to Nina Philadelphoff-Puren's (2003) findings that frequently rape judg-ments demonstrate their reprobation of victims by identifying other actions the victims might have taken to avoid their rapes. Philadelphoff-Puren argues that this is a highly disempowering strategy as it requires the victims to operate as if they already knew they were going to be raped. His Honour's comments also seem to evidence the argument made by Susan Griffin in her 1971 essay, 'Rape: The All-American Crime', in which she notes, '[t]he fear of rape keeps women off the streets at night. Keeps women at home. Keeps women passive and modest for fear that they be thought provocative' (Griffin 1971, p. 35).

It is also worth returning to Carol Smart's comment that the repetition of rape horror stories can in themselves be seen as a form of pornography that is damaging

24 *The 'Sydney gang rape' trials*

to women. The threat of rape has not only played a vital role in shaping female sexuality. At the same time, the eroticism of rape has been consistently reinforced and recreated in popular culture and particularly pornography. For this reason, a number of feminist scholars have argued for rape trials to also be seen as contributing to a blurring of the line between rape as violence and rape as sex.

Rape trials: 'Pornographic vignettes'?

Aside from the need for victims to assert an 'ideal victimhood' in the face of highly damaging legal discourses, feminist legal scholars have also argued that the trial process provides for the re-degradation/violation of women by the eroticised and sexualised narratives developed and proposed. Through the re-telling of the rape, women are forced to accept and utilise sexualised language to describe their experience. Through being forced to speak publicly of their breasts, their vaginas, their anuses and the injuries inflicted on these body parts by the perpetrator, rape trials turn into what Carol Smart describes as 'pornographic vignettes': 'It is not just that they [victims] must repeat the violation in words, nor that they may be judged to be lying, but that the woman's story *gives pleasure* in the way that pornography gives pleasure' (1989, p. 39). In support of this argument Smart discusses the work of Anna Clark (1987), who has traced the emergence of the rape trial as 'pornographic spectacle' (Smart 1989, p. 40) with greater and greater emphasis placed on the victim providing a detailed account of every aspect of her violation, which is then widely reported to the public through the media.

Appeal court: R v Aem; R v Kem; R v MM [2002] NSWCCA 58 (13 March 2002)

Aside from its graphic descriptions of the rapes, discussed above, the Appeal Court in AEMs/KEM/MM also noted in its judgment: 'JH was menstruating at the time of the multiple assaults. As a result of the repeated offences of forcible penile vaginal intercourse, the tampon she had inserted prior to the offences was forced up into her cervix and had to be removed by a doctor' (para. 20). While it is assumed that this was mentioned in order to stress the level of violence experienced, it also provides an example of the 'pornographic nature' of the rape trial in which the most intimate details of a woman's body and bodily functions are presented in a public forum (Ehrlich 2001; Smart 1989; MacKinnon 1987). As Susan Ehrlich points out: 'It is perhaps only in pornography that the intimate details of a man removing a tampon from a woman's vagina . . . would be expressed in a public forum' (Ehrlich 2001, p. 20). Similarly, the public restatement of such an intimate aspect of the victim's body as the fact that she was menstruating and wearing a tampon is something that would normally be considered completely outside of the scope of 'decent' public discussion. For it to be the source of judicial comment is not only humiliating for the victim, it reinforces her 'tainted' status due to its perceived immodesty (Ehrlich 2001, p. 21).

The 'Sydney gang rape' trials 25

Furthermore, this example seems to lend support to Jennifer Temkin's critique of legislation that provides a graded approach to sexual assault on the basis of seriousness (as is the case in NSW): By emphasising the increased seriousness of the assault based on the level of extrinsic violence, one is left with the impression that the real crime is the extrinsic violence rather than the sexual intercourse without consent (Temkin 2002, p. 98; see also Heath 1998, p. 23). The seriousness of depriving a woman of sexual agency, autonomy and subjectivity becomes a secondary issue, if it is considered at all. Instead, the law once more conforms to a conceptualisation of female sexuality in which a certain degree of coercion is considered 'part and parcel of a woman's sexual life' (de Carvalho Figueiredo 2004, p. 223).

Justice Finnane: R v Chami, M. Skaf, Ghanem, B. Skaf, unreported judgment, District Court of New South Wales, 15 August 2002

In the context of the Bilal Skaf trial, this identification of the potentially pornographic nature of rape trials emerges even more clearly. Even as Justice Finnane condemns the horrendous sexual violence of the rapes, his sentencing remarks simultaneously conjure images often associated with standard heterosexual pornographic films. In establishing the horrific nature of the crimes he considers it necessary to go into explicit detail of exactly how each assault was carried out. A few examples from the sentencing judgment follow:

- In explaining the second assault on the victim, 'Miss A', he states: 'He then had oral sex with her for the second time. He ejaculated in her mouth and she spat out the semen on the ground';
- With reference to the second gang rape incident involving a victim identified as 'Miss D', Justice Finnane states: '. . . she was forced on to the ground. The men surrounded her, pulled her clothes off and put their hands all over her body, some of them penetrating her vagina with their fingers';
- In relation to the third gang rape incident, involving the victim identified as 'Miss C', Justice Finnane notes:

> Chami [one of the accused] then got in the back seat, unzipped his pants, sat next to her, pulled his penis out and put a condom on it. She said: 'You're not going to do it too?' To which he replied: 'Fuck me.' He then pushed her on her back, pulled up her skirt, pulled down her underwear completely and spread her legs as far as possible and had vaginal intercourse with her.
>
> (ABC 2002c)

The choice of language used by Justice Finnane to describe the rapes is significant. In their linguistic analysis of Canadian rape judgments, Coates et al. remarked on the continued use by judges of terms most frequently associated with (and more

26   *The 'Sydney gang rape' trials*

appropriate to) consensual sex (1994, p. 191). In particular, they seek to problematise the use of the term 'intercourse', arguing, 'its [intercourse's] dictionary definitions emphasise mutuality and communion of this act' (1994, p. 193). This has the effect of placing the acts in the interpretative framework of sex first and foremost, rather than in the interpretative framework of assault.

Once again Justice Finnane's sentencing judgment seems to support MacKinnon's (1987) argument that rape should not be characterised simply using the frame of violence but requires attention to the specific sexualisation/eroticisation of certain types of violence. In particular, it points again to the continuum of domination assumed to be natural within normative gender and sexual identity: 'Dominance eroticized defines the imperatives of its masculinity, submission eroticized defines its femininity' (1989, p. 130; see also Awkward 1995; Griffin 1971). The fact that Justice Finnane's description of rape could so easily be re-configured into a pornographic heterosexual script suggests a disturbing inability on the part of the law to fully conceptualise the nature of the violation and violence experienced by victims of rape. Also noteworthy, in each of the judges' sentencing remarks they specify the moment and circumstances of ejaculation. This further reinforces MacKinnon's argument that the nature of the violation experienced by women who have been raped becomes overlaid with what has been considered by men to be the nature of sex: penetrative intercourse and male orgasm (MacKinnon 1987, p. 87).

It is for this reason that an increasing number of feminists working on the relationship between rape laws and women's experience of rape have argued that law reform in itself cannot provide an answer. Rather, through analysing the discourses and narratives utilised by the law to understand and explain rape, it becomes clear that it is the very constructions of normative female and male sexuality that require revision. Equally, the law cannot be seen as simply expressing existing constructions but must be seen as directly implicated in their constitution.

'Rape as a weapon of war': The symbolic communal dimension to sexual violence

Not only are Justice Finnane's sentencing remarks disturbingly graphic, they also invoke stereotypical tropes to understand the motives for the rapes. These are also quite distinct from those utilised by Justice Sully. In a very detailed editorial piece in the *Sydney Morning Herald*, Sarah Crichton and Andrew Stevenson note:

> Court transcripts show Judge Finnane, in sentencing one of the rapists, feeling for the light switch that might illuminate the offences. Misogyny, contempt, drunken parties or even mass rapes by Japanese soldiers in Manchuria spring to his lips. The Bankstown rapes, he mused, are events 'you hear about or read about only in the context of wartime atrocities'.
>
> (Crichton and Stevenson 2002)

The 'Sydney gang rape' trials   27

This reference to war was the most overt judicial articulation of what became a common feature of other public responses to the rape (described further in Chapter 4). It highlighted the significance these rapes took on beyond horrific acts of violence against individual young women. By linking them to the emergent 'rape as a weapon of war' discourse being articulated in the international legal arena, a further distinction was drawn between these rapes and the more 'mundane' forms of sexual violence generally associated with 'peacetime' contexts: what two international lawyers have described as '"merely" undesired sex' (Schomburg and Peterson 2007, p. 127).[6]

This is made even clearer in what *The Daily Telegraph* reported to be Justice Finnane's ultimate conclusion: 'These cases concern one of the greatest outrages, in criminal terms, that has been perpetrated on the community in Sydney . . . military organised gang rape involving 14 young men' (Connolly 2008). These comments by Justice Finnane are perhaps the closest judicial endorsement of the discourses that expressed the strongest sense of outrage: those for which – as the later chapter on media responses will demonstrate – the central concern in these rapes was their potential to represent an attack on Australia. It is perhaps for this reason that of all the judges, Justice Finnane handed down the severest sentences. It is acknowledged that the alleged military metaphors employed by His Honour during the trial proceedings do not ultimately appear in his sentencing remarks. However His Honour does draw a rather alarming distinction between these gang rapes and other instances of similar crimes:

> As I have earlier remarked these crimes were carefully planned and coordinated. The degree of planning and coordination distinguishes these crimes from other cases of gang rape which have been reported from time to time, which are often, if not usually, perpetrated by intoxicated men who have seized an opportunity, which has been presented to them.
>
> (ABC 2002c)

This, as with Justice Latham's categorisation of the AEMs/KEM rapes as 'opportunistic', seems to suggest that it is the intention of the rapists that determines the seriousness of the crime, *not* the feeling of violation experienced by the victim. The complete erasure of the women from this discussion (they become 'an opportunity, which has been presented' to the men) means that once again only men emerge as active sexual agents. It also reinforces a troubling understanding of 'normative' sexuality through its acceptance of the notion that a group of men whose inhibitions were lowered could potentially be expected to engage in sexually violent behaviour. This is a problematic assumption for both men (they are all constructed as potential rapists, given the right circumstances) and women (their presence in the company of inebriated men could be interpreted as invoking some personal responsibility to protect themselves from rape).

28 *The 'Sydney gang rape' trials*

The 'cultural timebomb': Introducing the cultural dimension

Justice Hidden: R v MAK; R v MSK [2006] NSWSC 237
(5 April 2006)

While the other judges all dismissed attempts by both sides to assert some cultural specificity to the cases,[7] Justice Hidden did explore the issue in some detail in his written judgment. This was largely due to the submission by one of the defence teams of an expert report by anthropologist Professor Michael Humphrey. The report provided background information on the area of Pakistan the accused came from as well as a summary of Professor Humphrey's analysis of normal gender relations in that cultural context.

In particular, His Honour quoted Professor Humphrey's opinion that, ' . . . a gathering with unrelated teenage girls, unaccompanied by a male guardian would have been inconceivable in the offender's area of origin. He would seen [sic] them as "immoral or loose", and would have interpreted their very presence as sexually provocative' [para. 36]. His Honour also noted:

> [Professor Humphrey] added that the proposition, 'that a girl in this situation could take control by asserting her rights – i.e. saying no – would be very difficult in a patriarchal tribal culture where women are treated as dependents and legal minors'. In the case of [victim] CH, he noted that she had had consensual sexual intercourse with MMK [one of the accused]. Given the cultural requirement of chastity prior to marriage, he said that the offender's knowledge of her intimacy with his brother 'would have, at the very least, created enormous expectations that she might be also available to him'.
>
> [para. 35]

His Honour noted that the prosecution objected to the evidence on the basis that it was too generalised and was not based on actual knowledge of the particular accused's personal circumstances [para. 36]. Yet he saw this objection negated by the accused's testimony that Professor Humphrey's description was accurate and, 'he saw both victims as promiscuous and believed they had no right to repel his sexual advances' [para. 36]. This led His Honour to conclude, '[t]he argument that a cultural background such as that disclosed in evidence in the present case might bear upon sentence for sexual assault is unpalatable, but it is worthy of measured consideration and cannot be peremptorily dismissed' [para. 38].

Ultimately His Honour gave little weight to the cultural considerations in his decision on the basis that the accused had not raised his cultural background earlier in the trial process and, 'he was no stranger to this country' [para. 45]. As a result, His Honour was of the view that, '[the accused] must have had sufficient exposure to the Australian way of life to be aware that the place occupied by women in the traditional culture of his area of origin is far removed from our social norms'

The 'Sydney gang rape' trials   29

[para. 45]. This reasoning was similar to that of Justice Sully who, in also dismissing the cultural defence raised before him remarked:

> In our society to force a woman, any woman, to have sexual intercourse, is always and everywhere a base act and a major crime. It is not, ever or anywhere, a defence that the woman was flighty, flirtatious or simply foolish. That latter comment is especially to the point with boys and men from foreign ethnic cultures. The status of women in foreign countries is, in the end, a matter for the law and culture of those countries. The status of women in Australia is a matter for the law and culture of Australia.
>
> (*R v MSK; R v MAK; R v MMK; R v MRK* [2004] NSWSC 319, at paras. 48 and 49)

Although ultimately unsuccessful, the 'cultural defence' proposed and considered highlights another interesting and disturbing aspect to the 'K brothers' case. Not only did it provide support for right-wing commentators' linking of these rapes with broader questions of immigration and multiculturalism (as the later chapter on Paul Sheehan's book will demonstrate), it also raised some difficult questions about the relationship between feminism and multiculturalism.

A key critique of official policies of multiculturalism such as those adopted in many Anglo-Saxon nations is that they provide the opportunity to justify or excuse the further denial of women's rights. In her seminal essay, 'Is multiculturalism bad for women?' Susan Moller Okin (1999) argued that all too often 'respect for cultural difference' has been used to justify or legitimate male control over women. As she points out, the majority of cases in which culture is cited as a defence or a justification for differential treatment involve issues of gender, 'in particular, with male control over women and children' (1999, n.p.). In demanding, '[w]hen a woman from a more patriarchal culture comes to the United States (or some other Western, basically liberal, state), why should she be less protected from male violence than other women are?', Moller Okin presents a compelling argument. However, the simplistic division between 'gender' identity and 'cultural' identity is problematic as many postcolonial and Black critical race feminists have pointed out (Razack 2004, 1998; Moorti 2002; Yegenoglu 1998) and indeed, as responses to the 'Sydney gang rapes' demonstrated.

In accepting the evidence of Professor Humphrey, the court tacitly accepted an essentialised reading of 'true' Western Pakistani culture. It is not disputed that there is evidence of extremely patriarchal values and customs, which impose severe limits on women's lives and provide them with few avenues of redress. However, to accept this as a fundamental aspect of the ethnic culture reinforces two equally problematic views. One, that there is not and cannot be a non-patriarchal version of that culture or the possibility for contested versions of the culture. Two, it suggests that Australian society *does not* have a tradition of patriarchal customs and values, that Australian women have always experienced great freedom and autonomy and that the legal system has traditionally been highly receptive to the needs of women. As both the earlier analysis of judicial

30   *The 'Sydney gang rape' trials*

responses to the 'Sydney gang rapes' and those of others detailed later attest, these are highly debatable propositions. And yet – as I will argue further in the proceeding chapters – it became harder and harder to name the sexism within dominant Australian society, culture and institutions. As has happened elsewhere,[8] the association of misogyny with particular ethnic groups or cultural contexts served to mask the depressingly (near) universal culture of misogyny across societies. Instead we saw what Sherene Razack (1998) has described as 'the culturalization of sexism'.

On the one hand this silenced the various attempts – including by gang rape survivor Tegan Wagner herself – to open a broader discussion about the culture of violence against women (discussed further in the next chapters). On the other, once the problem was identified as one of culture, no other response from *within* that cultural context seemed possible. There could be no such thing as a 'feminist' Pakistani perspective, as the two become mutually exclusive. Rather, there becomes a need for the more civilised, 'feminist' Western legal institutions to impose a higher standard of behaviour. Making a similar point in relation to Norwegian responses to forced marriage, Razack writes, '[u]nassimilable, duplicitous, tribal and prepared to sell their daughters into marriage a life of continual rape, Muslim communities require the force of law to bring them into modernity' (2004, p. 138). In the context of the 'Sydney gang rapes' both Justice Hidden and Justice Sully conformed directly to this discourse. They did not seek to problematise the claim that the accused's culture would condone such behaviour, they simply asserted the pre-eminence of their own (more civilised) standard of behaviour.

This also seemed to highlight a key problem with Australian multicultural politics: the reliance on one essential(ist), 'authentic' version of (non-Western) culture. The fact that the 'expert' is not of the cultural background being discussed is an issue in itself. Following Talal Asad (1986, p. 163) the inevitable power relations (professional, national, international) involved in the process of 'cultural translation' cannot be dismissed, even as they remained unacknowledged by the Court in accepting the professor's report. It is not insignificant that the evidence accepted by the Court came from a professor of anthropology: postcolonial scholarship has long pointed to the centrality of knowledge production through disciplines such as anthropology to the colonial project (Dirks 2001). But perhaps more importantly for the purpose of this analysis is the question of why the dominant 'male' view of Pakistani culture is the only one presented? Is it to be accepted that Pakistani women would consider it an unproblematic suggestion that if they were to find themselves alone with men they did not know that rape would be inevitable?

Furthermore, the suggestion that due to the conservative nature of Pakistani society, once a woman had had sex outside of marriage with one brother she would instantly be deemed available to the other is a far from logical conclusion to draw. After all, sexual conservatism is also a cultural value accepted for men. The accuseds' actions in picking up women they did not know, drinking with them and proposing sex were hardly in keeping with their cultural norms. Yet there was no

The 'Sydney gang rape' trials 31

discussion at all of this. This seems to demonstrate a far too simplistic approach to what cultural tolerance actually means.

Conclusion

In conclusion, a reading of the judgments and sentencing remarks in the three sets of gang rape trials does seem to present a rather bleak outlook for the possibility of the law adequately addressing and reflecting the experiences of rape victims. Even in the context of cases that attracted extreme public condemnation, the legal actors demonstrated themselves to be remarkably incapable of challenging the dominant norms and rape discourses, which have been so long subject to critique. This would suggest Carol Smart's observation that '[w]e should not make the mistake that law can provide the solution to the oppression that it celebrates and sustains' (1989, p. 49) remains depressingly accurate. Ultimately the 'Sydney gang rape' trials seem to exemplify Sharon Marcus' argument that, 'courtroom trials assert first and foremost their own legitimacy and power to judge events, and only grant power to the vindicated party on the condition that the court's power be acknowledged' (Marcus 1992, p. 388). This observation becomes even more pertinent when we consider the narrative of the one gang rape survivor who has chosen to speak publicly: Tegan Wagner, to whose book I will now turn.

Notes

1 One creating a new offence of 'aggravated sexual assault in company', the other amending criminal procedure that had previously allowed unrepresented accused to cross-examine their victims.
2 It has frequently been observed in feminist analyses of rape cases that the seriousness of the violation is usually interpreted based upon the 'aggravating factors' of physical violence, increased vulnerability of the victim (essentially her age and sexual experience) and lack of prior relationship between the victim and the accused: see for example Débora de Carvalho Figueiredo's (2004) analysis of legal decisions in the United Kingdom.
3 *R v L* (1992) 174 CLR 379.
4 *R v Brown and Others* [1993] 2 All ER 75. Although see also *Wilson* [1996] 3 WLR 125 in which the consensual branding of a wife by her husband was permitted, leading commentators to question why a distinction has been drawn between the activities of a heterosexual married couple and those of equally consenting homosexual adults.
5 This is an argument I have made in relation to feminist engagements with international law: see Grewal (2015, 2012, 2010).
6 For a detailed discussion and critique of this development in international law, see Grewal (2015, 2010).
7 Although Dagistanli (2005) does make a significant point when she identifies Justice Sully's use of language in rejecting a cultural defence. Similarly to Justice Hidden, Justice Sully seemed to draw distinctions between Australian and 'foreign' attitudes to, and treatment of, women. For this reason, Dagistanli makes a similar argument regarding Justice Sully's remarks to my own in relation to Justice Hidden's judgment: both judges seem to accept (and indeed articulate) a certain backwardness in respecting women's rights associated with specific cultures, that is not at all applicable to Australia. The Appeal Court appears to have recognised this: In rejecting the cultural defence, Justice Grove (Hall J and McClellan CJ concurring) stated 'there was, and is, not the slightest basis for

32   *The 'Sydney gang rape' trials*

concluding other than that in both places, all women are entitled to respect and safety from sexual assault. The expression "cultural time bomb" was, to say the least, inappropriate and inapt. It would understandably be regarded as offensive by those who fell within the scope of its insult.' (*R v MAK; R v MSK; R v MMK* [2005] NSWCCA 369 at para. 61).

8 See Razack (2008, 2004) for examples from Canada, Norway and the UK. See also Volpp (2007) writing about the US.

3 'White angels' and 'Muslim misogynists'

Survivor and rapist discourses

Introduction

In this chapter, following on from the analysis of judicial discourses, I examine the discourses of victims and rapists as they emerged in the public arena. In particular, I will focus on gang rape survivor Tegan Wagner's intervention in the public debate on the rapes. Not only has Wagner been the most publicly vocal of the 'Sydney gang rape' victims, she is also the author of an autobiography released in 2007 in which – similarly to French rape survivor Samira Bellil (described in Chapter 8) – she describes both her experience of rape and her subsequent attempts to overcome its legacy. Aside from the obvious parallel with Bellil, which makes it a useful point for comparative analysis, Wagner's book provides a fascinating insight into the space available to rape survivors to narrate their experience, assert agency and receive redress. Meanwhile, a number of the accused rapists also gained notoriety as a result of their very public displays during the trial proceedings. Noting the mediated access I have to their voices (largely through media reports), I nonetheless analyse their actions and comments as contributors in their own right to the public discourse.

In analysing Wagner's account, as with that of Bellil, I want to clearly differentiate my critique of the discourses from any critique of these two women and their opinions. The horrific violence both experienced and the courage they have shown deserve respect. I will therefore proceed with a cautious acknowledgment that nothing I say seeks to diminish the right both women have to speak nor the admiration I hold for both as strong, brave women who have suffered great wrongs.

Seeking to analyse the rapists' discourses – indeed including them in this chapter – is also potentially a task fraught with danger. To begin with, it is necessary to stress that this is not an attempt to explain the rapists' behaviour or actions, to justify their actions through resort to portrayals of the men as victims themselves of racism, social exclusion, and economic marginalisation. All of these things may be true, but these men are not alone in facing such hardships, and yet not all men (or women) in this situation resort to violent and degrading attacks on others. At the same time, I also do not wish to demonise them further. It is true, their acts and their subsequent lack of remorse do not create an image that easily

34 *Survivor and rapist discourses*

invokes sympathy or a desire to engage. But by seeking to critically engage with their voices I am less interested in the words and/or actions of these particular men than the discursive frames they reveal.

'The making of me': The trial of Tegan Wagner

While for French gang rape survivor Samira Bellil her encounter with the criminal justice system forms a relatively minor feature of her book (discussed in Chapter 8), the majority of Wagner's narrative concentrates on her experience of the initial reporting of the rapes and then the trial process itself. In detailing this aspect of her experience, Wagner provides an excellent insight into the rape trial process. In comparison with Bellil, Wagner's assessment of the justice system in her book is also relatively positive. Although she is deeply critical of some aspects of the criminal trial process, overall she identifies the criminal prosecutions and ultimately the convictions as providing her with a sense of closure and justice:

> I was able to move on because I took the power back. I took those boys to court, I saw it through and I stared them down. It really is the best feeling, and that's why I tell every victim to come forward. Do something about it. Take back the power. Make them pay. Because once you have, you can move on.
>
> (2007, p. 242)

She notes that submitting herself to the justice system had its risks but asserts the value of having the 'truth' on her side and even advocates for other victims to also make use of the process. This provides a stark contrast with the remarks of 'Debra', also a rape victim who went through the Australian legal process in relation to a rape she suffered at the hands of an unknown stranger:

> That the legal system offers an avenue of justice is one of the greatest misconceptions and myths of sexual assault. Too often the legal system treats the crime as if it is an acceptable social interaction. This legitimises the crime and in doing so causes the victim to suffer further impact of the crime.
>
> ('Debra' 2003, p. 53)

It is in fact somewhat surprising in the context of all the research done on the damaging effects of rape trials to victims (often referred to as a 'second rape') that Wagner should ultimately express such optimism about the justice system's ability to protect and serve her interests. This anomaly becomes less surprising when read in the context of the rest of Wagner's reflections. First of all, Wagner's assertion of confidence in the 'truth' winning out throughout the book seems to contrast with her own observation that various versions of the 'truth' were presented during the trial and that throughout the process she was far from confident as to which version was being accepted: 'I spent a lot of time trying to work out what the jury were

Survivor and rapist discourses   35

thinking . . . Every so often I'd see one of them jot something down and I'd start racking my brains about how I'd acted, how I'd behaved, wondering if they were thinking that I was this little snot-nosed brat that just deserved everything she got.' (Wagner 2007, p. 178)

'Performing the victim'

In fact, Wagner is very astute in identifying the role required of her and utilising this to achieve the desired outcome (the conviction of her rapists). In her concluding chapter she notes:

> When you're the victim in a rape trial, what you're experiencing is an argument about what kind of person you are: whether you're a naïve fourteen-year-old who let herself get drunk and was preyed upon by a group of guys who'd done this before and would do it again in the most ruthless manner. Or whether you're a slutty fourteen-year-old who couldn't wait to offer a sexual smorgasbord to a bunch of guys she'd just met and whose only concern was that she might get pregnant. That may not be how the lawyers or the judge see it, but that's how I saw it. It was an argument about who Tegan Wagner really was. It was an argument I had to win.
>
> (2007, p. 239)

Even as she asserts the need to demonstrate 'who Tegan Wagner really was', she also recognises the need to perform a particular version of herself in order to win:

> Theatre made going to court every day just about bearable, because it helped me detach myself and stay focused on what the trial process was really about – presenting my case in the best way I could – and not letting myself get so swept up in the emotions that I broke down or started screaming obscenities at the boys or did any of the other things I would have loved to do, but which wouldn't have helped me win.
>
> But we did win. I told my version of the story, and a jury of twelve people agreed I was telling the truth.
>
> (2007, p. 241)

Her reference to utilising the skills she learnt in her theatre classes provides a wonderful parallel to post-structuralist and critical accounts of the courtroom as a performative arena. Far from being a neutral site in which the 'truth' is uncovered through a process of rational, unbiased reasoning, the courtroom has been increasingly recognised as a site of intense ideological struggle in which participants must compete to have their voices and perspectives heard and understood.[1] Furthermore, in order to have their voices heard, participants are often required to fit within the traditional repertoires already established and understood by the Court. Janet

36 *Survivor and rapist discourses*

Galbraith provides a particularly vivid description of the experience of a victim in the rape trial process in writing about her own court case:

> In the courtroom they put me into a box and placed stories upon me, told stories of me. They were searching for their truth *in* me. How were they to find this (in) me? Well, the night before I entered the witness box I was told by the police informant, 'It's all up to you Janet, it's all up to how you perform in the witness box, you just have to prove your innocence'. What performance was I to give and of what did I have to prove myself innocent? Innocent of making up a story? Every time I spoke, or was spoken, a story was being told; and, yes, the story/ies told were the stories already performed and which I would re-perform in an arena where the representations of rape and myself were limited by the discourses available. The script had already been written upon my entry into this room.
>
> (Galbraith 2000, p. 71)

In this description Galbraith identifies both the struggle between truths that emerge in the trial process and her feeling of being limited in the discourses she could utilise to perform her truth. As I have described in the previous chapter, judges rely heavily on particular categorisations of men, women and sexuality (see also de Carvalho Figueiredo 2004, p. 219). As a result, in order for the victim to achieve the desired outcome (presumably, successful prosecution and strong judicial censure of the accused), she must as much as possible adhere to the normative categorisations of 'woman' and 'rape victim' set out in judicial discourses. It has been identified that this is one reason why many women do not report their experiences of forced sex: either because they themselves are unable to view their experience as 'rape' due to its failure to fulfil certain conditions (for example, the use of force, by a stranger, against which they demonstrated strong resistance) or because they fear the ambiguity of their situation may mean others will not categorise their experience as 'real rape' (Wood and Rennie 1994, p. 145).

Throughout her book Wagner describes a torturous process whereby she is forced to conform to certain constructions of the 'ideal victim' and indeed the 'ideal young woman' in order to gain sympathy and support. She also demonstrates that not only was this support far from unconditional, it was also not immediately forthcoming. While arguably slightly less unpleasant than Bellil's experience (described in Chapter 8), Wagner's description of the initial reporting process also depicts an ordeal in which she was offered very limited sympathy/empathy:

> The whole process was pretty intimidating [reporting the rapes to the police]. I was still in shock, and I was completely exhausted, and the way they were questioning me made me doubt myself even more than I already had been. I really needed someone to reassure me that what I'd experienced *was* rape, because in spite of everything I still wasn't completely sure. . . .

> . . . .I needed someone to say to me, 'Yes, Tegan, you were raped, and you've done the right thing by coming here and talking to us.' But no one said it.
>
> (2007, p. 58)

Ultimately Wagner does establish a strong relationship with a number of legal figures involved with her case – one of the initial investigating officers, the solicitor assigned to her case and the victim support representative assigned to her in court – but she also points to incredible inadequacies in the counselling services offered to her. In a startlingly similar encounter to Bellil (described further in Chapter 8), Wagner details an attempt to utilise a children's telephone counselling service immediately following the rapes:

> . . . I rang the Kids Help Line and told my story, and when I'd finished, the lady on the other end said, 'You sound very calm for someone who's just been raped.'
>
> When bad things happen to me, once the worst is over I've always been able to calm down and think logically and process my thoughts thoroughly – and that's what I'd started doing. But the lady on the phone gave me the impression she didn't believe a word I was saying.
>
> (2007, p. 49)

This initial failure to find support impacted heavily on Wagner:

> . . . I was starting to doubt myself. What if I was wrong and Kerry was right? What if what had happened to me wasn't really rape? The lady at Kids Help Line hadn't sounded too sure. And the more I thought about it, the more I started to convince myself that it must have been all my fault. After all, I was drunk, and I'd kind of let the first one kiss me, and maybe if I'd really really tried I could have fought them off . . . The only reason I thought it might be rape was because the last guy, Mustapha, had slapped me across the face a few times and pushed me on the couch. If it wasn't for that one incident, I would've had myself convinced that it wasn't rape at all. I was fourteen and a virgin, I had no sexual experience, and I didn't even have a very clear idea about what rape was. And that night, all I could think about was how it must have been all my fault.
>
> (2007, pp. 49–50)

This description seems to fit within the broader findings of rape victims' feelings following rape. As Wood and Rennie (1994) discovered in their interviews with women who had experienced rape but had not reported it to the police, of the various strategies adopted by the women to make sense of their experience, self-blame featured prominently. Furthermore, the fact that Wagner not only worried about her own degree of culpability but associated rape as only 'real' when some other form of physical violence was involved (the slap from Mustapha) seems to evidence the frequent complaint by feminist theorists that the law maintains an

38 *Survivor and rapist discourses*

ongoing understanding of rape in which 'the real crime is the extrinsic violence rather than sexual intercourse without consent in itself' (Heath 1998, p. 22).[2]

Even as Wagner appears confident through the course of the book about the validity of her claim, her concluding chapter suggests that some of this may in fact be the result of hindsight, following the vindication she felt she received from the Court:

> I spent a lot of years having people tell me I couldn't have been raped, I was lying. I made the whole thing up. Now I've got a judgment in the Supreme Court of New South Wales proving that what I said was true. I *was* raped. I'm not lying. And now the whole world knows it.
>
> (2007, p. 242)

Her choice of wording is significant. The Court's judgment is not ancillary to the veracity of her rape claims; it becomes *the proof itself*. Thus, even as Wagner asserts a rightful sense of personal victory in having overcome the difficulties she encountered and achieving the outcome she desired, the extent to which the legal process was responsive to her needs is highly debatable. The fact that Wagner is ultimately successful does not turn so much on her ability to express her subjective experience on her own terms but rather the extent to which she is able to make it 'fit' within the dominant legal discourses on rape. Throughout the trial process she expresses her desire to fight back, whilst simultaneously acknowledging a need to 'play the victim' in order to achieve the desired outcome.

Even as she is disgusted by the unfairness of the process, she realises the importance of not throwing off the victim role completely and is careful in her choice of dress, her attitude in court[3] and her responses to questions.[4] Just as Bumiller (1998) details how the gang rape victim's testimony in the infamous 1984 New Bedford gang rape trial in the US both conforms to legal ways of understanding violence and yet embodies resistance to accepted modes of expression, so too the struggle between resistance and conformity can be identified in Wagner's actions and language.

'The fallen angel'

It is well documented that for rape prosecutions to be successful it is necessary for the victim to emerge as someone as 'unblameworthy' as possible (Bumiller 1998; Wood and Rennie 1994; Estrich 1987, 1986). Thus, a central feature of the trial process remains the testing of the extent to which the victim 'deserves' sympathy, depending on her actions in the lead up to the rape and whether her prior sexual and personal life conforms to that of an 'ideal' chaste femininity. As Bumiller explains, even as the rape victim may seek to resist legal conventions and their construction of her identity, she is always required to demonstrate a certain type of 'innocence' in order to demonstrate her worthiness of protection:

> The trial turns on her 'innocence of experience' or 'freedom from guilt'; this has powerful symbolic consequences, for it reinforces the presumption that

Survivor and rapist discourses 39

punishing violent men is justified to the extent that women are worthy of trust and protection. . . . The symbolic message is, in some degree, an expression of the legal system's high tolerance for violence against women and its low threshold for the measure of her unworthiness.

(Bumiller 1998, p. 39)

In all of Wagner's attempts to explain the causes, circumstances and subsequent impact of the rapes, she demonstrates an ongoing need to assert her blamelessness. It is perhaps not insignificant that the image on the front cover of Wagner's book is a close up of her face, innocent-looking, big blue eyes, strands of hair to frame her face and a bandana tied discreetly across her head: an image of virginal innocence with more than a passing resemblance to standard images of the Virgin Mary within Western iconography. This would seem to fit with Bumiller's (1998) theory that for rape victims to elicit sympathy they need to emerge as 'fallen angels'; virginal, asexual beings whose innocence has been violated.

A two-page spread in the *Sun Herald* on Wagner in late 2007 seems to further exemplify this point. The opening paragraph provides a description of an innocent, potentially religious young teenager: 'Six years ago, a school photograph of Tegan Wagner shows her as a young, naïve teenager, with a cross laced around her neck'. This is contrasted with an image of her following the rapes: 'A school photograph taken of the following year captures a startling difference: heavy black eye make-up, dark clothes, and hair pulled tight into corn rows. A marijuana leaf had replaced the cross' (O'Dwyer 2007). While the intention of these descriptions seems to be to demonstrate the emotional toll the rapes and the subsequent legal process took on Wagner, it is also noteworthy the extent to which they endorse a certain image of the rape victim: innocent to begin with, deprived of this innocence and suffering subsequently. It is through adopting this classic narrative of the young woman 'despoiled' that sympathy for Wagner is built.

In the context of the criminal trials, she describes a feeling of panic in preparing for her initial court appearance:

> The date for my trial had been set for 25 October 2004. I was both excited and anxious about going to court. I'd never been to court before and the whole thing was pretty scary. I had no idea what I should wear. I asked the police, and they joked, 'Don't wear anything that shows cleavage'. . . .
>
> . . . .I spent a lot of time worrying about how I should present myself. What shoes should I wear? How should I have my hair? Should I wear make-up? Should I try to seem older than I am, mature and reliable? Or should I go in my school uniform, to remind the jury that I'm still a schoolgirl?

(Wagner 2007, pp. 146–147)

The need to present the 'right' image seems to reinforce the assertions of feminist scholars that the trial process is a site of coerced gender performance. Similarly she describes the process of cross-examination as an ordeal, which required

40 *Survivor and rapist discourses*

all her strength to maintain composure and remain within the character of the 'ideal' victim and woman:

> Morison [one of the defence barristers] made me feel like a little piece of dirt who'd decided to tell a whole lot of lies about a nice bunch of boys because I was such an evil, lying, filthy little slut. It felt like the defence could say whatever they liked about me, and I couldn't do anything to hit back or even show how I felt, because it might harm my chances. I had to be sweet and nice and good and patient while the defence barristers made me out to be something I am not . . .
>
> (Wagner 2007, p. 159)

Having identified that she must 'play the game' she decides not to confront and directly challenge the dominant legal discourses and structures; she opts for a more subtle strategy of resistance. She cherishes brief moments of subversive satisfaction in her visual confrontation of her rapists,[5] her ability to hold off tears during cross-examination[6] and identifying mistakes made by the defence lawyers.[7] While the trial process she describes is far from an empowering experience, Wagner continually refuses to allow it to break her or diminish her sense of agency: while noting the particularly difficult cross-examination she endured at the hands of Mr Morison (involving 856 questions in total), she states:

> I felt so much better knowing I'd just stood up to him in front of the three people I will always hate. Morison had asked me the foulest questions and I'd been able to stand up to him. Knowing I'd made it through gave me a real sense of strength and accomplishment.
>
> (2007, p. 167)

Wagner does not choose the identity assigned to her of victim, but she is forced to adopt it in order to win the law's approval. Just as her initial sense of self-worth is destroyed by the male violence of rape, her only means of reasserting worth is through acceptance within the male violence of legal discourse. She is not unaware of the violence being perpetrated against her again but chooses strategically to endure this violence in order to emerge with a renewed sense of agency that she can then assert in her own words through her book. So too, Wagner expresses a feeling of regaining some agency and dignity not during the trial process but as a result of it:

> By the time Mustapha's barrister had finished cross-examining me I felt great. The ordeal was finally over and I was the happiest girl in the world. I was so ecstatic, I felt like doing cartwheels. It was finished. I'd come to court wanting to make the boys feel powerless, to make them feel that no matter what they tried, or what they threw at me, I was always going to be around and I was never going to let them get away with it. I was the reason they were in court, and I was the reason they were going to be made to pay for what they'd done.

Survivor and rapist discourses 41

They'd made me feel powerless, but now I had the power, and I'd used it to bring the full weight of the law down on their heads. And I was so proud of the fact that I'd actually done it.

(Wagner 2007, p. 169)

This suggests that while she is aware of the unjust aspects of the court process, she sees the strategic adoption of the victim identity as the only means for her to achieve a sense of (re)empowerment. One of the central feminist critiques of rape trials has been the overemphasis on interrogating and evaluating the victim's conduct. As a result, victims simultaneously emerge as key figures in the trial and as severely limited in the discourses available to them to express their subjective experience. Wagner's frustration at being cross-examined on matters which called her character and her sexual behaviour into question and not being able to respond as she would have liked seems to provide a poignant example of this critique.

In her analysis of the linguistic and discursive features of rape trials Susan Ehrlich (2001) identifies an institutional coerciveness within the legal process, which requires certain performances of (gender) identity. Furthermore, Ehrlich argues that the resources available for describing rape tend to be the same for men and women. As a result women are often left without the appropriate words to express their perspectives or their experiences. Even in the aftermath of the rapes (perhaps as a result of them and the trial process) Wagner seems to struggle between asserting her own sexual agency and being trapped in a discourse, which associates certain aspects of (female) heterosexual behaviour with disempowerment and degradation. For example, she notes:

That's one of the things people want to know about after you've been raped, but they're afraid to ask: what does it do to your relationships? Are you still interested in boys? Can you still have sex? I can't answer for everyone, but in my case the answer is definitely yes. Everybody has to learn how it's done. I had to learn too – I'm a normal girl, it's just that I had this horrible early experience to get past before I could enjoy it. There's stuff I won't ever want to do (which is why it was so ridiculous that Sabir [one of the 'K brothers'] tried to pretend I'd offered to do it 69-style with him – is there any woman who really likes to do that? I mean, *really?*). But I don't think the rapes have scarred me for life.

(2007, pp. 214–215)

On the one hand she demonstrates the resilience and strength Wood and Rennie (1994) allude to in their research on rape victims, by rejecting the permanent victim status. On the other (again possibly due to her experience of the rapes and the legal process) she describes her own sexuality in relation to a particular normative version of female sexual identity. The fact that she suggests no woman could enjoy certain sexual acts demonstrates an essentialised attitude to female sexuality and sexual identity, as well as potentially stigmatising those women who do not conform to these norms. It also reinforces dominant constructions of female sexuality

42 *Survivor and rapist discourses*

against which women's sexual behaviour is measured to determine the extent to which they are deserving of protection from sexual violence or coercion.

Violence against women: A game between men?

At the same time, Wagner does at one point provide an intuitive critique of gender identity construction. She notes:

> Gang-rape seems to be turning into a trend now – 'Let's get all my buddies together and show them how manly I am.' Whatever happened to the days when they'd just show each other how manly they are by decking each other? They might break a bit of furniture but it's replaceable, it's not going to cause some woman a lifetime of trauma. Gang-rape is like the latest fashion for criminals and we've got to stamp it out before it gets any worse.
>
> (2007, p. 225)

Although her comments regarding gang rape as a 'new phenomenon' are unsubstantiated and not supported by feminist scholarship on the subject, Wagner does show a perceptive insight into the relationship between normative (albeit problematic) masculinity and sexual violence and the centrality of the relationships 'between men' in the act of gang rape. In fact research into the specificities of gang rape have focused on the ways in which the act is used as a form of homosocial bonding (Cossins 2000, p. 111; Sanday 1990). The significance is to the male relationships with each other. The female body is essential only to disavow homosexuality and to provide an object over which the shared male power to dominate can be expressed. This is also clear in male responses to '*les tournantes*' discussed shortly.

Wagner also problematises female socialisation, arguing it is through pressure to conform to 'appropriate' modes of feminine behaviour that women's vulnerability to rape is created:

> As girls, we're taught that the most important thing is to make other people like us, so in group situations we're all so busy being nice we actually do things to hurt our own interests. We let guys take advantage of us, dominate us, bully us, and rape us because we're too afraid to stand up and say, 'You're a creep. I'm out of here.'
>
> (Wagner 2007, p. 240)

This is remarkably similar to Sharon Marcus' assertion that '[w]omen's non-combative responses to rapists often derive as much from the self-defeating rules which govern polite, empathetic feminine conversation as they do from explicit physical fear' (1992, p. 389). For Marcus, it is the 'script' that men have the power to rape and women are inherently rapeable that makes rape possible. Hence Marcus concludes that for rape to actually be prevented, the rejection of these 'self-defeating' notions is as imperative as the development of physical self-defence tactics (1992, p. 389). Unfortunately this is a response that flies in the face of female

Survivor and rapist discourses 43

socialisation as Wagner so accurately observes. Moreover this socialisation and the 'script' Marcus describes are reinforced by the legal system itself as the previous chapter on judicial discourses demonstrated.

The legal process as space for resistance?

At the same time, as well as being a site of coercion, the legal process may also provide a possible site of resistance and ideological struggle (Ehrlich 2001, p. 95). Even as victims are severely constrained in the identity they are forced to perform and the agency they are imputed, they may also potentially be able to utilise certain tools and reclaim a form of agency in their strategic performances of the identity of 'rape victim'. This is not to suggest that they can be seen to be completely empowered and autonomous legal agents (as dominant legal discourses would seek to assert), but it is to recognise that nor should they be read as mere passive victims. Instead, within the 'rigid regulatory frame' (Butler 1999), it is possible to identify attempts to co-opt and reinterpret dominant stereotypes in a way that creates the possibility for a positive outcome.

In Wagner's case, not only does she demonstrate exceptional strength of character and an intuitive astuteness for 'playing the game' throughout the trial, but she also manages to force recognition of herself as an individual rather than a mere symbol. A demonstration of this is her choosing to be named publicly. This can be read on the one hand as an act of revenge against her attackers, whose names remained suppressed, demonstrating a greater strength on her part and a refusal to accept humiliation (2007, p. 224). However, it can also be read as containing a message to broader society. In choosing to be publicly identified Wagner not only seeks to reject the stigmatisation associated with being a rape victim ('the fallen angel' whose innocence is irretrievably lost, as Bumiller describes it), she also rejects the general trend to treat rape victims as passive objects of comment:

> For the most part, references to the victim ignored her as an individual who had her own specific responses to rape. Either the victim was named by her formal legal status and demographic qualities (e.g. 'the complainant', 'young woman', '21 year old city woman'), or more elaborate discussion of the victim was carried out through references to 'generic' victims of rape (e.g. antirape activists' statements of solidarity with the victim and special reporting features about rape crisis centers' efforts to respond to the psychological trauma of victims).
>
> (Bumiller 1998, p. 40)

Wagner's act of defiance is thus not only directed at the rapists but also at the broader community, from whom she has also suffered extensive negative judgment:

> That night I was on every TV news service, and I was on the front page of all the newspapers the next day. I was glad, because it meant that my message

44 *Survivor and rapist discourses*

was getting out there. But if I'm honest, it was pretty satisfying for me personally, too. For one thing, I knew the boys would be watching from jail, and knowing it was me who put them there. For another, I'd had to put up with people calling me a liar for so many years, and now, finally, I'd been vindicated in the most public way. I'd won my case. It was in all the papers. Anyone who didn't believe me could read the reports and what the judge said. It was sweet revenge.

(2007, pp. 227–228)

Although she was forced to endure so many negative institutional and social responses to her rapes, the fact that she ultimately experiences the court case as a source of vindication and justice could be seen to provide a glimmer of hope in the face of feminist critiques that have dismissed the legal process as holding any possible advantages to women who have survived sexual violence. Certainly Wagner seems to consider it as unfortunate that she was forced to comply with rules she saw as unfair and disempowering but ultimately asserts a sense of victory. However, in many ways her ultimate conclusion is tragic. The fact that she was only able to confirm her rape through the judgment of the court demonstrates the continued fragility of women's words in and of themselves.

Further, the limitations placed on her throughout the legal process, which forced her to comply with dominant constructions of the ideal 'rape victim' (whilst successfully negotiated in her case), hardly present a desirable position for women attempting to gain redress for sexual violence committed against them. Even as she achieved a reasonably satisfactory outcome, far from the trial process being an empowering experience, much of what Wagner describes seems to reinforce Bumiller's conclusion in her analysis of the New Bedford gang rape trial: that ultimately major rape trials 'illustrate the vulnerability of the woman as an accuser in contemporary legal culture' (1998, p. 39).

One is also forced to question the extent to which Wagner's story was capable of being heard and endorsed due to the very specific characteristics of these particular rapes. As Janet Galbraith notes, '[t]he discourses which circulate around bodies constituted in relation to race, sexuality, gender and class condition the meaning of rape as well as the possibility of the event itself' (2000, p. 76). Thus, it is not only dominant constructions of sexuality and gender identity that emerge in legal discourses on rape. Race and class also emerge as informative categories within which the rape can be contextualised and understood.

Susan Estrich (1987, 1986) has demonstrated how the law differentially treats rape depending on the extent to which rapists and victims conform to normative constructions of 'real' rapists and 'real' victims. The fact that it is well documented that the majority of rapes are committed by people the victim knows (https://rainn.org/statistics, accessed 23 May 2016; Kelly et al. 2005; Cook, David and Grant 2001) is then to be contrasted with the rapes that are most frequently reported, prosecuted and convicted: those involving strangers, preferably Black or of a minority ethnic background and where violence is evident.

Survivor and rapist discourses   45

Similarly, Ehrlich notes that '[w]hile inter-racial rape cases make up a minority of rapes committed and brought to trial, when White women are raped by Black men (especially strangers) they are much more likely to obtain convictions than in cases where the perpetrator is White' (Ehrlich 2001, p. 19). This has the consequence of exaggerating the problem of inter-racial/stranger rape while simultaneously underplaying the magnitude of the problem of coerced sex that most frequently affects women's lives but is not seen as 'real rape':

> If only the aggravated cases are considered rape – if we limit our practical definition to cases involving more than one man, or strangers, or weapons or beatings – then 'rape' is a relatively rare event, is reported to the police more often than most crimes and is addressed aggressively by the system. If the simple cases are considered – the cases where a woman is forced to have sex without consent by only one man, whom she knows, who does not beat her or attack her with a gun – then rape emerges as a far more common, vastly under-reported, and dramatically ignored problem.
>
> (Estrich 1987, p. 10)

In the case of the 'Sydney gang rapes' we see that, contrary to the political, legal and media suggestions that their aggressive prosecution and harsh convictions demonstrated progress in institutional responses to sexual violence, in fact the outcome was as many feminist scholars would expect. Just as Catharine MacKinnon (1987) suggests in the context of the United States, the fact that the 'Sydney gang rape' victims came forward, reported their rapes and were able to gain prosecutions and convictions depended heavily on their ability to establish themselves as victims of 'real' rapes: victims of gang rape, by non-White men they did not know and involving some level of violence.

Resisting the 'law and order' rhetoric

It is for this reason that feminist scholars such as Julie Stubbs (2003) are sceptical about the value of 'law and order' approaches to rape law reform. This rhetoric tends to encourage harsher sentences and tougher policing but does little to challenge dominant understandings of the reasons for and causes of rape in the first place. Stubbs had the 'Sydney gang rapes' in mind when she commented:

> Law and order rhetoric . . . also often draws on images of dangerous, unknown 'others' and is implicated in reinforcing a view of sexual assault that is atypical, obscuring the level of violence by offenders who are known to the victim, and the level of sexual violence that occurs within the home.
>
> (Stubbs 2003, pp. 20–21, references omitted)

As will be demonstrated in the next chapter, the exceptionally horrific nature of the 'Sydney gang rapes' made it easy to mobilise majority outrage and condemnation. However, the fact that these gang rapes were exceptional and not reflective

46 *Survivor and rapist discourses*

of the vast majority of situations within which women suffer sexual violence meant that to focus on them detracted from addressing broader societal and structural issues. Sherene Razack adds, that emphasis on situations such as these serves to render violence against women the preserve of particular cultural groups: 'Once the violence becomes a property of immigrant culture, it cannot easily be uncoupled from debates about how to manage foreigners' (2004, p. 155). It is precisely this direction that the responses to the 'Sydney gang rapes' took, as the next two chapters document.

The invisible marker of whiteness

This is not to say Wagner herself subscribed to this conceptualisation of rapes. In fact she specifically rejects the significance of culture or ethnicity: 'The whole cultural issue wasn't an issue to begin with. With me, it wasn't. This was not about culture; this was about abuse against women.' (2007, p. 227) She also demonstrates a keen awareness of the possibility of her words being manipulated to support other agendas when she writes about refusing to do interviews on issues related to the Cronulla riots or the comments of Lebanese Australian imam, Sheik al Hilaly:[8] '. . . I didn't want people to look at what I've been doing and start saying, "It's all about race" as opposed to "It's all about assault". I didn't want people to think I was motivated by racism, because I'm not. I've never bought into the anti-Muslim thing. Australian guys rape women too.' (2007, p. 235)[9]

Yet, to what extent were the victims' personal attempts to make sense of their experiences reflected in the public discourse? And to what extent were the victims in fact placed in a position where their ability to obtain sympathy and support became contingent on subscribing to other discourses? As explored in the next chapter, an important aspect of media reporting on this case was the identification of the victims as 'ordinary, young (White) Australian girls'. This identification was in turn taken up by a number of commentators to create a symbolic significance of the girls as representative of Australia more generally.[10] While Wagner, in choosing to be named and have her image made publicly available, seems to attempt to reject this symbolic function of 'just any Australian girl', she struggles to achieve this. Even as she seeks to protect her narrative from manipulation, she is unable to guard against being appropriated as a symbol to support other agendas, as the analysis of Paul Sheehan's book in Chapter 5 will demonstrate.

Furthermore, other victims have found it harder to reject this dominant formulation of the rape script in which race/ethnicity became a central factor. In the context of the 'Sydney gang rapes' Wagner was not the only victim to seek to speak out about her experience. Victims in the AEMs/KEM rapes also gave interviews to the popular current affairs programme *60 Minutes* in which they described their anger and frustration at what they perceived to be an inadequate legal response to their suffering. In particular they expressed resentment at the fact that an 'accepted statement of facts' was presented to the Court, agreed to by both prosecution and defence lawyers but which the victims felt inadequately described their experiences (Channel Nine, 'Life Sentence', *60 Minutes*, 21 September 2002). A central feature of this was the removal of all references to racist motivations or abuse expressed by the rapists. One of the victims addressed the media outside the courtroom and reported the racist taunts of one of her attackers during the rapes (Albrechtsen 2004; Brearley 2002).

The extent to which the victims were able to mobilise support and sympathy due to the added dimension of race remains an unresolved question. To put it as Janet Galbraith has, '[w]ith this struggle of re-membering and re-telling, the practices, and particularly the racialising processes which produce a legitimised authentic raped and rapeable subject are shown to be constitutive of this subject according to a White supremacist, phallocentric and heterosexist legal economy.' (Galbraith 2000, p. 72) In her article, 'Processes of Whiteness and Stories of Rape', Galbraith explains her reason for writing about her own experience as a rape victim. She states that the article was a means of re-writing the stories told in court in the way she would have told them, given the opportunity.

While Galbraith details the many factors that worked against her as a rape victim in the criminal justice system (in particular her failure to live up to the expected standards of ideal bourgeois femininity), she does recognise herself as in a relatively privileged position by virtue of being White. For Galbraith, 'whiteness was a "valuable property", an asset in my interactions with the effects of rape and the White legal system' (2000, p. 88). She contrasts this experience with that of Roberta Sykes, as an Aboriginal woman and rape victim: 'In opposition to dominant notions of White womanhood she was constructed according to racist constructions of Aboriginal women's sexuality and availability' (Galbraith 2000, p. 88). In fact the prevalence of sexual violence on the bodies of Aboriginal women is both an important and silenced feature of Australian national history (Moreton-Robinson 2000; Behrendt 1993). This abuse of Black female bodies was both integral to the colonial conquest and remains unacknowledged and unaddressed. It provides an important backdrop against which the debates about the 'Sydney gang rapes' must be read.

Significantly, Galbraith writes of how Sykes' ability to access whiteness (through her mother's presentation of herself as a White woman) became a valuable means through which Sykes was able to gain access to the White legal system. In the context of the 'Sydney gang rapes' this poses interesting questions. A central feature of much of the mainstream discourse on the gang rapes was the characterisation of the victims as 'Australian'/'White'/'Caucasian'/'Anglo-Celtic' girls. Certainly among many of the right-wing commentaries on the rapes these terms were used interchangeably. However, it also seems to be something that others, including the victims themselves, were keen to assert.

An article that appeared in the *Sydney Morning Herald* on 14 September 2002, which seeks to present a reasoned discussion of the racial aspects of the cases (in relation to both racism against the victims and the perpetrators) notes, 'In the space of two months, seven teenage girls who identify as Australian – though two have Italian parents, one has Greek parents and one is part-Aboriginal – were abducted and pack raped . . .' (Crichton and Stevenson 2002). The significance of stating 'though' when discussing the ethnic origins of these young women (especially in

48   *Survivor and rapist discourses*

the context of the part-Aboriginal woman) re-affirms an impression that they are not 'typically' Australian. In a similar way to Jon Stratton's (1998) identification of how the markers 'Italian Australian', 'Greek Australian', 'Vietnamese Australian' serve to render Australians of Anglo-Celtic heritage as the invisible norm, here the certainty of the victims' Australianness seems in question when their particular ethnic origin is known.

At the same time the victims seem to realise the significance of 'being White' in their assertion of their 'Australianness', as if, like Sykes, they see this as their way of obtaining access to some standing within the dominant White legal institutions. In the *Sydney Morning Herald* article mentioned above, one of the victims is quoted as saying, 'The world isn't what I thought it to be – it isn't safe and females are punished for being Australian'. The fact that she structures her indignation in line with dominant discourses of the rapes as an 'attack on Australia' rather than in terms of a violation made possible by the misogyny which exists in Australian society (within both minority and majority ethnic communities) could be read as a strategic choice in order to situate herself as a 'believable rape victim' (MacKinnon 1987, p. 81), deserving of sympathy.

This need to be read as 'White/Australian' could have even greater significance for the victim of part-Aboriginal origin and for 'Kelly' (who is Maori). It has been argued by various postcolonial feminist scholars that in considering the different experiences of rape suffered by White and Black women, consideration must be given to the different stereotypes that have traditionally circulated about Black (particularly Indigenous) women's sexuality compared to White women (Behrendt 1993; Razack 1998, writing about the Canadian context; hooks 1994, 1992, 1990). Through looking at the descriptions used both by and about the 'Sydney gang rape' victims, we can see the ongoing legacy of this specifically racialised and sexualised national history.

Paul Sheehan, in discussing the 'K brothers' trial involving 'Roxanne' and 'Kelly' notes, 'Kelly's arrival on the stand brought a shift in tone, clarity and ethnicity. She was more given to slang. Her voice kept trailing off. And she was Maori, while Roxanne was pale-skinned and Anglo' (Sheehan 2006a, p. 84). This description in which 'Kelly's' ethnic origin, clarity and strength of character are all listed alongside each other seems to reinforce Galbraith's observation that race, gender, class and other power differentials cannot be read separately in the trial process but are intimately intertwined in producing a normative ideal of White heterosexual gendered identity.

In conclusion, the public discourses of the 'Sydney gang rape' victims, while demonstrating points of resistance, ultimately succumb to dominant discourses frequently utilised to explain rape. Rather than representing a progressive approach by the legal system and society more generally to addressing the impact of sexual violence, the victims are ultimately coerced into performing standard victim roles, which do little to challenge the sexist and racist underpinnings of dominant legal and societal constructions of rape. Sharon Marcus could almost be referring to the 'Sydney gang rapes' when she notes, 'White women often obtain legal victories at the cost of juries' giving currency to racist prejudices and to patronizing ideologies of female protection . . . [t]hese biases fabricate and scapegoat a rapist of color and implicitly condone the exploitation and rape of women of color' (1992, p. 388). Even Wagner, who shows incredible self-reflexivity and courage, struggles to separate the need to perform a particular identity for the law from her own articulation of her experience and identity.

'Protest masculinity'?: The rapists' discourses

Having noted the trial process' potential for reinforcing hegemonic discourses on sexuality, gender and ethnicity, it must also be acknowledged that the resort to culturalised language was not solely the domain of dominant discourses. The rapists themselves, both during the rapes and during the subsequent trials (and even after in some cases), sought to assert a cultural component to the rapes. Unlike the French context in which the 'gang rapist' of '*les tournantes*' remained a nameless, faceless threat, in Australia a number of the rapists themselves gained a certain level of personal notoriety. 'Bilal Skaf' has become a name associated with gang rape within Australian media discourses if not broader public discourses. So too, the 'K brothers' – whilst remaining unnamed – sought to assert their own voices throughout the trial process. The identity of the 'Leb gang rapist' is not one that has solely been imposed by dominant representations but one that was apparently embraced by the rapists themselves and – as I will discuss further in the next chapter – a minority of young Sydney men of Middle Eastern origin who subsequently paid tribute to the gang rapists in the form of online videos.

In this section I will focus on two specific features of the rapists' performed masculine identity, which emerged as central to both their own public discourses and the responses (both celebratory and critical) to their actions. The first is the alleged racial motivation behind their selection of victims and their racist taunts to the victims during the rapes. The second is their refusal to acknowledge any wrongdoing. This was reflected in their continued defiance and attempts to disrupt the trial process and – particularly in the context of the 'K brothers' – their attempts to present themselves as victims of racism or at least cultural misunderstanding.

Competing racisms

One of the most provocative aspects of the 'Sydney gang rapes' in media and political discourses was the allegation that in each of the cases, the victims had been targeted on the basis of their nationality (as 'Australian' girls) and been subjected to racial slurs during the rapes. As will be discussed in the next section of this chapter, it was this fact that served to justify in the eyes of many the linking of the crimes with questions of immigration, ethnicity and multiculturalism. It should be noted that there was also evidence of violence and misogynist remarks against women of the same background as the rapists: as discussed above, following her ending of her engagement to Bilal Skaf his fiancée was the subject of graphic drawings by Skaf depicting gang rape. So too, Paul Sheehan notes a number of instances involving violence against women within the K family, including

50   *Survivor and rapist discourses*

the physical assault of their sister, which provided the title for Sheehan's book.[11] However, this was only referred to in support of the characterisation of the rapists as pathological and did not dismiss the alleged racist overtones of their rapes. This was reinforced by statements reported by the victims made to them during the rapes and by a number of comments made by family and friends of the rapists during the trials. Following the AEMs/KEM trial one of the victims informed media outside the court that one of her rapists had told her, 'you deserve it because you are Australian' (Albrechtsen 2004; Brearley 2002). Similarly, victims in the Skaf rapes reported being called 'Aussie pigs' (Mazzocchi 2002; Sutton and Duff 2002), 'sluts' and told they would be 'fucked Leb style' (Albrechtsen 2004).

The 'anti-Muslim conspiracy'

At the same time, the term 'cultural time bomb', which was widely reported in the context of the potential for cultural defences to be argued in rape cases, was the result of a submission on behalf of one of the accused in the 'K brothers' rape trials. A similar submission was attempted by KEM in the AEMs/KEM case, although it was summarily dismissed by Justice Latham. In the context of the 'K brothers' case, their father did not assist their case when he was reported as having told one journalist, 'What do they [the victims] expect to happen to them? Girls from Pakistan don't go out at night' (Sheehan 2006a; Devine 2005) and asserted in court that his sons were not aware of the cultural norms of Australia (Wallace 2004a, 2004b). While AEMs/KEM pleaded guilty to the charges against them, most of the men in both the 'Skaf' and the 'K brothers' rapes refused to do so[12] and remained defiant and openly aggressive throughout the court process.

It was also widely reported that the 'K brothers' were asserting an 'anti-Muslim conspiracy', calling for the jury to be made up of Muslim jurors and claiming unfair bias on the part of both prosecution and defence lawyers as well as the judiciary. Even as there may have been grounds for arguing a certain racial bias on the part of the legal system, the manner in which the 'K brothers' sought to make their point resulted in their argument becoming entangled with general defiance and 'bad behaviour' in the courtroom on the part of many of the 'Sydney gang rapists' in the various trials. In both the 'Skaf' and the 'K brothers' trials, court reporters consistently reported the demeanour of the men as lacking contrition and appearing to be amused by the process. As mentioned in the previous chapter, in the context of the Skaf case, Justice Finnane noted in his sentencing remarks the fact that Bilal Skaf 'had conducted himself as if the proceedings were a joke' ('Rapist out of sight but not out of mind', *The Age*, 2 August 2003; ABC 2002c). Cindy Wockner of the tabloid newspaper, *The Daily Telegraph*, also reported Justice Finnane frequently admonishing the accused and sometimes their family members during the trial. For example, upon receiving a complaint about one of the men laughing and smiling while one victim was testifying, His Honour was reported as saying: 'I am not going to have the place [court] turned into a three-ring circus'. Wockner also claimed that 'at the end of one trial, late last year, one family member professed loudly in Arabic that it was not a crime to f . . . a White slut' and reported hearing a family member

Survivor and rapist discourses 51

of one of the accused call Crown Prosecutor Margaret Cunneen a 'slut' when she was cross-examining the accused (Wockner 2002).

In the 'K brothers' case the accused men's assertions of the 'anti-Muslim conspiracy' merged with the various court reporters' accounts of the men sniggering and behaving inappropriately during the proceedings. It was reported that the accused frequently interrupted the judges, at one stage threw fruit at the jury and shouted at and attempted to physically attack prosecution lawyers and two of the victims' mothers. A journalist with the *Sydney Morning Herald* who covered the trial, Natasha Wallace, also reported the accused treating the trial 'as a joke': 'mocking investigators and giving family members the thumbs-up when they testified in their favour'. She also reported that alongside demanding six Muslim jurors, they laughed out loud when found guilty (Wallace 2004b).

Similarly, Paul Sheehan, in reporting on the proceedings in both newspaper columns and subsequently in his book (analysed in Chapter 5), noted various claims and behaviour exhibited by the 'K brothers' which appeared highly inflammatory. For example, he quotes the response of one of the brothers to his conviction: '*Sami*: We did not commit this crime, your honour. This crime was committed against us. The police set us up because we are Muslims, your honour' (Sheehan 2006a, p. 161; see also Sheehan 2004). Sheehan also notes the behaviour of two of the brothers to the testimony of their father, Dr K: '. . . Sami and Amir spent much of their time buckled over with laughter. For the reporters in the court, it was an extraordinary spectacle, so the impact on the jury would have been considerable' (Sheehan 2006a, p. 146). Recounting the same incident in a newspaper article following Dr K's death, Sheehan quotes at length from the court transcript:

Crown: 'Who wrote this [statutory declaration]?'

Dr K: 'Who? You wrote it, maybe.'

This was greeted with great hilarity by the two defendants, MSK and MAK.

Crown: 'Everything you have said about the night, from start to finish, is a pack of lies, isn't it?'

Dr K: 'It's the truth . . . but we don't always remember. Can you put machine in my brain to recollect it?'

This caused his sons to double up with laughter.

Justice Sully directed a long-suffering gaze at them: 'Mr K has something he would like to contribute?'

They could not respond, such was their mirth . . .

(Sheehan 2006d)

This type of reporting was a frequent if problematic occurrence within Australian media coverage of the 'Sydney gang rapes' as I document in the next chapter. Through such descriptions, images of anti-social behaviour, misogyny and disrespect designed to shock the reader were simultaneously overlaid with a specific racial/ethnic context, for example through the various references to the

52 *Survivor and rapist discourses*

perpetrators speaking Arabic. However for the purposes of this discussion I want to focus on these reported acts and what they might tell us beyond evidencing deviant or horrifying behaviour. Assuming these are fairly accurate accounts of the rapists' behaviour, these actions would seem to have been highly counter-productive to the men's causes. It certainly did little to challenge the stereotypical image of the pathological deviant widely presented in media reports on the cases (as the next chapter will demonstrate) and made it very difficult for those who felt there were racist motivations behind focusing on these particular rapes to maintain much sympathy for them. So why did they behave in this way?

The refusal to admit guilt is not that surprising. Research on the attitudes of accused rapists has demonstrated they infrequently plead guilty and often present a lack of understanding as to the seriousness or criminality of their actions (Cossins 2000; Bowker 1998). However, what makes the behaviour of the Sydney gang rapists remarkable is the extent to which they actively sought to disrupt the legal process and adopted strategies of behaviour, which were undoubtedly damaging to their cases. One possible reading of the rapists' behaviour in court is a refusal to submit to the inherent violence of the law's discourse. The outrage their conduct elicited was largely based around the apparent acceptance of the neutrality and legitimate authority of the courtroom, which demanded respect of all those before it. And yet, the legitimacy of the courtroom is based completely on the effacement of its implicit violence:

> 'All who enter this legal system are constructed according to its normative and violent discourses. This "domination of the existent (a relationship of knowing) enacts a suppression or possession of the other' (Pugliese 1996, p. 23). The violence of this is rewritten as reason and law'.
>
> (Galbraith 2000, p. 74)

The rapists were no doubt aware of the racial imperative – which alongside the highly damaging evidence accumulated by the police – would work strongly against them. Certainly, by the time the 'K brothers' trial began, the general public sentiment was one of limited sympathy for young men of immigrant origin accused of raping 'Australian' girls. It is unlikely that the men would have been completely oblivious of the symbolic significance of their actions. Can the disruptive conduct of the rapists therefore be understood as them reject-ing that which the law assumed was already known about them? To accept the authority of the courtroom would have been to endow it with a legitimacy, which it perhaps does not deserve in light of its historical inability to counter the racist, classist and sexist structures, which have shaped both the law and society more generally.

As discussed above, two of the 'K brothers' were particularly vocal about their feeling of disadvantage in the legal process. They repeatedly asserted that there was an 'anti-Muslim conspiracy'. This included their defence lawyer, who they claimed had told them, 'All Muslims are rapists', leading to them defending them-selves (Sheehan 2006a, p. 62; Dagistanli 2005). They also stated that the legislation

Survivor and rapist discourses 53

passed removing the right of an accused to directly cross-examine their victim had 'only been changed for us . . . They change the laws because we are Muslims. To them we are not human beings' (Pelly 2003). As Selda Dagistanli documents from her observation of the trial, MSK told the Court:

> The government wants to play games with us. The government wants to enjoy this trial. This is not a fair trial. These laws were made because we are Muslim. This is racial discrimination from the government. This is not a fair trial because we cannot cross-examine the complainants who are very important to our case.
>
> (2005, p. 90)

Thus, could their actions be understood as a refusal to grant legitimacy to an institution they felt would fail them?

Yet the perception of disadvantage was not limited to the accused in each of these trials. As seen in the analysis of Tegan Wagner's description of the trial process, she too baulked at the extent to which she was forced to reframe her narrative and subjective experience into a form comprehensible to judicial discourse. Yet Wagner ultimately did just that. She strategically conformed to the image required of her in the courtroom in order to gain support for her cause. To use the Bourdieusian language of the habitus and the field, it would seem Wagner's strategic adoption of the role of 'ideal victim' displayed a good understanding of the 'rules of the game'. Thus, in exercising her agency, she both recognised the structural limitations imposed upon her and adjusted her behaviour accordingly to achieve the best possible outcome.

In contrast to Wagner, the rapists seemed to demonstrate *no* clear sense of the game and did little to aid their cause. Throughout the trial process the men in the 'Skaf' and 'K brothers' cases and their family members, friends and supporters did little to dispel the allegations of their racist attitude to broader Australian society. Rather than rebelling against the hegemonic categorisation of 'Muslim' as terrorist in the aftermath of 9/11 (a stereotype that many nations of the developed West have tacitly accepted and that has been repeatedly problematised by liberal, anti-racism activists and academics alike), Bilal Skaf in fact sought to draw upon 'War on Terror' discourses linking Muslims with violence and terrorism when he threatened Corrective Services Commissioner Ron Woodham (see the previous chapter).

The 'K brothers' even affiliated themselves with a 'Lebanese' identity, despite being Pakistani. One of the victims, 'Roxanne', reported that she had asked the 'K brothers' their nationality when she met them and had allegedly been told, 'Lebanese. We're all Lebanese' (Sheehan 2006a, p. 40). Another of the victims ('Kelly'), in her evidence to the Court, testified to a conversation between the men in the car following her rape:

Crown: What did the driver [of the car – MAK] say?
Kelly: They was, like, he wanted to kill us.

54 *Survivor and rapist discourses*

Crown: Can you remember what he said? If you can, try to say the exact words he said or as close as you can remember.

Kelly: Umm, he said, 'We have to kill them because', oh, like, he said, 'Okay, we have to get rid of them. We have to kill them', and Mohammed said, 'No, let's not kill them because the other boys are in prison'.

Crown: Did you know what they were talking about?

Kelly: Yes, I knew what they were referring to.

Crown: How did you know what they were referring to?

Kelly: Because at that time there was a lot of publicity about these other rapists [the Bilal Skaf gang-rape trials]

(Sheehan 2006a, p. 88)

Paul Sheehan reported that in asserting his claim of an 'anti-Muslim conspiracy', the oldest K brother (MSK) told the prison psychologist that the Skaf gang rape trials had been to promote the careers of the police and prosecutors involved and to discredit young Muslim men in Australia. MSK apparently also alleged that the evidence against Skaf had been fabricated (Sheehan 2006a, p. 62). In a separate incident involving indecent and physical assault by MRK, the victim alleged he had pushed her against a wall and told her, 'If a Leb wants to fuck you, you fuck them' (Sheehan 2006a, p. 160).

Sheehan adds to this the following description of the young men's physical appearance:

The K brothers certainly affected Lebanese-style haircuts. [MSK]'s head was shaved at the sides and back and he had a very short cut on top, with a bleached-blond fringe at the front.

[MRK] had a variation on this: shaved hair around the sides and curly hair on top, streaked with blond. He, too, had a fixation with the Lebanese street culture.

(2006a, p. 40)

Tegan Wagner also described the men as 'Lebanese looking' and gave a similar description of MMK's haircut (2007, p. 18). What Sheehan means by a 'fixation with the Lebanese street culture' is not clear, and he does not provide specific examples. There are of course reasons why identifying the 'K brothers' as adopting a 'Lebanese youth' identity could possibly be expedient for Sheehan (discussed in Chapter 5). However, the description of the 'K brothers'' appearance, dress and car[13] do seem to suggest an affinity for a particular version of 'Leb/ gangsta culture'. However along with the assertion of this particular ethnic identity, what emerges from the reports of the three sets of gang rape trials is that the men themselves seemed to embrace (or at least did not seek to challenge) the identity of the violent, misogynistic and racist young Muslim man. Moreover, they are not the only men who appear to have done this as I will elaborate on in the next chapter.

The 'young Lebanese Muslim man': Postcolonial habitus?

As discussed above, there is little doubt that gang rape survivor Tegan Wagner demonstrates a remarkable astuteness for how she must construct herself in order to achieve the outcome she desired. However, as also noted, she was aided by her racial advantage: the 'unmarkedness' of her whiteness (Frankenberg 2001). This racial advantage provided a means of helping to balance the disadvantage experienced by women in their encounters with the sexist institutions of the law. In itself it was not sufficient to guarantee her status and her credibility (as evidenced by the cross-examination ordeal she details), but it did provide a certain power, which she could capitalise on. While the other victims were not universally 'White', the relativity of 'whiteness' emerges clearly in the 'Sydney gang rapes' context. Despite their ethnically diverse backgrounds, the media discourses, which served to 'render them White', also provided them with access to the power and privilege that whiteness brings albeit at the expense of neutralising the harmful racist and sexist assumptions contained in the process.

In contrast, the rapists' 'ace' of masculinity (Galbraith 2000) was heavily countered by their racial profile and the inter-racial nature of their crimes. Furthermore, in a post-9/11 world where discourses on terror have cemented a link in the popular imaginary between Islam, violence and misogyny, the rapists conformed to powerful stereotypes. Perhaps they realised this and felt it pointless to passively accept what they already knew would be the outcome of their prosecution: harsh condemnation. Or, on the contrary, could their actions be read as them performing exactly the role expected of them?

Stuart Hall, in 'Cultural Identity and Diaspora', suggests the following ongoing relationship between colonial domination and the construction of identity of former colonised peoples:

> They [the West] had the power to make us see and experience *ourselves* as 'Other' . . . It is one thing to position a subject or set of peoples as the Other of a dominant discourse. It is quite another thing to subject them to that 'knowledge', not only as a matter of imposed will and domination, but by the power of inner compulsion and subjective conformation to the norm.
>
> (Hall 1990, pp. 225–226, emphasis in original)

Gutterman (1994) and Connolly (1991) similarly argue that 'specific facets of personal identity can be discursively inscribed on individuals so forcefully that an individual may have very little power or space in which to discursively challenge or reshape that particular aspect of his or her social persona' (Gutterman 1994, p. 222). Gutterman goes on: 'In the United States, where gender, racial, and sexual identities are so emphatically marked on individuals, there is often little discursive space to challenge these aspects of one's identity' (1994, p. 223). Here Gutterman draws on the Foucauldian notion that the individual must be seen as an 'effect of power' (1994, p. 219) or that the subject is in fact produced from within relations

56 *Survivor and rapist discourses*

of power (1994, p. 220). Gutterman's solution to this relies on the idea of performativity. Gutterman believes this provides an answer to the frequent critique of post-structuralist theory that its emphasis on the discursive construction of subjectivity ultimately provides little scope for agency. Yet, how does this relate when the performance in fact conforms to the very discourse that has constructed and dominated it?

For this reason I find a Bourdieusian analysis more helpful. In particular, drawing on the concept of 'symbolic violence' allows us to explain how it is that certain unequal power relations are maintained through their apparently 'common sense' or 'taken for granted' nature. Ciaran Cronin explains: 'The shared schemes of perception and evaluation incorporated in the habitus mask the arbitrariness of social divisions by inculcating belief in their legitimacy or naturalness'(1996, p. 65). While Cronin (and others) have argued that this understanding of human subjectivity seems to provide very limited scope for agency, the influential feature of Bourdieu's analysis is its recognition of the inter-relationship between history, social structures and the individual subject's identity construction and performance:

> [W]hile dominant agents have a vested interest in upholding the principles of 'vision and division' of the social world that legitimate their position of dominance, symbolic power also depends on the complicity of the dominated in the form of an immediate, unreflective, bodily adherence to these same principles.
>
> (Cronin 1996, p. 66)

Just as Bourdieu is concerned with the implications of class and gender on the embodied subjectivity of individuals, a concept of '(post)colonial habitus' recognises the ongoing implications of colonialism on the identities of both the former colonised and coloniser. Using this term I want to draw on and expand literary scholar Vivek Dhareshwar's concept of the 'colonial habitus'. Using Bourdieu's (1977) definition of habitus, Dhareshwar argues: 'The practices produced by the *habitus* appear "natural", not amenable to thematisation by the agents participating in it, although their participation is what sustains it. The specific form of colonial domination is, to a great extent, inseparable from this *habitus*.' (1989, p. 85). For this reason he argues:

> I think the hypothesis of a specifically colonial *habitus* is an extremely productive one for historians/anthropologists/sociologists. The works of Frantz Fanon and Albert Memmi and a few others can be seen as the programmatic exploration of the *habitus* as the site of colonial encounter and the cluster of power relationships which semiotize everyday behaviour in a particular fashion. Bhabha's psychoanalytic framework, methodologically refined and delimited, would be relevant in this context.
>
> (1989, endnote 20)

This is a revolutionary idea and one that seems to hold great potential in attempting to reconcile the apparent contradictions in the rapists' own identity construction and articulation. Can their discourses be read as resisting or conforming to dominant constructions of 'Muslim male youth' identity in Australia? Why do they seem frequently to emerge as such caricatures? And how can we conceptualise the function of stereotypes when they are not simply imposed by external discourses but are adopted and performed by the rapists themselves? For Dhareshwar this can be understood in the following way:

> The stereotypes that emerge out of the *colonial habitus* simplify the subject's relationship with himself/herself and with others not because they falsify reality, but because they impose 'an arrested, fixated form of representation that, in denying the play of difference . . . constitutes a problem for the *representation* of the subject in the significations of psychic and social relations' (Bhabha "The Other Question" 1983, p. 27).
>
> (Dhareshwar 1989, pp. 85–86)

In describing a 'postcolonial habitus' I argue that the social structures and relations of power created by colonial discourses continue to be embodied in individual subjectivity. This is also a circular practice for, at the same time, the continued reiteration of these discourses through the embodied practices of individuals serve to re-legitimate time and again the very power structures on which they are based.

This possibly provides a way to understand how it is that the rapists seemingly fail so completely to adapt to the rules of the 'field' within which they are required to operate. If habitus provides one with the capacity to adapt one's behaviour to maximise capital, then the rapists' actions in the context of the 'Sydney gang rapes' seem to demonstrate a complete inability to play the game. Yet if we are to accept that external discourses of racial hierarchy have the capacity to impact deeply on the identity formation of those deemed 'inferior' to the point that they themselves absorb images of themselves that are negative and disempowering, then the strategic adoption of a 'Lebanese Muslim' identity of violence, terrorism and disrespect for women and authorities, while still counter-productive, becomes comprehensible.

Intersecting racisms and sexisms

As discussed in the next chapter, many of the public responses from left-wing academics and media commentators in Australia, while condemning the sexist nature of the violence, refused to engage with the suggestion that the attacks were racially motivated or influenced. And yet, the rapists themselves did not seem to have expressed the same hesitation about drawing on racialised and racist stereotypes of both themselves and the women they raped. Even if the racist comments made to the victims can be discounted as simply further proof of the desire to humiliate them (an explanation, which in itself does not satisfactorily dismiss the concern that the rapes must be seen as acts of sexism *and* racism, which cannot be separated), the resort to racialised (and racist) stereotypes about normative female

58 *Survivor and rapist discourses*

behaviour espoused by both the rapists and those attempting to explain their behaviour warrants interrogation.

For example, the suggestion that the men chose victims from outside of their community on the basis that they were 'easier targets' (Brearley 2002) does not discount their racist assumptions about White women as more sexually available and promiscuous than Muslim girls. Furthermore, the 'K brothers' and at least one of the AEMs/KEM rapists attempted to suggest there was an issue of 'cultural misunderstanding' created by the victims' behaviour. The racist and sexist assumptions within these statements *cannot* simply be labelled the responsibility of either White or Muslim society. Rather sexism becomes a vehicle through which battles between different groups of racialised men are fought.

The striking feature of the rapists' discourse is not that it is a rebellion or rejection of existing power structures but that it in fact conforms to many of the stereotypes on which positions of dominance are constructed and legitimated: both racial and sexual. There is a startling commonality between the discourses of the rapists and many of their (predominantly but not exclusively male) critics. Both groups appear aware of the symbolic significance of the rapes (if not during, the rapists certainly seem to realise this afterwards), and both remain within the logic of 'inter-ethnic conflict and conquest' as they battle to dominate the public sphere. The gang rapes provide a means for the (male) 'Other' to communicate his resistance to (male) Australia, through the wrongful appropriation of bodies seen to both belong to and symbolise the nation of Australia. As a result, the punishment of the rapists becomes a means of reasserting White Australian masculine power just as the acts of rape and the defiance of the rapists appear to seek (unsuccessfully) to destabilise and challenge this dominant model of masculinity. The women emerge as passive objects of exchange. Not only is the act of gang rape an act 'between men', so too the subsequent interactions between the Sydney gang rapists and their critics emerge as a battle of masculinities.

In this context Tegan Wagner's comment (quoted above) in which she links gang rape with other 'masculine displays' of violence emerges as highly insightful. The feeling of exclusion and disempowerment she and a number of the other victims express becomes comprehensible. Just as their positions as victims in the gang rapes is suggested to be ancillary (merely a vehicle through which a process of homosocial bonding becomes possible through a heterosexual act: Sanday 1990), so too their voices in the subsequent discourses on the rapes are treated as being of less importance than the symbolic function the violation of their bodies performs for a communication between two groups of men.

As explained in the introduction to this chapter, in attempting to analyse the discourses of the rapists, the central issue of interest is their choice of language and their modes of attempted resistance to the dominant public and judicial discourses that 'explained' or responded to their behaviour. Their personal motivations are largely irrelevant, and it is accepted that these men represent a particularly disturbing and repugnant but also a marginal model of masculinity. Having unequivocally accepted the misogynist criminality of their actions, I propose that a possible reading of their discourses reinforces the argument that the 'Sydney gang rapes' must be read as acts in which sexism, racism and nationalism are all intertwined.

Notes

1 Since the 1960s the schools of Critical Legal Studies, Critical Race Theory and Feminist Theory have all contributed excellent analyses of how power relations operate in the context of the court process as well as identifying the embodied subjectivity that impacts on the actions and language of all the participants in the courtroom from judges and lawyers to jury members and the parties to the case.

2 For a detailed discussion of this in the context of Australian law reform, which has created a graded definition of sexual assault, see Temkin (2002).

3 She attempts to maintain her composure despite expressing repeatedly the desire to lash out and express her anger; in describing the evidence of Kerry, her former friend who had been at the 'K brothers'' house the night of the rape, she writes, 'I wanted to get up and shout at the jury, "She's a liar! Don't listen to her!" But I couldn't. I wasn't allowed to show any emotion or argue or do any of the things I was desperate to do . . . I really just wanted to get up and abuse the crap out of her, but I knew that if I did that the whole case would have to be restarted and I would've had to go through everything all over again. So I had to just suck it up.' (2007, p. 174).

4 Generally restraining herself to bare minimal responses, the most she allows herself in response to a series of aggressive questions is, '"If you don't mind me saying," I said, "that's complete bullshit!"' (2007, p. 163). Otherwise she maintains her composure and resorts to a sarcastic tone when attempting to resist the imputations put to her by the defence lawyers.

5 'I turned to look at the boys just to see if they could feel my telepathic waves of hatred' (2007, p. 160).

6 'I wasn't going to cry in front of them, I was going to win' (2007, p. 160).

7 'I couldn't help but chuckle as I watched him [Morison, the defence barrister] make a fool of himself. I just looked at him with a small grin and went, "Mmm." He'd avoided my question and he knew it. It was a little moment of revenge.' (2007, p. 161).

8 See the next chapter for details on these two events.

9 Following these remarks it is noteworthy that Wagner was in Cronulla the day of the riots. Her presence suggests either she is being disingenous in her book or that the events at Cronulla were more complicated than the 'moral panic'/ 'Islamaphobia' accounts presented by some left-wing academics (for example Poynting 2006). See the next chapter for further discussion.

10 For example – as discussed in the next chapter – right-wing media commentator Miranda Devine (2002) characterised the rapes as reflecting, 'a hatred for Australia's dominant culture and contempt for its women'.

11 *Girls Like You* does not in fact refer to the rape victims but was a comment made to Ms K by her brother just prior to his physical assault on her and reported in legal proceedings against him Sheehan (2006a, p. 1).

12 None of the 'K Brothers' pleaded guilty, and of the nine men charged in the Skaf cases, only three pleaded guilty.

13 The 'K brothers' drove a Subaru WRX Impreza: a car frequently associated within popular representations of 'gangsta' culture both within Australia and elsewhere.

4 'Talking race or racism'?

Public responses to the rapes

Introduction

In this chapter I examine the political, media and academic discourses responding to the 'Sydney gang rapes'. As noted in the previous chapter, the 'Sydney gang rape' trials provoked intense media scrutiny of the criminal justice system as well as opening up debate about the status of multiculturalism. The rapes also led to two pieces of law reform. I will start with an analysis of the political debate that accompanied this law reform before moving to an in-depth exploration of the various media discourses.

Initial political responses

As noted in Chapter 2, the sentences handed down in the AEMs/KEM case provoked a strong public reaction. Justice Latham's perceived leniency re-opened public debate about judicial disregard for community expectations. It also instigated the proposal of new legislation in the NSW Parliament on 4 September 2001 seeking to create a new offence of 'aggravated sexual assault in company', carrying a maximum life sentence (Johns et al. 2001).

Initially race/ethnicity did not seem to be the focus of official responses to the gang rapes. Rather the emphasis was on the inadequacy of judicial sentencing and the need for a tougher stance on crime. For example, Ian Ball, the president of the NSW Police Association, was quoted in an opinion piece in the Sydney broadsheet *Sydney Morning Herald* as stating: 'If the courts don't start to reflect community views and the views of the Parliament then at some point they're going to forget their right to judicial independence . . .' Similarly, then NSW Premier Bob Carr was quoted as saying: 'We need judges to be aware of the public's expectations in sentencing, especially in the serious categories of crime such as sexual assault and aggravated sexual assault. We also want a justice system sensitive to the concerns of the victim and the victim's family.' (cited in Johns et al. 2001, pp. 19–20).

This response fit within a broader 'law and order' discourse that had played a central role in political and public discourses for a number of years, particularly during the tenure of NSW Premier Bob Carr (Poynting, Noble, Tabar and Collins 2004; ADB 2003; Collins, Noble, Poynting and Tabar 2000). In this context Bob

Public responses to the rapes   61

Carr provided the following response to the AEMs/KEM case, quoted in the *Sun Herald*:

> As Premier I am committed to seeing judges get the message. Gang rape is a dreadful crime. The worst offenders should be in jail for life . . . We want to send a clear message from NSW families [to the judiciary] that judges must take a tougher attitude to people convicted of serious crimes. It is clear we need tougher legislation and a guideline judgment that the courts can follow for these terrible crimes.
>
> (Johns et al. 2001, p. 19)

The sentiment appeared admirable, a real attempt to address the traditional legal failure to treat sexual violence with sufficient seriousness. Yet Carr's deployment of the 'law and order' discourse raised a number of issues. The first was the focus on *gang rape* as a particularly horrendous crime. While apparently reflecting a greater commitment to addressing sexual violence, it in fact did not stray far from traditional social and legal responses. Gang rape not only reflects a relatively small proportion of rapes committed, it is also more likely to fit the dominant characterisation of 'real rape' as it generally does involve strangers and is associated with an extended ordeal including degradation of the victim (Franklin 2004). By limiting his condemnation to gang rape – although clearly relevant to the particular case – Carr did not open up a broader discussion of rape. This did little to challenge the broader issue of impunity, which has led to ongoing, normalised levels of violence against women.

At the same time, by framing the problem of gang rape within the rhetoric of 'law and order', Carr's response took on an implicit racial/ethnic dimension. Since at least the early 1990s the political and media emphasis on the need for stronger judicial responses to crime in NSW has frequently been tied up with debates surrounding ethnicity as a factor in crime and backlash against immigration and multiculturalism (see Poynting et al. 2004; ADB 2003; Collins et al. 2000). In the context of the gang rapes, this connection was later made explicit when Carr reportedly told a journalism student writing for an Arabic newspaper, '. . . what these violent rapists said when they committed the crime – they projected race into this argument' (ADB 2003, p. 61). Thus, the 'law and order' responses to the 'Sydney gang rapes' began to follow a similar trajectory to that identified by Sherene Razack in the context of Norwegian institutional responses to forced marriages, where responding to violence became inseparable from the management of immigration (2004, p. 155).

While (or perhaps because) the original trial judge in AEMs/KEM had sought to dismiss any racial/ethnic element to the case, this aspect became increasingly prominent as media, political and general public attention to the issue of gang rape grew. So too, criticisms of the justice system became increasingly entangled with the race/ethnicity debate surrounding the AEMs/KEM case. What followed was an oscillation between attempts to quell the rising wave of racially motivated and

62   *Public responses to the rapes*

frequently xenophobic mainstream public and media responses to the rapes, and blatant capitalisation of these very sentiments.

Introducing new legislation: The Crimes Amendment (Aggravated Sexual Assault in Company) Bill 2001 (NSW)

An excellent example of the equivocality of political discourses can be found in the parliamentary debate following the introduction of the proposed gang rape legislation.[1] Immediately following the AEMs/KEM trial and prior to the commencement of the 'Skaf trials', a bill was hurried through parliament proposing an additional crime be added to the *Crimes Act 1900* (NSW) specifically dealing with rapes committed concurrently and by multiple perpetrators. While NSW Attorney-General Bob Debus tried to distance the legislation from the 'Muslim gang rape' panic in his Second Reading Speech to the NSW Parliament,[2] the subsequent parliamentary debate became a struggle between those who sought to concentrate on race/ethnicity and those who sought to concentrate on gender.

For example, the member for Wentworthville, Pamela Allan, provided a powerful critique not only of the attempt to 'culturalise' the problem of rape but also the broader sexist attitudes prevalent within dominant Australian culture:

> At present there is an enormous amount of hysteria in the community relating to the perception that these rapes have been perpetuated by ethnic boys who hang around in ethnic gangs. One of the previous speakers in this debate referred to the crisis relating to the asylum seekers. In my opinion, it is a great tragedy that issues relating to ethnic communities already living in Australia and those seeking to relocate to Australia are currently running in tandem in the media. Rape is not a cultural problem. It is sad that in the current debate we are not reading about the continued incidence of pack-rape by, for example, Anglo-Celts in our community at the same time as we are reading about the problems involving supposedly ethnic gangs. It is not a cultural problem but a gender problem. Men have oppressed women for many thousands of years, and in some instances, unfortunately, that oppression takes the form of violence and physical assault.

Aside from attempting to shift the focus away from the race aspect and onto the gender aspect, Allan highlighted the media trend whereby the rapes were increasingly linked with broader immigration debates. Her condemnation of this trend is insightful, as is her identification of the more pressing problem: the ongoing impunity for violence committed against women. Unfortunately, while other MPs did reject the racialisation of the crimes and sought to defuse the intense negative attention focused on the Lebanese/Muslim population, Allan was one of the few voices to emerge that really problematised broader Australian conceptions of women's sexual and bodily integrity.

Public responses to the rapes   63

To exemplify her argument, Allan referred to a disturbing and sexualised email she received from a 'Mr Dowling', attacking her stance on the AEMs/KEM rapes and directly threatening Judge Latham. Commenting that she 'cannot fathom why a person who is so concerned about rape in the community would send such a violent email to me . . . He is not simply a father who is concerned about the welfare of his daughters', she went on to condemn Australian culture more generally:

> This is part of a culture that oppresses women. I am not suggesting that Mr Dowling is a rapist, but because of the vicious and sexual nature of the email that was sent to me as a public office holder, particularly in reference to Megan Fay Latham as a judge, one could almost extrapolate that this is part of a spectrum of violence and views on women that exist in our society.

Allan's ultimate statement of support for the legislation largely conformed to the dominant 'law and order' rhetoric and highlighted again the limited space for a socio-political feminist response: an issue I will return to in the concluding chapter of the book. However, by placing Mr Dowling's email in the public domain Allan did present an attempt to address the broader issue of sexual and sexist violence.

By way of contrast with Allan's intervention, Andrew Fraser, the member for Coffs Harbour, provided this commentary:

> The fact that a female judge handed down such a sentence makes it even more abhorrent to many people in the wider community. Also of concern is the plea bargaining entered into by the prosecution and defence counsel in which important facts were omitted, with the result that the girls were perceived by the court to have entered the vehicles willingly, when evidence has since shown that to be incorrect. Also, details of the ethnic nature of the crime were omitted and, despite what was said by the honourable member for Wentworth-ville, we need to look at those cultures . . .
>   . . . We do not excuse our electorates for ethnic-based crimes because we have a high ethnic population. Instead we say to them, 'We are Australians. This is the way we treat our women in Australia and this is what we would like to see you do.' There is evidence that there was an ethnic tinge to this crime. I am not saying it happens in every case, but let us not hide or excuse it, because it is totally unacceptable.

Not only did Fraser fail to address the issue of discrimination and violence against women across cultures, he contributed to gender stereotyping by suggest-ing that female judges should be expected to act differently to male judges. This is noteworthy when we consider the general legal feminist consensus that the very possibility that women judges could behave differently from their male counter-parts has frequently been used to justify their exclusion through the suggestion of judicial bias.[3]

64 *Public responses to the rapes*

Furthermore, in making the statement regarding, 'the way we treat our women', Mr Fraser did not in fact explain what indeed that treatment was or the 'we' he was seeking to represent. Instead he reinforced an androcentric vision of citizenship in which 'Australians' are men, and the women within the Australian national territory merely belong to these male citizens ('our women'). The member for Coffs Harbour was not the only participant in the debate to adopt this approach (for example, the member for Oxley made similar remarks).

At the same time there were also those, like Paul Lynch, member for Liverpool, who sought to dismiss the racial aspect, while highlighting the resulting racism such discourses produce:

> Another consequence of linking crime with ethnicity is that it affects a whole range of people in the community. There is no doubt that the Arabic and Islamic communities in Sydney, including those in my electorate, are absolutely horrified at the demonisation they have been subjected to by the tabloid press and some politicians who ought to know better. . . .
>
> . . . a series of threats have been directed at individual Islamic and Arabic families. Certainly a very serious threat was made against one large fairly well-known Islamic school in south-western Sydney that a gang of bikers was going to trash the school and rape most of the female students there. They are some of the consequences of the racist allegations that have been continually, regularly and persistently made.

Lynch went on to report the receipt by his office of letters filled with racist abuse. He also sought to draw attention to the wider context of rape within Australian society. However, what was perhaps most interesting from his observations was the vast number of public responses that did seek to focus on the gang rapes as racial attacks. Most specifically, the fact that the retaliatory threats made also frequently drew on the threat of sexual violence demonstrated the centrality of nationalism and ethnicity to the characterisations of these crimes. In this sense the rapes conformed to classic nationalist propaganda in which women's bodies are markers of communal boundaries and sexual contact/violence a means for inter-communal struggle (Nagel 2003; Yuval-Davis 1997).

Rapes as attacks on the nation

The relationship between rape and nationalism has a long history (Eisenstein 2000, 1996; Peterson 2000; Ramet 1999; Finlayson 1998, p. 98). With this in mind the responses are perhaps less surprising. However this had very particular implications on the ability to formulate a truly non-racist feminist response to the rapes. As Alan Ashton, the member for East Hills, also added:

> Honourable members might have seen a *Four Corners* retrospective that was televised a few weeks ago. It depicted some very Aussie blokes with some very interesting hairstyles in the late 1960s talking about gang-rape and how

Public responses to the rapes   65

it came about. This crime was not invented a few months ago in the south-western parts of Sydney. Rape was considered a prize for the victors of war. Victors would rape the wives or girlfriends of the vanquished enemy. Honourable members will recall the unfortunate rape of members of some of the different ethnic communities during the war in Bosnia. Rape was regarded as a means of offending or outraging communities defeated in war.

By framing his intervention around the language of rape as one of the 'spoils of war', Ashton provided powerful support to the proposition that the 'Sydney gang rapes' must be read as symbolising something more than horrendous acts of individualised violence. Utilising the logic espoused in the findings of experts in the former Yugoslavian wars, Ashton proposed that the rapists' actions must be read as much further-reaching: an assertion of victory or an attempt to destroy or demoralise an enemy, in this case the Australian community. The victims thus became symbols rather than individuals whose rights have been violated. As the property of (male) Australia, their rapes were not personal attacks but attacks on the nation. Furthermore, this logic was adopted not only by members of dominant Australian society but also more marginalised members, as the example of rap group 'Bass Hill Boyz' and the Youtube video, the 'Soldiers of Granville Boys' (discussed later in this chapter) illustrates. Thus, regardless of how well-meaning and well-justified attempts to dismiss race/ethnicity from the debate may have been, this became not only impossible but in fact counter-productive, as an analysis of right-wing media commentators' discourses will demonstrate.

Media discourses

The public sphere is a highly contested site of struggle within which the mass media has been identified as playing a central role in both the dissemination of different discourses and the validation of certain voices and perspectives over others (Kuhn 1995; Jakubowicz et al. 1994; Van Dijk 1992, 1991). An analysis of media responses to the 'Sydney gang rapes' provides an excellent example of this. In this section I turn to the media's reporting of the 'Sydney gang rapes', with particular focus on which perspectives emerged as most prominent and the terms of reference within which the debate was framed. In doing this it becomes clear that there were various discourses circulating in the debate but few, if any, commentators were able to grapple with all the issues at play at the same time and present a completely adequate response. The four key groups can be summarised as follows:

- Those who sought to concentrate on the sexism and misogyny of the rapes and in doing so, removed the emphasis on race;
- Those who used the language of 'women's rights' and claimed they were responding to the problem of 'violence against women' but drew on racialised stereotypes and generalisations in order to do so;

66 *Public responses to the rapes*

- Those who condemned the media and particularly right-wing commentators for racialising the crimes unnecessarily;
- Those who sought to link the rapes with broader issues such as terrorism, Islamic fundamentalism, immigration and multiculturalism by arguing it was the rapists that were racist.

From this, two broad trends emerged: 'anti-sexist' and 'anti-racist', each with a left- and right-wing angle. This polarisation of the debate is unsurprising when we consider that sexism and racism have frequently been read and treated as two separate issues: a concern postcolonial and critical race feminists have increasingly drawn attention to (Roux et al. 2007; Guillaumin 1992; Crenshaw 1991). However, the problem in the 'Sydney gang rapes' was that it became virtually impossible to propose a response to the rapes that condemned the sexism and racism espoused by members of both the dominant and marginalised groups without justifying the re-establishment of hierarchical power structures of gender and race. As British journalist David Fickling astutely put it: ' . . . those who care equally about misogyny and racism are left in an invidious position by the gang rapes of 2000: attack the racists, and you risk defending the rapists; attack the rapists and you risk siding with the racists' (Fickling 2002).

Initial reporting

Unlike the hesitation in most of the judicial responses and at least some of the political responses to the gang rapes, the mainstream media wasted little time in identifying a 'racial' aspect to the crimes. It was widely reported that the rapes had been committed by men who were 'Lebanese'/'Muslim' or 'of Middle Eastern extraction' (ABC 2002a) against 'White'/'Australian'/'Caucasian' women and alleged racist remarks had been made during the attacks. For example, a *Lateline* report on the ABC on 22 August 2001 stated, 'Reports of Lebanese men preying on young Caucasian women, gang-raping them in planned, horrific attacks, has caused an outcry, leading all the way to the highest levels' (ABC 2001). In a lengthy article on the Skaf rapes, journalists Sarah Crichton and Andrew Stevenson reported:

> Three sets of brothers account for half of those caught. Five are related by marriage. All were born, raised and educated in Australia and identify as Lebanese Muslims, or just 'Lebs', although two had mixed parentage.
>
> Some chose to add racial abuse to their rampage. The teenager raped on August 30 was called an 'Aussie pig', told she would be raped 'Leb-style' and asked 'does Leb cock taste better than Aussie cock?' by three of her assailants.
>
> (Crichton and Stevenson 2002)

Herein lay a major difficulty in attempts to dismiss race as an issue in these rapes: the fact that the victims, the police and the rapists themselves all seemed to

Public responses to the rapes 67

endorse if not a racist motivation, a racist element to the attacks. In a report on the ABC in 2002, journalist Jo Mazzocchi noted:

> The case revealed the workings of the gang who operated in Sydney's South west and clearly identified themselves as being of Lebanese Muslim backgrounds. Gang members used mobile phones to alert other gang members to come and join in the rapes and their victims were referred to as Aussie pigs.
>
> (Mazzocchi 2002)

Similarly on the ABC's news and current affairs programme, *The 7:30 Report*, it was reported:

> [JOURNALIST] TRACEY BOWDEN: The victims were all Caucasian women aged between 13 and 18, those convicted all Lebanese Muslim youths.
> BOB CARR, PREMIER (AUGUST 2001): The incidents had a similar MO, in that males of Middle Eastern appearance aged between 15 and 19 years old would operate in this fashion, that is entice girls into the car and effectively, in some cases at least, kidnap them.
> TRACEY BOWDEN: These were not spontaneous attacks.
> Once a woman was lured to a suitable location, the ringleaders would call their mates to the scene on their mobile phones.
> In evidence one young woman revealed that during the ordeal she was called an Aussie pig and told, 'I'm going to (bleep) you Leb style. . . .'
> . . . .While some members of the young men's Lebanese Muslim community resent the focus on their ethnicity, others acknowledge the problem and the need to address it.
>
> (ABC 2002b)

Mazzocchi went on to report that '[e]ven the police admit it was one of the worst cases they'd ever seen', and quoted Detective Inspector Kim McKay:

> KIM McKAY: In terms of frequency, in terms of the number of victims involved and number of offenders involved, and the quite serious nature of the violence that was levelled at these women, and the length of time they underwent their ordeal – yes it is definitely the most serious I have been involved in.
>
> . . .
>
> MAZZOCCHI: . . . The Salvation Army court chaplain who supported the victims, Major Joyce Harmer says the women will never forget what they've been through.
>
> (Mazzocchi 2002)

It is true that the police had done little to establish their reputation as impartial commentators, with Police Commissioner Peter Ryan having already been accused of enflaming racial tension through his ethnicising of crime in Sydney's

68 *Public responses to the rapes*

south-western suburbs. In particular his comment following a shooting attack on Lakemba police station in 1998 that it was the work of, 'the sons of the people who reduced Beirut to rubble' (Brearley 2002) had provoked justifiably angry responses from the community.[4] So too, as noted above, Premier Bob Carr had previously been accused of capitalising on racialised explanations, which served to undermine his credibility. However, the fact that individual police officers, court support officers, Crown Prosecutor Margaret Cunneen (Devine 2003) and the victims themselves spoke of the horrific (and racialised) nature of the attacks resonated with the Australian public as did the apparent lack of contrition and defiance of the rapists and their supporters (detailed in the previous chapter).

Cindy Wockner's article on the rapists' outrageous behaviour in court (discussed in the previous chapter) was shocking because it revealed a division between White Australian society and the Arabic-speaking community behind the gang rapists that was *not* only the product of dominant discourses *but also* the product of the rapists', their families' and their friends' own behaviour. So too, the erratic, contemptuous and disrespectful behaviour of the 'K brothers' in court did little to build sympathy for their case. This does not of course justify the generalisation that such behaviour is attributable to *all* Australians from Lebanese/Muslim/Middle Eastern backgrounds. However, it became clear that to exclude a discussion about race was potentially ignoring an arguably relevant issue. This point was convincingly made in an editorial in the national broadsheet, *The Australian*, on 24 August 2001. In the piece, entitled, 'Culture must be aired in rape debate', it was noted:

> The argument is not that Lebanese culture necessarily promotes rape. Or that Islam is inherently misogynistic. Or, indeed, that immigration breeds crime. The issue is the community's right to have a frank public discussion of a disturbing series of crimes and how to punish the perpetrators, and tackle the underlying causes.
>
> (cited in Johns et al. 2001, p. 27)

In response to this, it was proposed that there was a need for sensitive, balanced discussion of the racial issue in a number of Australian newspapers. Similarly, in an editorial piece in the *Sydney Morning Herald* on 23 August 2001 entitled, 'Taboos, stereotypes', it was argued:

> There should be no taboo in discussing crime occurring in any particular ethnic community. Equally, there must also be great care to avoid stereotyping, which can slip easily into racial denigration . . . The problem of ethnic crime gangs has not gone away . . . But it is disappointing that the experience of the years of confronting such crime honestly while not inflaming hatred and division by careless stereotyping has not prevented the latest ugliness . . . Terrible though they are, these assaults by young Australian men of Lebanese background have been hardly distinguishable from any number of others by packs of other young men over the years. To suggest otherwise is to cross the

Public responses to the rapes 69

line from proper, open discussion of social problems to dangerous, racial stereotyping.

(cited in Johns et al. 2001, p. 27)

The extent to which the subsequent media commentary on the 'Sydney gang rapes' succeeded in presenting a 'balanced' analysis of the significance of race to the rapes has been well documented (Grewal 2007; Gleeson 2004; Poynting et al. 2004; ADB 2003) and does not need to be reproduced in detail here. Suffice to say, the resort to racial stereotypes, over-generalisations and provocative references to war metaphor did little to present the 'Sydney gang rapes' in a way that allowed for sensitive exploration of their causes and consequences. The reports from reputable news agencies and journalists added weight to claims by the more openly right-wing commentators that these were 'racist crimes. They were hate crimes. The rapists chose their victims on the basis of race' (Miranda Devine, cited in *7:30 Report*, 15 July 2002). It also established as 'known' the ethnic identity of both the rapists and their victims (even as in the case of the latter at least, this turned out to be false: ADB 2003, p. 82, note 87).

Some commentators also picked up on reports of a phenomenon known as '*les tournantes*' in France and utilised them to demonstrate a cultural specificity to the crime of rape, based on its connection with Muslim immigrant populations (Priest 2004; Albrechtsen 2002; Brearley 2002; Sheehan 2001). Janet Albrechtsen went as far as to quote 'French experts' to support her claim that this was a problem of culture and religion. She was ultimately exposed by the media watchdog programme on the ABC, *Media Watch*, as having doctored her quotes.[5] However, by this stage the link had already been made. A proliferation of weblogs and articles appeared suggesting that the events in Australia must be seen as part of a broader mode of behaviour exhibited by Muslim men (see Dagistanli and Grewal 2012).

Those who attempted to play down the racial element of the crimes or to dispute the legitimacy of placing the blame on a whole community were accused of allowing misplaced multicultural sentiments and political correctness to 'morally blind' them, as it was the gang rapists who were the racists and had failed to show tolerance and respect. As associate editor of *the Age* Pamela Bone put it: '. . . multiculturalism requires the goodwill not only of the dominant culture but of all cultures. Tolerance of difference is a two-way street' (Bone 2002; see also Priest 2004; Albrechtsen 2002; Devine 2002; Sheehan 2001). Many of the responses from the Left, which sought to critique the racism inherent in many of the stronger condemnations of the rapes, were rejected in favour of 'telling it as it is' and 'bringing it out into the open': 'Talkback radio commentators and callers are speaking the truth, and any attempt by a minority community representative to put an alternative view is portrayed as attempting to cover up that "truth"' (ADB 2003, p. 63). Similarly the refusal of Justice Latham to acknowledge any racial/ethnic element in the AEMs/KEM rape cases was used by right-wing commentators Miranda Devine (2002) and Paul Sheehan (2001) to demonstrate a left-wing conspiracy to cover up 'the truth' about ethnic crime.

70 *Public responses to the rapes*

When Campbell Reid, editor of *The Daily Telegraph* tabloid newspaper, was accused of fear-mongering and racial stereotyping, he responded: 'It could be fear-mongering and racial stereotyping if no-one had been attacked' (ADB 2003, p. 60). The fact that there were a number of rapes, within a short space of time and they were linked (all made reference to being 'Leb', and the 'K brothers' adopted personae that drew on reports of the Skaf rapes) added weight to Reid's argument and recast those seeking to underplay the racial/ethnic element as the irresponsible ones. Attempts by the Left to argue that the only reason why these cases had attracted so much attention was due to the ethnicity of the perpetrator and racism within White Australian society appeared to underplay the truly horrendous nature of the attacks and to over-simplify the problem. After all, the gang rapes and murders of Anita Cobby and Janine Balding had also been the source of intense public attention and outrage, and in both those cases the perpetrators had been White. Former Sydney detective, turned *The Australian* columnist Tim Priest capitalised on this to attack not only the 'Lebanese gangs' responsible for the majority of Sydney crime but also multiculturalism and the Left more generally. In a remarkable reappropriation of the language of anti-racism, Priest commented:

> I wonder whether the inventors of the racial hatred laws introduced during the golden years of multiculturalism ever contemplated the possibility, that we, the silent majority would be the target of racial violence and hatred. I don't remember any race-based charges being laid in conjunction with the gang rapes of southwestern Sydney in 2001, where race was clearly an issue and racial slurs were used to humiliate the victims.
>
> (Priest 2004)

In response to this, the commentary provided by the Left was unable to provide a satisfactory critique due to its apparent reluctance to engage with the issue of racism on the part of the rapists. Instead it allowed commentators such as Priest to construct a new victim of racism: the White majority. In the same opinion piece, Priest launched a vitriolic attack on the NSW Anti-Discrimination Board:

> Unbelievably, a publicly funded document produced by the Anti-Discrimination Board, titled *The Race for the Headlines*, was then circulated. It sought to not only cover up race as a motive for the rapes but to criticise any accurate reporting on this matter in the media as racially biased. It worries many operational police that organisations such as the ADB, the Privacy Commission and the Council for Civil Liberties have become unaccountable and push agendas that don't represent the values that this great country was built on.
>
> (Priest 2004)

By invoking 'values', Priest's statement erased the violence of Australia's past, including the genocidal effects of settler colonialism and the openly racist 'White Australia' immigration policy amongst other things. However, his comments seemed to appreciate in value and insight with the inability of the Left to articulate

Public responses to the rapes   71

a response that managed to address the apparent racism of the rapists while explaining why the focus must remain on combating institutional racism and racism in the dominant mainstream community (something Ghassan Hage does attempt to do in his 2003 book, *Against Paranoid Nationalism*).

The reporting of the alleged racist remarks made by the rapists in fact provided the ideal opportunity for various right-wing commentators to link the gang rapes with broader anti-immigration and anti-multiculturalism discourses. It also provided the opportunity for radio commentators like John Laws to transfer the responsibility for racism onto the rapists and away from White society. According to Laws:

> This is our country. This is a country that we have worked hard and our forebears have worked hard to create. We've created it with strength of character. We've created it with goodwill, and we've created it with hard work, and we don't want people who have different points of view, to the point of view we have in Australia in relation to how we live our lives coming here and simply destroying it. And that's why I really want somebody to come clean. I want somebody to be brave enough to ring me up and say, yeah that's the way it is. We just hate White women. We just hate, or the reverse. But somebody's gotta come clean about this . . .
>
> (quoted in ADB 2003, p. 63)

In fact, the Sydney gang rapists and their supporters seemed to offer Laws exactly what he was asking for. Moreover, the gang rapists, their supporters and Laws appeared to share a common understanding of what constitutes 'an Australian'. The young men *did not* identify themselves as Australian, despite the fact that many of them were born in Australia and/or are Australian citizens. The rejection of the label of 'Australian' was thus not only the product of dominant discourses, it was a product of the rapists' own discourses and those of other young 'Muslim' men as well (as I will show in a moment).

Unfortunately, right-wing discourses on the issue emerged as persuasive because of this and because of the refusal of much of the Left to even entertain suggestions that issues of race might be relevant, unless it was to condemn White racism. Attempts by the Left to minimise the rapists' own racist behaviour were in fact highly counter-productive: On the one hand, it further justified the commentaries of those on the Right who had long asserted the blind political correctness of the Left as the reason for its irrelevance in Australian public discourse. On the other, it diminished the very real feelings of grievance that the individual victims and other members of the Australian community had.

One of the approaches taken by Poynting et al. (2004) in seeking to de-legitimise media discourses on the gang rapes was to point to the 'alleged' nature of the racist remarks, suggesting that these remarks had not been proven and may not in fact have been made (see also Poynting and Mason 2007, p. 78). This was an unsatisfactory response as it seemed to fly in the face of a number of the rapists' own comments and those of their families/friends/supporters. This only further supported

72   *Public responses to the rapes*

claims by the Right that preoccupations with 'political correctness' were leading those on the Left to hide the truth.

As Andrew Lattas (2007) and Judy Lattas (2007, p. 330) have also pointed out in relation to the events at Cronulla in 2005 (discussed further below), the tendency within responses from the Left to dismiss the furore caused by the gang rapes as simply a 'moral panic' (see below) was unhelpful as it served to diminish a very real feeling of grievance experienced. Just as Chapter 3 documenting Tegan Wagner's experience demonstrates, in considering some left-wing academic responses to the Cronulla riot, Judy Lattas highlights that the 'moral panic' account presented a far too homogenising impression of the situation by portraying racism as the only issue at stake. Her conclusion from interviews conducted with various young Shire residents is telling:

> It is not only gangs of Middle Eastern youths who carry the threat of sexual harassment, of course; this is recognised readily by the Shire people I spoke with. Nevertheless, the problem presented at Cronulla by their [the young 'Lebanese' men] specific forms of 'protest masculinity' remains for these schoolies [recent school leavers]; and while they reject the riotous 'protest' that the nationalist Right is celebrating, they clearly do not accept the Left's contention that it was all just a racialised scare mongering of the media.
>
> (Lattas 2007, pp. 330–331)

In the context of the 'Sydney gang rape' trials, the judicial and left-wing academic and political attempts to remove race completely from consideration of the cases was contrasted with both the continued reference by the rapists and the victims to the specific racial context within which they understood the rapes to have happened. This served to reinforce claims that the judiciary was out of touch with community values and fed the argument proposed by right-wing commentators that this was yet another example of 'political correctness gone mad'. For example, the right-wing columnist with *The Australian*, Janet Albrechtsen, argued that this was a legitimate debate as it was, 'talking race not racism' (Albrechtsen 2002).

Left wing anti-racist responses

In the meantime, while trying to re-focus the debate, many academic and left-wing media responses were unable to overcome the limitations of the highly polarised positions presented and assert a non-racist feminist response. For example, significant academic commentators on issues related to immigration, migrant populations and masculinity in Australia, Poynting et al. sought to draw on their already rich body of work documenting how 'out-of-control Ethnic gangs' and the 'Lebanese'/'Muslim'/'Middle-Eastern man' have been successfully used to both justify the maintenance of dominant hegemonic conceptions of Australian identity and externalise problems existing within Australian society over the last decade (Poynting et al. 2004; Collins et al. 2000). However, by treating the 'Sydney gang

Public responses to the rapes 73

rapes' as simply representing a new incarnation of this pre-existing discourse albeit in a sexualised form, Poynting et al. ran the risk of minimising the extreme sexism and the element of racism on the part of the rapists. Academic Paul Tabar expressed this concern:

> It is a shame that we have to be racist in order to recognise the rights of raped women. It seems to me the fact the rapists are an 'ethnic other' explains both the exceptional space given to the rape victims and the magnified outrage manifested by the dominant culture.
>
> (ADB 2003, p. 61)

But he seemed unable to propose an alternative that would not simply return to the trivialisation of rape and the mistreatment of victims. While none of the left-wing commentators went as far as characterising rape as *primarily* a problem of racism, the attempt to argue the significance of social and economic marginalisation to the rapists' display of 'protest masculinity' began to sound dangerously like a suggestion that the rapists were the victims. For example, the Anti-Discrimination Board of NSW in its response to the media reporting of the 'Sydney gang rapes', cited Professor Andrew Jakubowicz:

> . . . Yes it is inevitable that we would notice cross-cultural violence. What's interesting is, what sort of cross-cultural violence we notice and what we don't notice. When it's 'our women' being attacked by 'their men', we notice it deeply. When it's their young men being failed by the education and employment systems, we don't notice and we don't care.
>
> (ADB 2003, p. 59)

It is not suggested that it was the intention of either the Anti-Discrimination Board or Professor Jakubowicz to diminish the significance of the violence committed against the women themselves and indeed they emphasise this point in various other comments. Yet this attempt to counter an extreme act of sexualised and gendered violence with an argument relating to racism and social marginalisation did seem to dichotomise the two: as if sexism and racism are two evils to be measured against each other, rather than intimately connected concepts.

An editorial piece by David Brearley in *The Australian* in 2002 further demonstrates the points of conflict. As a means of countering the perceived ethnic relationship between crime and the 'Sydney gang rapes' especially, Brearley quoted both Ghassan Hage and Scott Poynting, scholars considered experts in the area. Yet once again, the arguments focused on 'moral panic' and 'protest masculinity' frameworks in which the economic disadvantage of the Western suburbs of Sydney and the alienation of the populations in these areas were emphasised.

While these issues are important, the issue of gender was all but excluded from the equation. In citing Hage's comment that '[t]he culture of social rejects is *always* a violent masculine culture', the article did not go further to consider the implications of this to women both within and outside of these areas. Just as in the

74 *Public responses to the rapes*

French context, where commentators on the disadvantages of life in the *banlieue* focused on the limitations placed on the lives of *banlieue* men (discussed further in Chapter 7), so too Brearley's analysis normalised a state of marginality for the women who not only experience similar economic and social exclusion but are subjected to the added discrimination of gender and sexual violence. Through identifying the acts as demonstrations of 'protest masculinity' and attempting to highlight the issues of economic and social disadvantage experienced by men of ethnic minority origins in the south-west suburbs of Sydney, the feminist argument was once again relegated to secondary importance.

Furthermore, it failed to come to terms with the interconnected nature of racial and sexual identities that were relevant to the victims' experiences. By focusing on the rapists these discourses re-inscribed the invisibleness of whiteness (by only considering racialisation in the context of the rapists, the victims emerge in left-wing discourses as without a racial marker) *and* inadequately responded to the racist and sexist construction of White female identity as sexually available: a construction that is as offensive and reductive as the discourses of the Right on the oppressed and repressed Muslim woman.

Left-wing feminist responses

At the same time, left-wing feminist responses did not fare much better. In an attempt to reclaim the debate to focus on the issue of violence against women, a number of commentators and experts working in the area of sexual violence publicly rejected the racialisation of these rapes and the risk of rape generally. On 22 August 2001 the NSW Bureau of Crime Statistics and Research issued a press release stating that sexual assault figures for the Bankstown area had remained stable since 1995, aside from a period of one month in 1999 when 70 rapes were reported, all of which were believed to have been committed by the same person. The press release also named this person to demonstrate that he was in fact an Anglo-Australian (ADB 2003, p. 58).

Similarly, the NSW Rape Crisis Centre sought to downplay the racial aspect and instead utilise the heightened public interest to further its own demands for reform and greater sensitivity to rape victims (Duff 2002). The *Lateline* episode referred to above, while noting the ethnic element of the crimes, went on to quote various politicians and community representatives rejecting the reference to race/ethnicity as an excuse and calling for harsh condemnation of the rapists as criminal individuals (ABC 2001). Kate de Brito also attempted to recontextualise the debate in *The Sunday Telegraph* by pointing out, 'It serves no one to generate fear about gang rapes in a particular part of Sydney when rape is happening under our noses, everywhere, every hour, every day. . .' (de Brito 2001).

Unfortunately, those who sought to concentrate on the issue of sexism often found their message appropriated for other agendas. For example, Karen Willis of the NSW Rape Crisis Centre and gang rape victim Tegan Wagner have both frequently been cited to justify the position of right-wing commentator Paul Sheehan (discussed further in Chapter 5). In a 2008 article on the potential release of one of the Skaf gang rapists, Mahmoud Sanoussi, Willis was quoted as saying that she was 'concerned about his release. The victims of the gang rapes would also be in fear. "It was a vicious, appalling crime," Ms Willis said' (Connolly 2008). While this is a fairly generic statement, which one would imagine Ms Willis frequently makes, its use in an article that once again referred to the allegations that the rapists asked a victim, 'if she liked it "Leb style"' potentially undermined her broader message. Just as the condemnation of Justice Finnane's delivery of a 55-year prison sentence to Bilal Skaf risked reverting to traditional legal discourses, which have underplayed the violence of rape, anti-rape activists saw their message appropriated for application to the specific situation of 'Lebanese/Muslim gang rapes' to the detriment of attempts to challenge *all* instances of violence against women.

Another article in January 2003 in *The Sun-Herald* reported Ms Willis as being enthusiastic about apparent increases in the rates of rape reporting. She was quoted as stating: 'With what happened last year, with the publicity surrounding the gang rapes, women feel they may get a fairer go. And they feel they are being honoured and treated with respect, which hasn't always happened in the past' (Keogh 2003). While she did attempt to contextualise the gang rapes, noting, '[g]ang rapes did not first happen last year', the fact that she drew on the Skaf gang rape trials as an example of victims being treated better seemed to miss the point that these victims were able to draw on racial (racist) stereotypes. As the feminist literature on rape has demonstrated, this is in fact not a new phenomenon and has generally not led to similar improvements for the vast majority of victims who do not fall into this category (George and Martinez 2002; Estrich 1987, 1986). It is understandable that Ms Willis would seek to draw out a positive message for rape victims, but the extent to which the media reporting of the Skaf rapes was really 'good' for victims of sexual violence is debatable.

In an article in *The Daily Telegraph* reporting the reduction of Bilal Skaf's sentence by an Appeal Court on the basis that the rapes were 'not in the worst case category', one of the victims was described as being, 'bewildered at how the justice system has let her down. "How can they get lenient sentences? What's the top of the range, how do you grade these things?" she asked her father' ('Gang rape victims betrayed', *The Daily Telegraph*, 17 September 2005). Similarly, the *Sydney Morning Herald* reported the reaction of Women's Health NSW executive officer, Denele Crozier, to the reduced sentence: '"How many times do women have to be constantly let down and disappointed by the legal system?". . . The "extreme" reduction in Skaf's sentence would confuse the community about the way rapists are dealt with by the law, she said' (Gibson 2005). In principle these were valid criticisms: all too often the gravity of the rape has been assessed on the basis of the actions and intentions of the rapist rather than the experience of the victim. Yet the suggestion in both of these articles that Skaf's reduced sentence was to be considered 'lenient' is misleading. Although significantly less than the 55 years he was initially given by Justice Finnane, the 28-year prison term remains a great deal longer than the majority of rape convictions. According to the Australian Bureau of Statistics in 2006, the average sentence for a sexual assault and related offences was 7.6 years (Clark 2007, p. 18). The statements by both the NSW

76   *Public responses to the rapes*

Attorney-General, Bob Debus, and the Opposition legal affairs spokesperson, Andrew Tink, that the Appeal Court's decision should be appealed to the High Court (Gibson 2005) seemed remarkable in the context of the NSW Rape Crisis Centre's statement that only 1 percent of rapes result in the perpetrator serving time in prison (NSW Rape Crisis Centre Annual Report 2004, p. 5).[6] This would seem to suggest that there were other, more pressing cases than one where the accused is already serving a significantly longer sentence than most. So why the intense concern regarding these rapes?

Right-wing 'feminist' responses

An illuminating contribution was offered by Miranda Devine, columnist for the *Sydney Morning Herald*:

> Yes, it is unfair that the vast bulk of law-abiding Lebanese Muslim boys and men should be smeared by association. But their temporary discomfort may be necessary so that the powerful social tool of shame is applied to the families and communities that nurtured rapists, gave them succour and brought them up with such a hatred of Australia's dominant culture and contempt for its women . . .
>
> (Devine 2002)

Devine's characterisation of the problem certainly pointed to some important contextual aspects in these gang rapes. When identifying communities and families who had 'nurtured rapists', she clearly did not envisage this including Australian families and the Australian community. This was striking as it suggested that rape was not a social problem within Australian culture. In a manner similar to that identified by Sherene Razack in the Canadian and Scandinavian context (2004, 1998), the problem of sexual violence became a cultural problem.

Devine was not alone in this. Then Prime Minister John Howard and Treasurer Peter Costello subsequently added weight to this conceptualisation of the problem through various remarks regarding Muslim immigration and integration in Australia (Grewal 2007; Albrechtsen 2006a; Ho 2007). Similarly, in an opinion piece in 2006 the long-time critic of feminism, Janet Albrechtsen, expressed her disgust at the 'moral blindness' of feminists, which she saw as caused by multiculturalism. For Albrechtsen, feminists had chosen to concentrate on 'banalities' such as unequal pay, glass ceilings, unequal distribution of domestic and childcare workloads while ignoring the significant problem of 'oppression meted out to Muslim women at the hands of Muslim men in Australia' (2006a, 2006b).

Yet in her detailed accounts of violence against Muslim women committed by Muslim men in various European contexts, Albrechtsen did not explain why her concerns were limited to the oppression 'at the hands of Muslim men'. While Muslim women are often held up as 'proof' of an inherent misogyny in Islam through representations of them as 'veiled victims' of their men, their culture and their religion, there has been little attention given to racist and gendered violence committed against Muslim women in Australia, despite it being widely documented by academics and human rights organisations (Browning and Jakubowicz 2004, p. 7; HREOC 2004, para. 1.5.1; ADB 2003, pp. 75–76). Following the media coverage of the 'Sydney gang rapes' the ABC news programme *Lateline* reported that there had been threats of retaliatory rapes against women of Middle Eastern origin (Grewal 2007). Equally, during the 2005 Cronulla riots an attack on a 14-year-old Muslim girl provided an interesting contrast to the justification that the riots were a result of anger regarding the lack of respect for women and sexually threatening behaviour of 'Lebanese Muslim' men at the beach (see below).

The *Sydney Morning Herald* reported on 12 December 2005: 'A bare-chested youth in Quiksilver boardshorts tore the headscarf off the girl's head as she slithered down the Cronulla dune seeking safety on the beach from a thousand-strong baying mob' (Murphy 2005). The symbolism of 'deveiling' the Muslim woman invokes imagery used by Frantz Fanon in reference to French colonial violence in Algeria: 'the rape of the Algerian woman in the dream of the European is always preceded by the rending of the veil. We here witness a double deflowering' (Fanon 1965, p. 45). Thus for Fanon the unveiling of Algerian women was to be equated with the rape of Algeria. While problematic for its rearticulation of the symbolic place of women's bodies to communal identity, Fanon's argument does help provide a context within which the Muslim *hijab*, sexual violence and colonial conquest are deeply interconnected. This is an argument I will return to in later chapters.

Overall, as these examples suggest, the appropriation of 'violence against women' as an issue by right-wing commentators had an extremely detrimental effect. Not only did it add to the already heightened racist, anti-immigration and anti-multiculturalism sentiment within mainstream Australian society, it also undermined the claims of women from both the dominant and marginalised communities in Australia that violence against women was a broader issue of concern. In the context of non-White women, violence perpetrated against them was neglected: when it was violence committed within the community it was utilised – as the above article by Albrechtsen exemplifies – to further demonstrate the inferiority of their culture and when it was violence committed by members of the dominant community it was ignored or downplayed.

However, it also placed women from the dominant community in a difficult position: through the placing of 'gender equality' in opposition to 'cultural tolerance', an anti-racist, feminist response to sexual violence by members of a marginalised group became impossible, while attempts to highlight and challenge the violence committed against women by men of the dominant group became subsumed in issues of race. As Raminder Kaur notes in her research on White women's experiences living in the predominantly non-White London suburb of Southall, all too often literature on whiteness has failed to account for the differences between male and female subjectivities (2003, pp. 201–202). In fact Kaur provides an extremely interesting insight into how White women living in a non-White area attempt to negotiate an identity and a lifestyle that is affected by both their visibility as a White minority *and* the doxa of White women as independent, sexually

78 *Public responses to the rapes*

available and somewhat lacking in moral principles. In doing this, Kaur highlights how gender and racial identity *cannot* be separated and how attempts to analyse one to the exclusion of the other provides a distorted picture. This distorted picture clearly emerged in the case of the 'Sydney gang rapes'.

Racism versus 'mere misogyny'

An interesting counter-point to the 'Sydney gang rapes' was a spate of scandals associated with various Australian sports teams that had periodically been reported over the same five years. As Nina Philadelphoff-Puren (2004) demonstrates, these rapes also employed significant nationalist rhetoric but in this case usually as a means of asserting male victimhood and silencing the female victims.

A remarkable justification for drawing a distinction between the two sets of gang rapes was provided by Janet Albrechtsen (2004):

> There is a frightening misogyny behind the alleged gang rapes by footballers. But beneath the gang rapes by the Lebanese Muslim boys, their family members who say they have done nothing wrong and the perpetrators still at large, is not merely misogyny but racism. Spot the difference.

Thus *mere* misogyny was to be contrasted with racism. This comment appeared to suggest that the protection of 'our women' had less to do with the significance of violence against women than to do with the threat of racial attack. Furthermore, the earnest refusal by then Prime Minister John Howard to, as he stated, 'put the boot in' on the basis that it was 'quite unfair' on players who had not been accused of anything to be subjected to 'generalisations' (Marks 2004; Wakim 2004) is to be contrasted with his comments regarding the problematic integration of Muslims due to their lack of respect for women (Grewal 2007). The insistence of women such as Karen Willis, Tegan Wagner, Paula Abood, Kate Gleeson and many others that violence against women was a topic worthy of serious attention in its own right, regardless of the racial context, were effectively drowned out. Instead, the battle became once more a battle between men: as the events of Cronulla in 2005 demonstrated.

'Protecting our women': Cronulla 2005

While the events at the Sydney beach suburb of Cronulla are deserving of detailed analysis in their own right,[7] they do require brief mention in this chapter due to the connections drawn between these riots and the 'Sydney gang rapes'. By way of background, on 4 December 2005 it was reported that two lifesavers had been beaten up by a 'gang' of four men following a dispute. Over the course of the next week the attack took on mythical proportions. A further attack on lifesavers was reported in the middle of the week and stories of 'Lebanese'/'Middle Eastern'/ 'Muslim' men disrupting Sydney's beaches abounded. A demonstration was organised for the following Sunday, in what Steve Price of radio station 2UE called 'a community show of force'. At the same time, express links were made between the 'Sydney gang rapes' and the events at Cronulla. For example, in a response to a caller on his talkback radio programme suggesting racism went both ways, Alan Jones was clear: 'Let's not get too carried away, Berta. We don't have Anglo-Saxon kids out there raping women in western Sydney' (Marr 2005). This tied in well with his earlier comments on the gang rapes where he had described them as 'first signs of Islamic hate against a community which has welcomed them. . .' (Fickling 2002).

This response perhaps most clearly demonstrates the symbolic value of the 'Sydney gang rapes' to a number of conservative commentators. In Jones' formulation, the rapes ceased to be the abhorrent actions of individuals and became the responsibility of an entire community (indeed an entire religion) whose members were all implicated. Simultaneously, the rapes were not violations of individual women but an attack on the Australian community. The victims were transformed from individual women into symbolic boundary markers of the Australian community and nation, and the rapes into further examples of the classic nationalist trope of violation of national borders (Finlayson 1998; Yuval-Davis 1997; Parker, Russo, Sommer, Yaeger 1992).

Interestingly, in interviews conducted by the ABC programme, *Four Corners*, with rioters, Islam's 'lack of respect for women' and the gang rapes were cited as motivating factors for their participation. 'Mark', one rioter, told the journalist:

> I don't know if you remember, but when they [Bilal Skaf and others] were being tried in the court, they were . . . they wanted him to be tried in an Islamic court – do you remember that? Yeah, 'cause they wanted him to be tried under Islamic law. Because they were saying that that's ok to do that [rape] to a woman.

> (ABC 2006)

While recognising the need for rioters to seek to excuse or justify their behaviour, this comment provides an excellent example of the extent to which the image of the 'Muslim gang rapist' has permeated Australian popular discourses. These comments were paralleled in headlines such as 'Terrorism, gang rapes behind riots: MP' (*Sydney Morning Herald*, 12 December 2005), which appeared in the media in the days following 11 December. Paul Sheehan in his book *Girls Like You* – analysed in detail in the next chapter – dedicated an entire chapter to the Cronulla riots and their apparent relationship to the 'Sydney gang rapes'. Through this characterisation the events of Cronulla were re-written from an act of White racism to a legitimate retaliation.

Furthermore, it was not only members of the public or even the media commentators who forged this link. The Cronulla riots provided an opportunity for members of both the NSW and the Federal governments to give their perspectives on and interpretations of the 'Sydney gang rapes' and the implications to be drawn more generally on young 'Lebanese'/'Muslim' male identity in Australia. For example, in discussing the causes of the Cronulla riots, the NSW Police Minister was reported as stating, 'I am concerned a small number of Middle-Eastern

80 *Public responses to the rapes*

males have a problem with respecting women and I think that was an underlying current . . .' (Ho 2007). By specifically referring to the issue of 'respect for women', following such intense public interest in the 'Sydney gang rape' cases over the previous four years, there was no possibility of *not* seeing the events as linked.

Then Treasurer and Deputy Leader of the Liberal Party, Peter Costello, also contributed to this discourse a year after Cronulla. In this intervening period another major 'scandal' involving the Lebanese community in Sydney became a source of intense media, political and public outrage. In October 2006 it was reported that the Mufti of Lakemba Mosque (predominantly attended by Sydney's Lebanese/Middle Eastern Muslim population) in Sydney's south-west, Sheikh Taj el-din al Hilaly had given a sermon likening scantily clad women to raw meat left out for cats (Kerbaj 2006). In an article on the front page of the *Sydney Morning Herald* on 31 October 2006, Costello was reported to have accused the Muslim community, through its continued support for the controversial Sheikh, of having led to the gang rapes and Cronulla riot: 'These kinds of attitudes have actually influenced people . . . So you wonder whether a kid like Bilal Skaf had grown up hearing these kinds of attitudes and you wonder whether kids rioting at Cronulla have heard these sorts of attitudes.' (Hartcher, Coorey and Braithwaite 2006). This provided a re-affirmation of the connection between Islam, the 2005 events in Cronulla and the gang rapes. It also reinforced the Right's suggestion that political correctness had blinded the Left. As Miranda Devine saw it, Sheikh al Hilaly's 'sermon of ignorance has done Australia a big favour' (Devine 2006). According to Devine, 'by revealing so unequivocally his primitive views of women, Hilaly destroyed the claims by cultural relativists that Sydney's series of gang rapes by Muslim men had nothing to do with culture or religion'. To reinforce this point, Devine referred to a speech by another Muslim cleric, Sheikh Feiz Mohammad, who allegedly told a congregation at Bankstown Town Hall that a rape victim had no one to blame but herself for 'display[ing] her beauty to the entire world'. Through linking the 'Sydney gang rapes' with outrageous comments by two Muslim clerics, Devine succeeded in calling into question the Left's commitment to women's rights and anti-racism.

Responses of the 'young Muslim man'

As the comments of the two Muslim clerics illustrate, it was unfortunately not only members of the dominant mainstream society that contributed to culturalising sexual violence. Alongside the repeated statements of condemnation of the rapes and rapists, there were also those within the 'Muslim community' (acknowledging that this is a problematic, overly homogenising label) – including some with positions of authority – who endorsed a view that these rapes did reflect an essential cultural difference between 'Muslim' and 'Australian' society. This was also asserted by family and friends of the rapists, as documented in the previous chapter. Added to this, in 2006 and 2007 various videos were discovered on the user-created content sharing internet website Youtube depicting young men of 'Middle Eastern' ethnic origin in Sydney's west paying homage to Bilal Skaf as a hero and disseminating violent, racist messages threatening Australia.

Public responses to the rapes 81

In December 2006 the commercial television programme, *A Current Affair*, reported on another Youtube video, this time by rap group 'Bass Hill Boyz' who claimed to be 'Lebs', came from the south-west of Sydney and were calling for mass violence against 'Australians'. An example of Bass Hill Boyz lyrics demonstrates a bold invocation of anti-Australian, anti-nationalist violence:

> You'll witness war, you'll see Scattered all over the beach, your family Just like that war in Gallipoli
> All you Aussies from Cronulla Get your fists fucking down Gonna take over your fucking town This is our town now, you dirty fucking Aussies
> (video available at http://pommygranate.blogspot.com/ 2007/01/wogs-all-ova-sydney.html, Accessed 12 December 2008)

In mid-2007 there followed an amateur video – the 'Soldiers of Granville Boys' – apparently made by male students from a high school in the west of Sydney. In this video, symbolic images, photos and music were used to glorify the actions of Bilal Skaf, acts of terrorism and ethnic crime. Skaf was depicted holding a gun against the backdrop of a map of Australia draped in a Lebanese flag and headed, 'Under new management'.

A subsequent newspaper article, detailing both the 'Soldiers of Granville Boys' Youtube video and the 'Bass Hill Boyz', provided further examples of the latter's lyrics. Aside from generally ridiculing 'Aussies' for their lack of visible symbols of wealth (sports cars and jewellery), the following reference to the 'Sydney gang rapes' was reported: 'I don't give a f . . . what you say about us Lebos . . . they didn't get gang-raped bro, I swear it wasn't us, those Aussie chicks wanted it, bro' (McIlveen 2007). As I have argued in the previous chapter, the articulation of a 'protest' masculine identity by young Muslim men in Sydney is in itself unsurprising. As some of the academic commentators quoted above have documented, stigmatisation of and discrimination against young men from Lebanese/'Middle Eastern' backgrounds has been a recurring feature of Australian public culture since the early 1990s. What is less comprehensible is the form the young men's protest has taken. As with the rapists, they have not only adopted stereotypical representations of themselves but the most negative and violent of these.

Bell hooks in her book, *Black Looks*, invokes the field of representation as a 'place of struggle' (1992, p. 3). For hooks, the failure to address the ongoing legacy of colonialism has resulted in many former colonised people trapped within representations of themselves that they have not chosen, nor have any control over but that are sufficiently internalised that they seem impossible to resist. My articulation of a 'postcolonial habitus' in the previous chapter makes a similar argument. Hooks is particularly conscious of 'the internalised colonisation' of young Black American men whose promotion of stereotypical self-images in rap music and film does little to resist or challenge the dominance of White supremacist patriarchy. As hooks points out: 'The very images of phallocentric Black masculinity glorified and celebrated in rap music, videos and movies are the representations that are

82 *Public responses to the rapes*

evoked when White supremacists seek to gain public acceptance and support for genocidal assault on Black men, particularly youth.' (hooks 1992, p. 109).

The fact that the 'Soldiers of Granville Boys' and the 'Bass Hill Boyz' both draw on 'US gangsta' culture makes the application of hooks' critique all the more pertinent. As with the US 'gangsta' identity, these groups of young Muslim men assert a solidarity and identity of resistance, which in fact neither seems to liberate them from racist nor sexist structures of domination. They play completely into the classic orientalist representation of Muslim masculinity as inherently violent, barbaric and misogynist: a representation which constructs White masculinity as civilised, enlightened and 'feminist' by comparison, thus justifying White superiority. To apply hooks' assessment of Black masculinity, the Sydney gang rapists and the young men in these videos seem to have, 'passively absorbed narrow representations of [non-White] masculinity, perpetuated stereotypes, myths and offered one-dimensional accounts' (1992, p. 89). Their conformity with – and embodiment of – the dominant construction of non-White, 'Muslim' masculinity seems to legitimate the perpetuation of the myths and stereotypes on which this construction is based. This effectively functions to not only justify the ongoing marginalisation of these men but also to enforce a type of masculinity against which *all* young Muslim men are measured: the 'Soldiers of Granville Boys' and their hero Bilal Skaf become the sole representations of young men of Lebanese/Muslim origins in Australia.

Finally, the hierarchical relationship *between men* is maintained with the traditional, sexist masculinity critiqued by feminists displaced onto these men, freeing up the 'Australian' man to embody a new apparently more sensitive, 'feminist' identity.[8] So deeply internalised are these discourses – the very discourses that allow for the maintenance of White male privilege and power – that the men appear completely incapable of resisting them or articulating anything close to an independent identity. By focusing their efforts at resistance on an assertion of aggressive, sexist hyper-masculinity, they do little to destabilise dominant power structures or the discourses that allow these power structures to remain intact. At the same time, the fact that these men were in turn held up as 'representative' of 'Lebanese Muslim masculinity' dismissed the possibility of any other articulation of a non-sexist, non-racist masculine identity.

An excellent example of a conservative commentator who capitalised on the divisions outlined above is Paul Sheehan. In detailing the case of the 'K brothers' Sheehan was able to draw on the language of 'women's rights' and not only justify his identification of race/ethnicity as central to the gang rapes but also utilise the actions of the accused in support of this. His portrayal of the rapes provides a fascinating narrative of the benevolent non-racist multicultural Western nation betrayed and violated by the barbaric 'Other'.

Notes

1 All references to the MP's comments are taken from the transcripts of the parliamentary debates. NSW Parliament, 5 September 2001. Available at www.parliament.nsw.gov.au/Hansard/Pages/HansardFull.aspx#/DateDisplay/HANSARD-1323879322-25064/HANSARD-1323879322-25029 [Accessed 29 August 2016].

2 '. . . This offence will apply to all offenders. It does not recognise the race, religion or sex of the offender or the victim; it simply recognises the heinous behaviour committed in groups in these worst category cases and makes available the maximum punishment in this State in appropriate cases': Hansard, NSW Parliament, 5 September 2001. Available at www.parliament.nsw.gov.au/Hansard/Pages/HansardFull.aspx#/DateDisplay/HANSARD-1323879322-25064/HANSARD-1323879322-25029 [Accessed 29 August 2016].

3 In a classic example of 'damned if you do, damned if you don't', female judges who have been identified as holding 'feminist' positions have frequently been mistrusted and subjected to scrutiny regarding their ability to be truly impartial (something which is generally assumed in the context of their male counterparts): see Rackley (2007). A poignant example of this is the attempt by a defence team in the International Criminal Tribunal for the Former Yugoslavia (ICTY) to appeal the decision of Justice Florence Mumba on the basis that her former membership of a UN expert group on gender and her statement that rape should be a war crime suggested the possibility of bias. Similarly, Canadian Supreme Court Judge Claire L'Heureux-Dubé's overturning of the lower court's decision to acquit in the *Ewanchuk* rape case and her express rejection of the negative stereotypes that still plagued rape complainants in court sparked mass public debate in which it was suggested, '[w]e shouldn't have to pay the salary of a radical feminist who sits on the bench and uses her position to promote her own personal agenda' (Backhouse 2003, pp. 172–173).

4 See Collins et al. (2000) for a more detailed discussion.

5 For full details see the Media Watch website: www.abc.net.au/mediawatch/rassial.htm, [Accessed 26 August 2003].

6 According to the Australian Bureau of Statistics 2005, of the estimated 47,500 rapes committed each year, only 9,500 get reported and only 450 of those result in successful conviction.

7 See the special edition of the *Australian Journal of Anthropology*, 2007, for some excellent contributions.

8 This is similar to the process described by Pierrette Hondagneu-Sotelo and Michael Messner (1994) in their work on displays of masculinity amongst Mexican immigrants in the US.

5 'Girls like you'

Introduction

As a columnist with the *Sydney Morning Herald*, Paul Sheehan emerged as a particularly prominent commentator on the 'Sydney gang rapes'. This is largely due to his detailed coverage of the final set of trials involving the 'K brothers'. Sheehan personally attended many of the court hearings and – alongside many editorial pieces – published a book, which provides an in-depth account of what transpired both in the lead up to and during the trials. Published in July 2006, shortly after the final sentences were handed down in the 'K brothers' trials, *Girls Like You* presents a part factual account, part polemic. Sheehan provides a detailed exploration of the rapists' background, the rapes and the subsequent trials using official court transcripts, interviews with the rape victims, their families and legal representatives as well as his own observations.

Aside from providing an interesting parallel to the book by Fadela Amara discussing '*les tournantes*' (Chapter 9),[1] Sheehan's book is one of the most detailed and widely referenced analyses of the 'K brothers' trials. It also led to Sheehan gaining a position of influence within the Australian public sphere. In October 2006 when the NSW parliament was presented with the *Criminal Procedure Amendment (Sexual and Other Offences) Bill* (introduced to improve the protections available to victims of sexual assault in criminal proceedings), Sheehan's book was referred to by a number of speakers in the parliamentary debate. The honourable Chris Hartcher, MP, in fact stated, 'I commend the excellent book by Paul Sheehan, which in a very readable fashion draws the public's attention to the many problems associated with such trials'.[2] It is unclear why Mr Hartcher should have chosen to recommend Sheehan's book above the extensive range of publications already in existence that demonstrate these issues and are frequently the work of specialist organisations like the NSW Rape Crisis Centre or the Australian Centre for the Study of Sexual Assault. What it does demonstrate is the extent to which Sheehan has emerged as an 'expert' in the area of sexual assault and the criminal justice system.

However, while Sheehan's text is presented as a positive effort to redress the current inadequacies of the legal system's handling of rape victims, arguably this is far from the outcome it achieves. Rather, through its use of highly stereotypical gendered and ethnicised imagery Sheehan manages to reinforce many of the dominant conceptions of rape that feminists have long sought to dismantle. What makes Sheehan's text worth deeper analysis is the very telling insight it provides into why the 'Sydney gang rapes' attracted so much attention. Sheehan's description of the victims, their lawyers, the rapists and their families provide excellent examples of how dominant constructions of gender identity, sexuality, nationalism and ethnicity played significant, overlapping and mutually reinforcing roles in the symbolic significance of the 'Sydney gang rapes'.

Creating victims and villains

A common observation within feminist critiques of the legal process in rape cases is the need to construct clear victims and villains in order for the prosecution to be successful (de Carvalho Figueiredo 2004; Wood and Rennie 1994; Estrich 1987, 1986). As discussed in Chapter 3, Tegan Wagner acknowledges this and describes her attempts to perform an 'ideal' victimhood, which she sees as necessary to secure the conviction of her rapists. Yet while Sheehan seems to be attempting to critique the Australian courts' treatment of rape victims, he makes a limited attempt at challenging these dominant narratives in his description of the various actors. Rather, he employs many of the standard rape tropes to build sympathy for the victims and outrage against the perpetrators and the legal system. This results in the perpetuation and reinforcement of the very myths long-identified as being the cause of inadequate legal responses to rape.

Description of the victims

Throughout the book Sheehan dedicates considerable attention to describing the victims, with much made of the fact that they were 'innocent girls'. Their dress, behaviour and limited sexual experience are all commented upon in constructing his narrative. For example, the fact that many of the girls identified themselves as virgins is emphasised. In particular, Sheehan paints an emotive impression of Tegan Wagner as a shy innocent girl:

> [Tegan] was very inexperienced in dealing with older boys and she'd never had a boyfriend. She was a virgin; in fact, she had never even kissed a boy. She was fourteen, barely into adolescence, a big, broad girl and self-conscious about her size. She'd also never drunk alcohol before . . .

> (2006, p. 24)

This description appears designed to ensure a sympathetic response from the reader; the very response Wagner admits she was afraid she might not receive. So too, he comments on some of the young women's dress at the time of the rapes, remarking: 'Neither ["Roxanne" nor "Cassie"] was provocatively dressed: it was winter, and they both wore trousers and zipped jackets' (2006, p. 39). Even more explicitly, he describes their underwear: 'Amir reached under her denim skirt and

86 *'Girls like you'*

pulled off her underpants. They were not low cut or a g-string, just a normal pair of girl's undies' (2006, p. 25). The significance of this information suggests that greater sympathy is owed to rape victims who are not sexually provocative or promiscuous, once again conforming to the traditional discourse on rape and the 'ideal' rape victim (Wood and Rennie 1994).

In relation to the young women who did not fit the image of the 'virgin' victim, either due to the fact they had had sex before or engaged in consensual sex with one of the 'K brothers', Sheehan considers it important to emphasise their naivety. In doing this he seems to attempt to counter any possible claims that the young women were inclined to engage in casual sex, as if to admit this would devalue their role as victims in the subsequent rapes (adhering once again to the 'fallen angel' trope discussed earlier). In the chapter dedicated to Cassie's experience, Sheehan begins by addressing what he considers to be an important issue in establishing Cassie's victimhood: 'You might wonder what a thirteen-year-old girl was doing out at 11.30 at night with four men, and having consensual sex with one of them. Where was her mother, or her father?' (2006a, p. 31)

The inference the reader is invited to draw is that such questions impact on how much sympathy Cassie can be afforded depending on how much blame she must be attributed for what happened subsequently. As discussed in previous chapters, this reflects the classic interrogation rape victims must endure in establishing their right to 'victim' status. Sheehan goes on to build the reader's sympathy (and apparently his own) through a detailed narrative setting out Cassie's relationship with Mustapha K:

> Cassie had known Mustapha for eight months . . . . He told Cassie he was starting to fall in love with her. Strong words for a thirteen-year-old to hear from a handsome seventeen-year-old guy. . .
>
> . . . Mustapha was whispering sweet nothings to Cassie. 'I love you', he told her. They repaired to his bedroom and, for the first time, they had sex. . .
>
> . . . Cassie was hysterical. She began screaming at him. The man who said he loved her had used her as meat, not just for himself but for other guys. She was thirteen, the softest of targets.
>
> (2006a, p. 32–33)

This utilisation of the classic script of the young woman being lured into sex under romantic pretences demonstrates Sheehan's conformity with dominant rape narratives. For Sheehan the necessity for the victim to be 'pure' and 'innocent' remains a fundamental feature in establishing their right to sympathy.

Description of the rapists

The romanticised descriptions of the victims as 'innocent' and 'pure'[3] also provide an excellent contrast to the dehumanising description Sheehan provides of the rapists. From the outset the book's highly emotive language leaves the reader in little doubt that the rapists are not 'ordinary young men'. Their criminality, deviance

'Girls like you' 87

and moral repugnance are evident from their initial descriptions. For example, in the opening chapter describing an incident of road rage involving two of the 'K brothers' (not involved in the gang rapes), the contrast between the Anglo-Australians 'boys' who Sheehan describes as acting with the 'honesty of inebriation' (2006a, p. 5) and the violent, menacing 'K brothers'[4] is stark. The reader is left with the first impression of young men whose anti-social conduct makes them appear virtually subhuman. Added to this, the detailing of the brothers' criminal behaviour prior to the rapes clearly separates them as deviants.

This creation of rapist as 'deviant' has served a very clear purpose: according to many feminist scholars it has helped perpetuate myths of 'real' rape such that it can never be understood as an act of a 'normal', socialised man (hence why relationship rape is so frequently ignored or justified). Sheehan's descriptions seem to mirror those adopted by many of the judges (detailed in Chapter 2). In fact Wood and Rennie seem to hit the nail on the head when they write:

> It is usually men who name the woman's experience, and they name it from their perspective. Thus, the situation in which a college boy rapes a woman whom he is dating is thrown into the realm of 'grey area stuff', and milder sounding names and descriptors are attached to this experience than the harsh-sounding word *rape*. In order for an experience to qualify unequivocally as rape, it has to be violent, perpetrated by a stranger (the acceptable villain), and acted upon a woman who is not dressed provocatively and if possible is a virgin (the acceptable victim).
>
> (Wood and Rennie, 1994, p. 145, emphasis in original, citations omitted)

As I have argued earlier in this book, the discourse of rape has been a vital feature in the construction of national identities and gender identities. This has led to a paradoxical situation. On the one hand male and female sexuality and sexual identity are structured around the potential to rape/be raped: a point clearly illustrated in the judicial discourses in Chapter 2. In turn this has impacted upon their relative status within the national space. The bodies of women and girls have largely been constructed as passive symbolic boundaries for the community and nation. This construction can be seen in some of the commentaries discussed in Chapter 4. On the other hand, there has been a disavowal of rape as a social phenomenon requiring a re-interrogation of gendered structures of power. Instead, rape has been relegated to the domain of deviance and criminality: a domain that does not include the coerced sexual encounters of 'normal' men and women. Again this is demonstrated in the judicial discourses detailed earlier.

In relying on standard rape tropes Sheehan further contributes to this representation of rape. This leads to him presenting a critique that seems to support feminist arguments but ultimately undermines them. For example, he makes the following pertinent observation:

> Sexual assault is a crime for which the majority of those victimised are never going to be able to get justice, no matter what reforms are made, because the

88 *'Girls like you'*

majority of attacks involve partners, friends, spouses, family members, and most of the time it is one person's word against another's.

(Sheehan 2006a, p. 331)

This seems to reiterate the literature in the area and highlight a central problem within societal and legal approaches. Unfortunately, this paragraph appears alone towards the end of the book. It is not explored or elaborated upon, and the fact that Sheehan has chosen to place his emphasis on rape scenarios that do not involve these complexities but are in fact examples of the types of rape that *do* result in conviction makes this statement appear rather token.

At the same time, Sheehan adds an extra dimension to the 'ideal' villain through his unashamed use of classic orientalist language. For example, while describing the appearance of one of the 'K brothers' he notes, '[h]is boiling eyes and hooked nose terrified Cassie' (2006a, p. 33).[5] This imagery invokes classic orientalist tropes described by Edward Said back in 1978 (Said 1995). Aside from this physical description, he describes with clear sarcasm the displays of emotion of various male members of the K family:

Soon after Dr K began giving evidence, he began to cry. He broke down when he described coming to Australia from Pakistan, hoping for a better life, and later, hoping for a better life for his sons.

This prompted the questioner, Sami, the doctor's son, also to begin crying. Then Amir began crying. So much nose-blowing was going on that the judge instructed a court officer to bring two boxes of tissues to the bar, one for the witness and one for the accused.

(Sheehan 2006a, pp. 145–146; see also p. 256 for another description of Sami crying)

The scene emerges as farcical. It also invokes reference to *The Arab Mind*: a previously discredited 1973 text that has regained prominence in the context of the War on Terror with media reports alleging that it has been used by US military personnel as a training manual for dealing with Arab prisoners (Puar 2005). In that text Raphael Patai (1973) dedicates an entire chapter to what he describes as the 'proclivity' of the Arab to exaggerated emotional responses. As a parallel, Sheehan's reporting of the male members of the K family's public displays of emotion are made to contrast strongly not only with the unemotional rationality of the courtroom but also the greater self-control demonstrated by rape victim Tegan Wagner during her testimony (2006a, pp. 216–236). Further employing the well-established tropes used historically by Western powers to justify colonial domination, Sheehan goes on to construct an image of the 'K brothers' as not only morally degenerate but sexually unrestrained,[6] cowardly[7] and subhuman[8].

Sheehan also provides vivid accounts of the two self-represented brothers' behaviour throughout the trials, observing, '[e]verything the brothers did was counterproductive' (2006a, p. 134). Aside from the almost comical incident involving one of the 'K brothers' throwing fruit at the jury, Sheehan documents every

'Girls like you' 89

gesture, facial expression and submission to create a picture of not only morally reprehensible but imbecilic personalities. In Sheehan's words these were 'bullies and cowards', a 'pack of liars' and 'smirking morons' whose 'witless arrogance and ignorance' had worked against them in court (2006a, p. 149).

Returning to the work of foundational postcolonial scholar Edward Said demonstrates how true to orientalist literary convention Sheehan remains: '[Arabs] are *only* capable of sexual excitement and not of Olympian (Western, modern) reason' (Said 1995, pp. 313–314). One could be forgiven for confusing Sheehan's construction of Amir or Sami K with Said's description of the 'Arab Oriental' as 'that impossible creature whose libidinal energy drives him to paroxysms of over-stimulation – and yet, he is as a puppet in the eyes of the world, staring vacantly out at a modern landscape he can neither understand nor cope with' (Said 1995, p. 312).

The 'cultural context' of rape

In fact, Sheehan's depiction of the entire K family consistently reinforces an image of disorder that permeates every aspect of their lives. In the opening chapter he provides a background to the K family's home city in Western Pakistan: 'The K boys had grown up in a village not far from the border with Afghanistan. They spoke Pashtu, or Pashto, a language which ignored the border and was one of the two official languages of Afghanistan. . .' (2006a, p. 16). In this description even their native language is presented as unruly and unpredictable: refusing to be restrained by neat national or even linguistic borders (hence the two names). Furthermore, the linking of the K family with Afghanistan is important. In the context of the 'War on Terror' and the 9/11 bombing of the World Trade Center, Afghanistan has come to represent violence, terrorism and Islamic fundamentalism in the Western imaginary. Sheehan draws on this imaginary as a means of situating the 'K brothers' within a culturally predestined paradigm:

> Violent history flowed through the city where the Ks were educated – Peshawar, the gun-running capital of the Middle East, a city of arms dealing, drug trafficking, political intrigue, Islamic fundamentalism and Taliban sympathies. Peshawar was basically a Pashtun city.
>
> The ethnic Pashtuns were the wellspring of the Taliban, the most extreme of Islamic fundamentalists, who took power in Afghanistan by force during the late 1990s, then harboured Osama bin Laden and his organisation as it planned the attacks of September 11, 2001.
>
> (2006a, pp. 16–17)

In providing this information, Sheehan sets the scene for the 'K brothers'' behaviour as if their cultural and ethnic background is enough to explain something about their subsequent acts. Sheehan's discussion of Pashtun culture is limited to emphasising the link between Pashtun culture, lawlessness and the Taliban (read as Islamic fundamentalism and terrorism). His concluding remarks regarding

90 *'Girls like you'*

the 9/11 attacks is a remarkable leap that allows the gang rapes to emerge as but one example of a violent and barbaric culture.

This 'cultural context' emerges even more clearly in Sheehan's many opinion pieces that must be read alongside his book. For example, in an article in the *Sydney Morning Herald* entitled, 'Cold-blooded law heats up cultural war', Sheehan (2005) ostensibly presents a critique of the judicial process. However, the inclusion of the term 'cultural war' and the specific examples he cites provides a limited context within which his comments can be read. It becomes difficult to see whether it is the legal culture he is referring to or 'Muslim' culture, with the majority of his examples being associated with the various 'Sydney gang rapes' and the express naming and detailing of Bilal and Mohammed Skaf's trial involving the gang rape of a young woman in Greenacre.

Similarly, in a piece entitled, 'Rough, slow justice for rape victims', published in the *Sydney Morning Herald* on 10 April 2006, he provides a detailed list of 'recent cases where judges have treated rape victims as cannon fodder' (Sheehan 2006c) suggesting a judicial disregard for the subjective experiences and rights of the victims. However, as he later acknowledges, he limits his description of the inadequacies of the legal system to cases involving Muslim defendants and non-Muslim complainants, which he suggests, 'represent the apex of thousands of instances of sexual harassment, or worse, in Sydney'. His statement that 'recalling the worst excesses because they help explain why only one in 10 of the 7000 sexual and indecent assault incidents reported to NSW Police each year results in someone being found guilty in court' is misleading in the extreme, when contextualised only through reference to cases involving Muslim perpetrators and non-Muslim victims. It does not reflect the reality documented by experts in the area: that the reason rape is so underreported, under-prosecuted and under-convicted is precisely because the majority of rapes do not fall within the category of 'real' rapes but are seen as merely examples of 'private relationships' gone wrong (Kelly et al. 2005; Cook, David and Grant 2001; Jaspard et al. 2001).

Finally, Sheehan's particular agenda emerges most clearly in an opinion piece in the *Sydney Morning Herald* in October 2006. In commenting on the Sheikh al Hilaly scandal (described in the previous chapter), Sheehan entitles his piece, 'Sheik's views show up the wider problem with Muslim men' (Sheehan 2006b). This title leaves little doubt of the general problem of misogyny and racism within the Muslim population in Australia. Further, he reports individual Muslim Australians expressing racist and sexist views to support his generalisations. Unfortunately, as discussed above, a central problem that has emerged in the Left's discourses on racism and multiculturalism is that there has been no safe space within which to critique racism and sexism by ethnic minority communities. The risk of providing further ammunition to the Right's attack on immigration and multiculturalism has led to a marked silence when the allegations of racism and sexism are directed towards communities also the subject of 'mainstream' Australian racism. It is this very silence that has provided the space for commentators like Sheehan to take the floor.

'Girls like you' 91

Merging misogyny with ethnicity

So too Sheehan's use of the term 'culture' throughout the book must also be situated within his apparent adherence to classic colonial and orientalist discourses. Alongside his description of Pashtun culture as inherently lawless, violent, barbaric and linked to terrorism, he also seeks to identify a specific gender context by observing, 'Pashtun culture was not noted for its embrace of feminism' (2006a, p. 17). To support this he draws on Christopher Kremmer's journalistic account of the Pashtun tribal code as allowing honour killings (2006a, p. 16). This contextualisation allows him to reach the conclusion that '[i]t was as if the Ks could not comprehend that Australian law applied to them or that Australian girls were not there for the taking' (2006a, p. 29). This is an interesting comment in light of the general disregard demonstrated towards violence against women as potentially criminal behaviour. So too, it is noteworthy in light of the highly sexualised descriptions he provides of the two Australian prosecution lawyers, Sheridan Goodwin and Margaret Cunneen (discussed further below). It raises the question, are Australian girls *never* 'for the taking' or are they simply not 'for the taking' of these 'Other' men?

Part of the answer may lie in Sheehan's subsequent restatement of Islam as significant to the equation. Admittedly, the significance of the family being Muslim emerges primarily as a result of the 'anti-Muslim' defence the elder two 'K brothers' attempted to present:

> These men were Muslim, however dubiously they practised their faith, and the father, Dr K, and the two eldest brothers, Sami and Amir, were convinced that the state machinery now working against them was anti-Muslim. They saw themselves as the victims of a racist society and a corrupt legal system. They regarded their actual victims as sluts.
>
> (2006a, p. 59)

However it is the link Sheehan draws between the 'K Brother's' allegations of racism with their apparent opinion of their victims that is strange. A possible explanation for it could be to reinforce the 'multiculturalism gone mad' argument discussed above in which a simplistic binary is created between 'cultural tolerance' and 'women's rights'. Sheehan appears to suggest that the 'K brothers'' claims of racism have to do with their belief in a right to free access to women's bodies: represented here as a feature of their culture. In this characterisation, the only thing that stands between women and their potential 'Muslim rapists' is the 'state machinery' of the Australian nation: a mirror of the physical encounter between Sami K and the Australian prosecution lawyers in the courtroom.

In describing an incident in court where Sami K is holding a knife he notes, 'The two women Crown lawyers, sitting nearby, both rolled their chairs away from him. A court sheriff moved up to the bar table. Everyone noticed' (2006a, p. 150). The added detail of the Crown lawyers being women (something we have already been told) seems largely irrelevant to this description until it is read in the context of a

92 *'Girls like you'*

later incident. Sheehan records how Sami K at one stage jumped out of the dock and charged at the bar table:

> Sami rushed across to the Crown's side of the bar table, to where the Crown solicitor, Sheridan Goodwin, was sitting. He grabbed the nearest implement he could find – a glass. As he raised his arm to throw, Goodwin ducked under the table. Sami ran past the empty jury box toward the public gallery. His targets were two women in the public gallery – the mothers of two of the rape victims.
>
> He threw the glass at the women, who ducked. The glass smashed just above their heads on the back wall. He grabbed the water carafe from the bar table and smashed the top of it against the table. As he did so, the Crown prosecutor, Ken McKay, grabbed him from behind in a bear hug. Two seconds later, a sheriff's officer helped restrain him . . .
>
> (2006a, p. 252)

The conclusion Sheehan is able to draw from this incident is 'Sami's true nature – he was a coward – had proved useful. Instead of physically attacking his closest antagonist, Ken McKay, he went for the women. As usual.' (2006a, p. 253). Aside from being a rather patronising and paternalistic representation of the women involved (their vulnerability assumed on the basis of gender), this comment highlights the extent to which race and gender are indivisible in Sheehan's account. The image of the Australian male court officers intervening to rescue Australian women from the cowardly and crazed attack of the Arab reads like a classic nationalist, orientalist script. In the process both female vulnerability (upon which gender order is built) and the 'national goodness' (upon which the hierarchy of ethnic groups is built) are maintained.

Added to this, not only does he make ample use of orientalist imagery in his description of the 'K brothers', so too are his descriptions of the 'K women' woven with classic orientalist tropes. Part I of the book is introduced by a quote from the youngest of the 'K brothers' and an explanation of its context: '"Shut up, you bitch, you slut. Girls like you, I know how to fix them up." – one of the 'K brothers', prior to an assault on his sister, 3 January 2004, after she had failed to make him dinner' (2006a, p. 1). Aside from this reference to the 'K sister', she is only mentioned again once when she is called to give evidence in defence of her brothers. The description is minimal; we are told she is a 16-year-old school girl, she testified in English and she is ultimately presented as a passive victim:

> Rather than attempt to grill the schoolgirl, the Crown merely established that ZHK [the sister] was in the thrall of the male culture in which she lived. When Cunneen [the Crown Prosecutor] asked why she had gone straight to her bedroom when someone had knocked on the front door, ZHK replied: 'Because . . . if someone comes to our house, we just go to our bedrooms because my dad told me to go . . . Because in my religion, we don't [meet], like, other boys or something.'

'Girls like you' 93

The sister was relegated to her room for the purposes of the trial. The Crown had bigger fish to catch.

(Sheehan 2006a, p. 145)

This description of the 'K sister' as a 'small fish' is patronising and belittling. In fact, the references to women in the K family throughout the book are few and tend to convey an image of faceless, objectified non-agents as well as, often, victims of the K family men. Aside from the reference to ZHK being assaulted by her brother, Sheehan also reports an allegation by another journalist, Lee Glendinning: 'She [Glendinning] also saw evidence of ongoing violence against the women in the family. "In one of [Sami]'s applications for bail, his wife arrived with a black eye and told the court through an interpreter that one of the brothers, [Junior], had hit her."' (Sheehan 2006a, p. 133).

Sheehan also notes that 'Dr K' – who he identifies as the 'patriarch' – at 36 married a 17-year-old Pakistani woman. The only other mention 'Mrs K' receives is towards the end of the book, where she is described and placed in direct contrast to rape victim Tegan Wagner:

Mrs K had finally arrived from Pakistan. She was wearing the distinctive veil, half-sari and leggings favoured by traditional Pakistani women.

Mrs K looked stone-faced when Tegan, with her shock of long curly hair and summery dress, walked to the well of the court to begin reading her victim's impact statement. . .

(Sheehan 2006a, p. 301)

This description is evocative but unoriginal in its metaphoricity. The use of these two women and their attire as a means of setting a clear visual division between 'Pakistani' and 'Australian' culture rearticulates classic nationalist and culturalist narratives, which draw on a symbolic value of women's bodies, dress and behaviour (Ware 2015; Stoler 2002; Yuval-Davis 1997; McClintock 1994). Equally, the imagery of the veil versus the free-flowing hair draws on the common Western trope of Muslim womanhood as based on oppression and submission that can be contrasted with the liberty and equality enjoyed by Western women.[9]

This is not the only place where the physical appearance of the women associated with the K family is a source of comment. In describing Sami K's wife, Sheehan notes, 'She spoke Pashtu, like everyone else in the family, and would testify via interpreter. She wore a headscarf and a long skirt' (Sheehan 2006a, p. 139) and again at a later date, 'Mrs K was a round-faced woman, veiled, with an ankle-length dress that barely revealed silver high heels'(Sheehan 2006a, p. 208). It is interesting to note the focus placed on her having a covered head and at the same time, in the second description, the ironic reference to her shoes: positioned to suggest a contradiction, possibly hypocrisy within Muslim identity. Meanwhile, a description of Yusef's widow and Mrs Sami K's sister, Musarat Gull, is also given, noting: 'She wore Western clothes. No headscarf. Tight jeans. She was pretty' (Sheehan 2006a, p. 178).

94 *'Girls like you'*

Sheehan also uses the opportunity of describing the victims to reinforce the 'Clash of Civilisations'[10] emphasis:

> If there were any doubts about the cultural subtext of these rape trials, they were removed when one of the victims, Roxanne, arrived to see the judgment handed down by the Court of Criminal Appeal in the appeal by Sami and Amir against their convictions.
>
> Roxanne arrived early. She waited outside Court 13A in the Supreme Court building, before the court was open.
>
> Around her bare neck hung a large diamanté-encrusted crucifix.
>
> (Sheehan 2006a, p. 165)

This is not the only reference Sheehan makes to the victims and their legal team being Catholic/Christian.[11] The characterisation of the 'K brothers'' cultural and ethnic background impacting on their actions can also be contrasted with his ethnicised and gendered description of the Australian prosecuting lawyers: 'Two women now faced the K brothers, two blondes, and they presented an immediate and significant threat' (2006a, p. 57). Sheehan clearly considers the lawyers' appearance and identity important as he goes on to dedicate some time to describing them.

Writing about DPP[12] lawyer Sheridan Goodwin, Sheehan notes, 'She was also a surfer chick. She lived by the sea and her long blonde hair was bleached by the sun – not by peroxide' (2006a, p. 58). The reference to Goodwin being a 'surfer chick' is noteworthy for its replication of an identity Kathy Lette and Gabrielle Carey (1979) problematise for its sexualised and demeaned status within the surfing community at Sydney's southern beaches. Yet, aside from endorsing a gendered and sexualised image, it is also significant for its ethnic and nationalist connotations. The reference to the beach and surf culture is a frequently deployed and stereotypical representation of the 'ideal Australian' that has been used to reinforce the dominant national identity as necessarily White.[13] This suggests a nationalist significance is attached to Goodwin's appearance. When read in the context of Sheehan's discussion of the Cronulla riots in 2005, this significance emerges even more clearly: by performing this (quintessentially Australian) 'beach identity', Goodwin becomes the embodiment of Australia. So too, her placement in opposition to the rapists secures their place *outside* the national space.

Added to this, the description of Crown Prosecutor Margaret Cunneen, makes even more explicit use of dominant Australian nationalist imagery:

> Margaret Cunneen was the antithesis of the Ks, a conservative Catholic. She was one of seven Irish-Catholic girls named Margaret Mary in her graduating class at Santa Sabina College. She still went to Mass every Sunday. Her three sons attended a Catholic school. She had a salty tongue, a black belt in tae kwon do and a fondness for beer.
>
> (2006a, p. 59)

'Girls like you' 95

Through this description Sheehan on the one hand reinforces the Irish-Catholic identity as typically Australian (he also links it with the image of 'the battler' through his description of Cunneen's toughness and the ever-present trope of the Australian beer drinker (Kirkby 2003)) and on the other, distances the 'K brothers' from the possibility of being Australian. Sheehan goes on to also add a sexualised element to Cunneen's identity: 'Cunneen was a particular favourite of the police, but not a favourite of the judges, in part because she was an industrial-strength flirt who could appear in court in high heels and sheer stockings, showing plenty of leg.' (2006a, p. 59). The relevance of this comment is left unexplained. Aside from presenting an impression of judges as overly conservative, it paints an image of Cunneen as a sexualised, feminine but independent woman: an image that sits in stark contrast to the dominant representation of the Muslim woman as veiled and oppressed.

The following highly emotive and melodramatic statement, which appears early in the book provides a remarkable insight into how Sheehan conceptualises the significance of these rapes:

> The first trial was set to commence on 15 September 2003. More than a trial was about to begin. The proceedings would turn into cultural warfare. Parliament had already intervened. Public passions would be inflamed. Women had been raped. And men were going to die.
>
> (Sheehan 2006a, p. 68)

Feminist scholars of nationalism have pointed to the very different relationship imputed to the nation and its male and female citizens (Carver and Mottier 1998). Sheehan perfectly exemplifies these classic roles through his imagery of women being raped and men dying. It is also the rearticulation of classic military propaganda. In this, Sheehan's imagery more clearly than any other commentator highlights the symbolic function these rapes served. He was not however the only one to draw on these tropes, as my earlier discussion demonstrates. Rather his account builds on and reproduces images that have a well-established history and contemporary valence such that the gendered, sexualised, nationalist figures he inserts barely register as problematic.

It can be concluded that for Sheehan the particular rapes that concern him have a very specific contemporary cultural context. Having examined the way in which Sheehan describes various actors, what emerges is the extent to which his descriptions draw on dominant discourses of gender and ethnicity to the point that the two are completely intertwined. This entangling of concerns relating to the protection of women's rights and the place of migrants in Australia is not incidental but seems to be cultivated by Sheehan in his selective and fluid use of the term 'culture'. His account of the rape trials emerges as not just *any* example of a broader problem within the Australian legal system – regardless of how he attempts to frame it – so much as the result of a highly specific cultural context. Sheehan frequently makes ambiguous use of the term 'culture' to allow himself to move freely between a critique of the Australian legal system and directed attacks on specific ethnic groups.

96   *'Girls like you'*

This is evident from the subtitle featured on the front cover of the book: 'Four young girls, six brothers and a cultural time bomb'. The full significance of the 'cultural time bomb' will be discussed shortly, but its inclusion within the title of the book provides the first indication of the angle the book intends to take. Similarly, despite the assertion on the cover of the book that it is dedicated to detailing the experiences of 'four teenage girls encountering a legal system loaded against rape victims', the back cover also specifies that these are not the victims of just any rape: 'Their [the rapists'] crimes took place against the backdrop of a violent cultural clash between young Muslim men and young western women' (Sheehan 2006a, back cover). By explicitly referring to 'Muslim' men and 'Western' women on the book's cover, the issue of the legal culture's disregard for rape victims is overshadowed by – or at least tied to – questions of ethnicity.

Competitive racisms and the 'anti-Muslim conspiracy'

As noted in Chapter 3, two of the 'K Brothers' were themselves instrumental in racialising/ethnicising their trials. Throughout the process they alleged that they were the victims of a racist conspiracy aimed at all Muslim men. In documenting these allegations Sheehan presents the most extreme conspiracy claims put forward by the brothers. The result is that the brothers' claims appear ridiculous, and this allows Sheehan to completely dismiss any claim of racism. When Sheehan makes the comment, '[Sami and Amir] were determined to make this a political trial' (2006a, p. 129), he removes all politicisation from other sources and lays the responsibility solely on the accused. At the same it seems to be Justice Sully's refusal to countenance political considerations (reflected in the legislative changes brought in just prior to the 'K Brothers' trial that denied them the opportunity to cross-examine their victims directly) that allows Sheehan to conclude, '[Justice Sully's] outburst allowed a glimpse of the Olympian grove from which judges look down on our representatives in parliament' (2006a, p. 133). In this context he performs a paradoxical move. One the one hand he appears to lament the failure of the Courts to adopt a more 'politically savvy' approach. Yet on the other he simultaneously rejects the possibility of external political factors influencing the legal process and criticises the 'K brothers' for alleging this.

At the same time, Sheehan suggests a possible conspiracy theory of his own:

> When the media learnt that two Muslim men, charged with multiple counts of gang-rape, intended to defend themselves and cross-examine their victims, it was a hot story. When they heard the reasons – because the defendants argued the Australian legal system was biased against Muslims – the impact was felt all the way to state parliament.
>
> Muslim men raping young non-Muslim women in significant numbers – dozens – was an emotive subject for the public, so much so that sections of the government, police, civil rights bureaucracies and the media, notably the ABC and SBS, sought to put a lid on the subject.
>
> (2006, p. 63)

'Girls like you' 97

Sheehan thus not only dismisses the 'K brothers'' claims of racism but presents an image of an overly tolerant society allowing its own anti-racism to be used against it. This reinforced the myth of the 'good White nation', identified by some scholars as providing a key fantasy on which Australian national identity has been built (Hage 2003, 1998; Rutherford 2000). As described in the previous chapter, this was a common theme among many right-wing commentators and was only enflamed by the attempts by certain news sources and commentators to play down the racist/ethnic aspects of the rapes, which the rapists themselves never sought to deny.

In noting that Sami and Amir K sacked their legal-aid barrister, Sheehan writes:

> Sami and Amir sacked their legal-aid barrister, claiming he had said that all Muslims were rapists. What the barrister, Joe Busuttil, had actually said, unwisely, was that many Australians believed all Muslims were rapists.
>
> (2006a, p. 62)

The fact that Sheehan merely characterises this comment as 'unwise' rather than offensive, leaves an impression with the reader that perhaps Busuttil's remark was not without some merit. This is further supported by Sheehan's later statement contextualising the 'K brothers' case: '[a] clear pattern of sexual assault and sexual harassment by Muslim men was beginning to register in the legal system and the public consciousness' (2006a, p. 64). His remark that '[t]here were also reports of rape and sexual assault increasing while other crimes declined', when read in the context of the previous paragraphs suggests a correlation between the increasing Muslim population and sexual violence, a claim that reflected similar suggestions by other right-wing commentators (discussed in the previous chapter).

This would appear to endorse Leti Volpp's analysis of discourses on cultural diversity in the United States. In looking at the ways in which cultural identity has been used historically in the United States to justify the exclusion of certain groups or individuals from citizenship, Volpp argues:

> If we consider this together with the fact that the perception of cultural behavior is subject to a kind of selective recognition – so that problematic behavior is thought to be characteristic of the culture of entire nations, rather than the product of individual deviants – we can see the perversity of current configurations of the relationship between citizenship and culture. One's cultural identity constitutes a predictor of problematic behavior. To be a citizen, one must not engage in problematic behavior. Both the cultural norms underlying citizenship and the problematic behavior of those who are already recognized as citizens are made invisible.
>
> (2007, p. 582)

Thus, not only is the 'K brothers'' behaviour to be understood as culturally determined, the 'K brothers' case provides a useful means of reinforcing who does and does not belong to the nation. The linking of rape with 'Muslim' culture sets

98 *'Girls like you'*

it apart from 'Australian' culture (which is constructed as tolerant, egalitarian and pro-feminist) and also justifies the continued exclusion of certain groups and individuals from holding a legitimate place in the Australian national space. Again Sheehan was not the only commentator to endorse this position: it is also implicit in a number of the judicial, political and media responses.

Sheehan's argument regarding the cultural aspect of the 'K brothers'' behaviour is reinforced when he discusses the final submission made on behalf of Sami K by his barrister on appeal, Stephen Odgers. Alongside the ongoing claim that Sami was suffering from a psychiatric condition, Odgers also sought to raise a cultural defence:

> The new evidence [of psychiatric disorder offered by his father, Dr K] does tend to establish he suffered from a disorder which, combined with his cultural conditioning, having essentially come out of Pakistan, a society with very traditional views about women, combined with his use of alcohol in parties where excessive drinking occurred, combined with his personality traits, which was clearly a factor in the commission of these offences, that in a sense the applicant [Sami] was a cultural time bomb.
>
> He was a man who came into a situation where it was almost inevitable that something like this would happen, I am not excusing what he did. The different perspective on what he did shows that his culpability was not as severe as the sentencing judge believed it to be . . .
>
> (Sheehan 2006a, pp. 291–292)

When asked by the appeal judges to further explain what the relevance of the expression 'cultural time bomb' was, Sheehan reports that Odgers added, "'If a person is transplanted from one culture to another with very little time to appreciate the norms of this culture . . .'", but does not go on to quote the full explanation, claiming 'His [Odgers'] response occupied more than a page of court transcript and said nothing' (Sheehan 2006a, p. 293).

The presentation of a 'cultural defence' is not new within the Australian criminal law and has been the subject of ongoing debate by legal scholars. Some scholars have argued its necessity in order to provide greater substantive equality to ethnic minorities faced with the generally monocultural discourse of the law. However, many feminist legal theorists have argued that aside from allowing judges to draw on essentialist stereotypes of cultures they do not belong to, 'cultural defences' are most frequently employed in ways which are detrimental to women (Phillips 2003; Okin 1999; Volpp 1994). The discussion of the judicial handling of cultural arguments in the 'K Brothers' case in Chapter 2 highlights this problem.

The identification of a straightforward dichotomy of 'feminism' versus 'multiculturalism' has frequently led to the claim that the two cannot exist alongside each other. However, as the discourses on the 'Sydney gang rapes' (and, as set out shortly, *'les tournantes'*) demonstrate, the juxtapositions of 'recognising of cultural diversity' against 'protecting women's rights' are formulated in ways that erase or under-emphasise the fundamental interconnectedness of racism and sexism. As a result, one is left with the impression that any attempt to reconcile both interests is doomed to fail. By focusing on the ethnicised aspects of 'cultural defence' claims, many scholars have failed to fully make the link with what has been recognised to be a general failure by the law to condemn violence against women and its implicit endorsement of dominant heteronormative gender stereotypes.[14]

In any event, in this case it appears the judges were extremely reluctant to grant any validity to Odgers' 'cultural time bomb' defence (2006a, p. 292). Yet, Sheehan, while critical of Odgers for raising the issue, is less inclined to completely reject Odgers' argument:

> Even though Odgers' argument about cultural conditioning was torn apart by the judges, and by the media the next day, he was right about one thing – Sami K was a cultural time bomb.
>
> The big question that hung over these proceedings was how many other cultural time bombs were ticking amid the Muslim male population living within the liberality of Australia? . . . In the previous five years, there had been a dozen proven gang rapes involving young Muslim men in Sydney. There had also been thousands of acts of sexual harassment or intimidation by young Muslims involving young women on or near beaches.
>
> (2006a, p. 294)

In referring to the beaches, Sheehan makes the necessary link to justify his final chapter, entitled 'Intifada'. He also presents an image of the 'K brothers' as representing not an aberration but an accurate representation of many other young Muslim/Middle Eastern men, while completely eliminating non-Muslim men from any consideration in terms of sexual violence and/or harassment. To reinforce this point, he also links the widely reported and outrageous remarks of an Islamic fundamentalist preacher, Sheikh Feiz Mohammed:

> Speaking to a packed crowd in the Bankstown Town Hall in Sydney on 18 March 2005, not far from where all the gang rapes involving Muslim men had occurred, Sheikh Mohammed left no doubt he believed young Western women invited the violence and humiliation that had befallen them. 'A victim of rape every minute somewhere in the world? Why? No one to blame but herself. She displayed her beauty to the entire world. She degraded herself by being an object of sexual desire and thus becoming vulnerable to man who looks at her for gratification of his sexual urge . . . Strapless, backless, sleeveless, nothing but satanic skirts, slit skirts, translucent blouses, miniskirts, tight jeans! All this to tease man and appeal to his carnal nature.'

It is interesting that Sheehan should quote this passage. After all, he himself dedicates a fair amount of attention to the attire of the young women when they were raped, suggesting he is not completely immune from prejudice against rape victims who are dressed 'provocatively'. In fact looking closely at the narrative

100   *'Girls like you'*

employed throughout the book, it is possible to say that Sheehan, the Sheikh and the Australian legal system seem to share a number of common understandings of gender identity and normative (hetero)sexuality. Aside from the rape victims' sexuality, behaviour and dress being a notable feature for each, the understanding they each employ of a female sexuality based on objectification, passivity and emotionality compared with the more carnal, aggressive male sexuality fits within standard constructions of normative heterosexuality, which in turn are central to the construction of both gender and national identity.

Admittedly, Sheehan does make a greater attempt than the Sheikh at problematising the assumptions associated with rape. He dedicates space to the views of Karen Willis of the NSW Rape Crisis Centre and cites her comment:

> 'I think the way the criminal justice system treats women who make complaints of sexual assault is appalling', she [Willis] said. 'The system is misogynist, embedded with myths about sexual assault, and it intimidates, degrades and mistreats women who are brave enough to come forward.'
>
> (Sheehan 2006a, p. 166)

He also provides some important statistics, emphasising the inadequacies of the legal system's approach to rape: '*Less than 1 per cent of sexual assaults lead to conviction*' (Sheehan 2006a, p. 167 emphasis in original). This leads him to conclude, '[t]his was the cultural context of all the K trials and the legal guerrilla warfare surrounding them' (Sheehan 2006a, p. 167). Yet, this appears within a chapter entitled 'Roxanne's Crucifix' in which he asserts at the outset that it is her wearing of this symbol that provides the 'cultural subtext of these rape trials' (2006a, p. 165). By merging the two references to culture (one ethno-religious, the other socio-legal) Sheehan capitalises on a genuine feminist critique and merges it with other agendas.

Equally, his description of the Court's rejection of medical evidence of severe vaginal injuries as necessarily evidencing lack of consent (discussed in Chapter 2) provides an example of a genuine problem within the criminal justice system's approach to sexual violence. As already discussed, he appears to be demonstrating a point made by many feminist legal scholars: the tendency within legal discourses to accept a construction of female sexuality as necessarily one of passivity and masochism. Yet ultimately this is not the issue he is concerned with. By detailing the cross-examination of Dr Jackson, in which it appears the defence is attempting to argue the injuries were the result of anxiety and inexperience on the part of Kelly rather than violence, Sheehan does not necessarily problematise the linking of female sexuality with pain. His final rather facetious comment, 'Virgins beware. In a court of law, vaginal injuries can be represented as evidence of inexperience, not violence' (2006a, p. 101), adds little by way of critique but simply reasserts his belief in the inadequacy of the law. It also misleadingly suggests that rape victims who are virgins are in fact further disadvantaged in court: a proposition in complete opposition to the bulk of feminist literature on the topic. If anything, this comment demonstrates Sheehan's resort to traditional conceptions of rape, reflecting male preoccupations with chastity (MacDougall 1998, para. 24).

Furthermore, it appears that for Sheehan, the Sheikh's remarks are significant not primarily for their misogyny. In noting that the Sheikh was speaking at Bankstown Town Hall, Sheehan comments:

> It was the same hall where Paul Keating, the champion of multiculturalism who declined to live among the melting pot of his own electorate, had greeted election victory and defeat. It was near the sites where, within a year, hundreds of young Muslim men would gather to form violent attacking raids on eastern beach suburbs, when this cultural time bomb would finally go off.
>
> (Sheehan 2006a, p. 295)

The threat posed by these 'cultural time bombs' is a national one. Through the introduction of an official policy of multiculturalism, which Sheehan suggests does not affect the lives of those advocating it (reinforcing the alleged divide between the 'ivory towers' of the elites – academics, judges, left-leaning politicians and media commentators – and the lived reality of 'mainstream Australia'), Australia has become vulnerable to penetration by violent outsiders in the same way as Australia's women have become vulnerable to sexual assault and harassment.

'Intifada': The 'nasty migrant' strikes again . . .

If the reader is left in any doubt as to Sheehan's belief in the culturally determined nature of the 'K brothers' gang rapes, this is settled by the final chapter. The title in itself says a great deal: 'Intifada'. In fact, this chapter deals with the events in Cronulla in 2005 in which White Australians congregated following a text message/talk-back radio campaign to 'reclaim the beach' from unwanted immigrant groups (for more on this, see Chapter 4). Aside from the fact that Cronulla was an unrelated event to the 'K brothers' case (except insofar as the 'Sydney gang rapes' were used by White protesters as one of the justifications for their violence), titling the chapter with such loaded imagery of presumed Arab violence is misleading in the extreme. It presents a further example of the re-writing of Cronulla away from an act of White racism towards a Muslim/Middle Eastern male threat to Australia. With the Muslim/Middle Eastern/Arab man once again positioned as the agent of violence, his position as a 'nasty migrant' against which Australian national goodness can be measured is assured.

I draw the term 'nasty migrant' from Ghassan Hage who, in a short section of his book, *Beyond Paranoid Nationalism*, asks 'are there such things as nasty migrants?' Referring to racism amongst migrants, Hage argues that this should not be dismissed but that the focus must remain on the types of racisms that are endowed with greater credibility and capacity through institutional power (2003, pp. 116–118). Agreeing with this, I think that Hage makes a more interesting point. He observes: 'when evil is at work, its opposite is always good' (Hage 2003, p. 116). While Hage is talking about the need to characterise victims of racism as 'good' by virtue of their victim status, this principle could equally be seen to apply in

102   'Girls like you'

reverse. The association of racism and violence with those identified as 'Middle Eastern' or 'Muslim' has allowed for a displacement of these traits away from White Australia, helping to reinforce the fantasy of the 'Good Nation' Jennifer Rutherford (2000) has so convincingly written about.

Added to this I see a second way in which the concept of the 'nasty migrant' can be operationalised in the context of the 'Sydney gang rapes'. As outlined in the previous chapter, some of the media commentators' outrage arose not because of the horrific violence suffered by individual women but because of the attack these rapes seemed to be on a community that had 'welcomed' them. In this sense I also see the 'nasty migrant' as representing the ungrateful subject, the one who refuses to accept the place of passive object of (White) Australian benevolence. In Sheehan's description of young Muslim men, I see both versions of this 'nasty migrant' in play.

In explaining the events in Cronulla in 2005, Sheehan – like a number of other right-wing commentators – succeeds in making 'common sense' links to the gang rapes:

> Sexual aggression was a subtext, as it always had been. During the rampage, a parked car with three girls inside was approached, the door pulled open and the girls told, 'We are going to rape you, you Aussie sluts.'
>
> Where was this coming from? There was a tension between two cultural worlds, between a male-dominated society that constrained the freedom of women, and a Western culture saturated with the imagery of sexuality and sexual promise.
>
> (Sheehan 2006a, p. 368)

This explanation connects the Cronulla riots with the gang rapes, reinforces the spectre of the 'young Lebanese/Middle Eastern/Muslim man' as gang rapist and generates a discourse in which feminism is understood as a Western virtue. When Sheehan refers to a 'male-dominated society', he seems to clearly be suggesting that Australia is *not* such a society. Yet, Sheehan's focus on an instance of sexist violence by men we are led to believe are 'Middle-Eastern/Muslim/Lebanese' (we are not told anything about their nationality or ethnicity), serves to mask the sexism and indeed sexual violence of White Australian beach-goers. Not only has Sydney male beach culture long been associated with (hetero)sexism and frequently violent hyper-masculinity,[15] but the attack by a surfer on a young woman wearing the *hijab* recounted in the previous chapter provides a striking contrast with Sheehan's narrative. Unsurprisingly, this instance of violence against women is not commented upon by Sheehan.

Perhaps the most telling quote Sheehan uses to explain his anger comes from Dr Michael Kennedy:

> 'We got north Lebanese, mostly peasants, mostly uneducated, mostly Moslem, who didn't want to be here in the first place,' Dr Michael Kennedy told me. He had worked with the Lebanese community for more than 20 years,

'Girls like you' 103

first as an undercover cop, then as an academic sociologist. He liked them, but he harboured no illusions. 'They come from a very patriarchal culture. They don't go in for the greater good. They are tribal. They are aggressive, they are in your face. And they are not grateful.'

(Sheehan 2006a, p. 368)

Not only does this quote serve to homogenise and essentialise an image of a 'Lebanese community', it reinforces what Hage (2003, 1998) has frequently argued underlies Australian nationalism whether in its right-wing, conservative, xenophobic or more liberal, multiculturalist guises. For the migrant to be accepted in Australia it is necessary to not only demonstrate commitment to Australia in a way that is not expected or is assumed to already exist in certain Australians (i.e. those of the dominant ethnic group), it is also expected that gratitude be shown. By stressing a communal/tribal/familial loyalty existing between individuals of minority ethnic or migrant backgrounds, their ability to demonstrate loyalty to the family of the Australian nation is called into question. This is a recurring theme in Sheehan's book, where he repeatedly notes the tendency of the K family to 'stick together', in a manner which is presented as beyond reasonable.

Conclusion

Capitalising on the apparent disjuncture between judicial and left-wing academic responses, which sought to play down or erase the racial/ethnic aspect of the rapes and the public and media focus on precisely this feature, Sheehan has positioned himself as a consistent and vocal critic of the legal process, its treatment of rape victims and the rapists themselves. In doing this he frequently utilises the term 'culture' to mean – interchangeably – legal culture (drawing on the 'law and order' rhetoric noted above, which presents the justice system as too lenient and out of touch with community values) and ethnic culture.

While Sheehan attempts to present his book as a defence of rape victims, his is a far from 'feminist' account. Despite the overwhelming quantity of literature dedicated to dispelling the myth of the 'real rapist' and seeking to draw attention to the need to reconceptualise societal understandings of 'normal' male and female sexuality, which allows most rapes to remain unpunished and often unrecognised, Sheehan settles for the easy stereotype of the 'rapist as sexual deviant'. Furthermore, not only does he not challenge the classic conception of what rapist and rape victims should look like, he adds the 'cultural' criteria that further limits the possibility of a full exploration of why rape occurs. As one reviewer of the book commented all too presciently, '[i]t would be disappointing, however, to see it [the book] used as evidence that only certain kinds of men are rapists, and only certain kinds of women victims' (Humphrey 2007, p. 19).

So did the French gang rape victims fare any better? Having explored an array of voices in the Australian context I will now turn to analysing the discourses on '*les tournantes*' in France.

104 *'Girls like you'*

Notes

1 Both present themselves as knowledgeable but objective bystanders in relation to the gang rape phenomena they are commenting upon. At the same time, they are situated very differently: While Sheehan appears to sets himself up as a representative of 'mainstream Australia', Amara is keen to emphasise her authenticity as a 'woman of the *banlieue'*. The relative impact that has on their narratives will be examined through the course of this chapter and Chapter 9.
2 Parliament of New South Wales, Hansard, 25 October 2006, www.parliament.nsw.gov. au/Hansard/Pages/HansardFull.aspx#/DateDisplay/HANSARD-1323879322-37443/ HANSARD-1323879322-37393, Accessed 29 August 2016.
3 This is not intended to suggest that the victims were not worthy of the sympathy they received: rather, it is to highlight the very specific roles they were required to play in order to obtain this sympathy.
4 Described as emulating 'the most lawless tribal subculture in Sydney's ethnic mosaic, the Lebanese gangs' (2006, p. 5) and contextualised by an account of their criminal histories.
5 See also his reference to Cassie calling Sami 'Hook Nose' (2006, p. 260) and his description of the 'wild-eyed accused rapist, shouting over the judge' (2006, p. 123).
6 He refers to a prison visit by one of the K brother's girlfriends during which she was filmed masturbating him (2006, p. 189).
7 Sheehan states three times that one of the brothers when confronted by the police lost control of his bladder: 'He promptly wet his pants': (2006, p. 21, p. 61 and again at p. 135).
8 'the [K] house was squalid' (2006, p. 21).
9 A powerful recent example of this can be found in the interactions between Ukrainian 'feminist' group *Femen* and Muslim women regarding the former's asserted concern for the oppressiveness of Muslim women's dress: see the 2015 special issue of the journal *Women's Studies in Communication*, 38(4) for a detailed discussion of the various positions.
10 The term 'Clash of Civilisations' of course refers to Samuel Huntington's 1993 theory, which has subsequently been employed in various contexts to explain the increasingly problematic relationship between the West and the Arab/Muslim world.
11 See also: '[Tegan] was in school uniform – blue, Catholic – and sat in a corner' (2006, p. 242).
12 Department of Public Prosecutions.
13 This is best captured in the events of Cronulla in 2005, discussed further in a moment. See also Elder (2007, pp. 303–307).
14 For example there has been extensive work done by feminist legal scholars on the ways in which the provocation defence has allowed for a tacit condoning of male violence against women: for example, see Coss (2006).
15 One only needs to look at Kathy Lette's and Gabrielle Carey's 1979 book, *Puberty Blues*, documenting teenage gender relations in the Sutherland Shire (within which Cronulla is situated) and the 2007 documentary on the Maroubra surf gang known as 'The Bra Boys' for vivid examples in popular Australian culture.

6 *La Squale*

'Feminising the *banlieue*'

Introduction

Whereas in Australia it was a series of highly mediatised criminal trials that provided the main reference point for media, political and other public discourses, these were not a significant feature of the French public discourses on '*les tournantes*'. Rather, the catalyst for the emergence of discourses on the so-called '*tournantes*' was a film released in 2000 entitled *La Squale ('The Tearaway')*. The film was heralded for presenting the *banlieue* from a 'female' or 'feminist' point of view (Barthe 2000; Lalanne 2000) and, while it was not widely viewed,[1] it did receive critical acclaim (it was nominated for a César[2]) and provoked intense media interest through its opening scene, which is a depiction of a gang rape. It was proclaimed that this film had finally lifted the veil of silence on another form of violence commonplace in the *banlieue*[3] (Chambon 2001b).

Furthermore, its presentation as part fact, part fiction (Barthe 2000; Chambon 2000) gave it status within public debates that went beyond simply an artistic work. The blurring of the line between 'documentary' and 'fiction' allowed the film's version of the 'reality' of '*les tournantes*' to become crystallised as a 'true representation' in public imaginings of the gang rapes and life in the *banlieue* more generally. An important illustration of this crystallisation was the adoption of the slang *banlieue* term '*les tournantes*' in mainstream discourse and its frequent use, even in quality print media such as *Le Monde* and *Le Figaro*.[4] What followed was an intense period of media interest in which '*les tournantes*' were reported as occurring in *banlieues* across the country at levels unimaginable and immeasurable due to the 'law of silence' associated with them. By way of a quantitative analysis of the main print media in France between 1998 and 2003, Laurent Mucchielli documents that this film both launched the previously unused term (he notes it had never been used prior to 2001) and led to it becoming a fairly regularly occurring term, along with mention of '*viols collectifs*' in the next three years (Mucchielli 2005, p. 17).[5]

Given its prominence within French public discourses on '*les tournantes*' and its presentation as a feminist, political and realistic insight into the *banlieue*, in this chapter I analyse *La Squale*. In particular I focus on the ways in which it represents gender identity, sexuality, race, disadvantage and violence. But first, in order to

106 La Squale: '*Feminising the* banlieue'

understand the significance of these claims it is first important to understand the role played by the *banlieue* in French public imaginary and discourse.

The *banlieue* and '*les violences urbaines*'

The *banlieue* has historically been a zone on the periphery, first separating the working classes and poor from bourgeois *intra-muros* society and later a zone of immigration (Rey 1996). The association of the *banlieue* with juvenile delinquency in media and academic discourse has been present since the 1960s (Lochard 2002, p. 34). However it was in 1981 and the '*Été Chaud de Min-guette*'[6] that the stigmatisation of the *banlieue* became crystallised within media discourse (Lochard 2002, p. 37; Peralva and Macé 2002, p. 18; Rinaudo 1999, p. 30).

At the same time, this image became ethnicised: 'During the "hot summer of the Minguettes", the media described an ethnicised universe in which the image of the immigrant and that of the "yob" became superimposed' (Rinaudo 1999, p. 30).[7] For example an article in respected left-wing news magazine the *Nouvel Observateur* at the time described the *banlieue* of Lyon as 'a hideout for angry young Arabs, unemployed and more or less delinquent' (Rinaudo 1999, p. 31[8]; see also Baudin and Genestier 2002, p. 114).[9]

Eric Macé and Angelina Peralva, in their analysis of the phenomenon of '*les violences urbaines*' ('urban violence') within media discourse, also note that the *Beur* movement which rose in the late 1980s to counter the effects of racism on the immigrant population served to further link the *banlieue* with those French residents of (predominantly) North African background within the public imagina-tion (Peralva and Macé 2002, p. 19). With the fragmentation of the *Beur* movement due to differences within its leadership and aims, the *banlieue* remained imagined as a site of social unrest with the young French residents of North African origin defined as those largely responsible.

From his analysis of televised representations of the *banlieue* from 1951 until 1994, Guy Lochard concludes that from 1989 on, the *banlieue* received increasing media attention and was increasingly associated with Islamic fundamentalism and the 'un-integratability' of certain immigrant groups (Lochard 2002, p. 39; see also Schneidermann 2003, p. 28). Thus, within current media and public discourse, the term *banlieue* has become a byword for areas inhabited by minority ethnic groups and particularly by Muslims or 'foreigners', especially 'Arabs'. As Mireille Rosello describes it:

> Those demonized *cités* are the symbolic crossroads where anti-Arab feelings crystallize around issues of housing: images of drug-ridden basements and of vandalized letter-boxes are ethnically encoded. Gradually, amalgams perme-ate French culture, certain types of housing are equated with violence or even terrorism, and immigration is reduced to a gendered caricature: to the menac-ing silhouette of armed young male delinquents.

> (Rosello 1997, p. 240)

La Squale: '*Feminising the* banlieue'   107

The fear of the *banlieue* has become a fear of the *étranger* in general, and more specifically a fear of the African, the North African/Arab first and foremost (Rey 1996, p. 11).

Furthermore, as the above quote from Mireille Rosello suggests, the *banlieue* has also been constructed as a highly masculinised space. Women were traditionally for the most part excluded from representations of the *banlieue*, just as they were generally ignored in scholarship and political debate on immigration and citizenship in France (Raissiguier 1999, p. 440). This has been true of both critical and sympathetic portrayals of the *banlieue*: a point I will return to in the next chapter.

In this context *La Squale* was identified as offering something new. By focusing on the lives of young women in the *banlieue* and making them the central characters, the film seemed to provide a missing perspective. The aim, the director Fabrice Génestal asserted, was not to further stigmatise *banlieue* residents nor capitalise on the already catastrophised issue of the *banlieue* and '*les violences urbaines*' (Chambon 2000). Rather it was to confront issues of racism and sexism in the *banlieue* (Barthe 2000).

Moreover, both cast and director spoke of the film as representing a reality that they had personally experienced. This led to the film being described as a 'testimonial: somewhere between fiction and documentary' (Chambon 2000). The director was situated as an expert on the *banlieue*, having both lived and worked as a teacher in various Parisian *cités*. In an article in Le Monde, following the statement 'La Banlieue, Fabrice Génestal connaît bien' ('The Banlieue, Fabrice Génestal knows well'), Génestal was quoted as stating:

> According to him [Génestal], the phenomenon of gang rape is the product of a macho and reactionary order which uses this practice as a type of 'initiation rite' for certain young people in disadvantaged suburbs. 'It happens in other places too but not in a manner that is as ritualistic or extreme. [In the *banlieues*] the practice has become completely normalised and valourised', laments Fabrice Génestal.[10]
>
> (Chambon 2000)

Meanwhile one of the lead actors, Esse Lawson, was interviewed by left-wing newspaper *L'Humanité* on 2 December 2000 and stated:

> The scenario is inspired by real events. I have friends who have been the victims of gang rape. We call it '*la tournante*'. Young people speak about it a lot amongst themselves. It has become unexceptional. But outside of that context no one knows anything and no one says anything. Through this film, we hope to lift this taboo. That doesn't mean that if you go to Sarcelles [Parisian *banlieue*] you will be beaten and raped.[11]
>
> (Barthe 2000)

So how did the film represent the 'hidden truth' of sexual violence in the *banlieue*?

108   La Squale: '*Feminising the* banlieue'

The story

The story centres around a young woman, Desirée, a recent arrival in a Parisian *banlieue* who struggles to find a place for herself and overcome her own insecurities caused by a lack of father figure and a difficult relationship with her mother. Rebellious and angry, she constructs an identity for herself as the daughter of legendary gang leader Souleymane who mysteriously disappeared years before but continues to hold a mythical status in the *banlieue.* This leads to her becoming the leader of her own female gang as well as developing a relationship with young gang leader Toussaint. Through this relationship, Toussaint's subsequent betrayal and Desirée's act of revenge, we are presented a graphic taste of life in the *banlieue.*

In particular, the film begins with a brutal gang rape perpetrated by Toussaint and a group of young men. We later discover that this is a regular practice in which Toussaint uses his charms to romance girls and then lures them into situations in which they are used as a body over which Toussaint and his gang bond. This representation of gang rape seems to both conform to the description given by survivors (such as Samira Bellil, discussed in Chapter 8) and sociological studies that have sought to understand the practice and significance of this particular type of sexual violence among young gang members in different contexts (Hamel 2003; Bourgois 1996)

However, in spite of the unquestionable reality of the violence depicted, from the outset, *La Squale* does little to challenge dominant discourses. The viewer is thrown into a chaotic, animalistic world in which senseless criminality, insults and physical violence are part of the quotidian. It seems to produce a similar effect to that critiqued by Henry Giroux in his analysis of Black 'ghetto' films in the US:

> In both pedagogical and political terms, the reigning films about black youth that have appeared since 1990 may have gone too far in producing narratives that employ the commercial strategy of reproducing graphic violence and then moralizing its effects. Violence in these films is tied to a self-destructiveness and senselessness that shocks but often fails to inform audiences about either its wider determinations or the audience's possible complicity with such violence. The effects of such films tend to reinforce for White, middle-class America the comforting belief that violence as both a state of mind and a site of social relations is always somewhere else – in that strangely homogenized social formation known as 'black' youth.
>
> (Giroux 1996, p. 43)

If the claim the film's aim was to confront issues of racism and sexism in the *banlieue*, it is unfortunate that it ultimately falls victim to a similar fate as many US films on Black urban youth:

> ... complex representations of black youth get lost in racially coded films that point to serious problems in the urban centers, but do so in ways that erase the

La Squale: '*Feminising the* banlieue'   109

accountability of the dominant culture and racist institutions on the one hand, and any sense of viable hope, possibility, resistance, and struggle on the other.

(Giroux 1996, p. 45)

Not only is the sociological reality of pervasive cross-societal sexual violence rendered invisible – with it being reduced to simply a reality of the *banlieue* – but the deeper critical message is lost through the reliance on well-accepted stereotypes and clichés. This is evidenced both by the crudely crafted characters and the lack of real feminist or anti-racist politics demonstrated. Let me treat each of these issues separately.

Hyper-sexual, violent Blacks; prudish, patriarchal Arabs and the civilised French: Reinforcing colonial sexual stereotypes

First, the characters within *La Squale* all too neatly conform to dominant racial prejudices and stereotypes and in ways that hark back to colonial days.

The Black characters

The image of the hyper-sexual Black man or woman has frequently been identified and critiqued by critical race and postcolonial scholars (hooks 2004, 1994, 1992, 1990, Mercer 1994). And yet in *La Squale* both of the primary sexual(ised) characters are Black: Toussaint, the 'rapist villain', and Desirée, the 'rebellious heroine'. Both are represented as having an easy and 'animalistic' sexuality, largely devoid of emotion. Even their physical appearance is notable: their taut, muscular bodies fitting uncomfortably well with the racialised accounts of the Black body so frequently problematised in critical race scholarship.[12]

The film is also populated with images of Black female aggression and sexual availability (as well as potential promiscuity). The local nightclub is overwhelmingly male with the few women present almost only Black women. So too, the 'bad girls' ('*les cailleras*') who Desirée befriends are all Black women except for one woman of South-East Asian appearance. These young women behave aggressively, preying upon the quieter, timider North African girls and the younger boys. Added to this, both Desirée's and Toussaint's mothers are single parents and Toussaint's older sister also has a baby and appears not to have a partner. Desirée's mother is extremely violent and hard. She ultimately confides that, after what seems to have been a gang rape in her adolescence she became highly promiscuous leading to her being unsure who Desirée's natural father was. This association of Black women with the stigmatised image of the "poor, single mother" does little to challenge dominant constructions of Black female identity or sexuality.

The North African characters

Meanwhile, the North African characters are also presented in highly stereotypical ways. The family structures depicted mirror the classic representations of North

110   La Squale: '*Feminising the* banlieue'

African immigrant homes: over-bearing brothers; weak, ineffectual mothers; absent fathers and oppressed sisters/daughters. The main male North African character, Anis, is complicit in the gang rapes but is teased for being unable to perform (contributing to the somewhat paradoxical orientalist image of the Arab as both sexually repressed and perverted). He, Leila's cousin and Yasmine's brother are all represented as uptight and controlling. Their masculinities emerge as fragile and dependent on their ability to police the women of their family. While Anis befriends Desirée and claims to 'respect women', he remains Toussaint's accomplice and stands by and watches the rapes apparently either incapable of seeing it as completely wrong or of resisting the pressure to be involved. Although he ultimately kills Toussaint, this is not in response to the latter's treatment of women. Rather, it is an act of revenge for what Anis believes to be Toussaint's betrayal in stealing the group's drugs. The male bond is therefore where his primary loyalty and concern lie. Moreover Anis, like Yasmine's brother and Leila's brother and cousin, conforms to the image of the possessive, patriarchal young *banlieue* man. He is fiercely protective of his sister, who he also infantilises, buying her a pink bunny for her birthday (which he subsequently gives to Desirée to comfort her after Toussaint has beaten her up).

The figures of the two main female North African characters, Leila and Yasmine, are those of virginal, naïve young women who are prey to the charming Toussaint. They are coy and easily flattered but essentially do not assert an active autonomous sexuality. Instead they are portrayed as victims. Moreover, both manifest classic stereotypical traits of 'Beurette' identity (discussed further in the next chapters). Yasmine is presented as the 'good Beurette': hard-working, obedient, virginal and intent on using the school system as a means of escaping the *banlieue*. Meanwhile, Leila's fate following her rape reflects the standard narrative of woe deployed in dominant discourses: as 'soiled goods', she is rejected by her family and forcibly sent back to the *bled* ('the village', presumably somewhere in North Africa) to be married off.

White characters

There are some White male faces within the film, which appear to attest to the ethnic mix of *banlieue*, but aside from Steve (the resident drug dealer) they do not emerge as significant characters in the film. For the most part the White members of the *banlieue* community remain nameless, and we are given no insight at all into their family lives, sexuality (although one of them does take part in the *tournante*) or gender relations. There are no White *banlieue* women portrayed at all. As a result, the inclusion of White *banlieue* residents seems superficial and adds little to re-conceptualising the *banlieue* as a site of economic and social marginalisation *without* a particular racial/ethnic identity.

The main role played by the White characters tends to be as representatives of 'mainstream' (read 'civilised') France: the teachers who seek to maintain order within the Republican school, the well-spoken and polite shop assistants on the Champs Elysées who are terrorised by Desirée and her group of friends, the ticket inspectors on the bus who catch Touissant and his friends fare evading, the doctor who informs Desirée that she is pregnant. In many ways these characters mirror Génestal's own relationship with the *banlieue*: while he claims to understand it well, he also situates himself *outside*, refusing to identify himself as one of the *banlieue* community. If the *banlieues* emerge as extra-territorial sites of control that mirror the former colonial territories (Tshimanga, Gondola and Bloom 2009, p. 5; Dubois 2000), then Génestal and his White characters are the colonial administrators.

Reinforcing the public/private divide of the *banlieue*

Through the *Beur* movement and the emergence of the *banlieue* as a notable site of cultural production, it has been argued that *banlieue* cinema and music provide an opportunity for re-opening debate on French society, relations of power and identity (Orlando 2003). In this regard, *La Squale* has frequently been compared with an earlier example of *banlieue* cinema, *La Haine*. Released in 1995 and telling the story of three young *banlieue* men from diverse backgrounds (one North African, one Jewish and one Black), *La Haine* presented a graphic and highly critical insight into the impact of institutional racism, police violence, poverty and discrimination on young men living in the French *banlieue*. It received huge critical acclaim and has gained a cult status both within France and internationally. So influential was the film on French society that it was reported that then Prime Minister Alain Juppé organised a special compulsory screening for members of his cabinet (Johnston 1995).

La Haine's powerful social critique was however limited. The film's narrative revolves around the homosocial bond of three marginalised young men of the *banlieue* in a world replete with racism and sexism. While challenging the White French demonisation of the *banlieue* and particularly its non-White male residents, the *banlieue* represented is devoid of any female agents. Mothers and carefully policed sisters make fleeting appearances, and the only interaction the men have with women is their botched attempt to flirt with bourgeois White French women at an art exhibition they have gate-crashed in central Paris. After failing to convince the women of their charms, the 'heroes' become aggressive and hostile. They rampage through the exhibition, destroying glasses and causing chaos before running off into the night. This scene reflects a classic example of the 'protest masculinity' used by many commentators to explain the sexism of marginalised men (also discussed earlier in relation to the 'Sydney gang rapes'). The ability (or rather inability) to access the women of the dominant society becomes both a symbol of their oppression and a site for resistance.

The positioning of *La Squale* as the 'sister' film (assisted by the fact that hip hop artist Cut Killer provided parts of the soundtrack for both) fails to address the fact that both films reproduce a version of the classic 'public/private' divide critiqued by feminists. *La Haine* situates its narrative between the *banlieue* and the idealised 'authentic French' space of central Paris and attempts to show the complex realities of men in the *banlieue* framed by the impact of racism, poverty and discrimination.

112   La Squale: '*Feminising the* banlieue'

Yet while *La Squale* was presented as the 'female follow-up', virtually all of *La Squale*'s narrative is confined to the *banlieue*,[33] making few comments on racism or other political and socio-economic factors of exclusion and instead concentrating on gender relations. Thus unlike *La Haine*, there is little by way of social commentary on the social, political and economic marginalisation faced by *banlieue* residents as a result of dominant French society nor the racism they may face. Moreover while the men in *La Haine* do demonstrate agency and resistance (however self-destructive) in their engagement with the world outside the *banlieue*, the women are relegated to the role of survival within the *banlieue*. They do not really challenge the status quo; they simply attempt to find a way to exist within it.

The most rebellious act is that of Yasmine who erupts at the breakfast table after having been subject to an attempted rape the night before. She throws the breakfast patisseries at her brother and pours coffee on the tablecloth. When her brother slaps her, she lashes out back at him and shouts that he will never touch her again before storming out. The fact that at the end of the film she is also in England with Desirée, apparently alone, suggests she has asserted some greater degree of freedom, but in order to do this we have been clearly shown that she has played the dutiful, virginal daughter and sister up until this point. She is also shown to be actively participating in school, which reinforces the dominant myth of the good young *Beurette*, who unlike her male counterpart, integrates and performs well within the education system (discussed further in the next chapters). The problems she faces are represented *not* as the result of dominant French society but the actions of men of the *banlieue*.

A 'feminist perspective' on the *banlieue*?

Considering the film was presented as a 'feminist' view of the *banlieue*, it is startling that the female characters in fact show very little gender consciousness. Ultimately when the women do rebel it is not in solidarity or out of a political or social consciousness but due to their personal grievances: Desirée because she has been rejected by Toussaint, Yasmine because she feels betrayed by Toussaint. Otherwise the women show no solidarity and in fact are highly competitive with – and contemptuous of – each other (this is particularly well-reflected in the relationship between Desirée and her mother).

The only real exceptions to this are the final scene when Desirée and Yasmine are shown holidaying together in England and one of the final scenes involving Desirée and her mother. These are the only two scenes where the women demonstrate any real connection with each other. Even then, in both cases the relationships are mediated through relationships with men. Desirée and her mother are openly hostile to each other throughout most of the film, and Desirée holds onto the belief that her father is the key to her happiness. She refuses to relate to her mother in any way, instead insulting her for not being good enough for Desirée's father to want to stay. In return, Desirée's mother throws back that it was rather because of Desirée that no man has stuck around. Equally, Yasmine and Desirée only bond through their relationship with Toussaint. It is only after their rivalry is

La Squale: 'Feminising the banlieue'   113

finished and Toussaint is dead that they are able to share any sort of friendship and then it is centred on the fact that Desirée rescued Yasmine from being raped and in return Yasmine pays for a trip to England for Desirée to abort the baby she is carrying by Toussaint.

This is contrasted with the male relationships: the sharing of not only Toussaint's rape victims but the subsequent sharing by the men of the tape recording of the rape outside the school gates provides a powerful example of the homosocial bonds between men of the *banlieue*. As noted above, it takes Toussaint's alleged betrayal of the group of men for Anis to take action against him. Otherwise, the men stick together and protect each other wherever possible: the distraction of Leila's cousin by Toussaint's group of friends to allow him to be alone with her is but one example. Even as Anis is disgusted by Toussaint's assault on Desirée, this is not sufficient for him to actively protest. And yet when it appears Toussaint has cheated him, he is willing to resort to murder.

At the same time, *La Squale* also exemplifies the identification of sex as a tool of domination, used both by men over women (the collective celebration of patriarchal privilege, Anne Cossins (2000) writes about) and, in certain circumstances, by men over other men. The proprietorial element to the rapes is well-illustrated through the use by Toussaint of his ring to brand his victims after he has raped them. Another example is the punishment handed out to Toussaint following his rape of Leila is his own anal rape by Leila's brother. He experiences this as a fundamentally humiliating attack, which leads him to be aggressive towards Yasmine (who witnessed the rape) and to demand that she swear not to tell anyone. As discussed in relation to Sully J's disturbing 'educational initiative' detailed in Chapter 2, this representation of rape reinforces its feminising and simultaneously subjugatory power.

Overall, for an apparently 'feminist' engagement with the issue of sexual violence in the *banlieues*, *La Squale* does little to trouble dominant stereotypes of appropriate 'victims' and 'villains'. Yasmine is clearly constructed from the outset as an innocent, obedient and chaste girl. Her compassion for her mother and for Toussaint and her modesty set her up as the 'ideal victim' that both mirrors the Australian discourses and resists feminist efforts to displace this common foundation on which many rape myths rely.

Furthermore, the division of women in the film according to their relative connections to powerful men does little to dispel proprietal constructions of female bodies or sexuality. For example, Desirée is only able to initially establish a standing within the group through her claim to be the daughter of the mythical patriarch of the *banlieue*, Souleymane. Later, she is able to maintain this status through her connection with Toussaint, who himself seeks to emulate the *caïd* (boss) identity: wearing a ring of the letter 'S'. It is also interesting that, once he establishes a relationship with Desirée, Toussaint does not suggest that she be made sexually available to other members of his group of friends. While he ultimately betrays her, this is done in a typical 'bad, cheating boyfriend' manner, as opposed to the intentional enticement and entrapment of the young women with whom he flirts. He is also fiercely possessive of her; when she dances with Leila's cousin in a

114 La Squale: '*Feminising the* banlieue'

nightclub it is not clear whether he reacts so angrily – shouting and shoving Leila's cousin – because of his recent rape of Leila, which he realises the male members of Leila's family will seek to avenge, or whether it is in asserting his proprietal right to Desirée as 'his woman' ('ma meuf'). In any event, the two possible reasons for his reaction can in fact be read together and both conform to proprietal notions of female identity in relation to men.

It is interesting to contrast the sexual relationship Toussaint has with the young women he lures and gang rapes with his sexual relationship with Desirée. With her they appear as equals and in fact, the final time they have sex it is Desirée who asserts dominance by sitting on top of him and holding him down by the neck. When he attempts to kiss her or take charge in any way, she pushes him down again. By this time she has already come up with her plan to frame him and is in fact in his room to plant the drugs she wants the others to believe he has stolen. Thus while she appears to use sex as a tool for asserting dominance, it is in fact her inability to take revenge on him herself that leads her to resort to tricking him, using her body.

Desirée on the one hand asserts a fierce independence (rejecting the sentimental offer to exchange necklaces with Toussaint) and yet on the other is repeatedly subjected to Toussaint's insults and physical assaults. Even though she and her friends are presented as aggressive and independent, they are constantly placed in second place to the men around them. Desirée is intended to be a forceful character, and yet she ultimately only acts in response to the two men in her life: her mysterious father and Toussaint. We are not shown what she herself desires out of life, except when we discover that she is pregnant, and she dreams of having babies with Toussaint thereby conforming to a stereotypical construction of femininity.

Similarly, while Yasmine does shown signs of resistance to the patriarchal and sexist demands of her family and while she seems bright enough to be aware of the insincerity of Toussaint's courting, she continues to perform her 'daughterly/ sisterly' duties, while at the same time ultimately succumbing to Toussaint's charms. As mentioned previously, she does increasingly fight back at home and even appears to gain a certain independence. However, we are not given any insight into what it is she seeks out of her life. Similarly, while her tenderness for Toussaint emerges after she witnesses his rape, we are never really clear as to the extent to which she is genuinely attracted to him and why. In the early parts of the film she appears to both recoil from and be flattered by his advances. When he touches her, we are not sure if she is consenting or too afraid to resist. She giggles and looks shy when he corners her against a tree on her way home from school. Other times, such as when they encounter each other on the bus, she looks ill at ease. Once they do begin to spend time together her feelings are still very unclear. She remains with Toussaint even though he is very rude to her. She also seems to be attracted to him and is only unwilling to enter into further intimacy out of fear of being discovered by her brother. For a young woman who otherwise presents herself as intelligent and aware of the dangers the *banlieue* holds, this complete reversal in her interactions with Toussaint seems to make little sense. Instead, it seems almost to play into the 'rape as romance' narrative in which the line between

La Squale: '*Feminising the* banlieue'   115

sexual attraction, fear and repulsion are increasingly blurred (Philadelphoff-Puren 2005). Thus, even the more assertive female characters are shown to have little agency and even less subjectivity.

The women also require the men to perform the acts of revenge on their behalf – either through having a brother/cousin who will stand up for them (even at the beginning when the tough girls encounter Desirée, and she refuses to be afraid of them, they suggest that her attitude derives from having a big brother who will protect her). Leila is avenged by her brother Samir and her cousin, but no sympathy or love is shown to her as a victim. Rather, the attack is seen as an attack on the family and the family's honour. Otherwise, even though Desirée masterminds the plan to destroy Toussaint, she is unable to carry it out herself but requires the active intervention of other men.

When the girls are discussing Desirée's impending abortion whilst lying on the beach in England, Desirée laughingly says that if it is a boy she will abort, and if it is a girl she will keep it. This seems to reinforce a belief that the violence, misogyny and criminality shown in the *banlieue* is a problem of masculinity. It also essentialises this masculinity, as Desirée does not suggest that she would seek to bring her son up differently but simply accepts as a fact that by the very nature of his being male, he will be a problem. This essentialist vision of *banlieue* masculinity and the fact that there are no decent men portrayed in the *banlieue* (the closest is Anis, and he is a drug dealer and complicit in the gang rapes) seems to fit a little too neatly with the hegemonic discourses that have defined the problems in the *banlieue* as caused by a hyper-virile masculinity.

Heralded as presenting a 'female/feminist perspective' on the *banlieue*, *La Squale* in fact presents some very disturbing images of not only the *banlieue* but of its residents. Through the recreation of racialised and sexualised stereotypes that hark back to colonial discourses, *La Squale* does little to disrupt dominant constructions of the *banlieue* as a site of criminality, violence and ethnic difference. Nor does it in fact challenge the construction of the *banlieue* as a masculine/masculinised space and that masculinity as inherently violent and misogynistic. Finally, by placing all the female characters in positions of dependence on the male characters, the construction of *banlieue* (read 'immigrant') women as 'victims' or 'dupes' of *banlieue* men is in fact reinforced.

Despite its problematic, sensationalist and reductive representation of the phenomenon of '*les tournantes*', *La Squale* was embraced within mainstream French public discourse for its presentation of what was understood to be a serious social problem. It sparked a period of intense media attention that sought to not only report on incidents of sexual violence in the *banlieue* but also to explain and understand the causes. I will now turn to analysing these discourses.

Notes

1 David-Alexander Wagner (2006) states that only 40,400 people went to see it in Paris and 58,000 in the whole of France.
2 The French equivalent of the Oscars.

116   La Squale: '*Feminising the* banlieue'

3 'Après la sortie – en novembre 2000 – du film *La Squale*, en partie consacré à la question des tournantes, le phénomène est sorti de la confidentialité.'

4 This did not pass without comment as an outraged letter to the editor of *Le Monde* by one reader, Sidonie Christophe demonstrates (*Le Monde*, 6–7 May 2001, p. 15).

5 By way of example, centre-left newspaper *Le Monde* held an online forum specifically dedicated to the subject of '*les tournantes*'.

6 'The Hot Summer of the Minguettes' – a series of uprisings that took place on the Minguettes housing estate on the outskirts of Lyon. This uprising was most notably marked by the images of cars set on fire by protesters.

7 'Lors de "l'été chaud des Minguettes", les médias décrivent un univers ethnicisé dans lequel l'image de l'immigré se superpose à celle du jeune voyou.'

8 'un repaire de jeunes Arabes en colère, chomeurs et plus ou moins délinquants'.

9 'les jeunes impliqués dans les révoltes urbaines ne sont pas tous d'origine étrangère, mais fantasmatique ment, on ne voit que des jeunes basanés'.

10 Selon lui [Génestal], le phénomène du viol collectif relève d' 'un ordre macho et réactionnaire' qui fait de cette pratique 'un rite d'initiation' pour certains adolescents des quartiers difficile. 'Ça existe ailleurs que dans les cités mais pas de manière aussi rituelle et extrême. Là, le passage à l'acte est banalisé et valorisé', déplore Fabrice Génestal.

11 'Le scénario s'inspire de faits réels. J'ai des copines qui ont été victimes de viol collectif. On appelle ça la tournante, les jeunes en parlent beaucoup entre eux. C'est devenu banal, mais au dehors on ne sait rien, on ne dit rien. Avec ce fim, on veut soulever un tabou. Mais ça veut pas dire que si tu passes à Sarcelles tu vas te faire frapper et violer.'

12 See for example Mercer's (1994) critique of representations of the Black male naked form within photography and pornography and hooks'(1992) essay, 'Selling hot pussy' on the commodification of Black female sexuality.

13 There are only 3 scenes which take place outside; of the two in France, one is when the girls raid a perfume shop on the Champs Elysées and the other when Desirée assists with a drug deal in a park, which appears to be outside the *banlieue* and which goes wrong. The final scene takes place in England, where Desirée and Yasmine have gone to procure Desirée an abortion.

7 The (sexually) lost *banlieues* of the Republic

Media responses

In his 2005 book Laurent Mucchielli provides a detailed critical analysis of both media discourse and empirical data available on the phenomenon of '*les tour-nantes*'. Building on this useful analysis, in this section I examine media reporting with a focus on the specific frames used to describe and explain the rapes. In particular I argue that the discourses can be divided between:

- those that drew on issues of ethnicity/religion/culture;
- those that suggested '*les tournantes*' were some sort of initiation rite or ritual;
- those that focused on the poverty/social marginalisation of the *banlieue*;
- those that identified '*les tournantes*' as a result of 'affective deficit' and '*la misère sexuelle*' (sexual deprivation) of the *banlieue*; and
- those that saw it as simply another manifestation of '*les violences urbaines*'.

Many of these discourses are inter-linked. However, first of all it is worth commenting on the use of the term '*tournante*' a little further.

Situating sexual violence: Use of the term '*les tournantes*'

It is interesting to consider the implications of the gang rapes being specifically identified according to a *banlieue* slang term rather than the more generic '*viol collectif*' or '*viol en réunion*', both of which were also utilised but less frequently or alongside '*tournante*'. It is argued that this is not incidental. By calling the gang rapes in question '*les tournantes*', they became specifically located. As noted in the previous chapter the term '*banlieue*' is a highly charged one in French public discourse: It is associated simultaneously with criminality, anti-sociality, aggressive masculinity and immigrant communities. As a result, the media use of a term originating in the *banlieue* is likely to immediately evoke a particular social context for readers. This is important as, unlike the Australian context – and attempts by unscrupulous right-wing commentators like Janet Albrechtsen and Paul Sheehan writing about the French context – race/religion/ethnicity were generally not *explicitly* identified as a factor in the rapes within quality media, even as discourses

118 *The lost* banlieues *of the Republic*

of race/religion do emerge on closer examination. This is a significant difference between the two contexts and one that points to the very different founding myths and subsequent approaches to immigration and ethnic diversity. In Australia the question of race has always been at the heart of debates about the Nation (even in the thinly disguised 'Australian values' rhetoric used more currently). However in France the centrality of civic notions of citizenship based on adherence to Republican values has been a crucial component of the imagined national identity (Silverman 1999, p. 128; Conklin 1997; Brubaker 1992; Weber 1976). As I will show, this does not mean race is *not* relevant. Rather that it can only be spoken of through the mediating language of the *banlieue* and/or breakdowns in civic relationships between citizens and/or citizens and the institutions of the State.

It should also be noted that the acceptance of '*les tournantes*' as a specific and serious problem of the *banlieue* was not completely uncontested. For example, Françoise-Marie Santucci in *Libération* cited two local government workers who questioned the true extent of '*les tournantes*' and asserted the broader nature of the issue of youth sexuality and violence beyond simply the *banlieue* context (Santucci 2001a). There was also one example of an attempt to employ the term '*tournante*' outside of the *banlieue* context: In an article appropriately subtitled, 'Les cités ne sont pas seules concernées' ('The *cités* are not the only ones implicated') in *Le Figaro* in 2001, Philippe Motta reported on a series of gang rape trials involving 15 accused. Yet he noted the setting is nothing like a *banlieue*. Rather, he describes a bourgeois French town of 3,000 'in which two thirds live very well',[1] implying that a simplistic account of poverty or ethnicity as causal factors could be insufficient. Motta also quoted the victims' lawyers linking these rapes committed by local 'bourgeois' children with the phenomenon of '*les tournantes*': 'the social context is different but the state of mind is identical'[2] (Motta 2001). Unfortunately, these attempts to open up the issue for broader interrogation were sporadic and isolated.

While *La Squale*'s director Fabrice Génestal, asserted that the film was intended to present a female perspective on life in the *banlieue* and highlight the specific difficulties faced by young women,[3] the feminist perspective also appeared to often get lost in subsequent media discourses on '*les tournantes*'. Instead, as Christelle Hamel has argued, the rapes often added weight to the asserted need for a stronger 'law and order' response to the *banlieue*: an issue that dominated the 2002 elections and reinforced the links drawn between urban unrest, ethnic minorities and immigration (Hamel 2003, p. 85).

Herein lies the first parallel – aside from temporal – with the emergence of public discourses on the 'Sydney gang rapes'. As discussed earlier, 'law and order' featured heavily throughout political and media discourses in the Australian context, as did issues of inter-ethnic relations and immigration. The linking of immigrant populations and crime is not unique to Australia and France, but both have had a very intense recent history with vast amounts of public discourse dedicated to the issue: through the mediating language of the *banlieue* in France (and its automatic association with immigrants discussed in the previous chapter) and 'the Middle-Eastern gangs' in Australia (discussed earlier). At the centre of

The lost banlieues *of the Republic*   119

both of these discourses it is specifically the young Muslim man who has been identified as particularly problematic. This problematisation has frequently drawn on longstanding representations of an antithesis between Islam and (Enlightened) Western values. As illustrated in the first part of this book, the repugnant figures of the particular gang rapists were overlaid with well-established orientalist imagery.

In the French context, the standard generalised orientalist tropes employed in the Australian context were further enhanced by France's particular colonial connection with the Muslim world (a point also relevant to the analysis of *La Squale*), more specifically, North Africa. Although no trials in France assumed the status of the 'Sydney gang rape' trials, the trial of eighteen (including two young women) residents of the Parisian *banlieue* of Argenteuil did attract a fair amount of attention in mid-2002, particularly in print media of the Left. The descriptions of the participants and the background context are illuminating. This is not only due to some possible parallels with Australian discourses on the 'Sydney gang rapes', but also because they potentially demonstrate the ongoing significance of France's historical colonial relationship with its largest immigrant communities (namely from the Maghreb).

The 'backward immigrant' versus 'enlightened France'

In her coverage of the Argenteuil gang rapes for *Le Monde*, Pascale Robert-Diard provides a vivid image of the *banlieue*: a site she describes as a 'parallel' and closed-off world into which the Court had to venture:

> [The Court] followed them [the *banlieue* residents] into the stairwells of filthy basements, into underground 'squats'. It immersed itself in their daily life, punctuated by scholastic failure and the constant movement between middle school, care [temporary housing provided by social services] and the police station. The Court listened to their fathers, Algerians or Moroccans for the most part, throwing up their arms in a demonstration of their powerlessness or incomprehension at the acts their sons were accused of. The Court tried in vain to get the mothers to speak, women often veiled who stated, 'I agree with my husband. . .'[4]
>
> (Robert-Diard 2002)

This evocative description is layered with images of decay, failure, delinquence: all fairly classic images of the *banlieue*. It is also heavily gendered and ethnicised to the point where all these issues become merged. The classic image of the *banlieue* is reinforced in this description: a space of criminality and scholastic failure, which by implication also means the failure to integrate into the French civic community, as the school is the means by which this is done (Déloye 1994; see Chapter 9 for further discussion). So too, the specific reference to Algerians and Moroccans reinforces the findings of scholars that the *banlieue* is coded with specific ethnic markers and linked to immigration (Baudin and Genestier 2002;

120   *The lost* banlieues *of the Republic*

Lochard 2002; Peralva and Macé 2002; Schneidermann 2003; Rinaudo 1999; Rosello 1997; Rey 1996).

Yet added to this specific ethnicisation of the *banlieue* and the crimes associated, it is also noteworthy that the problem of '*les tournantes*' is identified as predominantly associated with North Africans in France. This is done implicitly: For example, through reference to mothers wearing headscarves, a symbol immediately associated with Islam both historically and more recently as a result of the highly mediatised '*affaires des foulards*' or 'headscarf affairs',[5] even though this is not the only reason headscarves may be worn. There is also the reproduction of names with particular ethnic affiliations and origins: for example, 'Moustapha', 'Karim', 'Ousmane', 'Mouloud', 'Kader' (Geisler 2002; Tourancheau 2002a; Santucci 2001b; du Tanney 2001). And on occasion it is done explicitly through reference to the parents being of 'immigrant'/'Moroccan'/'Algerian'/'North African'/'Arab' background (Durand 2002; Pech 2002c; Robert-Diard 2002; Tourancheau 2002a) or the rapists being described as '*Beur*' (Tourancheau 2002a) or 'Maghrébins' (d'Arrigo 2001).

Thus even if '*les tournantes*' are characterised as a *banlieue* problem rather than overtly related to a particular religion or ethnicity, the reader is left in little doubt as to the specific communities the practice is linked to. Picking up Giroux's argument that 'media culture is the central terrain on which the new racism has emerged' (1996, p. 58), it is unsurprising that links between already problematised ethnic/immigrant communities and further examples of anti-social and criminal behaviour would present easy story opportunities. Furthermore, as Giroux observes: 'In the mass-mediated cultural spheres that shape individual and social consciousness, social and political causes of violence are often elided' (1996, p. 67). The consequences of this are not only the uncritical reproduction of racist stereotypes but the racialisation of 'law and order' discourses, which call for tougher approaches to crime. This has already been well documented in relation to the broader discourse of '*les violences urbaines*' in France (Peralva and Macé 2002), just as it has been in relation to 'Middle Eastern men' in Australia (Poynting et al. 2004; Collins et al. 2000, discussed in Chapter 4).

'*Voileurs et violeurs*': Men of the *banlieue*

Yet aside from the tendency to link crime with a racialised 'Other' – a trend visible in a wide array of national contexts – through the contextualising of '*les tournantes*' as a problem associated with North Africans, the French media representations are also able to draw on a wide array of well-established colonial and orientalist tropes. The example of Robert-Diard's above-cited description of the women as subservient (unwilling to express their own opinions, agreeing with their menfolk) and veiled, far from subtly demonstrates this through its evocation of the traditional orientalist and colonial image of the oppressed, hidden Muslim woman. Further, the reference to their headscarves serves to link '*les tournantes*' with the other issue that has frequently dominated contemporary French media and public discourses, particularly in relation to Muslim/North African immigrants and their

The lost banlieues *of the Republic* 121

children: the issue of the *hijab*. In an especially explicit example in *Le Monde*, an article on '*les tournantes*' by Pascale Krémer and Martine Laronche is accompanied by a cartoon depicting a young woman exclaiming, 'Ni Voile! Ni Viol! Que ça vous plaise ou non!' ('Neither veil nor rape! Whether you like it or not!') (Krémer and Laronche 2002).

While the linking of violence against women with Islam and particularly the *hijab* has been a feature of discourses on violence against women in various Western contexts (as highlighted in the discussion of the Australian context, see also Razack 2008, 2004), the particularly controversial and problematised place of the *hijab* in France – as well as its specific colonial implications – adds further weight to this image.

Gender relations formed an extremely important feature of French 'civilising mission' discourses in the colonial period. In particular, the identification of Islam as a site of female oppression was a feature of both official colonial authorities' discourses and the discourses of well-meaning French feminists of the metropole (Kimble 2006; Conklin 1999; Clancy-Smith 1999). These are points I will return to in Chapters Eight and Nine. It is therefore not incidental that issues such as the *hijab* and sexual violence allegedly committed by men of North African origin become not only inter-linked in French mainstream media discourses but also central sites of public attention and concern.

In another article – this time in the left-wing newspaper *Libération* – journalist Jacky Durand reports on the family of one of the young men convicted of the Argenteuil gang rapes. The picture she presents is one of 'cultural divide': the life inside the family home, which remains built on tradition, and the life outside, in which the young men are confronted with sexuality that they cannot understand or manage:

> In the parents' account there is an 'inside' and an 'outside', a sort of border which informs the contours of familial relations in the *cité*. Between the apartment and the street . . . 'Some parents still see the street as it was when they were children in North Africa; that is to say, where the older [kids/adults] watched over and took care of the younger [kids]. They don't seem to realise that this form of social control has disappeared in the *banlieues* of today', explains one social worker of Val-d'Oise . . .
> . . . After the trial one of the accused's parent confided his surprise: 'They asked me if I had taught my son about sex. I replied that there was enough on the radio, television, in the newspapers. I have never known a Muslim who speaks to his children about sex. It is a question of respect.'
>
> (Durand 2002)[6]

While apparently attempting to understand the problem, Durand in fact characterises the problem in a very similar manner to Republican feminists and administrators in colonial Algeria: The inability to speak openly about sex is portrayed as a reflection of the repressed and repressive sexuality of Muslims, which in turn demonstrated their backwardness in comparison with 'enlightened

122   *The lost* banlieues *of the Republic*

France'. This fascination with Muslim sexuality was an important feature of the colonial era during which the attention of colonial administrators, scholars and metropolitan feminists turned increasingly 'from the battlefield to the bedroom' (Clancy-Smith 1999, p. 155).

Durand is not the only journalist to be concerned with the apparent 'sexual repression' of North African immigrants residing in France. Marie-Estelle Pech, writing in centre-right newspaper *Le Figaro* is even less coy in making the link between cultural and religious practices and the problem of '*les tournantes*'. In an article dedicated to the *tournantes*, Pech quotes a teacher working in the Yvelines:[7]

> 'A young girl who follows the teachings of Islam cannot sit next to boys,' remarks Stéphanie, a middle-school French teacher in les Yvelines. 'My class is divided in two like in the Middle Ages with girls on one side and boys on the other . . . '
>
> (Pech 2002a).[8]

This description raises two issues. The first is the problematic assumption of the ability of a French – and one assumes non-Muslim – outsider to speak authoritatively on Islam. As noted in Chapter 2 in relation to the use of Professor Michael Humphrey as an 'expert' on Pakistani Muslim culture: this raises problematic links with the past collection of colonial knowledge. Stéphanie's generalised statement does not suggest any room for differing interpretations nor for recognition of Islam as a diverse and diversely practised religion. The second issue is the missing link between the seating arrangement of boys and girls and sexual violence. There appears in this explanation a taken-for-granted understanding that sexual conservatism, and more particularly Islamic practices, lies at the heart of sexual violence.

In another article published on the same day, Pech adds to this portrayal. She quotes a young woman who, she states, dated a high school student of 'Moroccan origin':

> They were quite pious people but more than that they were very polite (conservative/prudish), both verbally and physically. I made sure I always wore skirts to my ankles so as not to shock them. Last year I spent a couple of days in the village with them. On returning to France I was also shocked. Over there, anything to do with sex and sensuality is controlled, censored. The contrast is violent when one returns.
>
> (Pech 2002b)[9]

While in this case it seems we are to assume the family and the young man were 'decent', we are left with little doubt that the problem of '*les tournantes*' is a result of this uptight, repressed sexuality being confronted with the sexual freedom of French society. Equally, in the description of the first day of a trial involving a tournante, Patricia Tourancheau, writing for *Libération*, quotes the victim's lawyer stating that the

The *lost* banlieues *of the Republic*   123

parents in the audience were organised according to sex: 'the mothers, veiled with religious symbols, up at the back, in the last row and, further away the old Arab fathers well integrated into France'.[10] Paradoxically, the reference to 'well integrated' men sitting at a distance also conforms to the dominant explanation for the failure of France's policy of integration: namely the apparent reluctance or incapacity of some immigrants to integrate due to their incompatible religious and cultural beliefs (i.e.Islam). In this case the continuation of these traditional practices of segregation – and the concomitant resistance to integration into France – is established by the description of the code of the *banlieue* in which, 'the "chicks" don't mix with the "guys", under threat of finishing up in the basement, treated like a "whore" [ie. raped]'(Tourancheau 2002a).[11] Through this description an implicit link is drawn between what is seen as the traditional Muslim/Arabic practice of segregation of the sexes, the *hijab* and the young men's dysfunctional sexuality.

Even as the explicit resort to racialised arguments is rejected, the apparent 'affective deficit' described among young people of the *banlieue* becomes intimately connected with the traditional background of their parents. Similarly, the repetition of the idea, 'a girl who is seen [hanging out] in the street, is a slut' (Santucci 2001a)[12] – by both media commentators and young men and women of the *banlieue* themselves, it must be noted – evokes traditional colonial images of the women of North Africa and the Orient more generally, cloistered in harems: an image both erotic and submissive (Alloula 1987). The constant reiteration of the mother/whore dichotomy in articles explaining the attitudes of *banlieue* men and women towards female sexuality and identity seems to suggest that such a dichotomy has no place within French society. Just as in Australia, rape myths were deflected onto the Sydney gang rapists, a couple of controversial Muslim clerics and, by implication, Muslim men more generally, in France, rape myths emerge as the sole possession of *banlieue* (immigrant/Muslim) men. By contrast, the Republic is envisaged as an enlightened and sexually egalitarian space (Fassin 2006). As Fassin and others point out, this has played an important part in reinforcing dominant gender, sexual and racial hierarchies within the Republic in recent years (Fernando 2013; Guénif-Souilamas and Macé 2004).

By implying that the *banlieues* are 'far from the Republic' a moral justification is provided for the social and political exclusion of the *banlieue* and its residents. Meanwhile the Republic is reasserted as a site of law and order in which women's rights are protected. This characterisation – as also discussed in the context of the 'Sydney gang rapes' – allows for the prevalence of rape across society to be erased, to the detriment of *all* women: in the *banlieue* and outside. France – as with many nations – has a far from admirable history in addressing violence against women, as numerous scholars have documented (Fougeyrollas-Schwebel 2005; Mucchielli 2005, pp. 55–58; Jaspard et al. 2001). Equally, the official recognition of personal status laws of North African nations for immigrant communities living in France has been critiqued for legitimating gender inequality in migrant women's lives (Ticktin 2008; Winter 1995).

124   *The lost* banlieues *of the Republic*

'Tribal practices'

Aside from the suggestion that Islamic culture and traditions contribute to the problem of '*les tournantes*', there are also frequent references to 'tribal practices'. For example, Marie-Estelle Pech (2002a) explains that in the *banlieue*, 'girls and boys are contained within well-defined spaces and roles, all influenced by ancestral codes [of conduct]'.[13] This reference to 'ancestral codes' evokes images of traditional, tribal peoples: an image often associated with the Orient. Similarly, Robert-Diard refers to the *banlieue* residents as resentful of attacks on 'their clan' ('leur clan'). Once again the tribal imagery cannot be removed from its colonial implications: the backward, native savage. Even more remarkably there are references to sexual violence as a problem in the *banlieues* dating back to the 1980s and 'Zoulou' gangs (Geisler 2002). The explicit reference to African tribes adds to the image of *banlieue* residents as primitive, uncivilised natives: just as African tribes were seen by colonial administrators. Equally, Robert-Diard's reference to the law of the Republic being re-instated, even in the *banlieues* in opposition to their 'law of silence' disturbingly unself-consciously harks back to the language of the colonial 'civilising mission'.

As is also evident from the reference to 'Zoulous', the colonial imagery is not reserved for the North African individuals described. We are also told in the Argenteuil case that 'Fathia' – one of the young women accused of being an accomplice in the rapes – is a 'belle Africaine moulée dans sa minijupe' ('an attractive African, shapely in her miniskirt') who was responsible for injuring a policeman and hitting a cameraman (Tourancheau 2002a). In another article, she is described as a 'tigress' (Robert-Diard 2002). These images – as with that of Desirée in *La Squale* – conform all too easily with the image of the hyper-sexualised, aggressive Black woman (hooks 2004, 1994, 1992, 1990).

The tribal imagery can also be found in suggestions that '*les tournantes*' be seen as 'initiation rituals/rites'. While completely discredited by sociologists working in the area (Hamel 2003), this explanation did gain some currency through repetition (Chambon 2001b). Once again, this invokes images of African tribal rituals and practices, traditionally associated with primitive, uncivilised people in Western discourses. France's extensive colonial engagement with Africa and the Arab world provides a much richer array of stereotypes to draw upon in describing '*les tournantes*' than the generic orientalist images used in descriptions of the 'Sydney gang rapes'.

At the same time, the source of salvation and liberation is also not left in much doubt: '. . . these young girls, according to [sociologist] Caroline Vaissière, "imagine a prince charming who will inevitably be from outside the *cité*"'[14](Santucci 2001a). The fantasy of the 'Prince Charming' from outside 'rescuing' these young women has in fact been argued by some scholars to be a prevailing fantasy within dominant French national discourses (Hamel 2005). As further illustrated a little later, the idea of a man of the *banlieue* (and thus a man of immigrant/ethnic minority origin) being capable of truly respecting gender equality is seen as an impossibility. At the same time, the 'feminism' of France is unquestionable.

'La misère sexuelle' and the exceptional nature of French heterosexual relations

Along with representations of *banlieue* youth as segregated and lacking in sexual education, frequent reference is made to pornography as providing the only source of knowledge in relation to sex. This, it is explained, warps young peoples' opinions of what 'normal sex' is. In many ways this seems to be presenting the perspective adopted by radical feminist scholars such as Andrea Dworkin and Catharine MacKinnon: a position that is not without its limitations due to its inadvertent replication of conservative, right-wing discourses on sexuality and censorship (Mercer 1994, p. 133). However, there may be some value in opening discussion of how men, women and sexuality are constructed and represented in pornography for interrogating discourses on normative sexuality. As I argued in Chapter 2, there were disturbing resonances with classic pornographic representations of sexuality in the discourses of Australian judges, which seem to demand a revisiting of radical feminist critiques of dominant social and legal heteronormativity. Unfortunately, this is not the direction the discussions on pornography in the *banlieue* seem to take. Instead, it is suggested that the problem lies in the discrepancy between the pornography watched by young people of the *banlieue,* which they see as 'normal', and the 'excessively prudish' ways of their parents.

For example, Marie-Estelle Pech (2002a) of *Le Figaro* quotes nurse Benoît Félix asserting that these adolescents are not able to clearly understand the difference between sexual violence, paedophilia, rape and normal sexuality. While factually dubious, this implies that within broader French society these distinctions are unproblematic. The function of stating this distinction is that it reserves sexual deviance, perversity and violence as traits of *banlieue* society. By linking back to the ethnic/religious/cultural explanations set out above, what emerges is a picture of young *banlieue* (Muslim/North African/immigrant) men uncritically digesting violent pornographic images without the benefit of the more sophisticated and mature sexual education received by 'mainstream' French society. Once again we are presented with the image of the 'perverted Arab' described by Guénif-Souilamas and Macé as existing since the colonial period (2004, p. 60).

Complementary to this representation of the 'perverted Arab' is the 'enlightened Frenchman'. As I will elaborate on further in Chapter 9, France has prided itself on having cultivated a special relationship between the genders based on mutual admiration rather than competition: this has been the justification for rejecting the 'war of the sexes' language derogatorily associated with Anglo-Saxon feminist politics. And yet in the context of the *banlieue* it is precisely the 'war of the sexes' that is identified in interactions between *banlieue* men and women. The tacit suggestion within this explanation is that while French men are capable of reconciling degrading pornographic images with more healthy and respectful attitudes towards women, the men of the *banlieue* are not.

Moreover, the reason for this inability is that these men are not party to *l'exception française* in which the genders interact in a relation of complementarity. By contrast, interactions in the *banlieue* are violent, lacking in subtlety and

126 *The lost* banlieues *of the Republic*

romance and by extrapolation, 'unFrench': 'no one flirts, no one knows how to get to know the opposite sex anymore, how to experience desire for the opposite sex. To openly pursue a romantic relationship, for the boys is a demonstration of weakness, for the girls is to be perceived as "sluts"'.[15] (Krémer and Laronche 2002) Once again, the interconnections between gender and national identity emerge through the discourses on rape and sexuality.

This characterisation of the problem as retarded or incomplete sexual development is disturbing for two reasons. On the one hand, it conforms to the orientalist image in which Western sexuality is constructed as superior: restrained, civilised and mature in the face of the brutality and perversity of the Orient, thus reinforcing racial hierarchies. On the other hand, the suggestion that it is 'mis-education' and an inability to flirt/engage in romantic liaisons with the opposite sex that leads to rape diminishes the possibility of recognising sexual violence existing in broader, mainstream French society. Rape is an aberration and a sign of deviance, not associated with the 'normal sexuality' of enlightened, civilised France. This allows the very phallocentric power structures central to rape *and* normative constructions of gender and sexual identity to remain unchallenged. It also makes the commitment of the nation to gender equality almost beyond question.

While the framing of this discourse is situated within the very specific parameters of French national identity, this oppositional account of 'immigrant man's sexism/misogyny' versus 'mainstream man's greater feminist commitment' does have some points of convergence with the Australian discourses. For example, *Libération* journalist Patricia Tourancheau (2002a) provides this description of one of the accused in the Argenteuil gang rapes:

> Accused of at least six rapes, Mouloud, the youngest of seven children, affected by a speech impediment, 'shy and easily influenced', has been delinquent since his arrival in the ZUP [an administrative title for the housing estates] of Argenteuil [suburb of Paris] at age 13 in 1995. His psychiatric report described 'an adolescent stuck between a strict and religious familial culture which he seeks to respect, and the culture of the street, where an individual gains respect from other members of the group through acts of delinquence.[16]

This description of the accused bears a striking resemblance to the assertion of the eldest K brother's lawyer in the 'Sydney gang rapes' that MSK was a 'cultural timebomb' (see Chapter 5). The presentation of non-White men as 'victims of their culture' has been repeatedly critiqued by postcolonial and critical race feminists: the resort to cultural explanations for misogynistic and sexist violence has been rejected as reinforcing both racial and gender hierarchies in which non-White women always emerge at the bottom (Razack 2004, 1998; Narayan 1997; hooks 1992, 1990; Crenshaw 1991).

Further, this 'aberration/improper education' explanation reinforces the dominant heterosexual paradigm as neatly as the judges in the 'Sydney gang rapes'. The

The lost banlieues of the Republic   127

natural tendencies of heterosexual men and women are not interrogated, a fact which emerges even more clearly in the cited explanation of the problem provided by a nurse: 'On the one hand we have the young girl who wants to remain a virgin, on the other there is the boy who wants to have penetrative sex'.[17] In the context of the girls, the image presented is of someone desperate for affection and romance (hence her resort to images of 'Prince Charming', mentioned above). In the context of the boys, they are sexually voracious and in need of physical sexual gratification.

This uncritical reproduction of normative female sexuality (based on emotionality and passivity) and male sexuality (physical and assertive) does little to present a complex and complicated picture of relationships between men and women of the *banlieue*. And yet this is the closest point of convergence between those discussing '*les tournantes*' from 'outside' the *banlieue* and those seeking to either explain or protect young people of the *banlieue* from further stigmatisation. An example of this can be found in the comment by rapper Dadoo in an interview on the stigmatisation of the *banlieue* and '*les tournantes*' in particular in *Libération*: when asked what could be done to improve the situation between men and women in the *banlieue*, he responds that the solution is letting guys into clubs so they can pick up each weekend: 'When they are locked in the *banlieue* for a month and then suddenly see a chick in a miniskirt they lose it'[18] (Binet 2003).

This characterisation of the problem as associated with the men not getting their sexual needs met is highly problematic for the heterosexist, phallocentric assumptions it incorporates: assumptions which, as I have argued earlier, link rape with constructions of normative heterosexuality. Christelle Hamel makes a similar observation in her analysis of media and rapists' discourses on '*les tournantes*':

> The 'sexual deprivation' discourse [to explain the rapes] is inappropriate. Its use reveals above all how the norm of an insatiable masculine sexuality is widely shared. Moreover, it allows for the justification or at least the explanation of rape as simply the result of male sexual needs not being sufficiently met.[19]

(Hamel 2003, p. 91)

In rejecting the '*misère sexuelle*' explanation, Hamel points to the convergence between 'mainstream' discourses and those of the rapists themselves regarding what is seen as 'normal' male sexuality.[20] Added to this, she notes from her interviews with young men who have participated in gang rapes that the men adhere to a construction of their sexuality as 'particularly developed' and their having greater needs than other men. The conformity of this self-representation with orientalist representations of the over-sexed, predatory, perverted, deviant Muslim man is noteworthy: not because it is suggested that the orientalist representation is thus proved true but because it seems to point to a similar '(post)colonial habitus' as that identified in the context of the Sydney gang rapists.

128   *The lost* banlieues *of the Republic*

Discourses from the *banlieue*

In France there have been sociologists who have sought to conduct ethnographic fieldwork in an attempt to identify the young men's perspectives and reasoning behind '*les tournantes*' (Coutant 2007; Hamel 2003). Unfortunately, they have frequently uncovered discourses that provide little additional information or resistance to dominant public discourses. Parisian sociologist Isabelle Coutant expresses her dismay when, in conducting field research to challenge dominant representations of *banlieue* youth, she was presented with young people expressing similar points of view to those she set out to disprove: 'I had thought I was going to cast doubt on the image the media and politicians gave of suburban youth and I ended up realizing that in certain ways, I was on the contrary going to confirm and even approve that image' (2007, p. 4).

In relation to '*les tournantes*', she notes how she initially ignored the issue in her interviews, believing it to be more evidence of media sensationalism. When she changed her mind and asked her interviewees their opinion on the way in which the law and the media had approached the issue, she was alarmed to discover that they conformed to dominant public discourses. In particular, she remarks:

> ... both boys and girls felt that such practices ['*les tournantes*'] were relatively widespread. One of them had even got their sexual initiation that way ... neither the boys nor the girls I spoke with interpreted these '*tournantes*' as being rape. According to them, the girls more or less agreed to participate, either because they wanted to please their boy-friend, or had agreed to go down into the basement, etc.
>
> (2007, p. 4)

Teacher and activist Richard Moyon describes similar sentiments among his students when he raised the issue of '*les tournantes*' (2002). This, alongside the testimonies of women like Samira Bellil and others associated with *Ni Putes Ni Soumises* (discussed in the next chapters), would seem to suggest that the issue of '*les tournantes*' and the incumbent misogyny associated cannot be dismissed as simply a 'moral panic' created to further stigmatise the *banlieue* as Mucchielli (2004) seeks to argue in a similar manner to Australian left-wing critics of the 'Sydney gang rapes' discussed in Chapter 4.

Binary understandings of the banlieue: *Site of racism or sexism?*

At the same time, the attempt to explain the young men's behaviour has too often reproduced the unhelpful sexism versus racism binary, critiqued in the context of the 'Sydney gang rapes'. For example, Pech cites sociologist Daniel Welzer-Lang characterising the hyper-masculinity displayed by young men in the *banlieue* as a collective defensive mechanism, 'in response to the fear of unemployment, racism, a state of disenfranchisement and the lack of the possibility of exhibiting other attributes of virile masculinity'[21] (Pech 2002(a)). Broader reference to his theoretical work demonstrates Welzer-Lang's analysis of the significance of '*les tournantes*' is much more complex: he identifies the importance of French colonial history and representations of colonised male masculinity, the failure of the French education system to provide sex education to adolescents resulting in many of them – within or outside the *banlieue* – resorting to pornography for information and constructions of normative masculine and feminine (sexual) identity (Dhoquois 2003). However this is not reflected in the simplistic equation cited above, which reflects many mainstream media attempts to address issues of socio-economic marginalisation, gender and violence.

While Welzer-Lang's explanation as cited in Pech may have some valence, to adopt it uncritically is to reinforce the even further marginalisation of women and men who do not subscribe to this role but who also experience similar socio-economic disadvantage. Similarly, Laurent Mucchielli's structural account of economic disadvantage, scholastic failure and social exclusion as behind the rapes and his frequent reference to the imprudence of the victims risks re-affirming certain highly problematic stereotypical and essentialist understandings of masculine and feminine identity and sexuality.

In an illuminating example, *Libération* journalist Marie-Joëlle Gros (2003) provides an account of a meeting at a local high school between members of *banlieue* feminist association *Ni Putes Ni Soumises* and students and *banlieue* residents on the question of violence against women in the *banlieue*. What emerges is an impasse between those who concentrate on the risk of further stigmatising *banlieue* residents (in particular the young men) and those who assert that they are compelled to speak out against the misogyny and/or violence limiting the lives of women in the *banlieue*.

This dichotomisation has pitfalls for both sides: a point also identified in the Australian context. Those who are concerned about the risk of racial/social stigmatisation seem (intentionally or not) to almost downplay the violence against women in a similar manner to that bell hooks describes in the US Black civil rights movement: the demand for community solidarity is once again seen to be of greater importance than the individual women's protection of their rights. Meanwhile, those who assert their feminist message also risk co-option (willingly or unwillingly) through focusing on one of arguably many concerns affecting the lives of *banlieue* residents, including women: an issue that emerges clearly in the next chapters.

The clash is perhaps best captured in an exchange between a woman Gros describes as 'a mother of immigrant origin'[22] who is reported as arguing, 'We've had enough of our children being caricatured. Why do we always have to talk about what is going wrong?'[23], and one of the women with NPNS who responds, 'We have to condemn things that are bad, even if it is painful'[24] (Gros 2002). Trapped in this seemingly irreconcilable binary of racism versus sexism, the question that remains is how can the violence and misogyny of '*les tournantes*' be confronted *without* further demonisation of *all* men of the *banlieue*?

130   *The lost* banlieues *of the Republic*

Banlieue habitus

The attempts made by sociologists to conduct interviews with young people of the *banlieue* have equally provided little in the way of assistance. The explanations offered by the individuals themselves have tended to provide little insight that could easily be used in an anti-racist feminist response. Returning to Coutant's explanation of her research, she notes:

> One might think their [the interviewees'] words reflect the fact that they had internalised the public discourse: from that point of view, they were saying what they thought they were expected to say, given they knew how the subject was dealt with in the social arena. That hypothesis would have led me to keep quiet about what they told me.
>
> (2007, p. 4)

Her justification for this approach was that she had no desire to support the further stigmatisation of an already disadvantaged population. She ultimately concludes it is important to discuss the issue, albeit in a sensitive manner. However, the concern she raises poses significant questions about how such controversial and sensitive issues should be dealt with by the academy. This has particular resonance with the Australian context where, as noted in Chapter 4, there was a general reluctance on the part of academics to even engage with the suggestions of racial motivation, which dominated mainstream media commentaries.

The difficulty with this approach was that, in refusing to acknowledge race and instead concentrating on issues of economic and social disadvantage, academic commentators seemed to be contradicted by the discourses of the rapists themselves (who *did* assert a racial/ethnic aspect). This provided fuel for the already well-established argument that left-wing academia existed in an 'ivory tower' and was incapable of relating to 'real life' social phenomena. As left-wing intellectuals became seen as increasingly irrelevant and 'out of touch', this added to the apparent persuasiveness of conservative commentators who presented themselves as 'brave enough' to tackle the issues, albeit through reference to simplistic, racist explanations.

Similarly, the conformity of young *banlieue* residents with the same negative stereotypes also used to justify their stigmatisation is both troubling and highly interesting. For this reason Coutant's dismissal of the importance of her interviewees' opinions if based only on internalised public discourse is curious. If this is the case, it seems even more important that the reasons *why* and *how* this discourse, which is essentially damaging to the young people reiterating it, is internalised. How and why do people endorse versions of themselves and their identity that are counter-productive? By refusing to engage with this question Coutant seems to reinforce an impression of *banlieue* residents as passive dupes suffering from false consciousness, when in fact their articulation of identity provides an interesting insight into the relationship between individual subjectivity and structures of power. Central to this is the issue of how structures of sexism and racism

The lost banlieues *of the Republic*   131

interconnect to make resistance to one without reference to the other counter-productive and self-defeating.

This also draws back to what I have described in an earlier chapter as the '(post) colonial habitus' and how this impacts upon the manner in which young people in the *banlieue* are able to assert agency and/or resist dominant power structures that construct them as naturally deviant, violent, uncivilised and inferior. So too bell hooks' (1992) similar problematisation of what she terms the 'internalised colonisation' of young Black men in the US may provide a useful framework for analysing the constructions of identity articulated by both men and women of the *banlieue*.

As discussed in the 'Sydney gang rapes' context, hooks has argued that the promotion of stereotypical self-images in rap music and film by young Black American men does little to resist or challenge the dominance of White supremacist patriarchy. And yet it is this model of masculinity, which has frequently provided the basis for the 'protest masculinity' espoused by many of the young men who either participated in the rapes or sought to justify them. The influence of US 'ghetto culture' through rap/hip hop music and popular culture on the formation of (male) *banlieue* identity has received extensive scholarly attention. With France responsible for the second largest hip hop culture after the US (Mitchell 2001), the 'ghetto pimp' identity promoted in much of US hip hop culture finds its French counterpart within many of the most successful French hip hop acts: a notable example is NTM, one of the oldest and best established rap acts, whose name (*'Nique Ta Mère'* or 'Fuck your Mother') itself reflects the misogyny embedded in much of their music.

Furthermore, while in the case of the 'Sydney gang rapes' the assertion of some sort of 'masculine resistance' to racist domination by White Australia – as offensive as it is – may have been plausible, such an explanation is impossible in the context of '*les tournantes*'. As Abdel-Illah Salhi writes in an opinion piece in *Libération*:

> It is a bad time for Arabs. When they are not being hassled by the police, killed by racists or sullied by the likes of Azedine Berkane [attempted assassin of Paris Mayor Betrand Delanoë], they are the primary victims of their fellow Arabs: exemplified in the case of Sohane [burnt alive by young men in the *banlieue*] and the emerging phenomenon of '*les tournantes*' in the basement of the tenement blocks.[25]

> (2002)

Salhi makes a number of significant points here. In addressing not only external violence committed against 'Arabs' in France but also acts of violence by 'Arabs', most often against other 'Arabs', he identifies how these acts not only injure the victims but reinforce dominant negative stereotypes circulated linking 'Arabs' with violence. Stereotypes, which in turn contribute to the reinforcement and legitimisation of anti-Arab racism:

> The only thing left now is an automatic link between Arabs and delinquence, the *banlieue* and the scumbag. Because how can one not think of

132   *The lost* banlieues *of the Republic*

the incomparable [author] Houllebecq's reflection in *Des Particules Elémentaires* [*Atomised*], in which he suggests that violence is in fact inscribed
in the genes of Arabs.[26]

(Salhi 2002)

This seems to parallel the situation critiqued by Black scholars of Black-on-
Black violence in the US, which leads Poussaint to conclude, ' . . . it becomes safe
in the minds of many blacks to abuse their own people, while they remain internally fearful of confronting the White man' (1972, p. 74).

In the French case, this has particular resonance when one refers back to suggestions made by anti-colonial scholar Frantz Fanon regarding violence and crime in
the context of the French colonial occupation of Algeria. In *Wretched of the Earth*,
Fanon notes differences in the criminality of Algerians in France and those resident
in colonised Algeria. He remarks, 'in Algeria, criminal conduct by Algerians operates within a practically closed circle. They rob, destroy and kill each other. In France
on the other hand, the immigrant creates an inter-communal/inter-societal form of
criminal behaviour'.[27] For Fanon, the nature of colonisation is to divide, break, and
instil internalised feelings of inferiority in colonised subjects. Thus, in the context of
the French gang rapists, it seems possible to argue that the French colonial mission
has succeeded: These men do not seek to rape White French women from the outside
community, which has discriminated against them. Instead they express their rage
and hatred on the bodies of 'their own' women: fellow colonised subjects.

In any event, it seems that reference to the concept of the 'postcolonial habitus'
is once more relevant: the internalisation of colonial discourses, which devalue the
bodies and subjectivities of colonised subjects, seems one of the only means
through which the actions of the gang rapists can be understood; their disregard
for the bodies of non-White women mirroring the White disregard and violence
condoned by the racialised, gendered and sexualised colonial order. Further it is
significant that the victims Salhi identifies are women (and the perpetrators are
men), suggesting that racism and social and economic marginalisation are not the
only factors that require consideration and condemnation.

This is not to suggest that the misogyny is *only* a product of colonisation. If
anything, research on violence against women demonstrates the alarming (near)
universality of sexist, patriarchal and phallocentric power structures, albeit rede-
fined and constituted according to different cultural contexts. However, what reference to colonial power structures does allow is an understanding of how discourses
of nation, gender, sexuality and race/ethnicity must be seen as convergent and
mutually reinforcing. It is only through recognising this that both the significance
of events like '*les tournantes*' and the 'Sydney gang rapes' becomes clearer and
the reason why the formulation of adequate responses emerges as so difficult.

Homosociality in the banlieue

In reviewing her fascinating interviews with young men of the *banlieue*, many of
whom had participated in a *tournante*, Christelle Hamel notes, '[l]e viol collectif

The lost banlieues *of the Republic*   133

révèle combien la sexualité masculine est structurée par la hiérarchisation des sexes et par la solidarité entre hommes' ('gang rape reveals how much masculine sexuality is structured both through the creation of a hierarchy between the sexes and through an asserted solidarity between men') (2003, p. 91). She includes excerpts of her interviews in which the men refer to 'sharing' a woman as being simply an extension of their fraternal bond in which *everything* is shared. This, as Hamel points out, is a common feature of groups of men who place great value on homosocial bonding. She invokes the example of the American fraternities. The controversy surrounding a 'gang bang' tradition associated with Australian sporting teams (mentioned in Chapter 4) also comes to mind. Indeed the parallel is striking between Hamel's quote from 'Marouane' (one her interviewees) that the fraternal relationship between the men means, 'Tu fais tourner tout c'que t'as' ('You pass around (and share) whatever you have') and the comment by Grant Thomas, the coach of Australian Football League team the St Kilda Saints:

> There's a sense of camaraderie about a gang bang where you have a good mate and you will share a woman with a good mate. It's a very binding act with you and your friend, with you and your mate. The sense of camaraderie would probably be the biggest aspect of it. You do everything together.
>
> (Philadelphoff-Puren 2004, p. 44)

In all of these articulations, the woman is represented as a *thing*: an object to be possessed, exchanged, offered or taken by male agents. In the context of the discussion in previous chapters on the construction of nation, gender and normative sexuality, this is unsurprising: all of these discourses rely on the objectified passivity of the female body as a central feature. It is also here that similarities with the Australian media discourses can once again be identified: while in both France and Australia the bodies being violated are those of women, the significance of the rapes in public discourses seem to suggest that outrage regarding these rapes has more to do with regulating relationships between groups of men. Whether it is the need to 'protect our women' (as in the case of Australia) or the need to 'liberate their women' (as in France), the women themselves appear to serve more a symbolic role than to be considered active agents.

The construction of sexism as a cultural problem has not only been the result of dominant discourses of the Right but is too frequently endorsed by responses either from within the ethnic community or of the Left that appear to make excuses for existing gender orders and relations in ethnic minority/immigrant communities (often based on sexism and misogyny) under the guise of cultural tolerance. In fact, this tolerant, 'anti-racist' approach itself often makes resort to racialised (and racist) stereotypes of normative female and male identity and sexuality in order to articulate its position.

As a result, these positions not only fail to take into account the power structures operating within minority communities – where sexist interpretations of culture and tradition legitimate male domination but do not necessarily go unchallenged by women within the communities – it also justifies and legitimates racial

134 *The lost* banlieues *of the Republic*

hierarchies on the basis that White society *is* superior due to its greater commitment to gender equality. The inability of those seeking to oppose both racism *and* sexism to articulate a position that allows for the two forms of discrimination to be understood as mutually reinforcing means they remain unable to articulate a position that is not already set out within hegemonic discourses and which does not seek to privilege one identity (gender/race) over the other: an approach which only leads to the undermining of both.

That this normative view of sexuality is reproduced by both critics and defenders of the *banlieue* provides little opportunity for greater exploration and deconstruction of the categories of race or gender. The acceptance of a certain (sexist) sexual order as an essential characteristic of ethnic minority cultures by both dominant 'mainstream' French society and the communities themselves suggests that the sexual agency and autonomy experienced by French women is an inherent feature of French culture and civilisation. This conceptualisation of feminism as the exclusive domain of Western European women was frequently used as an example of European superiority throughout France's colonial period: a point I discuss further in Chapter 9.

This negates all examples – past and present – where women of dominant French society have been subject to discriminatory, sexist structures, practices and attitudes. Meanwhile, the endorsement of this view by ethnic minority communities serves to reinforce male patriarchal order within these communities, denies any possibility of a culturally-contextualised feminist politics to emerge and leads to women such as those affiliated with *Ni Putes Ni Soumises* being forced to straddle a space in which they must conform *either* to their ethnic identity *or* a (White) feminist identity. In writing about the first *affaire du foulard*, Etienne Balibar's remarks seem equally applicable to the issue of '*les tournantes*': 'Fatima, Leila and Samira were taken as hostages and became pawns between two antagonistic phallocracies' (*Libération*, 3 November 1989, cited in Lloyd 2003, p. 105). Again the battle becomes one 'between men'.

Notes

1 'Immeubles hussmanniens, parcs napoléoniens pour 3,000 habitants, dont les deux tiers vivent plutôt bien. . .'
2 'Le contexte social est différent mais l'état d'esprit est identique.'
3 '"C'est un parti pris féministe et engagé. On est du côté des victimes, des filles qui souffrent", affirme Fabrice Génestal' (Lalanne 2000).
4 'Elle [la Cour] les a suivi de cages d'escalier en souterrains crasseux, de caves en "squats". Elle s'est immiscée dans leur quotidien, ponctué d'échecs scholaires et de va-et-vient entre le collège, le foyer d'accueil ou le commissariat de police. Elle a entendu les pères, Algériens ou Marocains pour la majorité, levant les bras en signe d'impuissance ou d'incompréhension devant les faits reprochés à leurs fils. Elle a tenté, vainement, de faire parler les mères, la tête souvent couverte d'un foulard: "Je dis comme mon mari. . ."'
5 The public debates about the banning of the *hijab* (and other 'ostentatious religious symbols') that have raged since the late 1980s: see Scott (2007) for a detailed overview. This issue will also be discussed further in the next chapter.

The lost banlieues of the Republic   135

6 'Dans le récit de ces parents, il y a le "dedans" et le "dehors", une sorte de frontière qui dessine le contour des rapports familiaux dans la cité. Entre l'appartement et la rue. . . "Il y a des parents qui se représentent encore la rue comme ils l'ont vécue quand ils étaient enfants en Afrique du Nord, c'est-à-dire avec des anciens qui surveillaient et mataient les jeunes. Ils n'ont pas conscience que ce contrôle social a disparu dans les banlieues d'aujourd'hui", explique un animateur du Val-d'Oise . . .
. . . Après le procès, un parent d'accusé a confié son étonnement: "On m'a demandé si j'avais appris la sexualité a mes fils. J'ai répondu qu'ils avaient assez de la radio, de la télé, de la presse et de leurs mauvaises frequentations. Jamais je n'ai vu un musulman parler de sexualité avec ses enfants. C'est une question de respect.'

7 A *banlieue* of Paris.

8 '"Une jeune fille qui respecte les enseignements de l'islam ne peut pas s'asseoir à côté des garçons," remarque Stéphanie, professeur de français en 4e dans les Yvelines. "Ma classe est divisée en deux comme au moyen âge, les filles d'un côté, les garçons de l'autre. . ."'

9 ' C'étaient des gens assez pieux mais surtout très pudiques, tant verbalement que physiquement. Je faisais très attention à mettre des jupes jusqu'aux chevilles pour ne pas les choquer. L'année dernière, j'ai passé quelques jours au bled avec eux, pendant les vacances d'été. En revenant en France, j'ai moi-même été choquée. Là-bas, tout ce qui touchée au sexe et à la sensualité est contrôlé, censuré, le contraste est violent quand on revient.'

10 'Les mamans voilées avec la marque religieuse, en haut, au dernier rang, et, plus loin, les vieux pères arabes bien intégrés en France.'

11 'Les "meufs" ne se mélangent pas aux "keums", sous peine de finir à la cave, traitée comme une "pute".'

12 'Une fille qu'on voit dans la rue, c'est une pute.'

13 '[f]illes et garçons sont cantonnés dans des espaces et des rôles bien definés. Tout cela sous l'influence de codes ancestraux. . .'

14 '. . . ces jeunes filles, continue [sociologist] Caroline Vaissière, "imaginent le prince charmant, qui sera forcément extérieur à la cité"'.

15 'On ne flirte plus. On n'apprend plus à connaître l'autre sexe, le désir de l'autre. Afficher une relation amoureuse, c'est pour les garçons, se montrer en situation de faiblesse, et, pour les filles, passer pour des "putains".'

16 'Accusé de six viols au moins, Mouloud, benjamin de sept enfants, perturbé par un défaut de prononciation, "timide et influençable", a versé dans la délinquance à son arrivée dans la ZUP d'Argenteuil à 13 ans, en 1995. Son examen psychiatrique montre "un adolescent écartelé entre une culture familiale religieuse et rigoriste, qu'il s'efforce de respecter, une culture de la rue, òu chaque conduite délinquante apparaît comme un fait d'armes valorisant son auteur au regard des autres membres du groupe. "'

17 'Avec d'un côté la jeune fille, qui veut rester vierge, de l'autre le garçon, qui veut avoir un rapport sexuel avec pénétration.'

18 'Laissez entre les mecs des quartiers en boîte. Faites des lois là-dessus: que tous puissent draguer chaque week-end, et tout changera, direct. Des mecs qui ont tourné dans leur quartier pendant un mois et qui, tout d'un coup, voient passer une meuf en minijupe, ils ont les crocs.'

19 'Le discours de la misère sexuelle est donc inapproprié. Son emploi révèle surtout que l'abondance de l'activité sexuelle masculine est une norme largement partagée. En outre, il permet de justifier ou tout au moins d'excuser le viol en le présentant comme le résultat de l'insatisfaction des besoins sexuels masculins.'

20 Hamel's argument would also seem to be further supported by the Australian discourses: similar convergences between the discourses of the judiciary, commentators, the rapists and sometimes even the victims themselves emerge in relation to 'normative' male sexuality. Added to this is of course the implicit ethnic/racial element that has served to

136 *The lost* banlieues *of the Republic*

reinforce notions of the inferiority of the 'Other' man based on his sexual appetite and behaviours.

21 'en réponse à la peur du chômage, du racisme, à l'état de non-droit, à la souffrance de ne pouvoir exhiber d'autres attributes de la virilité'.

22 'Une mère d'origine étrangère'

23 'Y en a marre qu'on caricature nos enfants. Pourquoi on parle toujours de ce qui ne va pas?'

24 'Il faut dénoncer ce qui ne va pas. Même si ça fait mal.'

25 'Sale temps pour les Arabes. Quand ils ne sont pas malmenés par les flics, assassinés par les racistes ou souillés pas des Azedine Berkane, ils ou elles sont les premières victimes de leur compatriots, comme l'indiquent le cas Sohane et le phénomène grandissant des 'tournantes' dans les caves des HLM.'

26 'Il ne manqué plus que la preuve de l'existence d'un lien automatique entre Arabes et délinquance, banlieue et racaille. Car comment ne pas penser à cette profonde reflexion tirée des *Particules Elémentaires* de l'intraitable Houellebecq qui suggère que la violence est inscrite dans les gênes des Arabes.'

27 'en Algérie la criminalité algérienne se déroule pratiquement en cercle fermé. Les Algériens s'entre volaient, s'entre-déchiraient, s'entre-tuaient. En Algérie, l'Algérien s'attaquait peu aux Français et évitait les rixes avec les Français. En France par contre, l'émigré créera une criminalité intersociale, intergroupes.

En France la criminalité algérienne diminue. Elle s'adresse surtout aux Français et les mobiles en sont radicalement nouveaux.' (Fanon 1970, p. 225).

8 The *'beurette'* and the Republic

Introduction

So how did women of the *banlieues* respond? In this chapter I will examine the testimony of gang rape victim Samira Bellil. This will be followed in the next chapter by an analysis of the *banlieue* women's organisation with which she was associated, *Ni Putes Ni Soumises* (NPNS). As I stated in my introduction to the discussion of Tegan Wagner's book in Chapter 2, I wish to begin by reasserting the respect I have for Bellil. While I am critical of her narrative I do not intend this to be a criticism of her or her right to speak. Rather I hope it will be apparent that my critique is rather of the conditions within which she is able to process her experience and then able to speak and be heard.

Testimony of a survivor: Dans l'enfer des tournantes

Released in 2003 Samira Bellil's memoir, *Dans l'enfer des tournantes* ('In the Hell of the *Tournantes*') is narrated in the first person. In it Bellil details her experience of surviving a dysfunctional and abusive childhood, three gang rapes and an adolescence struggling to come to terms with her trauma without support. It provides a useful point of comparison with the autobiography of 'Sydney gang rape' victim, Tegan Wagner (discussed in Chapter 3).

'Ma propre verité': Self-narrative as 'truth'

While Wagner describes her engagement with the legal process as a battle of truths, Bellil demonstrates an awareness of the tension within autobiography between the objective and the impossibility of documenting 'the truth' (Boulé 2002; Hughes 1999). While there were attempts by both her collaborator left-wing journalist Josée Stoquart and the publishers to frame *Dans l'enfer des tournantes* as having broader significance (discussed below), Bellil is in fact quite explicit in her explanation of the book as a personal voyage. Having attempted various means of achieving a sense of closure of her past, she states that she finally came to the conclusion that 'my salvation would be [writing] a book'[1] (2003, p. 296). Bellil thus situates her book as a means by which she seeks to come to terms with her trauma and anger

138   The 'beurette' *and the Republic*

arising from both her experience of gang rape and the subsequent lack of support she received from family, friends, community and state institutions alike:

> I didn't want my story to remain a secret, locked in Fanny's [her psychologist] office. To get myself out of my misery it took me many years of hard work and a lot of suffering. Would it be fair that those responsible for this damage be allowed to sleep easily at night? That K and his mates [the perpetrators of two of her gang rapes], the lawyer, the children's advocacy service [that did not help her], social services and my parents should sleep easily? It would be too easy for me to just shut up, to appear happy, have children and never speak of it again. No I wanted to share the cost. There was no reason why I should have to pay for this all myself. So nobody had ever wanted to listen to me, well they would have to read me instead![2]

> (2003, p. 299)

She frames her book as an attempt to hold to account her rapists and the many individuals and organisations she sees as having failed her. She rejects the implication that her book is an act of revenge. Rather she identifies it as an attempt to finally make others aware of the personal suffering she perceives as having been ignored, played down and/or ridiculed. In this way her book bears a close resemblance to Wagner's text discussed in Chapter 3.

She also identifies the writing process as not simply one of self-presentation but of self-discovery:[3]

> Everything was expelled and written, clarified by Josée [Stoquart – her collaborator and mentor], reflected on again and then, finally, digested and integrated. Then the process would all start again, fed by new elements that had emerged. It was necessary to take the time to allow things to mature inside me and every stage had its meaning.
>
> Progressively, everything was set out and put in place, like a puzzle being pieced together. I recovered my memory and was able to situate events in my life that I had not been able to reconcile at the time. Horrible memories that I had suppressed came back to me. Memories which I was able to imbue with new meaning over the course of my evolution.[4]

> (2003, p. 302)

In this way, Bellil's account becomes a form of therapy in itself: an attempt to make sense of her experiences rather than simply re-telling them. In expressing her aims in writing this testimony, Bellil asserts:

> I have been honest and lucid, as much as I could be. I wanted to show the extent of the negligence of my family, those around me, my lawyer, social services who abandoned me as well as the traumas of the rapes. This book is about presenting my truth.[5]

> (2003, p. 300)

The 'beurette' *and the Republic*   139

In this statement she both accepts that her account cannot ultimately be a disinterested recounting of her life (hence her proviso, 'as much as I could be') but also asserts a certain essential truth behind her narrative: *her truth*. The fact that she identifies this as 'her truth' situates this autobiography as not simply a factual statement of events but a discourse of identity. As a result the reader is presented with an amazing insight into Bellil's habitus: her embodied subjectivity, her attempts at agency and the external structures of domination against which she struggles and which she also internalises.

However, before considering the truth Bellil seeks to assert, it is important to situate her text. Autobiography is marked not simply by the relationship of the individual author and their text. After all, the author and the text exist within a particular social context, which impacts on *which* voices are heard and *how* their texts are read. Bellil's status as a postcolonial French subject is significant here.

While Tegan Wagner's text is framed as the personal account of one (exceptional) individual,[6] Bellil's is presented as emblematic of the broader experience of women of the *banlieue*: her experience just one example of 'sexual violence that has become instutionalised and normalised in the *cités* (housing estates) and *banlieues* (working-class suburbs)'[7] (Bellil 2003, back cover). This could be seen as an attempt to draw on the testimonial tradition – discussed further in the next chapter – which has been used particularly by Latina and Chicana writers as a form of political activism. Yet, unlike the text by Fadela Amara discussed in the next chapter, which seems to consciously invoke this comparison, in the case of Bellil this seems to be more something imputed to her text by Stoquart and the publishers. This positioning of Bellil as representative is both a common feature of how non-White women's voices are heard and an extremely problematic one as I and others have argued elsewhere (Grewal 2012a; Narayan 1997). The ability to make this assertion of representativeness relies on an essentialised monolithic characterisation of what Chandra Mohanty (1997) has called the 'Third World Woman' (a point I will return to a little later). It also demands attention to the conditions within which certain subjects can speak and be heard.

Postcolonial scholar Gayatri Spivak writes:

> . . . if one looks at the history of post-Enlightenment theory, the major problem has been the problem of autobiography: how subjective structures can, in fact, give objective truth. During these same centuries, the Native Informant [was] treated as the objective evidence for the founding of the so-called sciences like ethnography, ethnolinguistics, comparative religion, and so on. So that, once again, the theoretical problems only relate to the person who knows. The person who *knows* has all the problems of selfhood. The person who is *known,* somehow seems not to have a problematic self.
>
> (Suleri 1992, p. 123)

Thus Spivak points out that not only is the concept of 'objective truth' in autobiography problematic, but added to this relations of colonial domination create

140   *The 'beurette' and the Republic*

further difficulties in how the truth of the former colonised subject can and should be read. For this reason, Spivak argues that the struggle of the subaltern to be heard in the postcolonial world must be positioned within this historical context of colonial relationships of power whereby gathering information from and of the 'native' provided a means of knowing and controlling the colonised. It is thus not insignificant that Bellil should be of Algerian origin.

Testimony and the role of the collaborator

In the context of testimonies of North African immigrants in France, Bellil's is not the first. As Hargreaves documents, the publishing of testimony of the North African experience in France is a genre that has been around since the 1970s (2006, p. 43). The first of these kinds of narratives to emerge were texts like 'Journal de Mohamed' and 'Une vie d'Algérien, est-ce que ça fait un livre que les gens vont lire?' ('The life of an Algerian, is that a book people are going to read?'), which sought to provide an insight into the lives of North African male immigrants living in France. With the case of the former text, 'Journal de Mohamed', while it was presented as providing Mohamed the opportunity to voice his experience to the broader French society, it was done through the medium of a sociologist, Maurice Catani, who transcribed and edited the transcripts of Mohamed's oral testimony, and an introductory remark was provided by the series editor to situate the text by giving some government statistics on immigrant workers (Hargreaves 2006, pp. 43–44).

Hargreaves goes on to trace the developments in these forms of narratives to identify a recently emerged group of testimonies, this time from the perspective of young women of immigrant origin. He documents five such testimonies published by second-generation Maghrebi women since 1990. Each of these has been with explicit collaborators, mainly journalists from the Left (Hargreaves 2006, pp. 46–47). Bellil's book is one of these. Hargreaves problematises this process of collaboration, questioning whether this echoes too closely colonial relations of domination through the reinforcement of stereotypes passed off as 'personal experiences' (therefore legitimate and authoritative) that have in fact been appropriated, regardless of the author's intentions.

Hargreaves' article provides a useful overview of the ways in which testimonies by postcolonial immigrants have been co-opted in France. However he ultimately distinguishes Bellil's experience to others, who he sees as more dispossessed. On the contrary, I argue that a closer reading of Bellil's text and the social context within which it is situated suggests Hargreaves' dismissal may be premature. While it is true that Bellil does claim control and ownership of her narrative, she is not spared Stoquart's asserted role as the intermediary through which she must speak to be heard. The very fact that Stoquart's remarks appear as a preface, which will be read prior to Bellil's own narrative, means the testimony has already been positioned.

Furthermore, Stoquart maintains a position of dominance in her explanation for how the book came to be written:

The 'beurette' *and the Republic*   141

I could have chosen to interview Samira and written her story myself but I preferred to let her write it. This was firstly because she has an intense and evocative style of expression. Secondly – and more importantly – because she already had a place to speak and to write provided her with another way to work on herself.[8]

(2003, p. 15)

In this way, she positions herself as the benevolent overseer, allowing Bellil to express herself in her own words but (implicitly) telling a story that Stoquart endorses. This is very clever. As Julia Watson and Sidonie Smith point out, '[r]eaders also have expectations about who has the cultural authority to tell a particular kind of life story, and they have expectations about what stories derived from direct, personal knowledge should assert.' (2001, p. 30)

Thus, it is not necessarily as an act of empowerment that Bellil is allowed to tell her story but the perceived increased authoritativeness the story has when told through the voice of someone directly implicated. A similar example of this is Paul Sheehan's use of transcripts of Tegan Wagner's words to provide authoritativeness to his 'common sense' linking of the gang rapes with problematic Muslim masculinity (discussed in Chapter 5). Ultimately in Wagner's case, she is able to assert her voice through her own autobiography and in doing so expressly rejects the link proposed by Sheehan (see Chapter 3). Bellil, as the later analysis will demonstrate, is less effective in this regard, thus increasing the impression of her role as one of the problematic 'native informant' identified by Spivak (above).

It is also important to reconcile the tone of the book which gives the impression of Bellil presenting an unadulterated self-narrative (it is written in a conversational style and draws heavily on slang) and the fact that it is presented as 'avec le soutien et la collaboration de Josée Stoquart' ('with the support and collaboration of Josée Stoquart'). In the words of Bakhtin: 'Language is not a neutral medium that passes freely and easily into the private property of the speaker's intentions; it is populated – overpopulated – with the intentions of others.' (Bakhtin 1981, p. 294). In this case Bellil's personal account and attempt to come to terms with incredible suffering must be read within the framework of the preface written by Stoquart:

It seems that within these areas, euphemistically called, 'sensitive', where the majority of the families are of immigrant origin, it is difficult to situate a place for the woman. Certain young men are pulled between the strict discipline of their cultural origins (religious fundamentalism, the untouchability of the woman, polygamy) and a cultural environment which is heavily eroticised . . . These adolescents have no point of reference and are not conscious of the gravity of their actions. For them, 'la tournante' is a game and the girls, the objects.[9]

(2003, pp. 12–13)

Through the positioning of Bellil's testimony within this broader social context, Stoquart reframes the book away from being an individual process of Bellil

142   *The 'beurette' and the Republic*

expressing her anger and seeking recognition of her suffering. *Dans l'enfer des tournantes* becomes emblematic of the situation of women in the *banlieue* and, more specifically, the problems associated with immigrant communities and their cultures. Furthermore, Stoquart's passing references to religious fundamentalism, polygamy and the situation of women contains a less than subtle implication of an ethnic/religious cultural context within which Bellil's abusive childhood and '*les tournantes*' should be read.

'*Liberating a being*'

In her celebration of Bellil's achievement, Stoquart promotes an image of individual liberation from the otherwise pitiful existence of young women in the *banlieue*: 'This book lifts the veil on the horrendous conditions within which certain young girls live, caught between two types of servitude: obedience which means being trapped in the home or the risk in the street of becoming prey to the gangs and their sexual savagery.'[10] (2003, pp. 11–12) The imagery evoked fits nicely within the dominant stereotype of the 'average Third World Woman', Chandra Mohanty identifies as central to Western (feminist) discourses:

> This average Third World Woman leads an essentially truncated life based on her feminine gender (read: sexually constrained) and her being 'Third World' (read: ignorant, poor, uneducated, tradition-bound, domestic, family-oriented, victimized, etc.). This, I suggest, is in contrast to the (implicit) self-representation of Western women as educated, as modern, as having control over their own bodies and sexualities, and the freedom to make their own decisions.
>
> (Mohanty 1997, pp. 258–259)

The particular terminology of 'lifting the veil' is not only evocative of the *affaires du foulard* that are read alongside – and linked to – the instances of sexual violence but also of the colonial preoccupation with the *hijab* (discussed earlier and in the next chapter). This image is cemented in the preface to Bellil's book with Stoquart presenting a self-congratulatory and patronising account of her role in 'liberating' '*la petite beurette*', an experience that gives Stoquart a personal sense of achievement: 'it is a great opportunity to help in the liberation of a being'[11](2003, p. 16). The echo of colonial Republican feminist rhetoric of liberation is striking. For example the famous French Republican feminist Hubertine Auclert – founder of the French Women's Suffrage movement – dedicated a book to considering the situation of women in Algeria (*Les Femmes Arabes en Algérie* 1900) in which she decried Muslim teachings and practices as reinforcing the segregation and mistreatment of women through forcing them into early marriage, polygamy and denying them access to education (Elhami Kaldas 2007; Clancy-Smith 1999). She in turn criticised colonial administrators for failing to take steps to limit the influence of Islam and militated for the freeing of Algerian women from the 'cages' within which their traditions and religion kept them trapped (Clancy-Smith 1999, pp. 167–172). Although Auclert was critical of the racism she saw within colonial Algerian society and expressed a strong solidarity for the plight of the women of Algeria, she did not reject the validity of the colonial enterprise: 'sisterhood for Auclert was imperial and hierarchical' (Clancy-Smith 1999, p. 170) and her imagining of the desires of Algerian women built around an envy of and desire to be French.

One is left with the impression from Stoquart's words that once again this poor 'Third World Woman' (Bellil, the *'petite beurette'*) was incapable of freeing herself but required rescuing, just as the colonised woman required the colonial 'civilising mission'. It also reproduces the divide between the feminist sophistication of Western women and the political immaturity of non-Western women, who therefore require schooling (Mohanty 1997, p. 260).

Yet Bellil's ability to challenge this relationship with Stoquart is questionable. As discussed above, Bellil states that writing the book was her idea: she explains the process as a form of self-therapy and notes that she was solely responsible for the first draft. However she goes on to add that her psychologist put her in contact with journalist Josée Stoquart, who acted not only as her collaborator but her mentor throughout the writing process.

While Stoquart apparently did not take an active role in writing the book, she was not completely uninvolved in the process: 'She decided that I alone should do the writing and she took responsibility for restructuring my drafts and shaping the text. She assured me she would support me throughout the writing process, through asking questions, challenging me and encouraging me.'[12] (2003, p. 301). Thus, throughout the writing process – from Bellil's description – Stoquart played a role in shaping the form Bellil's narrative took. Bellil describes a feeling of apprehension experienced each week when she presented her writing to Stoquart (2003, p. 303) and how the latter's interventions and comments impacted on her own self-perception ('How she listened, her questions and her reactions slowly changed my perception of myself')[13] (2003, p. 303). Thus Stoquart emerges as integral to the articulation and formulation of Bellil's own identity through the book.

Despite this remarkably passive positioning of herself in relation to Stoquart, Bellil is not unconscious of the risk of co-option. For example, she recounts an incident when she was asked to appear on a popular television programme and refused on the basis that she did not want to pour out her heart for the benefit of audience ratings and in support of people whose interests were not the same as her own (2003, p. 282).[14] Yet, while Bellil expresses a desire to confront not only the gang rapists and her family but also the public institutions, which she also feels let her down, Stoquart's message is far narrower: 'We have seen, since the 1980s, the rise in power of the phenomenon of the gang with the central figure of the little *caïd* for whom the number of gang rapes, "the trapping of a slut", as they call it, are a mark of status.'[15] (2003, p. 11) There is no mention of the failings of the justice system or state institutions and social services in this preface. Instead, Stoquart provides statistics of the number of reported gang rape cases involving minors, which can only be described as alarming, allowing her to conclude that Bellil's story is far from unique. The figure of the *'petit caïd'*[16] serves as the symbol of the suffering Bellil and many other young women in the *banlieue* have had to endure.

144   *The 'beurette' and the Republic*

This description can be contrasted with an incident Bellil recounts, following her first television appearance to talk about her book:

> I crossed a young guy dressed in baseball cap, baggy tracksuit and sneakers, typical of one of those the media call 'the young *caïds* [thugs] of the *banlieue*'. He knocked into me in the [train] carriage! I think ok, all the open arms and smiles I had been experiencing were too much. I prepare myself straight away with my guns blazing, ready to shoot down his words. But timidly and discreetly he says to me, 'You spoke brilliantly yesterday!' I frankly admit that in the space of a fraction of a second, I felt very stupid! And unfortunately the time it took me to realise, the doors of the carriage had already closed. I only just had time to give him a smile of thank you. Because coming from *one of those we frequently demonise too quickly*, it touched me deeply.[17]
>
> (2003 p. 306, emphasis added)

In recounting this anecdote Bellil seems to understand the risks associated with publishing her story as anything other than a personal testimony. This risk of stigmatisation and the need to move beyond stereotyping does not appear to affect Stoquart. Or perhaps, as Hargreaves (2006, p. 50) notes, the commercial and/or other ideological value of creating this clear enemy is too strong.

However, returning to Bellil's encounter with a television reporter, Bellil explains:

> [S]he 'advised' me not to talk about '*les tournantes*', or the reality of life in the *cités*, or the failed trial, or the organisation that is supposed to help children but in fact helps no one, because it risked being too shocking for the viewers. She also didn't want me to mention my difficulties with the [first, female] lawyer. I began to ask myself why I was even there. Sure, I wanted to tell my story in front of the whole country but not at any cost.
>
> (2003, p. 281)[18]

Bellil's anger about having to 'sanitise' her account is understandable. Furthermore, it adds weight to the question, why were '*les tournantes*' at one stage considered too shocking or provocative to talk about publicly and only a few years later a topic of national concern and debate? Perhaps part of the answer to this question can be found in Stoquart's reference to Bellil as '*la petite beurette*' (2003, p. 16).

'La petite beurette'

The label '*beur*', while initially a self-referential term used by young people in France of North African origin (and famously connected to the anti-racist activism of the 1980s) has increasingly been appropriated in mainstream public discourses. This has unsurprisingly led to its rejection by many of those it is meant to describe.

The 'beurette' *and the Republic*   145

As Hargreaves notes in relation to the comments of journalist Sophie Ponchelet, who collaborated on another published testimony of a Maghrebi woman:

> Ponchelet notes that many second-generation Maghrebis hate to be referred to as 'Beurs', but this does not prevent her from labelling Benaïssa as 'une jeune Beur'. . . . For Ponchelet and the publisher of the book, *Payot*, the commercial value of the 'Beur' label clearly outweighs sensitivity towards those who resent being designated in this way.
>
> (2006, p. 50, citations omitted)

By drawing on this commercial value associated with the '*beur*' identity, situating Bellil's account as that of a '*beurette*' could be seen as capitalising on the economic interest. However, it is also significant that the specific feminine form carries a particular ideological weight. Postcolonial feminists have pointed to the increasing appropriation of young Muslim women's bodies as battlegrounds in French public discourse on immigration, ethnicity and national identity (Fernando 2013; Guénif-Souilamas 2000). The '*affaires du foulard*' provide one example of this and, I argue '*les tournantes*' provide another. But even aside from these two particularly mediatised events, '*la beurette*' has emerged as a highly ideologically charged figure within the French public sphere: a point further elaborated upon in the next chapter on *Ni Putes Ni Soumises*.

It is worth noting that the increased concern with the condition of immigrant women in both mainstream and more right-wing conservative political discourses is a trend that has emerged throughout Europe since at least the 1990s, as well as in the developed West more generally (as my earlier discussion of Australia illustrates; see also Ewing 2008; Razack 2008, 2004, 1998; Akkermann and Hagelund 2007; Volpp 2007). However, in the French context the '*beurette*' has been particularly significant due to her compatibility with the language of Republican values. In her book, *Des Beurettes*, Nacira Guénif-Souilamas (2000) explores the emergence of three central themes in discourses on women of North African origin in France: the eroticisation of Arab girls' bodies,[19] the portrayal of their successes in school suggesting the triumph of integration (even when indicators point to the contrary) and the idea of a greater loyalty among young North African women to the French Republic than their male counterparts.

It is therefore significant that Stoquart should describe Bellil as, '*la petite beurette*'. Through this, Bellil is placed in the position that Guénif-Souilamas identifies as common to those young women categorised as '*beurettes*' who are 'put at the forefront of a reactionary movement that now has a single enemy: the macho suburban *garçon arabe*'(2006, p. 35). While Bellil attempts to resist this binary construction, Stoquart's preface places Bellil's narrative within a very constrained space through which she must negotiate her identity and her relationships with fellow French subjects of immigrant – specifically North African – origin.

This is significant for two reasons. The first is that an analysis of Bellil's narrative reflects her struggle between race consciousness and gender consciousness, positions

146 *The 'beurette' and the Republic*

constructed as oppositional by the *garçon arabe/beurette* paradigm. The second is Bellil's positioning as 'representative' of the situation of young women of immigrant origin in the *banlieue*. Based on research conducted by Nacira Guénif-Souilamas, Bellil's struggle to identify a place within which to frame her desire for freedom and equality is shared by many young women of North African origin in France. In fact Guénif-Souilamas details what she describes as the struggle between 'subjection and subjectivity' (2006, p. 34) young women of North African immigrant origin remain caught in, on the one hand seeking to establish a degree of independence and freedom from the restrictive patriarchal structures of their parents' home cultures, on the other struggling to find a place for themselves within 'mainstream' French society:

> I showed how they had interiorized the obligation to distance themselves from tradition to thus be seen as 'integrated' into French society. I stressed the fact that they were experiencing a double bind compelling them to express loyalty to two institutions normatively defined as opponents: their immigrant family and their assimilative nation-state.
>
> (Guénif-Souilamas 2006, p. 34)

This 'interiorisation' invokes reference to the Bourdieusian concept of *habitus* again, but this point will be discussed later. First of all, in considering the 'double bind', Bellil's experience is illustrative. Returning to my first observation, close analysis of Bellil's narrative demonstrates the ability to articulate a thorough class, gender and race consciousness cannot simply be implied by virtue of the woman's marginalised position. As Honor Ford-Smith notes in relation to gender and class consciousness in the context of 'grass-roots' women's organisations, there is a tendency to confuse class and sex origins with class and sex consciousness (Ford Smith 1997, p. 257). In seeking to articulate her frustration and sense of injustice, Bellil frequently struggles in terms of both her race consciousness and her gender consciousness.

Race consciousness

As Paula Stewart Brush describes in relation to the difficulties experienced by Black women in post-civil rights US:

> By assuming that women of color always know and everywhere resist racial oppression, we short-circuit activism and ignore the need to raise consciousness – to identify, name, and strategize resistance to racial oppression. In sum, if the assumption of race consciousness is not deconstructed, it will be left behind in theory and practice, to the detriment of both feminism and progressive race politics.
>
> (2001, p. 195)

In looking at a description of racism experienced by a Black female autobiographer, Brush argues the woman is 'without a discourse to explain her situation, to explain that and how this interpersonal situation is political. Indeed, she is without

The 'beurette' *and the Republic*   147

the words to name the kind of racism she experiences. Finally, she has no concerted form of resistance to offer.' (2001, p. 187) Brush uses this and other examples found in the writings of US Black women post-civil rights to question why the race consciousness of coloured women has been treated as a given. On the contrary she argues, just as Black feminists have sought to question White women's assumptions of White privilege, there is a need for race consciousness to be cultivated among coloured women to provide them with a response to the everyday racism and effects of race that they experience.

This analysis seems helpful when reading Bellil's book. For while Bellil is highly critical of the state institutions she encountered following her rapes, she never frames this in terms of racism. Nor does she call into question the racist assumptions about immigrant communities that rely on an apparent 'civilisational superiority' on the part of the dominant group. This is despite the fact that many of the incidents she describes provide ample evidence to counter the narrow focus of many public commentators on the sexism of the *banlieue* and its residents.

For example, following her lodging of an official complaint with the police, Bellil describes an encounter with an association, which defends the rights of children. She records her interview with the woman assigned to her case, who she finds to be cold, unsympathetic and critical. After telling the woman her age, she is met with more criticism ('At fourteen there is no reason to be out at such an hour!':[20] 2003, p. 84) and notes: 'When I think that she had done years of study, that she defended children who had been sexually assaulted and yet her comments were at the same level as those of my parents, it kills me'(2003, p. 85).[21] She goes on to add: 'the organisation which she represents is very well-known. There is even a famous French actress who did the advert . . . After this incident, I can't watch that ad without feeling the desire to vomit' (2003, p. 85).[22]

This passage is noteworthy for her relating of the similarities in response received from this educated woman from the 'French establishment' to that of her parents: uneducated, working class migrants. This passage alone would suggest that her condemnation of the gang rapes and her subsequent treatment is not limited to those within migrant communities but constitutes a wider problematisation of the treatment of victims of sexual violence. On the other hand, in concluding her description of her third rape, which takes place in Algeria (the previous two having occured in France), she notes:

> I realised that in this shit country [Algeria], there was no justice because the police worked on *bakshish* [bribes]. I had already understood, from the policeman's eyes, that it wasn't worth insisting, there was nothing to hope for. I left it all there. The two thousand kilometres which separated me helped me not to think about it again, to try and forget what I could feel. I consoled myself by thinking, that at least in France there was a functioning justice system.
>
> (2003, p. 136)[23]

Even as she subsequently relates extremely negative experiences with the French justice system and questions whether there is in fact such a thing as justice,

148   *The 'beurette' and the Republic*

this does not lead her to reject the French system altogether. She perseveres and ultimately does achieve a small victory through a victim's compensation claim. While she dismisses Algeria as holding nothing for her, she continues to struggle in France for recognition and justice. Perhaps in doing this she demonstrates what Hargreaves (1997) has identified as 'incorporation'; while she is not oblivious to the racism and sexism existing in France, she recognises it as her place and seeks to assert herself as belonging to France, in the same way that France belongs to her, giving her the right to continue to struggle to claim a public voice.

However it is not only Algeria as a foreign country that she seeks to distance herself from. In describing her childhood she draws sharp distinctions between the traditional and violent culture of her parents and the loving, peaceful and 'civilised' environment of the Belgian host family:

> My parents are very Europeanised immigrants. However the after-effects of their upbringing have remained with them. They always went back to these methods: slaps and punches to make oneself understood and a kick up the ass to ensure it had gone in! I am the product of two traditions: two completely contradictory modes of living. From my parents I received a traditional education in which nothing was ever explained to me without slaps or screams or spitting. At the same time I received a more European education as a result of my childhood in Belgium with the foster family where my mother placed me . . . There life was peaceful and gentle. Papa Jean and mama Josette were well-balanced, well-meaning people who gave me confidence and love.[24]

(2003, p. 58)

Aside from this idealised family life she associates with her 'more European' upbringing in her host family, in referring to a period when she was taken into state custody as a result of parental abuse, she states, 'I was happy to be there, with the "French", as they told me'[25] (2003, p. 108). In explaining why she became increasingly rebellious as a young adolescent she notes: 'How was I supposed to understand what was being imposed on me here [with her birth parents]: this education of slaps and prohibitions, this inequality between boys and girls, these invasive taboos – after what I had known with papa Jean and mama Josette?'[26] (2003, p. 67). While understandable in the context of her personal experience, when framed as a narrative representative of the broader experience of '*la beurette*', Bellil's simplistic dichtomisation of violence, inequality and misery in her North African family and happiness, love and respect in her European (Belgian) family is highly problematic. It seems to adopt exactly the binary between the 'backward' colonised women and the 'enlightened' Metropolitan women of colonial Republican feminist discourse. So too, it reproduces what Mohanty (1997) and other postcolonial feminists identify to be the assumption among many contemporary schools of Western feminist thought of the 'backward' Third World that requires the intervention of the 'advanced' West.

The result is that Stoquart is not alone in her characterising and stereotyping of the 'average Third World Woman'. In explaining her upbringing Bellil draws on

The 'beurette' and the Republic   149

very similar imagery to that used by colonial Republican feminists. As she sees it, it is her rebellion against the cultural background of her parents and her attempt to gain access to the freedom and independence of a French ('Western') woman that is the cause of her problems: a point also relevant to the later analysis of Fadela Amara's text. Bellil remarks:

> In fact, my mother would have liked to have raised me as she had been raised in the village [in Algeria], the tough way. That's how it is with my people: the girls get it smack in the face, without flinching. I know my mother has had a tough life, that she has been the victim of a culture that treats women like dogs.[27]

(Bellil 2003, p. 105)

Bellil sees her rejection of this role and her constant questioning of her position as a woman within the context of her immediate environment, populated for the most part with other people of immigrant (North African predominantly) origin as placing her in direct conflict with her family and the *banlieue* community. In describing the misery she experiences in her long-term relationship with boyfriend Lyes, she exclaims:

> I don't want a life spent waiting for my man with the fear that one day he'll just pack up and leave. I don't want to prepare couscous while he lives his life in the outside world. I don't want to have kids in this disgusting *banlieue*. I don't want to reproduce my mother's life, 20 years on.[28]

(2003, p. 224)

In rejecting the life of her mother and the women of the *banlieue* she sees around her, she largely places the blame on what she associates as North African culture and in particular North African men. While on the one hand she recognises that it is wrong to stigmatise *all* men of the *banlieue* (as her description of her encounter with the '*petit caïd*' following her first television appearance demonstrates), at the same time she remarks, 'In this fucking *banlieue*, the guys are all made with the same mold. Lyes is the standard model. "Good guys" are the exception' (2003, p. 225).[29] Similarly, while she is quoted in one article rejecting any link between her negative experiences with men and Islam (see Hargreaves 2006, p. 52), in another, when asked if she would ever enter into a relationship with a North African man, she exclaims, 'With anyone in the world sure, but not someone of my culture! He'll either be a [religious] fundamentalist or a scumbag!' (Le Vaillant 2002).[30]

Gender consciousness

It is not only in terms of race consciousness that Bellil struggles without a clear framework. Equally her experience of gender inequality and oppression is something she resists without being able to frame her position in a larger political or

150   *The 'beurette' and the Republic*

theoretical discourse. For example, her struggle to address dominant rape myths and her own negative self-judgment is evident in her description of the rapes. She insists on her level of resistance and describes the violence meted out to her by K, the initiator of the first gang rape and the rapist in the second: 'He didn't have any pity for me, he continued to hit me until I understood that there was no alternative for me other than to follow him if I wanted to stand a chance of staying alive' (2003 p. 30).[31]

Similarly to Wagner (see Chapter 3), in saying this she seems to feel the need to justify why she submitted and conform to the dominant conception of what constitutes 'real rape', that being a sexual act perpetrated by use of physical force. Her rage is palpable when she notes:

> How many people would later say to me: 'I would have done this in your place . . . One should always defend oneself . . . Surprise the attacker, give him a kick in the balls . . . ' etc. How many times have I heard these killer little sentences that filled me with guilt, these pitiless commentaries offered by people who have never been crippled by true fear.
>
> (2003, pp. 30–31)[32]

Yet while she sees this attitude as wrong, she also admits that a large part of her struggle to come to terms with her rapes was overcoming her own feelings of culpability:

> I thought I deserved what I had suffered because I wasn't a virgin anymore. For Muslims, to not be a virgin as a young girl is sacrilegious and I knew my father could kill me for this. I had slept with Jaïd. Plus I was a runaway and a thief. I didn't listen to either my parents or my teachers . . . I therefore didn't have the right to complain about being raped. I deserved it. That was definitely what people around me were saying, but it was also what I thought myself.[33]
>
> (2003, p. 69)

In writing the book she confronts this self-image and seeks to reject it but at the same time feels the need to stress both that she had only slept with Jaïd [the man responsible for her first gang rape] once and that she had been very much in love with him. She seeks to rebut the dominant Madonna/whore dichotomy within which rape victims are situated, yet at the same time cannot go as far as to assert a truly liberated position within which her own sexual behaviour is not at all relevant. Similarly, while she instinctively rebels against the stereotypes of gender behaviour imposed upon her, she struggles to articulate another conception of her subjectivity. She is critical of the restrictions placed on women of the *banlieue* and in particular those of North African origin:

> I felt trapped between the arbitrary obligations of my environment and my dreams of freedom. I wanted to be free, not to live as a submissive, not cloistered up at home, like those women I saw around me. I wanted the

The 'beurette' *and the Republic*   151

same freedom as a guy: to breathe, live life to the full, what could be more natural?[34]

(2003, pp. 24–25)

However she simultaneously appears to seek status and acceptance within those models of behaviour. For example, in her description of the beginnings of her relationship with Lyes she tells herself, 'I didn't hold any illusions. A chick like me was just for fun, smoke a joint with. With the baggage I carried, I wasn't a chick with whom to stay, to plan a future with, to marry' (2003, p. 153).[35]

In asserting her ultimate desired relationship she conforms easily to standard heteronormative constructions of gender identity and the idealised form of sexual and familial relationship on which the nation is premised (McClintock 1994): '[w]hat I want is a normal guy, who comes home in the evening, speaks to me, finds me beautiful, is interested in the education and upbringing of his children. Just a regular guy, you know!'[36] (Bellil 2003, p. 226) Her happiest description of a relationship is with a younger man she meets while completing a training course to work as an entertainer/activity organiser (*animatrice*) at holiday resorts: 'With him I was a woman, I was beautiful, even when I slept. He would wake me with breakfast in bed, kisses, bouquets of roses. He would take me to a restaurant and under my napkin, I would find a little surprise' (2003, p. 228).[37]

This conformity with all the dominant stereotypes of 'romance' is touchingly personal but also reproduces a construction of femininity and gender roles that, as I have argued earlier, do little to challenge dominant discourses on rape and in fact help to secure them. Of course Bellil is under no obligation to resist these stereotypes in the context of describing her own personal sentiments. However, it is important to remember that she has been presented as providing a 'feminist voice' (especially in her role as one of the figureheads of *Ni Putes Ni Soumises*). In reality Bellil's struggle with the restrictions, violence and injustice she experiences are largely unaided by feminist analysis. Ultimately her struggle to articulate her experience and fight for subjectivity remains within the boundaries of dominant discourses of race/ethnicity, gender and sexuality.

Between a rock and a hard place: How to reconcile the 'postcolonial' with the 'feminist'?

It would seem that the situating of Bellil – both through her own narrative and how her book is positioned – within the confines of the 'average' young woman of North African origin in France could be seen as evidencing Gayatri Spivak's (1988) argument that women of subordinated groups are limited in expression to the language of those who have subordinated them. It is not that the subaltern cannot speak at all but rather that she is constrained by the discourse of the dominant. I would argue that in the process it becomes all but impossible for her to construct an experience or an act of resistance in anything other than the very language that placed her in the subordinated position in the first place. The overlapping blindness within dominant Western feminism to White privilege, the complicity of certain

152   *The 'beurette' and the Republic*

feminisms with the colonial project and the symbolic use of women as markers of difference in the articulation of anti-colonial nationalism has led to a seemingly impossible situation for non-Western feminists. They are forced to do battle against multiple forms of domination simultaneously, all the while being accused of being traitors to their community and their race (Grewal 2012a, 2012b; Narayan 1997; Nasta 1991; Minh-Ha 1989). In the demands placed on her from various competing interests Bellil seems forced to choose, and her choice is ultimately a statement of her loyalty to the French Republic.

Bellil is not alone in facing this difficulty. As the prominent documentary maker of Algerian origin Yamina Benguigui described in reference to a negative response from the North African community to a documentary looking at the condition of Muslim women in France:

> There is a certain complex among men which is that we should show the positive side of the community. If we reveal problems we should accuse the political system; that is, we should show how France is treating immigrants and denounce the system. But to look at ourselves and to show what's happening to outsiders, that's going too far.
>
> (quoted in Derderian 2004, p. 153)

This serves to create divisions among young North Africans in France, which Guénif-Souilamas identifies as placing the women within a trap of various irreconcilable positions. So too, the '[p]itting [of] postcolonial children of immigrants against each other maintains a latent racism in the society at large and a self-hatred among the young' (Guénif-Souilamas 2006, p. 36).

Black critical race feminist bell hooks has written extensively about the perception that Black women were not supposed to speak out against their own oppression to show solidarity with Black men. I witnessed firsthand a more recent example of this in France. In 2007 a group calling themselves '*les féministes indigènes de la République*' issued a manifesto in which they decried both sexism and racism, asserted the mutual imbrication of these forms of discrimination and declared a new form of intersectional feminist politics (Grewal 2011, 2009). Connected to the highly vocal *mouvement des indigènes de la République (MIR)* that had since 2005 been pushing French society to acknowledge the ongoing colonial relationship it maintained with many of its ethnic minority members, *les féministes indigènes* developed a powerful postcolonial feminist critique of French society. Having followed their work with great enthusiasm, when I happened to be in Paris in June 2009 I contacted the group's main spokesperson (and leading member of *MIR*), Houria Bouteldja, and organised to meet her. Over coffee I raved about the wonderful work they seemed to be doing until Bouteldja politely interrupted me. Sadly, she told me, *les féministes indigènes* were dead. When I asked, completely dejected, why, she confided that they had experienced difficulty getting the support of the men within *MIR*. 'We have to concentrate for now on the decolonising work', she stated. It seemed addressing homophobia and sexism was too contentious and risked splitting the movement but, she argued, that would come later.

The 'beurette' and the Republic   153

When I pointed out that this logic had been proven false in relation to the US civil rights movement (as hooks and other Black feminists have so powerfully shown), she simply shrugged with a rather tragic smile on her face.

I recount this story to acknowledge the difficult position women like Bellil have often found themselves in and to express sympathy for her predicament. In making my critique I wish to make clear that I am less concerned with Bellil's chosen strategy than the conditions within which she makes that choice. It would seem that the colonial violence described by Frantz Fanon by which colonised turns on colonised in desperation and a sense of disempowerment instead of challenging the coloniser (1970, pp. 215–228) remains a position that is far from reconciled in the context of discourses of gender and race in France. Not only is that true in the context of the discourses of young _banlieue_ men (discussed in the previous chapter) but it also emerges in Bellil's discourse as well as that of _Ni Putes Ni Soumises,_ detailed shortly.

A comparative example can be drawn from hooks' discussion of the Anita Hill sexual harassment case in the US (1992, p. 83). Hill, a Black woman, was pitted against her alleged harasser, Clarence Thomas, a Black male candidate for appointment to the Supreme Court:

> [U]ltimately, the nature of the hearings suggest that there is still no place within White supremacist capitalist patriarchy for a discussion of black gender relations that would enable black women and men to confront questions of power and domination, of black male sexism and black female resistance. For, to a grave extent, the spectacle of the Thomas hearings had little to do with any desire on the part of the American public to determine whether or not Thomas was a worthy candidate for the Supreme Court or to truthfully examine his coercive relations with black female subordinates.
>
> (1992, p. 83)

Hooks draws this conclusion from the ways in which the cases were made by both sides. In particular, she notes:

> Hill was never disloyal to patriarchy, or, for that matter, to the institution of White supremacy. Instead she expressed her loyalty consistently by the manner in which she appealed to the system for justice. By appropriating her as a feminist hero, women, and White women in particular, show that they are more interested in positioning Hill in support of a feminism that she never espoused.
>
> (1992, p. 83)

Similarly, Bellil's positioning as a figurehead for a feminist association and a representative of young women of the _banlieue_ is done largely without her having asked for such a role. As she explains in detail, her speaking out was an act of personal vindication. To position her as an authoritative voice on gender and race relations is not only to place a great burden on her but also – through her ultimate inability to negotiate the two roles without contradiction and resort to

154 *The 'beurette' and the Republic*

generalisation – she is co-opted to promote other ideological agendas. As a result, I both feel great sympathy for Bellil and also urge for greater caution in accepting her narrative uncritically.

Problematising the authority of experience

Bellil's case also highlights the need to problematise the emphasis placed on 'lived experience' within some postcolonial and critical race feminist theory. Even as power structures and dominant discourses may be challenged within that lived experience, without the theoretical framework and the situating of this narrative within the broader social, historical and political context, ultimately the power of the challenge can easily be lost – as it is in Bellil's case – subsumed within the dominant understandings and discourses.

Questioning postcolonial feminism's frequent reliance on 'lived experience' as the foundation for political and theoretical claims, Sara Suleri writes: 'While lived experience can hardly be discounted as a critical resource for an apprehension of the gendering of race, neither should such data serve as the evacuating principle for both historical and theoretical contexts alike' (1992, p. 119). In light of the above discussion of the ideological weight given to '*la beurette*', Suleri's comments seem prescient. While Bellil's account may be an attempt to express her own lived subjectivity, it still exists within a broader social and historical context, as does Bellil herself.

Suleri goes on to explain: 'Lived experience, in other words, serves as fodder for the continuation of another's epistemology, even when it is recorded in a "contestatory" position . . .' (1992, p. 123). In recognising this, the uncritical privileging of the postcolonial woman's voice by virtue of her postcolonial status becomes highly problematic, both in terms of the reduction of the various possible voices and positions that this woman may assert and in the responsibility it places on the individual woman to demonstrate a complete race/gender consciousness. In this way, the postcolonial female identity becomes a double-edged sword. On the one hand, as Sidonie Smith and Julia Watson point out:

> . . . identity confers political and communal credibility. In such cases, a previously 'voiceless' narrator from a community not culturally authorized to speak – the slave, the nonliterate, the child, the inmate of a mental hospital, the formerly colonized, for instance – finds in identification the means and the impetus to speak publicly. Richard Wright, for example, in narrating his autobiography *Black Boy (American Hunger): A Record of Childhood and Youth*, explicitly situates himself vis-à-vis racialized communities, both black and White, inviting his reader to accept his narrative as authoritatively representative of an African American 'boy'. Similarly, James Baldwin negotiates his identity as a 'native son' in *Notes of a Native Son* . . .

(2001, p. 28)

The 'beurette' and the Republic   155

However, they also note: 'As the cases of Wright and Baldwin suggest, not all "experience" is accorded social and cultural recognition or legitimacy' (Smith and Watson 2001, p. 28).

Moreover, the recognition or legitimation of a 'lived experience' remains outside of the control of the subject himself/herself. As Jean-Pierre Boulé documents in relation to his review of AIDS literature, 'the texts were framed as part of the dominant discourse of social and sexual regulation aiming to preserve the dominant form of monogamous heterosexual relationships' (2002, p. 143). Thus, following Guénif-Soulimas's insightful identification of the centrality of the figure of '*la beurette*' as a model of French integration and her male counterpart, '*le garçon arabe*' as the antithesis, Bellil's utility becomes clear. It is only through subscribing to a model of normative heterosexuality and a commitment to Republican values that her voice is legitimated. As Henriques et al. observe: 'Particular discourses set parameters through which desire is produced, regulated and channelled' (Boulé 2002, pp. 143–144).

This selective recognition of 'authenticity' is not limited to the French context. As Kadiatu Kanneh discusses in her article, 'Marketing Black women's texts: the case of Alice Walker', the identification of Black women as marketable authors has been tied up with their positioning within the promotion of certain discourses:

> The marketing of Black women's texts in the late twentieth century is reliant on the particular and continuing viability of Black women as political subjects, on specific cultural and critical notions of Black female literary identity. . . . There are specific reasons why Black women as authors occupy a significant, even radical imaginary. The packaging of texts by Black women writers in contemporary terms relies on the foregrounding of authorial identity, on emphasising the race and gender of the author to signal authenticity. . .
>
> (Kanneh 1998, p. 145)

Thus it can be concluded that as the privileging of the postcolonial woman's 'lived experience' opens the possibility for manipulation to reinforce dominant hegemonic discourses and epistemologies, not all 'lived experiences' can or will be recognised. In engaging with Gayatri Spivak's question of whether the subaltern can speak, it seems in Bellil's case, as Peter van der Veer comments in relation to controversial Dutch Somali author and former member of Parliament Ayaan Hirsi Ali, '[t]he subaltern can speak, but in order to be heard she has to express the feelings of the dominant community' (van der Veer 2006, p. 121).

At the same time, as Mohanty (1997) identifies, the figure of the 'average Third World Woman' is constructed as a singular, monolithic subject. While this works to reduce subaltern women's status to that of an object of Western discourses (feminist or other), making generalisations possible, so too it positions any subaltern woman who does speak as speaking on behalf of *all* subaltern women. Thus Bellil, in seeking to assert her own personal struggle, is forced into a position of representation. As Laurent Mucchielli describes in his book looking at media

156 *The 'beurette' and the Republic*

treatment of the *tournantes* phenomenon: 'the media quickly made this individual story the symbol of a whole nation'[38] (2005, p. 22). She no longer speaks from her own point of view but *on behalf of all* other young women of the *banlieue*. This is made clear from both the preface to her book and the reception her book received.

Yet, just as Bellil is not alone in negotiating this difficult position caught between loyalty to an ethnic identity, a national identity and a gender identity, nor is her response the only possible way in which this problem is negotiated. However it is the one that is ultimately privileged over others in that Bellil is allowed a public space within which to voice her struggle while others are not. So why is this? And why, when the rapes she survived happened 14 years before and in between she had generally experienced rejection, dismissal and blame from family, friends and state institutions alike, did she suddenly emerge as a national figure: the 'representative *beurette*' *par excellence*?

As Mohanty point outs, through the process of homogenising different groups of Third World women, all marginal forms of resistance are erased. This has been the major criticism of Bellil's book and *Ni Putes Ni Soumises* more generally; that, through their representations of North African/Muslim/ immigrant women as oppressed and providing French Republican feminism as the solution, they have excluded the possibility for any other form of resistance. Indeed, it has further stigmatised women who do not conform to this ideology.

Furthermore, through its attempts to promote the liberation of the voice of the 'Third World Woman', postcolonial feminism has become complicit in a simplification of non-White female identity. As a 'native informant', Bellil's account seems to reiterate some of the worst orientalist stereotypes that justified colonial violence and domination and ongoing racism. As a result Bellil's text poses significant difficulties for postcolonial feminist scholarship. Much of the literature of this school of thought has concentrated on the nature of Western feminism and its complicity with colonialist or racist discourses in attempting to speak for or understand the experience of the subaltern or 'Third World Woman'. Writers such as Chandra Mohanty and Trinh Minh-Ha have thus asserted the importance of the postcolonial woman reclaiming the right to speak for herself. However, as Sara Suleri (1992) points out, postcolonial feminism's insistence on asserting who has the right to speak for whom leads to what she sees as an artificial emphasis on 'authenticity', calling for only she who is in the position to speak. This uncritical legitimation of an 'authentic' voice is not without its problems, as Bellil's text suggests. As Suleri goes on to explain:

> The coupling of *post-colonial* with *woman* . . . almost inevitably leads to the simplicities that underlie unthinking celebrations of oppression, elevating the racially female voice into a metaphor for 'the good'. Such metaphoricity cannot exactly be called essentialist, but it certainly functions as an impediment to a reading that attempts to look beyond obvious questions of good and evil.
>
> (1992, p. 758)

The 'beurette' and the Republic   157

In over-privileging the postcolonial/subaltern woman's voice, postcolonial feminists are placed in an impossible position when dealing with a text like Bellil's. To critique her is to counter the very foundation of their assertion that she must be allowed to speak in her own voice, without the intervention of either Western feminists or non-Western elites. However, to unquestioningly accept her narrative is to reinforce the very discourses they have been so critical of in Western feminist thought. This is a tension I have tried to work through in relation to controversial Dutch Somali writer Ayaan Hirsi Ali (Grewal 2012a).

While it is of course of interest to promote the right of the subaltern/'Third World Woman' to assert her own voice, this promotion should not be done uncritically. It is necessary to recognise that within dominant hegemonic discourses a 'Third World Woman' who does claim a voice and speaks will often become responsible for not only the manner in which her own personal experience is understood and situated but as a *porte-parole* for *all* non-White women, as if there could only be one manner in which their identity can be experienced. With this comes a responsibility for the individual woman to demonstrate a highly developed and sophisticated sense of both class and gender consciousness. In failing to recognise that this may often not be the case, postcolonial feminist theory is left incapable of responding to positions and forms of resistance, which may not in fact be of benefit to their broader struggle or theoretical aims.

In her essay, 'Experience', Joan Scott also highlights the problem with over-privileging experience as an authoritative answer to the question of difference. Instead she argues the experience is, in fact, the question that needs to be explored. We are already aware that difference exists. What remains to be concluded is how subjects are positioned and their experiences produced through discourse. 'It is not individuals who have experience', she writes, 'but subjects who are constituted through experience' (1992, pp. 25–26). Consequently, evidence of experience becomes less a means of contesting ideological systems than a means of reproducing them (1992, p. 25). Applying Scott's analytical framework, it becomes imperative to not simply accept Bellil's experience as a self-evident truth but to situate it and interrogate what her assertions tell us about how she constructs her identity, her knowledge and her experiences: her '(post)colonial habitus' (see also McNay 2004 for further justification).

As already discussed in earlier chapters, I believe Bourdieu's concept of habitus can be meaningfully linked with postcolonial theory in an attempt to understand how the violence of colonialism and its legacy continues to affect the postcolonial subject. This is not to present this subject as a mere passive victim: a construction critiqued and rejected above. Bourdieu's theory of habitus is dynamic. As a result, it takes into account both the external structures and relations of domination that become internalised by the individual subject *and* the methods deployed by that subject to assert his or her agency and resist these external power structures.

Unfortunately, as the previous interrogations of the (post)colonial habitus have demonstrated, the outcomes of this habitus and the action it engenders have unfortunately been far from liberating. Yet it is only through reading Bourdieu alongside postcolonial scholarship that the ongoing significance of colonial relations of

158   *The 'beurette' and the Republic*

power is intelligible. Attempts to assign colonialism as a relic from the past become problematic when we consider how the identity of postcolonial subjects is not only still represented through resort to colonial tropes and stereotypes but also sometimes (and not uncritically) constituted by the subject *herself/himself* in these terms.

In much the same way that the discourses of the various non-White male actors in the 'Sydney gang rapes' and '*les tournantes*' reflect an internalisation of both racist and sexist power structures, which ultimately lead them to perform an identity that frees them (and others) from neither, so too Bellil's habitus reflects the colonial dichotomisation of 'women's rights' (associated with Europe) and 'backward tradition' (associated with colonised cultures). It seems she has internalised the 'civilising mission' language to such an extent that she cannot articulate an identity that embraces both her ethnicity and her gender.

Again, as stressed in the analysis of the gang rapists' discourses, the intention here is not to extrapolate this to a more generalised explanation of the identity of women of immigrant origin in France. However, herein lies the problem. Even as the essentialisation of identity is critiqued, called into question and challenged, in the context of both the Sydney gang rapists and Bellil, the fact that they emerge as the strongest voices means they become the figures against which *all* those they supposedly represent (as articulated by dominant discourses) become measured. Paradoxically, while the suggestion that the rapists reflect the attitude of all young Muslim men is generally rejected within left-wing academic commentary, the question of how to both acknowledge the validity of Bellil's account of her own experience, while questioning its broader applicability remains a tricky one.

Part of the difficulty Bellil's book produces for postcolonial feminist theory is that to critique her is to comply with patriarchal modes of anti-racism (as bell hooks and Benguigui describe it, the need to demonstrate loyalty to 'her menfolk') while to endorse her voice leads to an embracing of, to borrow and slightly reframe Spivak's (1988) comment, the 'Brown women needing to be saved by White men from Brown men' type discourses. In either case, Bellil's voice is not heard as that of an individual subject struggling to find a position of agency between the misogyny, racism and marginalisation she experienced but becomes emblematic of something wider: the voice of the 'Third World Woman', which is either to be ignored or valued without question.

Furthermore, the pitting of 'good White feminist France' against 'bad, backward, traditional, violent and misogynist Algeria' has left many women of immigrant background stuck in a no-man's land. By associating Bellil's experience of sexual violence and gender oppression with the culture of the *banlieue* (which is ethnically coded), her testimony conforms to a discourse that is counter-productive both in terms of addressing sexual and gender-based violence and racism in France. Her individualisation of her suffering allows this to occur in a way that it claims to be legitimate and 'authentic' as her lived experience and therefore unquestionable. However, the selective reading she is given and even at times her own apparent emphasis on one aspect of the injustice she experienced, that being the lack of support she received from her family and the *banlieue* (read immigrant/*Maghrebi*)

The 'beurette' *and the Republic*   159

community more generally over the injustice she has faced due to institutionalised racism and sexism allow her narrative to support rather than challenge dominant structures of power and the oppression they produce.

Conclusion

Although Bellil's book at first glance provides an excellent parallel to the autobiography of 'Sydney gang rape' victim, Tegan Wagner, in attempting to analyse the two books, Bellil's seems to pose more complex theoretical problems than Wagner's. While as noted above, Wagner's account is framed as a personal narrative of an exceptional situation, Bellil's account is characterised as representative of life for young (North African) women of the *banlieue*. Perhaps this is because, even though the 'Sydney gang rapes' have taken on a mythology of their own, the fact that there is no specific term for these rapes means Wagner's tale is not automatically linked to the discourses that emerged on the 'Sydney gang rapes'. However a more disturbing reading of this difference would be that, whereas Wagner's account is presented as individual, Bellil's can only be read as collective. The individual subject space is once more reserved for those who – as part of the dominant group, namely White – are unmarked by difference.

While Wagner, as a White woman, experiences limits on her ability to assert independent agency, she is still seen as a person in her own right. Meanwhile, Bellil is positioned in the doubly disadvantageous position of a woman *and* of ethnic minority origins. As a result, she is *prima facie* seen as a passive, voiceless entity. This impression is perhaps added to by the fact that there is no apparent intermediary in Wagner's recounting of her story: her story is presented as her own. Yet in Bellil's case, hers is framed by a preface by journalist Josée Stoquart, in which a cultural context is provided to her story, and she is situated as but one of many whose experiences are reduced to being the same.

Bellil's apparent disempowerment and marginalisation thus calls into question the efficacy of many of the assumptions underlying both feminist and anti-racist activism in contemporary France. The mid-1980s marked a period of increased anti-racist activism with the emergence of the *Beur* generation, who sought to assert their place in contemporary French society. While the *Beur* movement centred its claims around the discourse of '*droit à la différence*', the focus of their activism was the discrepancy between the official rhetoric of integration and the reality of social exclusion experienced by ethnic minority communities in France. Closely aligned with the *Parti Socialiste*, the leaders of the most prominent anti-racism organisations such as *SOS Racisme* remained loyal to the language of 'Republican values'.

It is therefore unsurprising that Bellil's indignation and anger concentrate on the denial of these principles of equality she understands as owed to her as a French citizen. Race is a reason for this denial but, while she is critical of the lack of institutional support and protection she receives, she remains unable to fundamentally challenge the Republican principles that are supposed to provide her with equality and justice but that so clearly fail her. Even at the end of her book she

160 *The 'beurette' and the Republic*

draws on the symbolic significance of the *Marche des femmes contre les ghettos et pour l'égalité* organised by *Ni Putes Ni Soumises* in 2003 in which she is a figurehead finishing at Place de la République in Paris (2003, p. 308) as a way to restate her commitment to official French national myths and principles and situate her protest within these without ever calling them into question. This commitment to the French Republic emerges even more clearly in the discourse of *Ni Putes Ni Soumises* and the association's founding president, Fadela Amara.

Notes

1 'ma délivrance sera un livre'.
2 'Je ne voulais pas que mon histoire reste au secret, dans le bureau de Fanny. Pour sortir de mon malheur, il m'a fallu des années d'efforts et beaucoup de souffrance. Serait-il juste que les responsables de ce gâchis dorment tranquilles? Que K et ses potes, que l'avocate, que l'association et les services sociaux, que mes parents eux aussi dorment tranquilles? Ce serait trop facile pour tous que je me taise, que je parvienne à être heureuse, que je fasse des enfants et qu'on n'en parle plus! Non, je veux partager la facture. Il n'y a pas de raison que je la paye seule. Puisqu'on n'a jamais voulu m'écouter, on va me lire!'
3 I would like to thank Professor Akeel Bilgrami for introducing me to these terms as a means of clarifying an important distinction that should be drawn when analysing autobiographical work.
4 'Lorsque tout avait été extirpé et écrit, clarifié par le regard de Josée, réfléchi de nouveau puis, enfin, digéré et intégré. Ensuite, tout recommençait, alimenté par de nouveaux elements. Il a fallu installer du temps pour que les choses mûrissent en moi et toutes ces étapes avaient leur sens.
5 'J'ai été sincère, j'ai été lucide, le plus que j'ai pu. J'ai voulu montrer à quel point la negligence de ma famille, de mon entourage, de l'avocate et des services sociaux m'a délinguée, en plus des traumatismes des viols. C'est de ma propre vérité qu'il s'agit dans ce livre.'
6 The backcover of Wagner's book reads: 'On June 14, 2002, Tegan Wagner, then 14 years old, thought she was going to a party with friends. Instead, she found herself trapped in a house with a group of older boys she had never met before. She was gang-raped that night by three brothers.'
7 'la violence sexuelle qui s'est instituée et banalisée dans des cités et des banlieues'.
8 'J'aurais pu choisir d'interviewer Samira et d'écrire moi-même son histoire. J'ai préféré la laisser écrire. D'abord parce qu'elle a un mode d'expression intense et imagé, ensuite et surtout parce qu'elle a déjà un lieu de parole et qu'écrire est un autre travail sur soi.'
9 'Il semble que dans ces quartiers que l'on dit pudiquement 'sensibles', où la majorité des familles est issue de l'immigration, il soit difficile de donner sa place à la femme. Certains jeunes sont pris entre le rigorisme de leurs origines culturelles (intégrisme religieux, intouchabilité de la femme, polygamie . . .) et un environnement culturel très fortement érotisé. . . . Ces adolescents n'ont plus aucun repère et ils n'ont pas conscience de la gravité de leurs actes. Pour eux, la "tournante" est un jeu et les filles, des objets.'
10 'Ce livre lève le voile sur la condition insupportable de certaines jeunes filles qui y vivent, tiraillées entre deux servitudes: obéir en restant enfermées à la maison ou risquer, dans la rue, devenir la proie des bandes et de leur sauvagerie sexuelle.'
11 'c'est une grande chance que de participer à la libération d'un être'.
12 'Elle décida que c'était à moi seule d'écrire et qu'elle se chargerait de restructurer mes textes et d'en reprendre la forme. Elle m'assura qu'elle me soutiendrait tout au long de l'écriture, par ses questions, ses confrontations et ses encouragements.'

The 'beurette' and the Republic 161

13 'Son écoute, ses questions et ses réactions ont petit à petit changé ma vision de moi-même.'

14 'sa seule préoccupation à lui, c'est l'audimat'.

15 'On assiste, depuis les années 80, à la montée en puissance du phénomène de bande, avec une idéalisation de la figure du petit caïd pour lequel le nombre de viols en réunion, les 'plans pétasse', comme il les nomme, est un titre de gloire.'

16 The term *caïd* is frequently employed in the context of young men of the *banlieue*, to signify the 'gang leader'. It is interesting to note that the term was used in the colonial context to identify the North African colonial officer who was charged with enforcing the colonial regime over local people and answerable to the French. When considering the evolution of the use of this term in French, one is left wondering whether the underlying idea of the *caïd* as the intermediary and ultimately the fallguy for France remains.

17 '... j'ai croisé un jeune mec: casquette-survêt-basket, typiquement l'un de ceux que les médias nomment "les jeunes caïds de banlieue". Il me bouscule dans le tram! Je me dis alors que tous les bras ouverts vers moi et tous les sourires étaient trop beaux! Je m'apprête déjà à sortir mon "lances-flammes" pour l'incendier en paroles, mais timidement et discrètement il me dit: "Eh! T'as parlé mortel hier! " J'avoue franchement que l'espace d'une fraction de seconde, je me suis sentie très conne! Et malheureusement, le temps que je réalise, les portes du tram s'étaient déjà refermées. J'ai à peine eu le temps de lui faire un sourire pour le remercier. Parce que, venant *d'un de ceux que l'on stigmatise souvent trop vite*, cela m'a profondément touché.'

18 'elle me "conseille" de ne pas parler des "tournantes", de la réalité des cites, du process loupé, de l'association d'aide à l'enfance qui n'aide personne, car cela risquerait de choquer les téléspectateurs. Ell ne veut pas non plus qu'on mentionne mes déboires avec l'avocate. Je commence à me demander pourquoi je suis là. Certes, j'ai envie de témoigner devant la France entière, mais pas à n'importe quelles conditions.'

19 Adding to Guénif-Souilamas' research, a cursory review of the internet seems to support the view that the label '*beurette*' has become a highly eroticised and sexualised term. While a Google search for the term '*beur*' delivers results associated with ethnic minority radio, arts and anti-racism projects, the term '*beurette*' delivers almost solely pornographic and sex sites. See also Hamel (2005, pp. 97–98).

20 'Mais à quatorze ans on a rien à faire dehors à cette heure-là!'

21 'Quand je pense qu'elle a fait des années d'études, qu'elle defend les enfants aggressés sexuellement et que ses commentaires ne dépassent pas le niveau de ceux de mes parents, ça me tue.'

22 'L'association qu'elle représente est super connue. Il y a même une grande actrice française qui en fait la pub... Après cet episode, je ne peux plus regarder cette pub sans avoir envie de vomir.'

23 'J'ai compris que dans ce pays de merde, il n'y a aucune justice, car la police fonctionne au bakchich. J'avais déjà compris, dans les yeux du flic, que ce n'était pas la peine d'insister, qu'il n'y avait rien à espérer. Je laisse tout là-bas. Les deux mille kilomètres qui m'en séparent m'aident à ne plus penser, à tenter d'oublier ce que je peux ressentir. Je me console en pensant que, au moins en France, il y a une justice.'

24 'Mes parents sont des immigrés, très européanisés, pourtant des séquelles leur sont restées de leur education. Il fallait agir comme avec eux: faire comprendre à coups de taloche, à coups de poing et à coup de pied au cul pour que ça rentre bien dans la tête! Je suis le fruit de deux traditions, de deux modes de vie complètement contradictoires. J'ai reçu de mes parents une éducation traditionelle que l'on ne m'a jamais expliquée autrement qu'avec des coups, des cris ou des glaviots. J'ai reçu aussi une éducation plus européene, issue de ma petite enfance en Belgique, dans la famille d'accueil où ma mère m'avait placée... Là-bas la vie était douce et tranquille. Papa Jean et maman Josette étaient des personnes équilibrées et bienveillantes qui m'ont donné amour et confiance.'

25 'j'étais heureuse d'être ici, chez des 'Français' comme on me disait'.

162   The 'beurette' and the Republic

26 'Comment comprendre ce qu'on m'imposait ici, cette éducation faite de taloches et d'interdiction, cette inégalité entre les garçons et les filles, ces tabous envahissants, après ce que j'avais connu chez papa Jean et maman Josette?'

27 'En fait, ma mère aurait voulu m'élever comme elle avait été élevée au bled, à la dure. Chez nous, c'est comme ça, les filles s'en prennent plein la gueule sans broncher. Je sais que ma mère a eu la vie dure, qu'elle a été victime d'une culture où la femme est traitée comme un chien.'

28 'Je ne veux pas d'une vie à attendre mon mec, avec la hantise qu'il se fasse coffrer un jour ou l'autre. Je ne veux pas preparer la tchout-choucka pendant qu'il vit sa vie dehors. Je veux pas faire des mômes dans cette banlieue pourrie. Je ne veux pas reproduire ce qu'a fait ma mère, avec vingt ans d'écart.'

29 'Dans cette putain de banlieue, les mecs sont tous fabriqués sur le même moule. Lyes est un modèle courant. Les "gars biens" sont des exceptions.'

30 'Avec toute la terre d'accord, mais pas avec quelqu'un de ma culture! C'est soit un religieux soit une racaille!'. It is also worth noting that she uses the term 'racaille', as used by Nicholas Sarkozy, then Minister for the Interior in his controversial 'cleaning the *banlieue*' statement (discussed in the final chapter).

31 'Il n'a aucune pitié pour moi, il continue à me frapper jusqu'à ce que je comprenne qu'il n'y a pas d'autre issue pour moi que de le suivre, si je veux garder une chance de rester en vie.'

32 'Combien de personnes me diront plus tard: "Moi, j'aurais fait cela à ta place . . . On peut toujours se défendre . . . Suprendre l'agresseur, lui metre un coup de pied dans les couilles . . .", etc. Combien j'en ai entendu de ces petites phrases assassins qui me trouaient de culpabilité, de ces commentaries sans pitié faits par les gens qui n'ont jamais été sous l'emprise de la vraie peur.'

33 'Je pense mériter ce que j'ai subi parce que je ne suis plus vierge. Chez les musulmans, ne plus être vierge pour une jeune fille est un sacrilege et je sais que mon pere pourrait me tuer pour cela. J'ai couché avec Jaïd. De plus, je suis fugueuse et voleuse. Je n'écoute ni mes parents ni mes profs . . . Je n'ai donc pas à me plaindre de m'être fait violer. Je l'ai cherché. C'est bien sûr ce qui se dit autour de moi, mais c'est aussi ce que je pense de moi.'

34 'Je me sentais tiraillée entre les obligations arbitraires de mon milieu et mes rêves de liberté. Je voulais être libre, ne pas vivre soumise, ni enfermée à la maison, comme celles que je voyais autour de moi. Je voulais la même liberté qu'un mec: respirer, croquer la vie, quoi de plus naturel?'

35 '. . . je ne me fais pas d'illusions. Une meuf comme moi, c'est pour rigoler, taper un joint. Avec le lourd dossier que je traîne, je ne suis pas une meuf avec qui on reste, on projette un avenir, on se marie.'

36 '[c]e que je veux, c'est un mec normal, qui rentre le soir, me parle, me trouve belle, s'intéresse à l'éducation de ses enfants. Un mec normal, quoi!'

37 'Avec lui je suis femme, avec lui, je suis belle, même quand je dors. Il me réveille avec des petits déjeuners au lit, des bisous, un bouquet de roses. Il m'emmène au restaurant et sous ma serviette, je découvre parfois une petite surprise.'

38 'La presse . . . fera rapidement de cette histoire individuelle le symbole de tout un pays.'

9 *Ni Putes Ni Soumises*
The new 'voice of the *banlieue*'?

Introduction

Samira Bellil's book was released shortly prior to a nationwide march entitled, '*Marche des femmes contre les ghettos et pour l'égalité*', in which she participated as a figurehead. This march was organised by – and marked the emergence into 'mainstream' French public space of – the *banlieue* feminist organisation *Ni Putes Ni Soumises (NPNS)*. Also in this year (2003), a text bearing the same name as the organisation was published by the organisation's then-president, Fadela Amara, in collaboration with left-wing journalist, Sylvia Zappi.

This text, written in a style that is both memoir and political manifesto, provides an overview of Amara's life, her analysis of the situation of women in the *banlieue* and the history of *NPNS*. While much of the critique in the previous chapter of Bellil's book is also relevant to Amara's book, Amara's text as a more overtly political document raises a number of other issues. Furthermore, *NPNS* has emerged as a highly publicised organisation and is frequently represented in French public debates on issues associated with the *banlieue*, sexism, immigration and Islam. It is therefore important to look at how the organisation presents its message to identify how and why it has become so prominent.

Manifesto for women of the *banlieue*?

Amara's text is presented as an 'insider' account of the situation of women in the *banlieue* (see Amara 2003, back cover). As has already been outlined in the previous chapter in relation to Bellil's testimony, Amara's recounting of her experiences cannot be read in a vacuum. It requires an interrogation of the social context within which she writes. Elaborating on this, Joan Scott writes:

> Subjects are constituted discursively, but there are conflicts among discursive systems, contradictions within any one of them, multiple meanings possible for the concepts they deploy. And subjects have agency. They are not unified, autonomous individuals exercising free will, but rather subjects whose agency is created through situations and statuses conferred on them. Being a subject means being 'subject to definite conditions of existence, conditions of endowment of agents and conditions of exercise.' These conditions enable

164   Ni Putes Ni Soumises

choices, although they are not unlimited. Subjects are constituted discursively, experience is a linguistic event (it doesn't happen outside established meanings), but neither is it confined to a fixed order of meaning.

(1992, p. 34, references omitted)

For this reason Scott argues that it is essential to reject any easy separation between 'experience' and language. Instead, an interrogation of the stated subject identity and experience creates possibilities for identifying features within the discursive framework through which certain positions are more achievable and/or acceptable than others. In the context of both Amara and Bellil, their articulations of their ethnic and gender identities and the paradigm within which they situate their struggles provides an invaluable insight into the fundamental assumptions underpinning French national identity and its relationship with constructions of ethnicity, gender and sexuality. Both women's narratives are historical and contextual. They constitute, as Scott explains, 'productions of knowledge of the self, not reflections either of external or internal truth' (1992, p. 36).

Just as Scott explains in her analysis of Samuel Delany's autobiographical text, Amara and Bellil's narratives are both (and inextricably) personal and public. Their experiences can be read neither as wholly autonomous acts of agency nor as wholly determined acts of historicity. In fact, it is the tension that exists between these two extremes in both cases that provides a fruitful site for exploration. Once again, reference to the concept of '(post)colonial habitus' is helpful. In Scott's words: '[e]xperience is at once always already an interpretation and is in need of interpretation' (1992, p. 37). Having already analysed the specificities of Bellil's text, I now want to examine Amara's narrative.

The politicisation of 'personal experience'

While there are many similar concerns raised by Bellil's and Amara's texts, in the case of the latter the significance of adopting Scott's critical approach to experience would seem even more pressing. This is due to Amara's apparently conscious and intentional positioning of her narrative as authentic, legitimate and authoritative. She does this by explicitly linking her political and theoretical analysis with her own personal lived experience (2003, p. 13).[1] The first chapter, in which she describes her childhood and personalises her account of the problems of the *banlieue* with reference to her family members, blurs the line between this book being a form of memoir and a political manifesto.

In doing this she seems to consciously position her text as a form of political testimonial: a genre which has been widely used within Latina and Chicana literature as a means of, as Lynda Marín explains, 'writing from the margins' (1991, p. 51). In distinguishing testimonial literature from other forms of self-narrative, George Yúdice provides the following definition:

[A]n *authentic* narrative, told by a *witness* who is *moved* to *narrate* by the *urgency* of a situation (e.g., war, oppression, revolution, etc.). Emphasizing *popular oral discourse*, the witness portrays his or her own *experience* as a *representative* of a *collective memory* and *identity*. *Truth* is summoned in the cause of *denouncing* a present situation of exploitation and oppression or *exorcising* and *setting aright* official history.

(Gugelberger and Kearney 1991, p. 4, emphasis in original)

Through its immediacy and resistance to political marginality, the testimonial genre has been adopted as a popular form of resistance for Indigenous peoples in Latin America against state-sanctioned violence. Through their recounting of their own life experiences, they have sought to situate and affirm the struggle of a people. While essentially autobiographical, testimonial literature has been characterised as a genre in its own right due to the positions of power, both available to, and within which, the giver of the testimony is situated. Marín contrasts the testimonial with other traditional narrative and literary forms in the following way:

Those privileged to belong to the dominant class, race and/or gender write Scripture, literature, autobiography, or ethnography. From the point of view of privilege, the testimonial has been seen as the means by which those who are not privileged tell about themselves and particularly about their struggle against the powers that claim privilege over them.

(1991, pp. 51–52)

Certainly the appeal to a collective identity can be seen within both Bellil and Amara's work. However, while Bellil explains her reasons for writing her account in terms of a personal struggle to address and overcome her experiences, Amara's book is more in the tradition of Latin American women's testimonial literature. These testimonies have generally talked in terms of personal experience, while always making clear the extent to which their stories and experiences are interchangeable with so many others to whom they feel a sense of solidarity. Marín provides the example of the testimonial of the Mayan activist Rigoberta Menchú, in which Menchú states:

I'd like to stress that it's not only my life, it's also the testimony of my people . . . The important thing is that what has happened to me has happened to many other people too: My story is the story of all poor Guatemalans. My personal experience is the reality of a whole people.

(Marín 1991, p. 52)

In relation to Amara's text, the reader is also given the impression that Amara speaks not only of her own experience but also of the experience of women in the *banlieue* more generally. This is enhanced by reference to her work with the *Fédération Nationale de la Maison des Potes*[2] and her summaries of conversations and anecdotes relating to the young *banlieue* residents with whom she has worked.

This linking of the personal with the broader public and political sphere is pertinent. Much of the academic analysis and commentary on the testimonial genre as

166   Ni Putes Ni Soumises

used by Chicano/as and Latino/as has celebrated it as a political tool whereby the disadvantaged, marginalised and forgotten groups are able to assert a voice and be heard. Yet, as with Bellil's book, Amara's narrative highlights some problematic assumptions underlying the discursive paradigm within which she situates both her identity and her experiences. While Gugelberger and Kearney assert that '[t]estimonial literature is emerging as part of a global reordering of the social and economic contexts of power/difference within which "literature" is produced and consumed' (1991, p. 6), the issue remains whether in fact only certain voices can be heard.

Doubtless, testimonial literature has provided a source of liberation and agency for both colonised peoples broadly and women specifically.[3] So too, the existence of such a genre, which as Yúdice elaborates is now studied in various disciplines, is in itself a powerful challenge to hegemonic discourses and structures of power. However an uncritical celebration of the testimonial as being that not of one speaker but rather 'an allegory of the many, the people' (Gugelberger and Kearney 1991, p. 8) raises the question: do 'the people' all want to be represented in this way?

The very distinction being drawn between the individualism of the Western writer, as an author who speaks for him or herself, and the collective voice presented by the 'Third World' writer of testimony would also seem to create problematic binaries that serve to remove the agency of many who may choose to frame their stories differently, while imbuing the provider of the testimony with the immense responsibility of representation. Yúdice appears aware of this risk when he seeks to distinguish between representation and an exercise of what he calls 'a means for establishing solidarity' (1991, p. 27). However, it is highly debatable whether this helps overcome the difficulties raised by testimonies which, while acting as sources of agency and bearing witness, are read in a way that justifies other forms of oppression or the reinforcement of hegemonic discourses. Yúdice's insistence that this representation takes place in 'the absence of domination through instrumental rationality' (1991, p. 27) does not address how the narrator of the testimonial is able to both utilise aspects of Western literary form and at the same time reject it.

Whatever Amara's intentions may be in providing her testimonial, the context within which she is read remains that of the French (Western) literary tradition. She appears to explicitly seek to engage this audience through the explanations she provides and the language she employs (stopping to clarify Algerian/*banlieue* culture and expressions throughout). This is not a book by an 'insider' written for an 'insider' (something which perhaps arguably could be the case for Bellil based on her unclarified use of *banlieue* terminology).

So too, Yúdice's celebration of the role of the politically sympathetic editor/collaborator who works with the subaltern witness to destabilise the concept of the author fails to consider the implications when this editor is themselves from the Western institutional tradition. Or when this editor is politically sympathetic to some of the concerns of the subaltern witness and maintains a position of power in how the concerns are framed. In the context of Amara's text, we are told that it is written in collaboration with Sylvia Zappi. However, unlike Bellil's text where the collaborative relationship is explained in detail, it is unclear what role Zappi played in the production of Amara's text. Furthermore, aside from the fact that Zappi is a member of the editorial team of *Le Monde*, we are given no more information regarding her position on these issues and her motivation for becoming involved in the *NPNS* project.

As Scott explains, privileging experience as a form of evidence, existing outside of any discursive construction ironically leads to a reproduction rather than a contestation of ideological systems:

> When experience is taken as the origin of knowledge, the vision of the individual subject (the person who had the experience or the historian who recounts it) becomes the bedrock of evidence upon which explanation is built. Questions about the constructed nature of experience, about how subjects are constituted as different in the first place, about how one's vision is structured – about language (or discourse) and history – are left aside.
>
> (1992, p. 25)

She concludes: 'The evidence of experience then becomes evidence for *the fact of difference* rather than a way of exploring *how* difference is established, how it operates, how and in what ways it constitutes subjects who see and act in the world' (1992, p. 25, emphasis added). Whether the assertion of experience as evidence is intentional, as appears to be the case with Amara, or less conscious, as Bellil's book suggests, both are imputed an autonomous and reified agency. They are attributed an ahistorical race and gender consciousness which masks, or at least neutralises, the reality of the many conflicting claims and subject positions they negotiate both internally and externally. Similarly the extent to which, in adopting particular political and personal subject positions, Bellil and/or Amara are read as speaking on behalf of all women of the *banlieue*/North African women points once again to the dangers in postcolonial theory of too wholeheartedly embracing the authentic and therefore 'good' postcolonial subject.

Many of these concerns have already been raised in relation to Bellil's book so I will not elaborate further. Instead, taking experience as both an interpretation and a representation requiring interpretation, it becomes interesting to analyse how Amara frames her calls for redress of the economic and social marginalisation of *banlieue* residents and her feminist message. By doing this, not only do significant underlying assumptions contained within dominant constructions of citizenship, gender, sexuality and ethnicity become apparent, but hopefully so too the vital importance of reading experience and the constitutive identity it entails within a historical and social context.

The immigrant woman versus the French woman

As noted in the previous chapter, a major criticism of Western feminist theory by postcolonial feminist writers has been its tendency to place in juxtaposition the 'backward' and traditional 'Third World Woman' with the 'liberated', modern

168 Ni Putes Ni Soumises

woman of the West. As was also discussed, this critique is rendered difficult when it is the 'Third World Woman' herself who voices this approach. While Bellil's narrative appears to do this quite unself-consciously, Amara is more cautious in her acceptance of the binary between the 'backward Third World Woman' and the 'liberated modern Western woman'. Instead she appears to oscillate between recognising similar experiences of patriarchal oppression across ethnic groups and situating her own struggle for freedom within the confines of Kabyle/Algerian culture.

In her introductory chapter, when describing her father she expresses a sympathy with him despite his strict, authoritarian approach to her. She frames this by positioning him as living in France in terms of geographical location only. Otherwise, due to the closed nature of the immigrant community she states:

> My father had a fairly simple conception of each person's place: men and women were certainly equal before the law but men outside and women at home! This was his vision of the world, inherited from his Kabyle education. A very common viewpoint among immigrant workers. When my father arrived in France, how could he understand that this model was no longer the approach of the modern society which welcomed him – where women could go out, work, organise their lives – when he moved into a housing estate almost exclusively inhabited by other immigrant workers from the Maghreb? Kabyle fathers, like him, came from a patriarchal and macho society where men had the obligation to take care of the needs of women.
>
> (2003, pp. 15–16)[4]

While characterising Kablye society as patriarchal and macho, she does not problematise the situation of women in French society. On the contrary, she situates the traditional and patriarchal society of Algeria in direct contrast and opposition with 'modern' French society in which women are emancipated. Considering her father arrived in France in the 1950s (Amara 2003, p. 17) this lack of interrogation of the situation of women in French society is strange. After all, women had only been granted the right to vote in France in 1944, and the *Trentes Glorieuses* with the emphasis on re-population led to a period of increased attention on women's role within the family and the re-affirming of patriarchy.[5]

Amara does note that the lack of freedom experienced by herself and her sisters was the same as many women of her generation, immigrant or not (2003, p. 15).[6] However by providing an explanation in terms of her parents' cultural traditions, Amara appears to reinforce the dichotomy often drawn in Western discourses on immigration between the 'backward' tradition of immigrants and the 'modern' enlightened (in this case French) State. This impression is reinforced later in the book when she describes the inequality of treatment of boys and girls within the family unit. While again, she notes that this is not limited to families of immigrant origin (2003, p. 41),[7] she first of all qualifies her critique of her parents with: 'One can't blame them, they were conditioned this way by their culture'(2003, p. 41).[8] This same explanation is not offered for French families; rather their patriarchal structures are situated in the context of the increased patriarchialisation of the *cité* (2003, p. 41). This, in the context of the slippage in popular French discourse between *banlieue* and *étranger/maghrébin*, does little to challenge dominant discourses which problematise immigration and ethnic minorities on the basis of an espoused 'feminist' concern.

Furthermore, while Amara asserts that the patriarchal domination of all women in the *banlieues* is her concern, she provides an explanation for the rage of young men of immigrant origin only:

> They live in a veritable state of schizophrenia: kings within the family and non-existent nothings outside. This lack of appreciation outside contributes heavily to their feeling of being excluded, rejected. They experience an intense feeling of injustice, which translates for those of immigrant origin into a feeling of not belonging to the Nation.
>
> (2003, p. 42)[9]

By framing this exclusion in terms of immigration and the Nation, Amara's analysis does not provide an explanation for the behaviour of the *français de souche*. This is interesting to note alongside the depictions of inter-personal relationships in the film, *La Squale*, discussed in Chapter 6. Here also, while there are a few White male characters included to demonstrate the ethnic mix of the *banlieue*, they are not substantial, and there is no exploration of their family relationships and gender dynamics in the film (aside from the fact that one of them does participate in the gang rapes), unlike the Black and North African characters.

So too, Amara provides the platform on which considerations of patriarchy and female oppression are tied up with immigration and national identity. Through feeling excluded from the Nation, she explains, young men of immigrant origin in the *banlieue* must assert their authority over the women of the *banlieue*. Therefore, the implicit solution to this is acceptance within the Nation, where, by giving a male sense of worth, respect and equality between the sexes becomes possible. This appears to echo the rhetoric of the Black Power movement in the US in which anti-racism was framed within the assertion of Black male patriarchy. As bell hooks has repeatedly argued (1994, 1992, 1990), this approach holds little benefit for women and in fact reinforces traditional constructions of heteronormative gender and national/ethnic identity. However, a look at the broader contemporary social and political context within which Amara asserts her feminist message provides some clues as to why she would frame her discourse in this manner.

'*Liberté, égalité, laïcité!*': The paradoxes of French Republican values

In terms of both feminist and anti-racist struggles in France, there has been an increasing division between those who continue to situate their discourses within the rhetoric of Republican values (emphasising the value of the principles and

170 Ni Putes Ni Soumises

contrasting these with a reality which does not properly apply them) and those who have in fact increasingly questioned the very foundation of Republican values, arguing that in fact it is the values themselves that have been used to legitimise and normalise inequality and hierarchies of power. For example, the *Parité* movement of the 1990s[10] began by explicitly problematising Republican universalism and equality and highlighting the historical exclusion of women from the public sphere. As one of the founders of the movement, Claude Servan-Schreiber, noted in an interview with the *New York Times*, '[e]xclusion of women has been part of France's political philosophy since the Revolution' (Scott 2005, pp. 3–4).

Similarly, the anti-racist association, *mouvement des indigènes* (famously associated with the 2004 blockbuster film, *Indigènes*, on the situation of soldiers from the colonies during the World Wars), has framed much of its political rhetoric around highlighting the hypocrisy contained within French Republican claims and situating these claims within the context of French imperialism (see Grewal 2011 for more on this). Discussing a book released in 1999 entitled *Françaises* and profiling six women from diverse ethnic backgrounds, Mireille Rosello points to a 'changing relationship between a historically universalist French tradition and two categories (gender and ethnicity) that challenge, in different ways, the utopian ideal of a genderless and, even more persistently, raceless Republican subject' (Rosello 2003, p. 97).

However, many authors have also pointed to the failure of anti-racist and feminist movements to profit from their interconnected challenge to dominant hegemonic discourses. While both have sought to challenge the universal abstract citizen, they have tended to do so by concentrating on only one aspect: the race or gender of this citizen. Moreover, it would seem that this lack of unity is more than merely an opportunity missed. For example, the *Parité* movement, while initially adopting innovative ways of challenging the gender bias underpinning French universal abstract citizenship, ultimately came to base its argument on the indivisibility of two mutually dependent sexes as the only truly universal difference. In particular pro-*Parité* philosopher (and wife of then *Parti Socialiste* Prime Minister Lionel Jospin) Sylvaine Agacinski emerged as the primary voice for the movement (Scott 2005).

Unlike some of the original proponents of *parité*, Agacinski relied on a much more essentialist and less radical process of reasoning in her support for the concept of *parité*. Not only did she describe the only one essential, 'truly universal' difference to be that of sex (dismissing other concerns of ethnicity, religion, amongst other things, as muddying the waters: Agacinski 2003, p. 18), she also sought to reclaim a femininity based on the image of the maternal. It was the devaluing of this role that was the problem she argued (Scott 2005, p. 117). So too, she celebrated the apparently exceptional French relationship between the sexes, based on complementarity:

> Men and women, here much more than elsewhere, have always sought to understand and to please one another, and they have not scorned borrowing

Ni Putes Ni Soumises   171

from one another qualities that are flaws in their own sex: a man with no grace or a woman without strength of character bothers us.

(Agacinski 1998, p. 159)

This statement presents a fascinatingly heteronormative and essentialised vision of gender identity (based on incredibly conservative norms) and, in this, Agacinski was not alone. In a book released in 2003, feminist historian Mona Ozouf also celebrated the lives of ten exceptional French women as representative of a broader tendency in French society towards a 'belief in love', which 'prevents the relationship between men and women from being interpreted as a war between sexes' (Ozouf 2003, p. 234). Through this a particular nationalist narrative emerged in which *l'exception française* was reasserted in the form of France's unique gender relations. Meanwhile the challenge to Republican universalism became limited to recognising the essential difference between male and female founded on reproductive difference.

As a result, rather than opening up space for identifying and addressing the various types of discrimination within the Republic, Republican feminism ended up in direct conflict with other social and political movements. The obvious heteronormativity of the *Parité* movement placed it in opposition to the contemporaneous *PaCS* movement seeking recognition of same-sex relationships (Raissiguier 2002; Fassin 2003). Meanwhile its rejection of all other forms of difference led to a pitting of feminism against anti-racism similar to that described in the Australian context earlier in this book.

It is therefore unsurprising that, while Amara claims to seek reform of both the racist and sexist structures impacting negatively on the lives of women of immigrant origin, she struggles to achieve this through her reliance on Republican feminist principles. This is precisely because the concerns of 'feminism' and 'women's rights' have been placed in direct opposition to 'tolerance of cultural diversity' within dominant discourses. The 2004 *affaire du foulard* provides an excellent example. As noted earlier, the issue of '*le foulard*' – the Muslim headscarf or *hijab* – has been a source of public controversy since the 1980s.

However while the original debate focused on the place of 'conspicuous religious symbols' ('*les signes religieux ostensibles*') within the avowedly secular space of Republican institutions like schools, over the ensuing decade the terms shifted. In December 2003 Fadela Amara, Samira Bellil and many other prominent members of *NPNS* joined a petition signed by Republican feminists and published in *Elle* magazine supporting a proposed law banning the *hijab* from schools. This petition (later republished in popular news magazine *L'Express*) was framed around the idea that the *hijab* was primarily a symbol of the submission of women, which had no place in a Republican institution that promoted equality. The issue of *laïcité* was also mentioned in connection with this position, but first and foremost it was asserted that such a measure was necessary to protect young girls from the pressure of male community and religious leaders and, even more so, from young Muslim men who increasingly sought to police the bodies and sexuality of young women in the areas in which they lived. This merging of discourses of

172   Ni Putes Ni Soumises

Republican *laïcité*, French exceptionalism and concern for gender equality both drew on a rich colonial history and became a key feature of contemporary national(ist) rhetoric.

In relation to the former, the *hijab* had long been a source of concern for metropolitan feminists and colonial administrators alike. On the one hand it was seen to symbolise the backwardness (and therefore inherent inferiority) of the colonised population, reinforcing French civilisational superiority and right to dominate. On the other it represented a potent symbol of resistance, perhaps best illustrated by Fanon in his 1965 essay 'Algeria Unveiled' and the 1966 film, *The Battle of Algiers*, in which fully covered women became key resources for the anti-colonial resistance, smuggling weapons past check-points under their robes (Mas 2006; Ardizzoni 2004, p. 631; Khedimellah 2004, p. 79). As a result of this mixed signification, throughout the history of the French colonisation of Algeria there were many attempts made to remove the veil from colonised women. As the French anti-colonialist, feminist movement *des Féministes indigènes de la République* highlighted, the ritual mass-unveiling of women in marketplaces or town squares across Algeria represented a potent symbol of submission to French cultural and physical might (Bouteldja 2006). Whether done in the name of 'emancipation' or to allow the coloniser to see into the 'closed sanctuary' of Algerian intimate familial space (Clancy-Smith 1999, referring to the work of colonial ethnographer General Eugène Daumas), the discourse of the undeniable superiority of 'French civilisation' was ever-present.

Meanwhile, as discussed in the previous chapter, Republican feminism has had a long historical intertwinement with the colonial project. For metropolitan French feminists the liberation of their downtrodden Muslim sisters led them to criticise colonial administrators not for the latter's racist attitudes and practices towards colonised peoples but rather their failure to fully enact the 'civilising mission' (Kimble 2006). Even as they were fighting for a complete overhaul of the French Civil Code back in France, for many Republican feminists it was the application of this Code in the place of Islamic law that held the key to Muslim women's emancipation (Clancy-Smith 1999).

Added to this, *laïcité* provided a crucial tool for the maintenance of colonial order and authority. As colonial administrators increasingly abandoned the idea of creating French citizens out of France's colonised populations, Islamic practices became a useful justification for the denial of citizenship rights. While Jewish Algerians were granted full citizenship in 1870 under the Crémieux Decree (*Décret no 136, 24 October 1870*), Muslim Algerians retained the status of 'subjects' and were required to apply to be 'naturalised' upon demonstrating a 'French way of life' (Weil 2003, pp. 6–7). This distinction was largely justified on the basis of the horrendous status of Muslim women. As Paul Cuttoli, mayor of Constantine and a leading opponent of a 1935 bill that proposed to extend citizenship rights to Muslim Algerians, asserted, 'the indigenous woman must see the end of this shocking inequality that exists between the man, the male, the lord, and his companion' before the indigenous man could be considered sufficiently civilised to hold French citizenship (Bowlan 1999, p. 184).

Ni Putes Ni Soumises   173

In contemporary discourses both *laïcité* and gender equality have been claimed as (exceptionally) French values. For example, Éric Fassin quotes a French government website explaining the Republican concept of equality:

> The principle of equality between men and women is a fundamental principle of French society. Both parents are equally responsible for their children. Women have the same rights and obligations as men. This principle applies to all, French citizen or foreigner. Women are subject to neither the authority of their husband, their father nor their brother in relation to matters such as, for example, working, opening a bank account or going out. Forced marriage is prohibited and monogamy and bodily integrity are protected by law.
>
> (Fassin 2006, para. 8)

These are admirable sentiments that unfortunately serve to mask the reality of gender inequality, which continues to impact on women's lives in France. As both the *Parité* movement and broader research regarding violence against women statistics in France show,[11] the recognition of women as equal and equally valued citizens is yet to be guaranteed. So what is the significance of these espoused principles? According to a number of scholars this claim for true democratic equality between the sexes, far from being aspirational, serves a very real ideological purpose: a means through which to re-establish dominant order in an increasingly diverse postcolonial France (Fassin 2006; Guénif-Souilamas 2006; Hamel 2005). It is within this context that *NPNS* has emerged, and this has inevitably impacted the message the organisation has been able to convey.

In March 2004 *NPNS* published the following manifesto on their website to accompany their nationwide demonstration:

> 6th March 2004 is the occasion in Paris and the whole of France to see march all those who wish to say loud and clear that without equality between men and women, the whole spirit of the Republic is in danger. To tolerate inequalities between the sexes is to cede to those who want to break France up through divisive communitarianism. It is now more than ever important to continue to fight for equality because we want to live together! Living together is only possible if and when we ensure respect of this fundamental right, which belongs to every human being, woman or man. The right to live in equality, dignity and respect. We denounce all forms of oppression and discrimination against women. At the same time, our feminist mission is also a fight for secularism: gender equality cannot be achieved if secularism is abandoned. Our movement, throughout France, has been trying for the last year to organise resistance to all forms of sexism, violence against women, obscurantism, fanaticism, which precarity and exclusion make more possible. So Saturday 6 March, let Paris be the capital of the Enlightenment, of feminism, of secularism and social progress.
>
> (NPNS 2004)[12]

174   Ni Putes Ni Soumises

By using the language of 'communitarianism' *NPNS*' message becomes focused on the question of ethnic diversity in France and the threat *this* is understood to pose to the otherwise egalitarian society. So too, feminism is inextricably tied up with French Enlightenment, modernity and secularism. The parallels between this discourse and that of the 'civilising mission' discourse central to the French colonial project are stark. As mentioned both above and in the previous chapter, feminism as an export of the West was a central feature of the 'civilising mission' used to justify the colonial enterprise. And in no other imperial project was the 'civilising mission' as central as it was in the French. Alice Conklin writes: 'Of course all European powers at the end of the nineteenth century claimed to be carrying out the work of civilisation in their overseas territories; but only in Republican France was this claim elevated to the realm of official imperial doctrine' (1997, p. 1).

Meanwhile, as I have also sought to show above, in the postcolonial context the 'clash of civilisations' discourse that has dominated French (and other Western) encounters with Islam has increasingly drawn on the issue of sexual equality as its justification. While this co-option of the language of 'women's rights' in response to the West's relationship with Islam and Muslims within and outside of Western nations is not specific to France,[13] the manner in which this discourse is framed relies heavily on the specificities of the French Republican tradition. The demonised figure of '*le garçon arabe*' is juxtaposed against both the exemplary principles of the Republic and the idealised figure of '*la beurette*', the model of successful integration, whose only obstacle to full modern Enlightenment is the patriarchal and misogynist traditions of her culture of origin.[14]

In framing their claim to be '*insoumises*' around the issue of the *hijab*, *NPNS*, however unconsciously, has promoted a discourse alarmingly similar to that used in relation to the 'liberation' of Algerian women through the removal of the *hijab*. In the context of France's historical relationship with Islam and the *hijab* in particular, the manner in which Amara and *NPNS* more generally condemn the *hijab* is illuminating. In asserting her rejection of the *hijab* as a symbol of female oppression, Amara begins by stressing her commitment to secularism: 'I, who place great value on fundamental freedoms, think that the religious practice is legitimate when it is freely chosen, without pressure or constraint, but above all when it is done in accordance with respect for the communal rule which is laïcité' (pp. 47–48).[15]

She goes on to discuss three reasons why the *hijab* is worn in the context of the *banlieue*. The first is the affirmation of a religious identity: the girls and women who wear the *hijab*, 'like a standard/banner' (2003, p. 48).[16] Her dismissal of this group is made clear by her statement that, in declaring their Muslim identity (also described as communitarian, with all the negative connotations contained in this term) these girls and women 'have the impression through this of being appreciated and respected'.[17] The implication is that this impression is, at best, misguided. Her description of the second and third groups of women and girls wearing the *hijab* is less subtle.

First, she describes those who wear it as doing so 'like an armour designed to protect them from masculine aggression', and goes on to add, 'under their "armour", they wear tight-fitting, revealing clothing, but these must not be seen in the *cité*. It is terrible to conceive of in a country of freedom' (2003, p. 48).[18] This statement highlights an important issue. The assumption by some men of the right to police the bodies and behaviour of women and girls is a genuine problem. This emerged in the discussion in Chapter 7, and I have personally heard this firsthand. As one woman living in a *banlieue* in Lille described to me, she was unable to leave her building without being spat at and called a 'slut' by young men.

However this is not purely a problem of the *banlieue* or of Muslims. As my earlier discussion of the 'Sydney gang rapes' demonstrated, the assumptions about 'proper' female comportment and attire are important foundations for rape myths that seem to exist across societies. Moreover the binary image of sexualised, tight-fitting clothes on the one hand and the *hijab* on the other leaves little space for a more profound feminist critique of societal obsessions with what women do or do not wear. Rather than seeing the possible sexist links between the sexual objectification of female bodies through revealing clothing and the demand for female chastity assumed by modest clothing, Amara simply reproduces the classic discourse of the *hijab* as a tool for denying female freedom.

In conforming to dominant representations of the *hijab* and the dichotomous position of the women who wear it as either victims or pawns, Amara reinforces a static and disempowering version of Muslim female agency. She leaves no room for Trinh Minh-ha's suggestion that '[i]f the act of unveiling has a liberating potential, so does the act of veiling' (1997, p. 416).[19] This un-nuanced analysis also does not sit well with observations such as that made by Hanifa Cherifi, a national mediator on issues related to the *hijab*. In an interview with *Le Monde* in 1999, Cherifi expressed her surprise when at one mediation the young women of Moroccan origin told her that in wearing the *hijab* they were disobeying their parents but obeying God and the Koran (Interview with *Le Monde*, 10 January 1999, cited in Dayan-Herzbrun 2000, p. 73).

Amara however reserves her strongest statement for this third group of women wearing the *hijab*, who she refers to as the 'green (Islamic) fascists' ('les soldates du fascisme vert'). She is scathing of their assertion of liberation through wearing the *hijab* and argues that these women are in fact 'dangerous to democracy' (2003, p. 48). In a manner similar to the events of 13 May 1958 during which the public unveiling of many Algerian women was staged in town squares across Algeria as a sign of their approval of colonial power (Bouteldja 2006; Dayan-Herzbrun 2000, p. 78), the veiling or unveiling of women of immigrant and ethnic minority origin becomes a means of demonstrating commitment to the French nation. As I argued above, *laïcité*, female emancipation and the civilisational superiority of the French Republic are all inextricably enmeshed.

In this context *NPNS* emerges as the ideal, demonstrating its commitment to the Nation through its endorsement of both Republican feminism and *laïcité*. In the process, other women of immigrant and ethnic minority origin have found themselves further marginalised. Activist with the association '*Femmes françaises et musulmanes engagées*' ('French women and active Muslims') and co-author of the book, *L'une voilée, l'autre pas* ('One veiled, the other not'), Saida Kada describes how in the national left-wing newspaper, *Libération*, she was accused in wearing the hijab of being, 'an accomplice to masculine domination and thus to gang rapes and other acts of barbarism' (Bouzar and Kada 2003, p. 145).[20] She also quotes a journalist from the local left-wing feminist newspaper, *Lyon Femmes*, who stated, 'the headscarf and the gang rapes come from the same contempt for women' (2003, p. 145).[21]

This has led French critical race and postcolonial feminists to critique the concentration on specific forms of sexism identified as belonging to a particular ethnic, racial or religious group (Roux, Gianettoni and Perrin 2007; Delphy 2006; Hamel 2005, 2003). In a similar argument to Razack (2004) discussed earlier in this book and my own earlier analysis of the 'Sydney gang rapes' (see also Grewal 2009), Christine Delphy (2006) has pointed to the ways in which this 'processus d'altérisation' ('process of othering') in France has served to hide hierarchies and power imbalances within society. This 'favours the stigmatisation of and discrimination against, not only people of immigrant origin but also women, the lower classes, homosexuals and perhaps even all subordinated groups' (Roux et al. 2007, p. 107).[22] The particular problem posed by an organisation like *NPNS* is that this process of othering becomes something not simply done by those within dominant society but also by those from more marginal or disadvantaged groups. As I have argued in relation to Dutch Somali woman Ayaan Hirsi Ali (Grewal 2012a), this requires those of us committed to a simultaneously anti-racist and feminist politics to construct our critique carefully. Even if we accept that there may be a certain degree of self-interest in the promotion of particular messages and impressions, the problems being pointed to are nonetheless real. While critics have identified Amara as a political opportunist,[23] many of the women (and men) associated with the day-to-day community level activities of *NPNS* are not. They are ordinary people who are struggling to respond to a variety of forms of discrimination and structural violence. It is for this reason that rather than simply dismissing *NPNS* I have sought to contextualise their message within France's historical and current socio-political setting.

Heterosexist feminism and the reinforcement of normative feminine identity

Returning to Amara's strong condemnation of the *hijab* and any form of feminine or feminist identity that adopts it, this leads to a consideration of the sort of feminine identity she promotes instead. It is also significant to consider the name of the association as it gives a deeper insight into the version of femininity being celebrated. By asserting that they are not '*putes*' the feminist framework within which they place themselves becomes explicitly limited. It is not a revolutionary claim for complete sexual autonomy that they are asserting. Rather – as with the Republican feminism of the *Parité* movement described above – *NPNS* ultimately conform to a normative conception of femininity that does not advocate complete sexual freedom. Nor does it seek to promote solidarity with a female sexuality that does not comply with dominant discourses that assert the centrality of heterosexual relationships and result in the propagation of the (patriarchal) family.

As Bellil demonstrates in her expression of her ideal relationship, the desire is simply one for a degree of respect and a lack of violence. While understandable, it is hardly a radical message. *NPNS* certainly does not seek to challenge the very structures of sexuality and family relations which many feminists argue require critical re-evaluation if the gender order is to really be disrupted. As Fassin observes in relation to the proponents of *parité*, sexual equality was reserved for gender equality only and based not on a recognition of the socially constructed nature of gender but rather a biologically determined role primarily promoted through motherhood (Fassin 2003, p. 32: he refers to Agacinski's article in support of this point).

If Amara asserts a rejection of a submissive female identity, she also endorses a certain type of femininity as 'authentic' and unproblematic. The nature of this femininity is perhaps particularly evident in her description of the various approaches adopted by girls in the *banlieues* to counter male aggression. In a section entitled, '*les "soumises", les masculines et les transparentes*' ('the "submissives", the masculines and the invisibles': 2003, p. 43), Amara briefly explains how each of these categories of girls and young women survive life in the *banlieue*. The first and the last are characterised by a lack of presence. They are seen as conformist and present little in the way of an identity according to Amara. The middle group is identified as the girls who choose to adopt male forms of behaviour and dress, which Amara clearly finds highly problematic:

> . . . dressed in tracksuits and sneakers, inconspicuous clothing to not appear feminine, and who use violence as a form of expression. These girls are very violent in their manner of speaking and their behaviour. They deal [drugs], fight – including with men – and don't hesitate to insult, to hit. Without ever showing a tenderness, which would be perceived as a sign of weakness. They are often worse than the men because when they attack they can prove to be harder and more sadistic. They have the same way of thinking and living as the worst machos: they act as if they had to 'come to the table'. To survive, to be respected, they believe it is necessary to always hit harder than the guys around them.
>
> (2003, p. 45)[24]

There are a number of noteworthy points in this description. The first is Amara's assumption that these young women's choice of clothes is a rejection of their femininity. In making this argument, Amara seems to demonstrate what Judith Butler (1999) has identified as the requisite disavowal of sexual 'sameness' central to the maintenance of dominant gender identity. Second, in critiquing their behaviour, Amara notes a number of times that these women or girls are worse than the men: more sadistic and tougher, more macho, more violent. It is possible to feel her disgust at this behaviour and her simple conclusion is that these women respond in this way as a result of their relationship to men of the *banlieue*. In doing

178   Ni Putes Ni Soumises

this, she first reinforces the undesirability of this behaviour generally but also specifically as a feminine trait.

Second, she imputes a lack of agency onto these women and a falseness to their identity that is highly questionable. While it does seem to accord with Samira Bellil's explanation of her behaviour (as discussed in the previous chapter), it seems somewhat reductive to assume that were these women to be allowed to express their femininity, they would do so in a way that was not violent or aggressive. The very fact that she describes these women as '*les masculines*' reinforces the binary heteronormative constructions of gender identity (men as the aggressors, women as passive recipients). As I described in Chapter 2, this logic was also drawn on by the Australian judges and led to a reinforcement rather than challenging of dominant narratives on rape.

However perhaps this articulation of normative gender identity provides a clue in answering the question: why have *NPNS* been so successful? As Joan Wallach Scott comments in France, 'republicanism and certain styles of heterosexual interaction are so intertwined that a critique of one is taken as an assault on the other' (Scott, 2003, p. 9). *NPNS* clearly seeks to challenge neither. Similar to other prominent Republican feminists, such as Mona Ozouf and Sylvaine Agacinski mentioned above and public intellectual Elizabeth Badinter (also a vocal advocate for the *hijab* ban), they instead celebrate a form of feminism that embraces *l'exception française*. As explained above, in this form of feminism there is no battle of the sexes, associated with the US feminist tradition, but rather a relationship of mutual dependence and appreciation. The emphasis on the Republican mythology of *l'exception française* as the foundation for this feminist statement highlights both the inextricability of constructions of national identity from constructions of gender identity in France and the centrality of heterosexuality to both.

The concentration of *NPNS* on the issue of sexual liberation has also contributed to the general eroticisation of the image of '*la beurette*' and to the creation of a sexual hierarchy between men. Christelle Hamel explains:

> Sexuality is thus a means of comparing people of immigrant origin to 'native' French men. The ethnicisation and racialisation of sexual and sexist violence, reinforces the inferiority of the former by stigmatising them and transforms the latter into the more desirable man. As a result, the decision of women of a minority group to choose a partner from their own or the other group is interpreted respectively as an invalidation and a validation of the assumed desirability of 'Arab' men. This message transforms every young woman of immigrant origin into an eroticised object of male sexual competition in which categories of 'ethnicity' or 'race' are drawn upon to symbolically situate the men involved.[25]

(Hamel 2005, pp. 97–98)

The body of '*la beurette*' is appropriated and turned into an erotic object over which the struggle for power between men is fought. Far from being a liberating discourse, this discourse reinforces traditional gender and national hierarchies.

Ni Putes Ni Soumises   179

Paradoxically, *NPNS*, far from rebelling against patriarchal order even just within the *banlieue*, has adopted a message that in fact conforms to and reinforces it.

Revisiting Republican integrationism

So why have these women of North African origin adopted a form of feminist discourse so heavily implicated in racist and colonialist language of the past? As I stated above, I do not accept the simplistic explanation that they are either co-opted dupes or self-interested opportunists. Instead I think it requires a deeper critical analysis of the frames they both access to make their claims and within which their claims are heard. For example, it is informative to consider Amara's assertion of her 'Frenchness' and the extent to which this has framed her political message. From the outset Amara distinguishes clearly between Algeria, which she sees as the country of her parents (they chose to remain Algerian citizens) and as unfamiliar[26] and France, which she identifies as her country. As she states in the beginning of her book:

> I am very attached to the region of my birth and if, one day, in the current debate about the withdrawal into communities (*repli communautaire*), someone asks me to define myself, obliging me to fit within a certain category, well at the end of the day I would define myself as an Auvergnate!
>
> (2003, pp. 13–14)[27]

In stating this, she appears to seek to demonstrate her loyalty. However her sense of belonging is not done with complete confidence. While she asserts that she felt no problem of identity as a child ('Yes, my name is Fadela, but I was born in France, at Clermont-Ferrand in 1964':[28] p. 18), the 'Frenchness' of her childhood is something she is at pains to establish:

> Like many kids, my childhood was filled with the classic fairytales, by the stories and legends where ogres occupied a prevalent place. Like many primary school students I read *Poil de Carotte* [French children's story], *the Little Prince*, I loved listening – on audio cassette – to the story of Peter and the Wolf, recited by the marvellous voice of Gérard Philipe [very popular French actor of the 1950s], with whom I was in love for a long time. Christmas was an equally important celebration for us . . . and every year I waited impatiently for Father Christmas to arrive with presents and candies . . . Easter was the same . . .
>
> (2003, pp. 18–19)[29]

Similarly she is at pains to repeat her love for French literature and culture, claiming that this was her sole inspiration during her school years. Her being born in France and holding nationality is not sufficient for her to feel she can convincingly assert that she is French. Rather, it is necessary for her to also demonstrate a cultural incorporation of what it is to be French. This is unsurprising in light of

180   Ni Putes Ni Soumises

her subsequent description of the disjuncture between her own experience of her identity and her realisation that this was not necessarily reflective of others' perceptions. She describes shock when considered to come from 'elsewhere' and gives an insight into a feeling of living in between: unconnected to the culture of her parents and yet not allowed to feel completely at home within the culture of her birth. A particularly striking anecdote she recounts provides a powerful demonstration of this marginal and ambiguous position she finds herself in:

> It was in the cradle of the Republic, the primary school of my childhood that I truly felt like a foreigner for the first time. The day when a well-meaning teacher, wanting to count the foreign children in the class, asked me to raise my hand. And yet, according to the Evian Accord, I had French citizenship.
>
> (2003, p. 19)[30]

Amara is very conscious in pointing to the ironic fact that it should be within the principal institution responsible for creating the French citizen (Déloye 1994; Weber 1976) that she first experienced exclusion. The Third Republic (1871–1940), drawing on the principles of Enlightenment philosophy, placed great emphasis on the creation of a sense of civic national citizenship, '[d]etached from parochial origins, belonging to no gender, race or nation, and guided by a blind faith in the connection between reason and civilisation, the new "Man" ... (Silverman 1999, p. 128), and this was conceived of as possible only through a highly centralised and freely available public education.

In recounting her experience of this institution, Amara appears to question the reality behind the myths of civic nationalism and Republican integration. She highlights an important tension between the apparent civic nature of French citizenship and the ethnic conception of nationalism and belonging. Yet, rather than rejecting these myths, she in fact draws on the language of Republican values in her defence:

> Deep inside myself, I knew with certainty that this wasn't France. My France – shared by many people of immigrant origin – is Enlightenment France, Republican France, France of Marianne, the Dreyfusards,[31] the Communards [members of the 1871 Paris Commune] and the Maquisards [members of the WWII resistance]. In short, the France of liberty, equality and fraternity. A secular France where the only principle which prevails is the development of consciousness and nothing else.
>
> (2003, p. 19)[32]

There are a number of ways in which to read this reclaiming of French Republican values and nationalist myths. This could potentially be an empowering position: by calling on the state institutions to act true to their founding principles. However, as numerous critics have pointed out (and as the subsequent mediatisation of *NPNS* appears to attest), this commitment to Republican values may not serve the desired purpose. As already discussed, the Republican myths of freedom, equality and solidarity have historically been used as a means of justifying incredible state violence both within the Hexagon and throughout France's colonial empire. Similarly, the WWII myth of resistance has been used in an attempt to wipe away the realities of the Vichy regime and the anti-Semitic violence committed independently of the Nazi occupation. It is therefore curious that Amara centres her political statement around upholding the 'true' Republican values on which *l'exception française* is built. One of the central paradoxes of Republican integration becomes apparent; Amara both represents the reality of cultural integration of a whole generation of French citizens of immigrant origin and the rejection by the Republic of these citizens based not on their cultural affiliations but their visible racial difference.

As I stated in Chapter 7, the most frequently cited reason for France's failure to integrate its immigrant communities is the new immigrants' apparent reluctance or incapacity to integrate due to the incompatibility of their cultures and religion (namely Islam) with democratic Republican principles. It is not incidental that within debates about 'immigrants' it is generally those from the Maghreb and particularly Algeria that are identified as the most problematic (Howell 2008; Derderian 2002; Stora 2002, 1999; House 1996, p. 220; Hargreaves 1995, pp. 152–159; Jelen 1991, p. 9). This belief in the unwillingness of certain immigrant groups to be integrated is in stark contrast to the findings of sociological research, which seems to suggest Amara's position is more representative. Various scholars both within and outside of France have documented a high level of cultural integration among second and third generation French residents from immigrant backgrounds. This is particularly amongst those of North African origin who predominantly speak French, are open to inter-marriage, adhere to French cultural values and norms and have birth rates that increasingly mirror White French birth rates (Laurence and Vaisse 2006; Tribalat, Simon and Riandey 1996; Tribalat 1995).

Instead it is in terms of social and economic mobility that immigrant communities have had limited success. As the *Beur* movement of the 1980s sought to demonstrate, it was not through active attempts to maintain other cultural or national affiliations that particularly second and third generation residents of immigration origin remained outside mainstream French society. Rather the problem was the widespread social and economic exclusion, segregated housing policies and the stigmatisation of the *banlieue*, which as I also explained in earlier chapters has become a symbol of both criminality or deviance and immigrants.

Although *NPNS* initially appeared to be attempting to revive the activism of the 1980s (and indeed Amara was a member of the original *Beur* movement), their concentration on sexism seemed to make it impossible for them to simultaneously critique economic and racial discrimination. If *La Squale* as the 'sister film' to *La Haine* sacrificed class and race critique to focus on gender, the same could be said of *NPNS* as the 'sister' of an organisation like *SOS Racisme*. *NPNS*' message became caught within the dominant rhetoric of French Republican exceptionalism in a way that reinforced rather than challenged the sexist, racist and colonialist foundations on which the Republic was built. At the same time, as with *La Squale*,

182 Ni Putes Ni Soumises

their visibility also contributed not to illuminating the problems of residents of the *banlieue* but rather further fixing dominant stereotypes.

Public reception of *NPNS*: Reinforcing the link between *banlieue*, immigrant, Islam and violence

The intense publicity *NPNS* has received has had two major consequences. The first is the further association of Islam with the *banlieue*, through the conflation of *banlieue* women and Muslim women. In one of many examples, a discussion on Muslim women's sexuality on the French television channel *Arte* on 8 February 2005 featured representatives from *NPNS* as *banlieue*/Muslim women. Furthermore, the most visible faces of the organisation are all women of Mahgrebin origin: in particular Bellil; the now deceased patron of *NPNS* and famous victim of gang rape, Loubna Mélaine who has also published a co-authored testimonial about her mother; Amara the founder; and subsequent presidents of the Association, Asma Guenifi and Linda Fali, all of whom are of Algerian descent. The second has been, through the association's often highly critical stance on Islam and its vocal support for the *hijab* ban, a reinforcement and perpetuation of the links currently drawn within French popular discourse between sexism, violence, Islam and the *banlieue*.

As a result, a number of academics and activists have been deeply critical of the association. Guénif-Souilamas and Macé (2004) argue *NPNS* has done little to challenge the racist and stigmatised representations of the *banlieue*. Instead, the association has further justified colonialist and racist discourses on the 'Arab'/Muslim and reinforced French patriarchal order. Certainly, the association seems to have done little to address the fact that representations of *banlieue* women are reduced to one of two positions: that of victim or of pawn of male domination.

By remaining within the paradigm of Republican values, *NPNS*' attempts to address the issue of discrimination and violence against immigrant/*banlieue* women have been limited to that perpetrated by 'their own' men. The *banlieue* is re-affirmed as a site of intersection between violence, misogyny, immigration and Islam, thereby justifying its residents' continued marginalisation. So too, the blind adherence to Republican values without situating them within the context of France's colonial and racist past, the continued pre-eminence of dominant patriarchal order and current anti-immigration and Islamaphobic trends allows for the reinforcement of dominant hegemonic identity and power structures.

In her critique of US feminist and civil rights movements, which have concentrated on equal access to state structures and institutions without actually challenging the system itself, Angela Gilliam writes, 'Neither movement has as its basis the transformation of the system at its roots' (1991, p. 216). This criticism seems to also capture the problems with *NPNS*. Neither Amara nor the organisation more generally question the validity of Republican values but simply claim greater access to them. As a result *NPNS* can hardly be seen as reflective of calls for radical change. In fact it remains very neatly within the confines of dominant public discourse.

Ni Putes Ni Soumises   183

The 1980s and 1990s in France were marked by a series of crises of representation and challenges to the Republican model. The *Parité* law represented a significant – if ultimately largely symbolic – victory for the feminist movement. The *Beur* movement in the 1980s, the revisiting of issues such as the use of torture in the Algerian War, improved pension arrangements for World War I and II soldiers from the former colonies and the increasing visibility of ethnic minorities in many areas of French social, cultural and political life have all impacted on the traditional French construction of its national identity. So too, with the *PaCS*, the heterosexual order on which Republican order has implicitly rested, has also been destabilised. It is therefore arguable that the reassertion of a heteronormative Republican national identity by an association embodied by immigrant women has provided a useful means of re-establishing dominant order.

Notes

1 'Mon histoire personnelle a sans doute beaucoup pesé dans ma manière d'analyser la situation des filles.'
2 An anti-racism activist education and training centre that works with young people in the *banlieue*.
3 Some scholars going so far as to argue that as a genre it is specifically female (Gugelberger and Kearney 1991, p. 8; Marín 1991).
4 'Mon père avait une idée assez simple de la place de chacun: les hommes et les femmes étaient certes égaux devant la loi, mais les hommes dehors et les femmes à la maison! C'était sa conception du monde, héritée de son éducation kabyle. Une vision très courante parmi les travailleurs immigrés. Quand mon père est arrivé en France, comment pouvait-il se rendre compte que ce modèle n'avait plus cours dans la société moderne qui l'accueillait – où les femmes pouvaient sortir, travailler et organiser leur vie – puisqu'il s'est installé dans une cité abritant presque exclusivement des travailleurs immigrés originaires du Maghreb? Les pères kabyles comme lui venaient d'une société patriarcale et machiste où les hommes avaient l'obligation de subvenir aux besoins de la femme.'
5 See Claire Duchen's 1994 book, *Women's Rights and Women's Lives in France 1944–1968* for an excellent overview of this topic, in particular Chapter 3.
6 'Mes sœurs et moi, nous ne pouvions pas sortir comme nous voulions. Situation à laquelle étaient confrontées nombre de femmes de ma génération, immigrées ou non.'
7 'J'ai été étonnée de constater que ce fonctionnement se retrouve à l'identique dans des familles de souche française.'
8 '[o]n ne peut pas leur en vouloir, ils ont été conditionnés ainsi par leur culture.'
9 'Ils vivent de fait une véritable schizophrénie: rois au sein de la cellule familiale et inexistants, niés, dehors. Cette absence de reconnaissance extérieure contribue fortement à leur sentiment d'être exclus, rejetés. Ils éprouvent un sentiment d'injustice majeure, qui se traduit pour ceux issus de l'immigration par le sentiment de ne pas appartenir à la Nation.'
10 A movement seeking an amendment to the Constitution to require equal representation of men and women in all French publically elected offices. This movement was launched at the end of 1993 following the revelation that France was second to last out of the EU nations in terms of women in decision-making roles with a dismal 4.3 percent of public officials women. For detailed discussion of the movement and its outcome, see Wallach Scott (2005).
11 For example, see Jaspard et al. (2001) for the first national study on violence against women.

184   Ni Putes Ni Soumises

12 'Le 6 mars 2004 est l'occasion, à Paris et dans toute la France, de voir défiler fraternellement toutes celles et tous ceux qui veulent dire haut et fort que sans égalité entre femmes et hommes, c'est tout l'esprit républicain qui est en danger. Tolérer les inégalités entre sexes, c'est abdiquer devant ceux qui veulent faire basculer la France dans le morcellement et le repli communautaire. Il faut plus que jamais continuer le combat pour l 'égalité parce que nous voulons vivre ensemble! Vivre ensemble n'est possible que si nous obtenons le respect de ce droit fondamental, dont dispose chaque être humain, femme ou homme, de vivre dans l'égalité, la dignité et le respect. Nous dénonçons toutes les formes d'oppression et de discrimination faites aux femmes. Dès lors, notre combat féministe est aussi un combat laïque: l'égalité femme/homme ne peut pas progresser si la laïcité recule. Notre mouvement, partout en France, essaye depuis plus d'un an d'organiser la résistance à toute forme de machisme, de violences faites aux femmes, d'obscurantisme, d'intégrisme, que la précarité et l'exclusion favorisent. Que le samedi 6 mars prochain, Paris soit la capitale des Lumières, du féminisme, de la laïcité et du progrès des consciences.'

13 See for example Bahramitash (2005, pp. 223–237) for a discussion of the US context; Razack (2004, 1998)

14 For a full discussion, see Guénif-Souilamas and Macé (2004).

15 'Moi qui suis très attachée aux libertés fondamentales, je pense que la pratique religieuse est légitime quand elle est librement choisie, sans pression ni contrainte, mais surtout quand elle s'inscrit dans une démarche de respect de la règle commune qu'est la laïcité'.

16 'comme un étendard'.

17 'ont ainsi l'impression d'être reconnues et respectées'.

18 'comme une armure censée les protéger de l'aggressivité masculine . . . [s]ous leur 'armure', elles portent des vêtement moulants, des décolletés, mais il ne faut pas que ce soit vu dans la cité. C'est terrible à imaginer dans un pays de liberté'.

19 And indeed an example can be found in the context of revolutionary Iran when educated, middle-class, Westernised women, rebelling against the banning of the *hijab*, adopted it as a symbol of resistance to the Shah and in solidarity with those promising a new, less corrupt regime (Tohidi 1991; see also Paydar 1995).

20 'complice de la domination masculine et donc des viols collectifs avec actes de barbarise.'

21 'e foulard et les viols collectifs relèvent du meme mépris pour les femmes.'

22 'qui favorise la stigmatisation et la discrimination non seulement des personnes d'origine étrangère, mais aussi des femmes, des classes inférieures, et des personnes homosexuelles, peut-être meme de tous les groupes dominés'.

23 And she has certainly been very successful: appointed as Secrétaire d'Etat chargée de la politique de la ville (Secretary of State for Urban Policies) in 2007 and then Inspectrice générale des affaires sociales (Inspector General for Social Affairs) in 2011, she remains a prominent political figure within France.

24 ' . . . habillées en jogging et baskets, tenue passe-partout pour ne pas assumer leur féminité, et qui utilisent la violence comme expression. Ces filles sont très violentes dans leur parler et dans leur comportement: elles rackettent, se bagarrent – y compris avec les hommes – et n'hésitent pas à insulter, à frapper. Sans jamais un geste tendre, qui serait perçu comme un signe de faiblesse. Elles sont parfois pire que les hommes, car quand elles agressent, elles peuvent se montrer beaucoup plus dures et sadiques. Elles ont la même façon de penser et de vivre que les pires des machos: elles font comme si elles les "posaient sur la table". Pour exister, être respectées, elles se croient obligées de frapper encore plus fort que les mecs qui sont autour d'elles.'

25 'La sexualité est donc le lieu d'une evaluation des descendants d'immigrés à l'aune des hommes français dits "de souche". L'ethnicisation et la racialisation des violences sexuelles et sexists infériorisent les premiers en les stigmatisant, ce qui transforme les seconds en hommes plus désirables. Dès lors, la décision des femmes du groupe

Ni Putes Ni Soumises   185

minoritaire de choisir pour partenaire un homme de leur group ou de l'autre groupe est interprétée respectivement comme l'invalidation et la validation de la prétendue moindre désirabilité des hommes dits "arabes". Ce message transforme chaque fille d'origine immigrée en objet erotisé d'une concurrence sexuelle masculine mettant en jeu des hommes symbolisant des categories dites "ethniques" ou "raciales".'

26 'c'est un pays que je connais mal' (2003, p. 17).

27 'Je suis très attachée à ma région d'origine et si un jour, dans le débat actuel sur le repli communautaire, on me demandait de me définir, en m'obligeant à entrer dans une certaine catégorie, et bien, au bout du bout, je me définirais comme Auvergnate!'

28 'Certes, je m'appelais Fadela, mais j'étais née en France, à Clermont-Ferrand, en 1964.'

29 'Comme beaucoup de gosses, mon enfance fut bercée par les contes de fées classiques, par des histoires et légendes où les ogres avaient une place prépondérante. Comme beaucoup d'écoliers, je lisais Poil de carotte, Le Petit Prince, j'avais adoré écouter – en cassette audio – l'histoire de Pierre et le Loup, racontée par la merveilleuse voix de Gérard Philipe, dont je fus longtemps amoureuse. Noël était également une fête importante pour nous . . . et chaque année, j'attendais avec impatience la venue du Père Noël pour les cadeaux et les friandises . . . Pour Pâques, c'était pareil . . . '

30 ' . . . c'est dans le creuset de la République – l'école de mon enfance – que j'ai véritablement senti pour la première fois que j'étais une étrangère, le jour où une institutrice voulant recenser les élèves étrangers, et pensant certainement bien faire, m'a demandé de lever la main. Et pourtant, selon la loi issue des accord d'Évian, j'avais la nationalité française.'

31 Intellectuals who protested the anti-Semitic treatment of French soldier Alfred Dreyfus.

32 ' . . . au fond de moi, je savais avec certitude que ce n'était pas cela la France. Ma France à moi – partagée par bon nombre de personnes issues de l'immigration – c'est la France des Lumières, la France de la République, la France de Marianne, des dreyfusards, des communards, des maquisards. Bref, la France de la Liberté, de l'Égalité et de la Fraternité. Une France laïque où le seul principe qui prévaut est le progrès des consciences et rien d'autre.'

10 Conclusion

I started this book with a series of questions that arose as I watched the debate on a specific set of gang rapes in France and Australia. As I have shown through my engagement with the different public discourses on these rapes, there were both important specificities to the responses in each nation and some interesting commonalities. In particular, while the forms of the discourses varied in both countries, a series of key concerns emerged in each. These broadly focused on questions of 'normal' gender identity and sexuality, race and culture and the identity of the nation in the face of diversity. In this the final chapter of the book I return to exploring the significance of the 'Sydney gang rapes' and '*les tournantes*' to constructions of gender, race and the nation in Australia and France and to consider what broader lessons these events may hold for those of us living in Western liberal democracies and committed to an anti-racist, feminist politics.

'Real rape' and the reinforcement of heteronormative gender identity

In both countries what went largely uncontested in the condemnation of these rapes were the normative constructions of gender identity and heterosexuality that made them possible. No discussion took place about how ideas of 'normal' masculine or feminine behaviour and sexuality might actually contribute to the perpetuation of rape. Rather, the way in which these incidents of sexual violence were characterised and responded to – while presented as demonstrating a 'feminist' sensibility – in fact conformed to classic heterosexist and patriarchal scripts. The various actors and commentators did not challenge – and in fact stabilised – a version of heteronormative gender and sexual identity in which women and girls are constructed as passive sexual objects requiring protection and men and boys are aggressive sexual agents prone to violence and conquest. Despite years of feminist work highlighting the rape myths that have served to both facilitate rape and to ensure inadequate redress to rape victims, there was little resistance to or questioning of these myths by any of the actors in the 'Sydney gang rapes' or '*les tournantes*'. We can therefore conclude that the reason these rapes secured the level of condemnation they did was due in part to their ability to fulfil the criteria of 'real rape'.

Conclusion 187

At the same time, it was not simply that these rapes could conform to dominant images of what 'real rape' looks like that they attracted widespread attention and condemnation. An important feature of both country's discourses was the narrowing of the focus to sexual violence committed by *particular* men: in the case of Australia, young 'Muslim' men; in the case of France, *banlieue* men.

The 'young Muslim man' and the 'good White nation'

The focus on the misogyny and sexist violence of particular men had a number of effects. First, it diverted attention away from the more widespread reality of violence against women committed by men across national, ethnic and social groups. As we saw in both the Australian and French cases, attempts to use these gang rapes to trigger a broader debate about both sexual violence and the inadequate social and legal responses ultimately became subsumed by the horror of these particular incidents. Instead commentators like Paul Sheehan capitalized on public concern to further demonise Muslim men and communities by suggesting that they were the reason levels of sexual violence were so high. In both countries the rapes were also used to justify stronger and harsher 'law and order' responses by the State, which in turn have led to the further stigmatisation and policing of already marginalised communities. It is a tragic but illustrative fact that Fadela Amara went on to serve as a junior minister in the government of François Fillon/Nicholas Sarkozy, the latter who famously suggested the 'scum' of the *banlieues* should be 'cleansed' using a high power pressure hose (Grewal 2011, p. 232).

Indeed even as actors such as those associated with *NPNS* began with a broader agenda to combat all forms of discrimination faced by the women of the *banlieue* (including racism and socio-economic exclusion), the frame within which they were able to both speak and be heard was too heavily saturated with existing imagery of the violent, sexist North African *banlieue* man. Thus, the second effect of the construction of *particular* men as sexist and sexually violent was that it justified a range of racist responses to their communities. It also became increasingly difficult to fight the racist generalisations being made about Muslims and the demands for either their greater policing or their expulsion without appearing to excuse horrendous acts of sexual violence. This resulted in the debate increasingly being posed as one in which anti-racism was necessarily in conflict with anti-sexism.

Pitting anti-racism against feminism

In relation to the racism versus sexism dichotomy, in each context the particular emphasis was different: in France, the exclusion of discourses of race meant that the focus became on gender relations albeit through a particularly racialised lens. In Australia the discourse of 'cultural tolerance' meant the discussion focused more on the future of multiculturalism with the particular gender dimension subsumed into the classic positioning of women's bodies as symbols of the nation. However what was common to both nations' discourses was the apparent

188   *Conclusion*

inability of commentators to articulate a simultaneously anti-racist *and* feminist response.

In both contexts 'women's rights' also seemed impossible to articulate outside a framework of Western liberalism. This led in Australia to respect for women's rights seeming to conflict with multicultural commitments to respect for diversity. In France, it meant that non-White women's activism either had to conform to a model of Republican feminism or be abandoned in the name of community solidarity to combat racism. In fact this setting up of a divide between '(women's) rights' and culture is a feature not just of these two national contexts but has also been well documented in other nations as well as within the sphere of international rights politics. In debates about the universality or cultural relativity of international human rights standards, it has been women's rights that have often provided the core site of conflict (Grewal 2016). The various responses to the 'Sydney gang rapes' and '*les tournantes*' show the deeply embedded conviction that feminism is inherently a product of the West, and (non-Western) culture is inherently patriarchal. At the same time, while commentators such as the judges alluded to an apparent 'respect for women' inherent within Australian society, the relative space actually given to a feminist politics in both countries itself requires deeper interrogation.

The possibility for a feminist politics

In fact in the French context there seemed to be greater space for a feminist response to the rapes than there was in Australia. In the latter the 'feminist' (or rather pseudo-feminist) discourse was by and large co-opted by conservative right-wing commentators, who have generally been unsympathetic if not openly antagonistic towards feminist politics in other situations. The attempts made by feminist figures such as longstanding anti-rape activist Karen Willis to focus debate on sexual and gender-based violence were too often appropriated and repositioned to focus on the specific threat posed by Muslim men. So too while Tegan Wagner's book is an articulate and insightful account that in many ways reinforces feminist analyses of rape and societal and legal responses, she does not seem to find a place for herself within a broader feminist politics.

It is also noteworthy that the only female voices in the debate were White. No non-White female voices were ever presented with the 'Muslim community' represented either through (male) 'community leaders' or 'representatives' or young Muslim men. This I would argue is reflective of the particular gendered and raced construction of the Australian nation. Since its foundation as a settler colonial nation the mythology relied upon in the articulation of national identity has been explicitly White and masculine. This can be clearly seen through all of the classic images of the 'ideal Australian': the 'battler' Bushman, the 'digger' (or ANZAC) and the surfer. Each represent a highly masculinised identity operating in spaces in which women are generally completely absent. As one author describes it: '[Australia's] public persona is a brotherhood summed up as mateship, an ideological representation of rough egalitarianism and "innocent male virtue" . . . It is a fraternity which

Conclusion   189

excludes Aboriginal men and male migrants from non-English-speaking backgrounds, and women from all backgrounds' (Pettman 1995, p. 67; see also Kirkby 2003).

Meanwhile the anxieties about keeping Australia 'White' that have lingered since the early days of colonisation and particularly with the advent of Asian immigration often manifested in concern about the possible sexual threat posed by non-White men. In this imagery the body of the White woman was simply symbolic and representative of the White community (Elder 2007, pp. 120–122, 2003; Batrouney 2002, p. 43; Pettman 1995). This exclusion of women has also informed the model of multiculturalism adopted by the State. Not only did this model reinforce the centrality of a White Anglo-Celtic identity as at the core of the nation, as numerous scholars have demonstrated (Gunew 2004; Jayasuriya, Walker and Gothard 2003; Hage 2003, 1998; Rutherford 2000), it also relied on a patriarchal approach to culture that is incapable of seeing or hearing women. Through the complicity of patriarchal elites from within different ethnic minority communities, this has led to non-White women being rendered virtually invisible in the public sphere.

The chanelling of all critical responses to sexual violence back through the framework of law and legal institutions also undermined the possibility for any radical disruption of the status quo. Thanks to the extensive work of critical legal scholars on the violence of law and its investment in maintaining rather than disrupting hegemonic power arrangements, this should not be surprising. However it is symptomatic of a larger crisis of left-wing politics in Australia, where it is not only feminists but a variety of social and political movements (including, for example, Indigenous and refugee rights) that have been seduced by the promise of the law only to ultimately be bitterly disappointed. This seems to suggest we need to heed Brown and Halley's unease back in 2002 writing about the US context:

> . . . that the left's current absorption with legal strategies means that liberal legalism persistently threatens to defang the left we want to inhabit, saturating it with anti-intellectualism, limiting its normative aspirations, turning its attention away from the regulatory norms it ought to be upending, and hammering its swords into boomerangs.'
>
> (2002, p. 5)

For Brown and Halley this points to a need to defend the project of left critique and resist the reduction of left political horizons to the project of law reform. As discussed earlier in the book, Australian feminist scholars have similarly expressed reservations about investing more in the project of law reform as a response to rape without a shift in social norms. The judicial discourses and Wagner's powerful account of her experience of the rape trial process seem to amply demonstrate the validity of these concerns. I see this as posing a challenge for those of us operating within the Australian public space to become more creative in our politics: feminist, anti-racist or other.

190 *Conclusion*

In this sense France provides an interesting contrast. As we have seen *NPNS*, an association with popular roots, led by non-White women asserting a feminist position has emerged as a significant player in French public debate. This could suggest a more generative and accommodating space for both social movements in general and feminist politics in particular. And certainly France has seen a wide array of such activism outside of the formal legal and political institutions of the State (a point I will return to in a moment). However I think such an optimistic reading can be tempered by a close reading of the ways in which *NPNS*'s message has been framed for it to achieve the status it has.

Notwithstanding the important everyday work being done at the level of *banlieue* communities, which I do not wish to dismiss, *NPNS* has not been an entirely progressive contributor to the French public sphere. As we saw, the narrowing of the association's focus to the misogyny and violence of the *banlieue* (read Muslim) man in fact allowed for a complete erasure of the sexism or patriarchy of dominant French society. At the same time, it helped support the further problematisation of *banlieue* men whose sexuality, criminality and anti-sociality all justified ever harsher policing and ever more violent exclusion by the Republic. The 2006 riots and State responses provide a good case in point.[1] This alongside the articulation of a form of mainstream feminist discourse that focused on (heteronormative) complimentarity of the sexes has served to legitimate hegemonic gender relations and neutralised challenges to dominant institutions.

Added to this, the relationship between French Republican feminism and the Arab and Muslim world requires colonial contextualisation. With the 'civilising mission' more central to the French imperial project than arguably any other European colonial power, Republican feminists provided an important ally to colonial adminstrators. This legacy while unacknowledged remains clearly visible within contemporary feminist discourses that focus on the problem of *banlieue*/immigrant/Muslim male attitudes and behaviour. Meanwhile non-White women have often found themselves co-opted as 'native informants' and/or symbols of successful integration, legitimating processes of domination in the name of the French Republican civilising mission.

The ongoing project of decolonisation

Various scholars have pointed to France's unresolved relationship with its imperial past (Tshimanga et al. 2009; Howell 2008; Blanchard, Bancel and Lemaire 2005; Dubois 2000; Stora 1999). This was powerfully illustrated in the attempt in 2005 to pass a law to teach the 'positive aspects' of French colonialism in schools.[2] While ultimately revoked due to widespread protests, the move indicates how deeply ingrained the fantasy of the civilising mission is in Republican mythology. On the one hand this continues to inform French approaches to questions of citizenship, recognition of difference (particularly Islam) and the place of residents from former colonised nations (namely Africa and the Maghreb). On the other, the legacies of the colonial project continue to haunt the Republic with its former colonised populations both highlighting the realities of imperial violence and representing an ever more visible part of French society (Grewal 2011, 2009). Within this context it is perhaps unsurprising that '*les tournantes*' were represented as symptomatic of particular cultures (namely North African and Muslim) and described using barely disguised orientalist language. Nor is it surprising that the 'solution' seemed to be a return to the more 'enlightened' form of Republican sexual relations. To counter this requires a critique that goes beyond the 'moral panic' response proposed by scholars like Mucchielli. It necessitates a much more sustained postcolonial critique and deconstruction of the founding myths of Republicanism.

In the Australian case, I see the concept of the 'nasty migrant' that I introduced in Chapter 5 as a useful device to deconstruct the 'colonial hauntings' (to paraphrase Gunew (2004)) within the national psyche. On the one hand the 'nasty migrant', in his violent rejection and indeed violation of the dominant community's 'welcome' (through his violent and racist attack on its women) exposes the regulatory core of Australian race relations. Through the positioning of the rape victims as 'White' and the identification of these rapes as an attack on the community, public discourses on the gang rapes were able to draw on and rearticulate classic settler colonial concerns about maintaining racial purity and dominance. Meanwhile the 'nasty migrant' also served the simultaneous function of shoring up the fantasy of 'goodness' of White settler society (Rutherford 2000, p. 15) by becoming the repository of racism, misogyny and violence. This speaks to a deep seated anxiety at the heart of Australian national identity, which struggles to legitimate its whiteness in the face of challenges from both Indigenous Australia and the reality of increasing ethnic and cultural diversity.[3]

Global Islamophobia

As I also stated in the introduction, while some of the discourses could easily be applied to the ways in which other non-White men are positioned in relation to sexism and sexist violence, the fact that there was a particular problematisation of Muslim subjects in both nations' public discourses is significant. While in the French case this can be explained by France's particularly troubled relationship with Islam and its Muslim former colonies/colonial subjects, Australia has not had such an extensive historical interaction with Islam or the Muslim world. And yet the stereotypes deployed in both contexts were strikingly similar. This would seem to support the argument that orientalist imagery has penetrated the West in general in ways that extend beyond the initial points of encounter.

The rapes and their responses also appear to reinforce the argument made by Poynting and Morgan that Islamophobia is/has become a globalised phenomenon with 'the racialized "Muslim Other". . . the pre-eminent "folk devil" of our time' (2012: p. 1). While in this book I have been critical of applying a simple 'moral panic' frame to analysing why these rapes attracted such attention (for reasons detailed in Chapters Four and Seven), the rapes clearly drew on and have been

192   *Conclusion*

used to support an ever greater demonisation and stigmatisation of Muslims. This is evidenced in the number of anti-immigration, anti-Muslim websites in various parts of the West that have sought to capitalise on these rapes to promote their message (Steyn 2002; see Dagistanli and Grewal 2012 for more). A similar trend is emerging again in response to the alleged sexual attacks by North African/Arab migrants and asylum seekers in Germany in early 2016 (McMah 2016; Richards 2016). This global Islamophobia is both a continuation of historic antagonism between the West and Islam – drawing on orientalist imagery and colonial discourses as discussed above – but also emerges as both justification for and result of contemporary geopolitical factors such as the War on Terror and neo-colonial interventions in the Middle East.

The postcolonial habitus

A final important if deeply troubling feature of the rapes was the ways in which the non-White actors themselves endorsed the racist, orientalist identities assumed within dominant discourses. As I have shown, not only did the Sydney gang rapists perform the worst stereotypes assumed of them (a fact one could write off as simply further evidence of their clear deviance) but so too did groups of young men in Sydney who sought to align themselves with the rapists. This version of 'protest masculinity', as some commentators described it, not only reproduced sexist and racist attitudes towards others but also towards themselves. Similarly, in the French context, both *banlieue* men and women seemed to accept a particular version of their identity as tied to inherently backward, barbaric traditions associated with their ethnic origins. The only escape from this, both seemed to agree, was through incorporation into White French society and its values.

In attempting to understand this behaviour I have developed a concept of a 'postcolonial habitus'. If Bourdieu has provided us with a tool – in the form of the habitus – to understand and reconcile the competing processes of structural domination and individual agency, then adding the colonial dimension allows us to also factor in historical conditions that necessarily shape both. In the case of the various non-White actors involved in the rapes and subsequent debates in both countries, the 'postcolonial habitus' allows us to see them as neither passive dupes nor as completely free, autonomous agents. Rather their struggles to articulate an identity for themselves that is not already shaped by racist assumptions demonstrate the ongoing significance of colonial power in the lives of postcolonial subjects. It cannot be coincidental that the male performances of their identity fit so neatly within the orientalist representations of the 'perverted, misogynist, barbaric Arab' critiqued so powerfully by Edward Said (1995). Nor is the fact that Samira Bellil sees the roots of her oppression to lie in the backwardness of her parents' culture, however understandable in light of her personal experiences, a position that can or should be taken at face value. Rather, as I have argued elsewhere I think these discourses require us to 'further interrogate how the legacies of colonial racial and gender orders continue to be rejuvenated and reproduced through the bodies of postcolonial subjects' (Grewal 2012a, p. 589).

Towards a new anti-racist-feminist politics

To conclude, a key argument is that the image of the 'misogynist Muslim' has been a very useful political tool. He has allowed for the construction of an image of a 'feminist' Australian/French society by comparison. This reinforces the inherent inferiority of 'Muslim' culture by contrasting it with the 'enlightened' values of the West (in this case specifically Australia and France). It denies the possibility of an internal feminist critique within Muslim communities that does not automatically subscribe to this discourse of Western superiority. It also removes the requirement for any deeper interrogation of constructions of gender and (hetero)sexual identity within dominant society and institutions. White patriarchal order remains essentially unchallenged. Added to this, the linking of particular cultures with acts of sexual violence provides the opportunity to link social problems of crime with concerns regarding immigration and ethnic diversity. This serves to undermine challenges to dominant constructions of national identity and the demands of recognition and equality by ethnic minorities. These demands can be rejected not through open acts of domination and racist oppression but in the name of a benevolent desire to protect the rights and safety of women.

Through both the rapes themselves and the subsequent responses to them, women's bodies were confirmed as sites of battle 'between men'. This allowed for hierarchies of civilisation to be asserted based on the apparently 'inferior' sexuality of non-White men. It also allowed the threat of sexual violence to be transformed from one faced by individual women to one faced by the community and the nation. This created tension in both feminist and anti-racist responses as they seemed to struggle not to conflict and undermine each other. For this reason I find it helpful to return to the words of seminal Black feminist scholar bell hooks:

> Sexism has always been a political stance mediating racial domination, enabling White men and black men to share a common sensibility about sex roles and the importance of male domination. Clearly both groups have equated freedom with manhood, and manhood with the right of men to have indiscriminate access to the bodies of women.
>
> (hooks 1990, p. 59)

Eloquently capturing what I see to be a key dimension of the rapes and their responses in both the contexts I have examined, hooks also suggests the importance of an intersectional politics as the only way forward.

While hooks was writing more than 20 years ago and the rapes and the debates they generated that I have chosen to concentrate on in this book occurred a decade or more ago, current events (particularly the debates in Germany discussed earlier) suggest that the lessons they raise for us remain as pressing today as ever. These lessons require us to reject the condemnation of violence against women if limited to only certain acts and certain groups. In this sense France has provided some interesting and potentially illuminating examples in recent times. For example

194 *Conclusion*

NiqaBitch who in 2010 created a piece of performance art that involved wandering the streets of Paris and visiting political landmarks dressed in short *niqabs*, hot-pants and high heels. In their slogan, 'Half Bitches, Half Submissives', they presented a clear critique of *NPNS* and the narrow types of femininity the organisation seemed to endorse. And while I am still undecided about their choice of presentation, their statement does question both the further intervention of the State into women's lives and the reduction of feminist issues to one of the niqab (Guidi 2015). The attention they generated presents at least one attempt to highlight both the continuum of sexism across communities and the political instrumentalisation of women's bodies.

I have also written about the movement *les féministes indigènes de la République*, who in 2007 presented a manifesto in which they declared themselves both the beneficiaries of French feminism and the daughters of anti-colonial heroines such as Solitude[4] and Jamila Bouharid.[5] (Grewal 2009, 2011). Over their short life, *les féministes indigènes* provided creative and insightful critique of the culturalisation of sexism and the importance of an intersectional politics that took into account race, class and gender. Unfortunately the movement has ultimately disbanded (for reasons I discussed in Chapter 8). However it is precisely this type of approach that seems so necessary if we are to generate possibilities for anti-racist feminist politics. Similarly promising was the far less publicised movement '*Ni Proxo Ni Macho*' (Neither Pimps nor Machos) that also emerged in the *banlieue* alongside *NPNS* and focused on male critiques of violence against women and particular modes of masculinity. It is through highlighting, documenting and supporting these alternate movements that a less divisive and distractive type of anti-racist and anti-sexist politics becomes possible.

In Australia there is a need to pay much greater and sustained attention to the deep-seated sexism within mainstream society. In a now famous speech in 2012 then Prime Minister Julia Gillard presented a damning critique of the misogyny she saw within Australian political life. It is this that I see as providing one of the greatest barriers to addressing violence against women across dominant and minority communities. For a start, this is through the placement of men in the position of constantly speaking for women (as was quite evident in the 'Sydney gang rapes') and then speaking about what for men is the most important aspect of the violation. In turn, the engagement with minority communities and the negotiation of 'tolerance' or 'respect' for difference currently takes place through the lens of a shared commitment to patriarchal order. This is either through the sexist assumptions about other cultures adopted by members of the dominant community (such as the assumed submissiveness of Muslim women) or through engagement with 'community leaders', who are almost invariably conservative male elites. This framework makes it virtually impossible for women and other marginalised or discriminated groups within ethnic minority communities to emerge as 'authentic' and legitimate voices. To combat this requires not only sustained critique of the racist assumptions underlying Australia's dominant nationalist myths but also the deep-rooted sexism on which they equally rely.

Notes

1 See Tshimanga et al. (2009) and the website http://riotsfrance.ssrc.org/ [Accessed 24 May 2016] for a range of scholarly perspectives on the 2005 French riots, many of which document the explicit links drawn (and conflations) by politicians and public commentators between migrant cultural practices such as polygamy and extended families, Islam, sexual dysfunction, scholastic failure and the violence.

2 *Loi française no 2005–158 du 23 février 2005 portant reconnaissance de la Nation et contribution nationale en faveur des Français rapatriés*, Article 4 – ' . . . Les programmes scolaires reconnaissent en particulier le rôle positif de la présence française outre-mer, notamment en Afrique du Nord, et accordent à l'histoire et aux sacrifices des combattants de l'armée française issus de ces territoires la place éminente à laquelle ils ont droit.' This law passed but was subsequently repealed in January 2006 due to intense public pressure (Howell 2008, p. 59).

3 In this sense I am reminded of Elizabeth Povinelli's (1998) reflections on the device of 'shame' regarding indigenous dispossession that served to solidify the Australian state as inherently White (Anglo-Celtic) in a way that both constantly set up Indigenous Australians as 'Others' (to be reconciled with) and excluded all other immigrant arrivals (who could not be 'embedded' and 'implicated' in the national history in the same way). While drawing on a different set of affects, the need to set up a White core that simultaneously contains and manages the racialised others of the Indigenous and the Immigrant is, I would argue, symptomatic of the same anxiety.

4 A leader of the Guadeloupe slave uprising.

5 Hero of the Algerian war.

Bibliography

Adkins, L. and Skeggs, B. eds. 2004. *Feminism after Bourdieu*. Oxford: The Sociological Review, Blackwell.

—— 2004. Reflexivity: Freedom or habit of gender? In Adkins, L. and Skeggs, B. eds. *Feminism after Bourdieu*. Oxford: The Sociological Review, Blackwell.

Agacinski, S. 2003. The turning point of feminism. In Célestin, R., DalMolin, E. and de Courtivron, I. eds. *Beyond French Feminisms: Debates on Women, Politics, and Culture in France, 1981–2001*. New York and Basingstoke: Palgrave Macmillan.

—— 1998. *Politique des sexes*. Paris: Seuil.

Akkermann, T. and Hagelund, A. 2007. 'Women and children first!' Anti-immigration parties and gender in Norway and the Netherlands. *Patterns of Prejudice*, 41(2), pp. 197–214.

Albrechtsen, J. 2006a. Heed the PM's call for women's rights. *The Australian*, 6 September 2006.

—— 2006b. Human rights can no longer be sacrosanct. *The Australian*, 13 September 2006.

—— 2004. Let us not overlook the race factor. *The Australian*, 17 March 2004.

—— 2002. Talking race not racism. *The Australian*, 17 July 2002.

Alexander, M.J. and Mohanty, C.T. eds. 1997. *Feminist Genealogies, Colonial Legacies, Democratic Futures*. New York and London: Routledge.

Alloula, M. 1987. *The Colonial Harem* (translated by M. Godzich and W. Godzich). Manchester: Manchester University Press.

Al-Shahi, A. and Lawless, R. eds. 2005. *Middle East and North African Immigrants in Europe*. London and New York: Routledge.

Amara, F. 2003. *Ni Putes Ni Soumises*. Paris: Éditions La Découverte.

Anti-Discrimination Board of New South Wales (ADB). 2003. Race for the headlines: Racism and media discourse, 13 February 2003. Available at: www.lawlink.nsw.gov.au/adb.nsf/pages/raceheadlines [Accessed 1 April 2004].

Ardizzoni, M. 2004. Unveiling the veil: Gendered discourses and the (in)visibility of the female body in France. *Women's Studies*, 33, pp. 629–649.

Asad, T. 1986. The concept of cultural translation in British social anthropology. In Clifford, J. and Marcus, G.E. eds. *Writing Culture: The Poetics and Politics of Ethnography*. Berkeley, Los Angeles and London: University of California Press.

Australian Associated Press (AAP). 2008. Skaf: 'Brand Name' for gang rapist. *Sydney Morning Herald*, 22 June 2008.

—— 2007. Be sensitive to rape victim filmmakers urged. *Sydney Morning Herald*, 28 January 2007.

Bibliography 197

——— 2007. Misgivings over gang rape film. *Sydney Morning Herald*, 29 January 2007.

——— 2006. Cleric's comments condemned. *Sun Herald*, 26 October 2006.

——— 2006. Deport rape comment cleric, says Goward. *The Age*, 26 October 2006.

——— 2005. Terrorism, gang rapes behind riots: MP. *Sydney Morning Herald*, 12 December 2005.

Australian Broadcasting Corporation (ABC). 2006. *Four Corners*, 13 March 2006. Available at: www.abc.net.au/4corners/content/2006/s1590953.htm [Accessed 31 October 2006].

——— 2002a. Criminal gang or Islamic gangs? *Media Watch*, 9 September 2002. Available at: www.abc.net.au/mediawatch/transcripts/090902_s2.htm [Accessed 3 November 2006].

——— 2002b. Ethnicity linked to brutal gang rapes. *The 7:30 Report*, 15 July 2002. Available at: www.abc.net.au/7:30/content/2002/s607757.htm [Accessed 28 September 2007].

——— 2002c. Sentencing of Bilal Skaf. Unreported judgement of the District Court of New South Wales, transcript, 15 August 2002. Available at: www.abc.net.au/4corners/stories/s675775.htm [Accessed 29 August 2016].

——— 2001. Ethnic crime under Sydney scrutiny. *Lateline*, 22 August 2001. Available at: www.abc.net.au/lateline/stories/s351038 [Accessed 28 September 2007].

Awkward, M. 1995. *Negotiating Difference: Race, Gender and the Politics of Positionality*. Chicago and London: University of Chicago Press.

Backhouse, C. 2003. The chilly climate for women judges: Reflections on the backlash from the *Ewanchuk* case. *Canadian Journal of Women and the Law*, 15(1), pp. 167–193.

Bahramitash, R. 2005. The war on terror, feminist orientalism and orientalist feminism: Case studies of two North American bestsellers. *Critique: Critical Middle Eastern Studies*, 14(2), pp. 223–237.

Bakhtin, M.M. 1981. Discourse in the novel. In Holquist, M. ed. *The Dialogic Imagination: Four Essays* (translated by C. Emerson and M. Holquist). Austin, TX: University of Texas Press.

Barthe, B. 2000. Banlieue, les meufs contre-attaquent. *L'Humanité*, 2 December 2000.

Batrouney, T. 2002. From 'White Australia' to multiculturalism: Citizenship and identity. In Hage, G. ed. *Arab-Australians Today: Citizenship and Belonging*. Carlton, VIC: Melbourne University Press.

Baudin, G. and Genestier, P. eds. 2002. *Banlieues à Problèmes: La construction d'un problème social et d'un thème d'action publique*. Paris: La documentation Française.

Behrendt, L. 1993. Aboriginal women and the White lies of the feminist movement: Implications for Aboriginal women in rights discourses. *Australian Feminist Law Journal*, 27(1), pp. 27–44.

Bellil, S. 2003. *Dans l'enfer des tournantes*. Paris: Denoël Impacts.

Benabdessadok, C. 2004. Ni Putes Ni Soumises: de la marche à l'université d'automne. *Mouvements*, 1248, pp. 64–74.

Bigo, D. and Guild, E. eds. 2005. *Controlling Frontiers: Free Movement into and within Europe*. Aldershot and Burlington: Ashgate.

Binet, S. 2003. Des rappeurs et rappeuses face aux propositions des Ni Putes Ni Soumises: 'Ça devrait être une cause nationale'. *Libération*, 4 October 2003.

Blanchard, P., Bancel, N. and Lemaire, S. eds. 2005. *La Fracture colonial: la société française au prisme de l'héritage colonial*. Paris: La Découverte.

Bloul, R. 1998. From moral protest to religious politics: Ethical demands and beur political action in France. *Australian Journal of Anthropology*, 9(1), pp. 11–30.

198   *Bibliography*

Bone, P. 2002. Rape: The debate we have to have. *The Age*, 24 July 2002.

Boulé, J.P. 2002. *HIV Stories: The Archaeology of AIDS Writing in France, 1985–1988*. Liverpool, UK: Liverpool University Press.

Bourdieu, P. 2003. Symbolic violence. In Célestin, R. et al. eds. *Beyond French Feminisms: Debates on Women, Politics, and Culture in France, 1981–2001*. New York and Basingstoke: Palgrave Macmillan.

——— 2000. *Pascalian Meditations* (translated by Richard Nice). Oxford: Polity Press and Blackwell.

——— 1998. *La Domination Masculine*. Paris: Seuil.

——— 1982. *Ce que parler veut dire: l'economie des échanges linguistiques*. Paris: Fayard.

——— 1977. *Outline of a Theory of Practice* (translated by Richard Nice). Cambridge, UK: Cambridge University Press.

——— 1972. *Esquisse d'une théorie de la pratique*. Genève: Librairie Droz.

Bourgois, P. 1996. In search of masculinity: Violence, respect and sexuality among Puerto Rican crack dealers in East Harlem. *British Journal of Criminology*, 36(3), pp. 412–428.

Bouteldja, H. 2006. De la cérémonie du dévoilement à Alger (1958) à Ni Putes Ni Soumises: l'instrumentalisation coloniale et néo-coloniale de la cause des femmes, 18 June 2006. Available at: www.indigenes-republique.org/spip.php?page=imprimerandid_article+152 [Accessed 1 June 2007].

Bouzar, D. and Kada, S. 2003. *L'une voilée, l'autre pas*. Paris: Éditions Albin Michel.

Bowker, L.H. ed. 1998. *Masculinities and Violence*. Thousand Oaks, London and New Delhi: SAGE Publications.

Brearley, D. 2002. Ethnicity and bad publicity a volatile mix. *The Australian*, 9 May 2002.

British Broadcasting Corporation (BBC). 2016. Germany shocked by Cologne New Year gang assaults on women, 5 January 2016. Available at: www.bbc.com/news/world-europe-35231046 [Accessed 8 June 2016].

Brod, H. and Kaufman, M. eds. 1994. *Theorizing Masculinities*. Thousand Oaks, London and New Delhi: SAGE Publications.

Browning, J. and Jakubowicz, A. 2004. Respect and racism in Australia: Discussion Paper No. 2. *Racism Monitor*. University of Technology, Sydney. Available at: www.fairgo.net [Accessed 3 November 2006]

Brownmiller, S. 1975. *Against Our Will: Men, Women and Rape*. New York and Toronto: Bantam Books.

Brubaker, R. 1992. *Citizenship and Nationhood in France and Germany*. Cambridge, MA: Harvard University Press.

Brush, P.S. 2001. Problematizing the race consciousness of women of color. *Signs*, 27(1), pp. 171–198.

Buddie, A.M. and Miller, A.G. 2001. Beyond rape myths: A more complex view of perceptions of rape victims. *Sex Roles: A Journal of Research*, 45(3/4), pp. 139–161.

Bumiller, K. 1998. Fallen angels: The representation of violence against women in legal culture. In Daly, K. and Maher, L. eds. *Criminology at the Crossroads: Feminist Readings in Crime and Justice*. New York and Oxford: Oxford University Press.

Butler, J. 1999. *Gender Trouble* (10th edition). New York: Routledge.

Butler, J. and Scott, J.W. eds. 1992. *Feminists Theorize the Political*. New York and London: Routledge.

Caldas-Coulthard, C.R. and Coulthard, M. eds. 1996. *Texts and Practices: Readings in Critical Discourse Analysis*. London and New York: Routledge.

Carty, L. 2008. Rapist sparks jail alert. *Sydney Morning Herald*, 14 September 2008.

Bibliography 199

Carver, T. 1998. Sexual citizenship: Gendered and de-gendered narratives. In Carver, T. and Mollier, V. eds. *Politics of Sexuality: Identity, Gender, Citizenship*. London and New York: Routledge.

Carver, T. and Mottier, V. eds. 1998. *Politics of Sexuality: Identity, Gender, Citizenship*. London and New York: Routledge.

Célestin, R., DalMolin, E. and de Courtivron, I. eds. 2003. *Beyond French Feminisms: Debates on Women, Politics, and Culture in France, 1981–2001*. New York and Basingstoke: Palgrave Macmillan.

Césari, J. 2005. Ethnicity, Islam and les banlieues: Confusing the issues. *Social Science Research Council (US) web forum*, 30 November 2005. Available at: http://riotsfrance.ssrc.org/ [Accessed 24 May 2016].

Chambon, F. 2001a. Dix jeunes gens comparaissent aux assises pour une 'tournante'. *Le Monde*, 26 April 2001.

——— 2001b. Les viols collectifs rélèvent la misère affective et sexuelle des cites. *Le Monde*, 24 April 2001.

——— 2001c. Une fille qui se fait "tourner" dans le quartier, c'est elle qui l'a cherché. *Le Monde*, 24 April 2001.

——— 2001d. À Besançon quatre mineurs soupçonnés d'avoir violé une jeune fille de treize ans. *Le Monde*, 24 April 2001.

——— 2000. 'La Squale', une fiction militante pour alerter l'opinion. *Le Monde*, 29 November 2000.

Chambon, F. and Laronche, M. 2002. Pour les garçons, celle qui fume dans la rue ou qui n'est plus vierge, c'est une pute. *Le Monde*, 25 October 2002.

Chatterjee, P. 1993. *The Nation and Its Fragments: Colonial and Postcolonial Histories*. Princeton, NJ: Princeton University Press.

Chesterton, S. 2007. Plea for change to rape script. *Daily Telegraph*, 7 May 2007.

Christophe, S. 2001. Tournante. *Letter to Le Monde*, 6–7 May 2001.

Clancy-Smith, J. 1999. Islam, gender, and identities in the making of French Algeria, 1830–1962. In Clancy-Smith, J. and Gouda, F. eds. *Domesticating the Empire: Race, Gender and Family Life in French and Dutch Colonialism*. Charlottesville and London: Virginia University Press.

Clancy-Smith, J. and Gouda, F. eds. 1999. *Domesticating the Empire: Race, Gender and Family Life in French and Dutch Colonialism*. Charlottesville and London: Virginia University Press.

Clark, H. 2007. Judging rape: Public attitudes and sentencing. *Aware: Australian Centre for the Study of Sexual Assault Newsletter*, No. 14, June 2007, Australian Institute of Family Studies, pp. 17–25.

Coates, L., Bavelas, J. and Gibson, J. 1994. Anomalous language in sexual assault trial judgements. *Discourse and Society*, 5, pp. 189–206.

Collins, J. 1998. Language, subjectivity, and social dynamics in the writings of Pierre Bourdieu. *American Literary History*, 10(4), pp. 725–732.

Collins, J., Noble, G., Poynting, S. and Tabar, P. 2000. *Kebabs, Kids, Cops and Crime*. Annandale, NSW: Pluto Press.

Commission of Experts on the former Yugoslavia established by the UN Security Council, Resolution 780 (1992), *Final Report*, UN Doc. S/1994/674 (27 May 1994). Available at: www.his.com/~twarrick/commxyu1.htm [Accessed 7 July 2008].

Conklin, A.L. 1999. Redefining 'Frenchness': Citizenship, race regeneration, and imperial motherhood in France and West Africa, 1914–40. In Clancy-Smith, J. and Gouda, F. eds. *Domesticating the Empire: Race, Gender and Family Life in French and Dutch Colonialism*. Charlottesville and London: Virginia University Press.

200   *Bibliography*

——— 1997. *A Mission to Civilize: The Republican Idea of Empire in France and West Africa, 1895–1930*. Stanford, CA: Stanford University Press.

Connell, R.W. 2002. *Gender*. Cambridge, UK and Malden, MA: Blackwell Publishers and Polity Press.

——— 2000. *The Men and the Boys*. St Leonards, NSW: Allen and Unwin.

——— 1995. *Masculinities*. St Leonards, NSW: Allen and Unwin.

Connolly, E. 2008. Evil rapist back on the street. *The Daily Telegraph*, 15 June 2008.

Connolly, E. and Moran, J. 2007. Film outrage. *Daily Telegraph*, 28 January 2007.

Connolly, W.E. 1991. *Identity/difference*. Ithaca: Cornell University Press.

Cook, B., David, F. and Grant, A. 2001. Sexual Violence in Australia. *Australian Institute of Criminology Research and Public Policy Series No. 36*, Canberra: Australian Institute of Criminology.

Coss, G. 2006. The defence of provocation: An acrimonious divorce from reality. *Current Issues in Criminal Justice*, 18(1), pp. 51–78.

Cossins, A. 2000. *Masculinities, Sexualities and Child Sexual Abuse*. Boston and The Hague: Kluwer Law International.

Costello, P. 2006. Solar rebates, solar energy, Muslim cleric's comments on women. Interview with Melissa Doyle and David Koch, *Sunrise*, Channel 7, 26 October 2006. Available at: www.treasurer.gov.au/tsr/content/transcripts/2006/157.asp [Accessed 1 November 2006].

——— 2004. Address to National Day of Thanksgiving Commemoration, Scots Church, Melbourne, 29 May 2004. Available at: www.treasurer.gov.au/tsr/content/speeches/2004/007.asp?pf=1 [Accessed 3 November 2006].

Couldry, N. and Dreher, T. 2007. Globalization and the public sphere: Exploring the space of community media in Sydney. *Global Media and Communication*, 3(1), pp. 79–100.

Coutant, I. 2007. The sociologist, the juvenile delinquent and the public arena: An ethnographic investigation in the Parisian suburbs of the early 2000s. Paper presented at *Ethnofeast III: Ethnography and the Public Sphere Conference*, Instituto Superior de Ciências do Trabalho e da Empresa, Lisbon, 20–23 June 2007. Available at: http://ceas.iscte.pt/ethnografeast/panels.html#icoutant [Accessed 10 December 2008].

Cowdery, N. 2005. Current issues in the prosecution of sexual assault. *University of New South Wales Law Journal*, 12. Available at: www.austlii.edu.au/au/journals/UNSWLJ/2005/12.html [Accessed 12 December 2008].

Crenshaw, K. 1991. Mapping the margins: Intersectionality, Identity politics and violence against women of color. *Stanford Law Review*, 43, pp. 1241–1299.

Crichton, S. and Stevenson, A. 2002. Crime and prejudice. *Sydney Morning Herald*, 14 September 2002.

Cronin, C. 1996. Bourdieu and Foucault on power and modernity. *Philosophy and Social Criticism*, 22(6), pp. 55–85.

Crossley, N. and Roberts, J.M. 2004. *After Habermas: New Perspectives on the Public Sphere*. Oxford and Malden, MA: Blackwell Publishing.

Crowley, J. 2005. Where does the state actually start? The contemporary governance of work and migration. In Bigo, D. and Guild, E. eds. *Controlling Frontiers: Free Movement into and within Europe*. Aldershot and Burlington: Ashgate.

Dagistanli, S. 2005. Consent, the 'lascivious Arab' and standards of reasonableness in legal and official discourses. *Conference on Racism in the New World Order*, Southern Cross University, Hyatt Regency, Coolum, Queensland, 8–9 December 2005. Available at: www.usc.edu.au/NR/rdonlyres/EBFE0A88–2291–4CEF-AF83–735E11E494A4/0/RacismsConf2revised.pdf [Accessed 10 November 2008].

Bibliography   201

Dagistanli, S. and Grewal, K. 2012. Perverse Muslim masculinities in contemporary orientalist discourse: The vagaries of Muslim immigration in the West. In Morgan, G. and Poynting, S. eds. *Global Islamophobia: Muslims and Moral Panic in the West*. Surrey, UK: Ashgate.

d'Arrigo, J. 2001. 'Tournante': le calvaire d'une jeune handicapée. *Le Figaro*, 25 May 2001.

Dayan-Herzbrun, S. 2000. The issue of the Islamic headscarf. In Freedman, J. and Tarr, C. eds. *Women, Immigration and Identities in France*. Oxford and New York: Berg Publishers.

de Beauvoir, S. 1949. *Le deuxième sexe*. Paris: Gallimard.

'Debra'. 2003. The self-confessed perpetrator and the Australian legal system that sanctioned a crime. *Women Against Violence*, 14, pp. 53–61.

de Brito, K. 2001. Rape is not an issue of ethnicity. *The Sunday Telegraph*, 26 August 2001.

de Carvalho Figueiredo, D. 2004. Representations of rape in discourse of legal decisions. In Young, L. and Harrison, C. eds. *Systemic Functional Linguistics and Critical Discourse Analysis: Studies in Social Change*. London and New York: Continuum International.

de Langhe, A.C. 2001. Violences: sept jeunes juges à Versailles pour des abus sexuels perpétrés en groupe sur une adolescente – Viols collectifs: l'odieux rituel des 'tournantes'. *Le Figaro*, 2 May 2001.

Déloye, Y. 1994. *École et Citoyenneté. L'individualisme républicain de Jules Ferry à Vichy: Controversies*. Paris: Presses de Sciences Po.

Delphy, C. 2006. Antisexisme ou antiracisme? Un faux dilemma. *Nouvelles Questions Féministes*, 25(1), pp. 59–83.

Derderian, R.L. 2004. *North Africans in Contemporary France: Becoming Visible*. New York and Basingstoke: Palgrave Macmillan.

——— 2002. Algeria as a *lieu de mémoire*: Ethnic minority memory and national identity in contemporary France. *Radical History Review*, 83, pp. 28–43.

Devine, M. 2006. How a vile sermon of ignorance has done Australia a big favour. *Sydney Morning Herald*, 29 October 2006.

———2005. Absent father who bred a gaggle of monsters. *The Sun-Herald*, 24 July 2005.

——— 2003. Betraying the rape victims. *The Sun-Herald*, 30 November 2003.

——— 2002. Racist rapes: Finally the truth comes out. *The Sun-Herald*, 14 July 2002.

Dhareshwar, V. 1989. Self-fashioning, colonial habitus, and double exclusion: V.S. Naipaul's *The Mimic Men*. *Criticism: A Quarterly for literature and the arts*, XXXI(1), pp. 75–102.

Dhoquois, A. 2003. Les rapports de sexe dans les banlieues. *Comme la Ville* (Ministère délégué à la ville et à la rénovation urbaine), 10, pp. 30–32.

Dirks, N.B. 2001. *Castes of Mind: Colonialism and the Making of Modern India*. Princeton: Princeton University Press.

Dubois, L. 2000. *La République Métissée*: Citizenship, colonialism, and the borders of French history. *Cultural Studies*, 14(1), pp. 15–34.

Duchen, C. 1994. *Women's Rights and Women's Lives in France 1944–1968*. London and New York: Routledge.

Duff, E. 2002. Crisis centre says gang rape a problem across all races. *Sun-Herald*, 21 July 2002.

Duncan, N. ed. 1996, *Bodyspace: Destabilizing Geographies of Gender and Sexuality*. London and New York: Routledge.

Duparc Portier, P. 2006. Media reporting of trials in France and in Ireland. *Judicial Studies Institute Journal*, 6(1), pp. 197–238.

202   *Bibliography*

Durand, J. 2002. La 'tournante' d'Argenteuil et l'incompréhension des parents: 'Pas mon fils, il n'a pas pu faire ça. *Libération*, 5 November 2002.

du Tanney, P. 2001. Une bande de violeurs aux assises. *Le Figaro*, 25 April 2001.

Dworkin, A. 1995. *Intercourse*. New York: Free Press Paperbacks.

Easteal, P. ed. 1998. *Balancing the Scales: Rape, Law Reform and Australian Culture*. Sydney: The Federation Press.

Ehrlich, S. 2001. *Representing Rape: Language and Sexual Consent*. London and New York: Routledge.

——— 1996. *Hatreds: Racialized and Sexualized Conflicts in the 21st Century*. New York and London: Routledge.

Eisenstein, Z. 2000. Writing bodies on the nation for the globe. In Ranchod- Nilsson, S. and Tétreault, M.A. eds. *Women, States and Nationalism: At Home in the Nation?* London and New York: Routledge.

——— 1996. *Hatreds: Racialized and Sexualized Conflicts in the 21st Century*. New York and London: Routledge.

Elder, C. 2007. *Being Australian: Narratives of National Identity*. Crows Nest, NSW: Allen and Unwin.

——— 2003. Invaders, illegals and aliens: Imagining exclusion in 'White Australia'. *Law Text Culture*, 7, pp. 221–250.

Estrich, S. 1987. *Real Rape: How the Legal System Victimizes Women Who Say No*. Cambridge, MA: Harvard University Press.

——— 1986. Rape. *Yale Law Journal*, 95(6), pp. 1087–1184.

Ewing, K.P. 2008. *Stolen Honor: Stigmatizing Muslim Men in Berlin*. Stanford: Stanford University Press.

Fairclough, N. 2003. *Analyzing Discourse: Textual Analysis for Social Research*. New York: Routledge.

——— 1995a. *Critical Discourse Analysis: The Critical Study of Language*. London and New York: Longman.

——— 1995b. *Media Discourse*. London and New York: E. Arnold.

——— 1992. *Discourse and Social Change*. Cambridge, MA: Polity Press.

Fanon, F. 1970. *Les damnés de la terre*. Paris: François Maspero.

——— 1967. *Black Skin, White Masks* (translated by C.L. Markmann). New York: Grove Press.

——— 1965. *A Dying Colonialism* (translated by Haakon Chevalier). New York: Grove Press.

Fassin, D. and Fassin, É. eds. 2006. *De la question sociale à la question raciale? Représenter la société française*. Paris: La Découverte.

Fassin, É. 2006. La démocratie sexuelle et le conflit des civilisations. Multitudes, 26(3), pp. 123–131.

——— 2003. The politics of PaCS in a transatlantic mirror: Same-sex unions and sexual difference in France today. In Célestin, R., DalMolin, E. and de Courtivron, I. eds. *Beyond French Feminisms: Debates on Women, Politics, and Culture in France, 1981–2001*. New York and Basingstoke: Palgrave MacMillan.

——— 1999. The purloined gender: American feminism in a French mirror. *French Historical Studies*, 22(1), pp. 113–138.

Fernando, M. 2013. Save the Muslim woman, save the republic: Ni Putes Ni Soumises and the ruse of neoliberal sovereignty. *Modern and Contemporary France*, 21(2), pp. 147–165.

Fickling, D. 2002. Racially motivated crime and punishment. *The Guardian*, 23 September 2002. Available at: www.guardian.co.uk/elsewhere/journalist/story/0,7792,797463,00. htm [Accessed 29 August 2003].

Bibliography 203

Finlayson, A. 1998. Sexuality and nationality: Gendered discourses of Ireland. In Carver, T. and Mottier, V. eds. *Politics of Sexuality: Identity, Gender, Citizenship*. London and New York: Routledge.

Ford Smith, H. 1997. Ring ding in a tight corner: Sistren, collective democracy, and the organization of cultural production. In Alexander, M. J. and Mohanty, C.T. eds. *Feminist genealogies, colonial legacies, democratic futures*. New York: Routledge.

Fougeyrollas-Schwebel, D. 2005. Violence against women in France: The context, findings and impact of the Enveff survey. *Statistical Journal of the United Nations*, ECE 22, pp. 289–300.

Fowler, R. 1991. *Language in the News: Discourse and Ideology in the Press*. London and New York: Routledge.

Frankenberg, R. 2001. The mirage of an unmarked whiteness. In Brander Rasmussen, B. and Nexica, I.J. eds. *The Making and Unmaking of Whiteness*. Durham, NC: Duke University Press.

Freedman, J. and Tarr, C. eds. 2000. *Women, Immigration and Identities in France*. Oxford and New York: Berg Publishers.

Friedman, L. 2004. The day before trials vanished. *Journal of Empirical Legal Studies*, 1(3), pp. 689–703.

Galbraith, J. 2000. Processes of whiteness and stories of rape. *The Australian Feminist Law Journal*, 14, pp. 71–89.

Galligan, B. and Roberts, W. 2004. *Australian Citizenship*. Carlton, VIC: Melbourne University Press.

Gaspard, F. 2002. Où en est le féminisme aujourd'hui? *Cités*, 9, pp. 59–72.

Gaspard, F. and Koshrow-Khavar, F. 1995. *Le Foulard et la République*. Paris: La Découverte.

Geisler, R. 2002. Sordides 'tournantes' dans le XVIIIe arrondissement. *Le Figaro*, 3 August 2002.

George, W.H. and Martínez, L.J. 2002. Victim blaming in rape: Effects of victim and perpetrator race, type of rape, and participant racism. *Psychology of Women Quarterly*, 26, pp. 110–119.

Gibbs, S. 2003. Rapist out of sight but not out of mind. *The Age*, 2 August 2003.

Gibson, J. 2005. Sentence slashed: Gang rapes not 'worst category'. *Sydney Morning Herald*, 16 September 2005.

Gilliam, A. 1991. Women's equality and national liberation. In Mohanty et al. eds. *Third World Women and the Politics of Feminism*. Bloomington and Indianapolis: Indiana University Press.

Giroux, H.A. 1996. *Fugitive Cultures: Race, Violence and Youth*. New York and London: Routledge.

Gleeson, K. 2004. From centenary to the Olympics, gang rape in Sydney. *Current Issues in Criminal Justice*, 16(2), pp. 183–201.

Greenfield, C. and Williams, P. 2001. 'Howardism' and the media rhetoric of 'Battlers' vs 'Elites'. *Southern Review*, 34(1), pp. 32–44.

Grewal, K. 2016. *The Socio-Political Practice of Human Rights: Between the Universal and the Particular*. London: Routledge.

——— 2015. International Criminal Law as site for enhancing women's rights?: Challenges, possibilities, strategies. *Feminist Legal Studies*, 23(2), pp. 149–165.

——— 2012a. Reclaiming the voice of the 'Third World Woman': What happens if we don't like what she has to say? The tricky case of Ayaan Hirsi Ali. *Interventions: International Journal of Postcolonial Studies*, 14(4), pp. 569–590.

——— 2012b. Australia, the feminist nation? Discourses of gender, 'culture' and nation in the 'K brothers' gang rapes. *Journal of Intercultural Studies*, 33(5), pp. 509–528.

204 *Bibliography*

—— 2011. The natives strike back: '*L'Appel des Indigènes de la République*' and the death of republican values in postcolonial France. In McCormack, J., Pratt, M. and Rolls, A. eds. *Hexagonal Variations: Diversity, Plurality and Reinvention in Contemporary France*. Leiden: Brill.

—— 2010. Rape in conflict, rape in peace: Questioning the revolutionary potential of international criminal justice for women's human rights. *The Australian Feminist Law Journal*, 33, pp. 57–79.

—— 2009. 'Va t'faire integrer!': The appel des feministes indigenes and the challenge to 'republican values' in postcolonial France. *Contemporary French Civilization: A Journal Devoted to All Aspects of Civilization and Cultural Studies in France and the Francophone World*, 33(2), pp. 105–133.

—— 2007. The 'Young Muslim Man' in Australian public discourse. *Transforming Cultures eJournal*, 2(1), pp. 116–134.

Griffin, S. 1971. Rape: The All-American crime. *Ramparts*, 10, pp. 26–35.

Gros, M.J. 2003. Ni Putes, Ni Soumises, Ni Comprises. *Libération*, 6 March 2003.

Guénif-Souilamas, N. 2006. The other French exception: Virtuous racism and the war of the sexes in postcolonial France. *French Politics, Culture and Society*, 24(3), pp. 24–41.

—— 2003. Ni Pute, ni soumise ou très pute, très voilée? *Cosmopolitiques*, 4, pp. 53–65.

—— 2000. *Des Beurettes: aux descendantes d'immigrants nord-africains*. Paris: Bernard Grasset.

Guénif-Souilamas, N. and Macé, É. 2004. *Les féministes et le garçon arabe*. Paris: Éditions de l'aube.

Gugelberger, G. and Kearney, M. 1991. Voices for the voiceless: Testimonial literature in Latin America. *Latin American Perspectives*, 18(3), Part I., pp. 3–14.

Guidi, D. 2015. Artistic reactions to contemporary controversies related to Islam. In Toğuşlu, E. ed. *Everyday Life Practices of Muslims in Europe*. Leuven, Belgium: Leuven University Press.

Guillaumin, C. 1992. *Sexe, Race et Pratique du pouvoir*. Paris: Côté-femmes.

Gunew, S. 2004. *Haunted Nations: The Colonial Dimensions of Multiculturalisms*. London and New York: Routledge.

Gutterman, D. 1994. Postmodernism and the interrogation of masculinity. In Brod, H. and Kaufman, M. eds. *Theorizing Masculinities*, Thousand Oaks, California: Sage Publications.

Haase-Dubosc, D. 1999. Sexual difference and politics in France today. *Feminist Studies*, 25(1), pp. 183–210.

Hage, G. 2003. *Against Paranoid Nationalism: Searching for Hope in a Shrinking Society*. Annandale, NSW: Pluto Press.

—— ed. 2002. *Arab-Australians Today: Citizenship and Belonging*. Carlton, VIC: Melbourne University Press.

—— 1998. *White Nation: Fantasies of White Supremacy in a Multicultural Society*. Annandale, NSW: Pluto Press.

Hall, S. 1990. Cultural identity and diaspora. In Rutherford, J. ed. *Identity, Community, Culture, Difference*. London: Lawrence and Wishart.

Halley, J. and Brown, W. 2002. Introduction. In Halley, J. and Brown, W. eds. *Left Legalism/Left Critique*. Durham, NC and London: Duke University Press.

Hamel, C. 2005. De la racialisation du sexisme au sexisme identitaire. *Migrations Société*, 17(99–100), pp. 91–104.

—— 2003. 'Faire tourner les meufs': Les viols collectifs: discours des médias et des agresseurs. *Gradhiva*, 33, pp. 85–93.

Bibliography   205

Hancock, L. 2003. Wolf pack: The press and the Central Park jogger. *Columbia Journalism Review*, 41(5), pp. 38–42.

Hargreaves, A.G. 2006. Testimony, co-authorship, and dispossession among women of Maghrebi origin in France. *Research in African Literatures*, 37(1), pp. 42–54.

———— 1997. Resistance at the margins: Writers of Maghrebi immigrant origin in France. In Hargreaves A.G. and McKinney, M. eds. *Post-Colonial Cultures in France*. London and New York: Routledge.

———— 1995. *Immigration, 'Race' and Ethnicity in Contemporary France*. London: Routledge.

Hartcher, P., Coorey, P. and Braithwaite, D. 2006. Sheik falls on his sword. *Sydney Morning Herald*, 31 October 2006.

Heath, M. 1998. Disputed truths: Australian Reform of the sexual conduct elements of common law rape. In Easteal, P. ed. *Balancing the Scales: Rape, Law Reform and Australian Culture.* Sydney: The Federation Press.

Hirschl, R. 2008. The judicialization of mega-politics and the rise of political courts. *The Annual Review of Political Science*, 11, pp. 93–118.

Ho, C. 2007. Muslim women's new defenders: Women's rights, nationalism and Islamophobia in contemporary Australia. *Women's Studies International Forum*, 30, pp. 290–298.

Hondagneu-Sotelo, P. and Messner, M. 1994. Gender displays and men's power: The 'new man' and the Mexican immigrant man. In Brod, H. and Kaufman, M. eds. *Theorizing Masculinities*. Thousand Oaks, CA: Sage Publications.

hooks, b. 2004. *We Real Cool: Black Men and Masculinity*. New York and London: Routledge.

———— 1994. *Outlaw Culture: Resisting Representation*. New York and London: Routledge.

———— 1992. *Black Looks: Race and Representation*. Boston, MA: South End Press.

———— 1990. *Yearning: Race, Gender, and Cultural Politics*. Boston, MA: South End Press.

House, J. 1996. Muslim Communities in France. In Nonneman, G., Niblock, T. and Szajkowski, B. eds. *Muslim Communities in the New Europe*. Reading, Berkshire: Ithaca Press.

Howard, J. 2005. Press conference, Phillip Street, Sydney, 13 December 2005. Available at: http://pmtranscripts.dpmc.gov.au/release/transcript-15612 [Accessed 25 May 2016].

———— 2001. Australia Day Address, 25 January 2001. Available at: http://pmtranscripts.dpmc.gov.au/release/transcript-12364 [Accessed 25 May 2016]

Howell, J. 2008. Reconstituting cultural memory through image and text in Leïla Sebbar's *Le Chinois vert d'Afrique*. *French Cultural Studies*, 19(1), pp. 57–70.

Hughes, A. 1999. *Heterographies: Sexual Difference in French Autobiography*. Oxford: Berg Publishers.

Human Rights and Equal Opportunities Commission (HREOC). 2004. *Isma – Listen*, Report of National Consultations on Eliminating Prejudice against Arab and Muslim Australians. Available at: www.humanrights.gov.au/publications/isma-listen-report [Accessed 25 May 2016].

Humphrey, M. 2007. Culturalising the Abject: Islam, Law and Moral Panic in the West. *Australian Journal of Social Issues*, 42(1), pp. 9–25.

Jakubowicz, A., Goodall, H., Martin, J., Mitchell, R. and Seneviratne, K. 1994. *Racism, Ethnicity and the Media*. St Leonards, NSW: Allen and Unwin.

Jaspard, M., Brown, E., Condon, S., Firdion, J.M., Houel, A., Fougeyrollas-Schwebel, D., Lhomond, B., Maillochon, F., Schiltz, M.A. and Saurel-Cubizolles, M.J. 2001. Nommer et compter les violences envers les femmes: une première enquête nationale en France. *Populations et sociétés*, 364, pp. 1–4.

206 *Bibliography*

Jaworski, A. and Coupland, N. eds. 1999. *The Discourse Reader*. London: Routledge.

Jayasuriya, L., Walker, D. and Gothard, J. eds. 2003. *Legacies of White Australia: Race, Culture and Nation*. Crawley, WA: University of Western Australia Press.

Jelen, C. 1991. *Ils feront de bons Français: Enquête sur l'Assimilation des Maghrébins*. Paris: Éditions Robert Laffont.

Johns, R., Griffith, G. and Simpson, R. 2001. Sentencing 'gang rapists': The Crimes Amendment (Aggravated Sexual Assault in Company) Bill 2001. *NSW Parliamentary Library Research Service*, Briefing Paper No. 12/2001.

Johnston, S. 1995. Why the Prime Minister had to see La Haine. *The Independent*, 19 October 1995. Available at www.independent.co.uk/arts-entertainment/why-the-prime-minister-had-to-see-la-haine-1578297.html [Accessed 14 May 2016].

Kampmark, B. 2003. Islam, women and Australia's cultural discourse of terror. *Hecate*, 29(1), pp. 86–106.

Kanneh, K. 1998. Marketing Black women's texts: The case of Alice Walker. In Simons, J. and Fullbrook, K. eds. *Writing: A Woman's Business – Women, Writing and the Marketplace*. Manchester and New York: Manchester University Press.

Kaur, R. 2003. Westenders: Whiteness, women and sexuality in Southall, UK. In Andall, J. ed. *Gender and Ethnicity in Contemporary Europe*. Oxford and New York: Berg Publishers.

Keaton, T.D. 2006. *Muslim Girls and the Other France: Race, Identity Politics, and Social Exclusion*. Bloomington and Indianapolis: Indiana University Press.

Kelly, L., Lovett, J. and Regan, L. 2005. A gap or a chasm? Attrition in reported rape cases. *Home Office Research Study*, 293. Available at: http://webarchive.nationalarchives.gov.uk/20110218135832/rds.homeoffice.gov.uk/rds/pdfs05/hors293.pdf [Accessed 24 May 2016].

Keogh, K. 2003. Finally, some good news comes from a terrible crime. *The Sun-Herald*, 12 July 2003.

Kerbaj, R. 2006. Muslim leader blames women for sex attacks. *The Australian*, 26 October 2006.

Khedimellah, M. 2004. Corps et inconscient collectif voilés: Enjeux de la similitude et de l'alterité. *Cosmopolitiques*, 6, pp. 75–93.

Kimble, S.L. 2006. Emancipation through secularization: French feminist views of Muslim women's condition in interwar Algeria. *French Colonial History*, 7, pp. 109–128.

Kirkby, D. 2003. 'Beer, glorious beer': Gender politics and Australian popular culture. *Journal of Popular Culture*, 37(2), pp. 244–256.

Krémer, P. and Laronche, M. 2002. La condition des jeunes filles s'est dégradée dans les quartiers difficiles. *Le Monde*, 25 October 2002.

Kuhn, R. 1995. *The Media in France*. London and New York: Routledge.

Lacey, N. 2001. Social policy, civil society and the institutions of criminal justice. *Australian Journal of Legal Philosophy*, 26, pp. 7–25.

Lalanne, J.M. 2000. La Banlieue vue des meufs. *Libération*, 29 November 2000.

Lattas, A. 2007. 'They always seem to be angry': The Cronulla riot and the civilising pleasures of the Sun. *The Australian Journal of Anthropology*, 18(3), pp. 300–319.

Lattas, J. 2007. Cruising: 'moral panic' and the Cronulla riot. *The Australian Journal of Anthropology*, 18(3), pp. 320–335.

Laurence, J. and Vaisse, J. 2006. *Integrating Islam: Political and Religious Challenges in Contemporary France*. Washington, DC: Brookings Institution Press.

Law, I. 2002. *Race in the News*. Hampshire and New York: Palgrave.

Lawler, S. 2004. Rules of engagement: Habitus, power and resistance. In Adkins, L. and Skeggs, B. eds. *Feminism after Bourdieu*. Oxford: The Sociological Review, Blackwell.

Bibliography   207

Lazar, M.M. ed. 2005. *Feminist Critical Discourse Analysis: Gender, Power and Ideology in Discourse.* Basingstoke, Hampshire and New York: Palgrave Macmillan.

Le Vaillant, L. 2002. Profil: Samira Bellil, 29 ans. Victime de 'tournantes' dès 14 ans, elle tente de s'en sortir en publiant un récit autobiographique. *Libération,* 7 October 2002.

Lette, K. and Carey, G. 1979. *Puberty Blues.* Carlton, VIC: McPhee Gribble.

Lewis, A.E. 2003 *Race in the Schoolyard: Negotiating the Color Line in Classrooms and Communities.* New Brunswick, New Jersey and London: Rutgers University Press.

Lloyd, C. 2003. Women migrants and political activism in France. In Andall, J. ed. *Gender and Ethnicity in Contemporary Europe.* Oxford and New York: Berg Publishers.

Lochard, G. 2002. La question de la banlieue a la television francaise: mise en place et evolution d'un conflit de representations. In Amorim, M. ed. *Images et Discours sur la Banlieue: Questions vives sur la banlieue.* Paris: Éditions érès.

Mac An Ghaill, M. 1994. The making of Black English masculinities. In Brod, H. and Kaufman, M. eds. *Theorizing Masculinities.* Thousand Oaks, CA: Sage Publications.

Macdonald, M. 2003. *Exploring Media Discourse.* Abingdon: Arnold.

MacDougall, G.J. 1998. Systematic rape, sexual slavery and slavery-like practices during armed conflict. *Final Report to the Sub-Commission on the Promotion and Protection of Human Rights* 50th session, 24 June 1998, E/CN.4/Sub.2/1998/13. Available at: www.unhchr.ch/Huridocda/Huridoca.nsf/0/3d25270b5fa3ea998025665f0032f220?Opendocument [Accessed 3 March 2006].

MacKinnon, C.A. 1997. Rape: On coercion and consent. In Conboy, K., Medina, N. and Stanbury, S. eds. *Writing on the Body: Female Embodiment and Feminist Theory.* New York: Columbia University Press.

––––––– 1989. *Towards a Feminist Theory of the State.* Cambridge, MA: Harvard University Press.

––––––– 1987. *Feminism Unmodified: Discourses on Life and Law.* Cambridge, MA: University of Harvard Press.

Marcus, S. 1992. Fighting bodies, fighting words: A theory and politics of rape prevention. In Butler, J. and Scott, J.W. eds. *Feminists Theorize the Political.* New York and London: Routledge.

Marín, L. 1991. Speaking out together: Testimonials of Latin American women. *Latin American Perspectives,* 18(3), pp. 51–68.

Marks, K. 2004. And they call it a British disease. *The Independent on Sunday,* 7 March 2004. Available at: www.findarticles.com/p/articles/mi_qn4159/is_20040307/ai_n12751183 [Accessed 1 November 2006].

Marr, D. 2005. Alan Jones: I'm the person that's led this charge. *The Age,* 13 December 2005.

Mas, R. 2006. Compelling the Muslim subject: Memory as post-colonial violence and the public performativity of 'secular and cultural Islam'. *The Muslim World,* 96, pp. 585–616.

Mazzocchi, J. 2002. Final gang member in Sydney rape case gets sentenced. AM, ABC online, 12 October 2002. Available at: www.abc.net.au/am/s699823.htm [Accessed 30 September 2003].

McClintock, A. 1994. *Imperial Leather: Race, Gender and Sexuality in the Colonial Conquest.* New York: Routledge.

––––––– 1993. Family feuds: Gender, nationalism and the family. *Feminist Review,* 44, pp. 61–80.

McClintock, A., Mufti, A. and Shohat, E. eds. 1997. *Dangerous Liaisons: Gender, Nation, Postcolonial Perspectives.* Minneapolis and London: University of Minnesota Press.

208   *Bibliography*

McIlveen, L. 2007. High school pupils linked to race hate images. *The Daily Telegraph*, 24 January 2007.

McMah, L. 2016. Police list reveals extent of Cologne's New Year's Eve crimes. *News. com.au*, 22 January 2016. Available at: www.news.com.au/world/europe/police-list-reveals-extent-of-colognes-new-years-eve-crimes/news-story/ff82e71448a5ebe6eb-4c4bd58251ced6 [Accessed 8 June 2016].

McNay, L. 2004. Agency and experience: Gender as a lived relation. In Adkins, L. and Skeggs, B. eds. *Feminism after Bourdieu*. Oxford: The Sociological Review, Blackwell.

——— 1999. Gender, habitus and the field: Pierre Bourdieu and the limits of reflexivity. *Theory, Culture and Society*, 16(1), pp. 95–117.

Mercer, K. 1994. *Welcome to the Jungle: New Positions in Black Cultural Studies*. New York and London: Routledge.

Miller, N. 2016. Migrant crisis: Crime spree sees shift in Germany's attitude towards refugees. *Sydney Morning Herald*, 17 January 2016. Available at: www.smh.com.au/world/cologne-weekend-feature-nick-miller—seo-here-20160114-gm62sa.html [Accessed 8 June 2016].

Minh-Ha, T. 1997. Not you/like you: Postcolonial women and the interlocking questions of identity and difference. In McClintock, A., Mufti, A. and Shohat, E. eds. *Dangerous Liaisons: Gender, Nation, Postcolonial Perspectives*. Minneapolis and London: University of Minnesota Press.

——— 1989. *Woman, Native, Other*. Bloomington, IN: Indiana University Press.

Mitchell, A. and Sutton, C. 2003. Gang rapist's horror drawings of girlfriend. *The Sun-Herald*, 20 July 2003.

Mitchell, T. ed. 2001. *Global Noise: Rap and Hip Hop Outside the USA*. Middletown, CT: Wesleyan University Press.

Mohanty, C.T. Under Western eyes: Feminist scholarship and colonial discourses. In McClintock, A., Mufti, A. and Shohat, E. eds. 1997. *Dangerous Liaisons: Gender, Nation, Postcolonial Perspectives*. Minneapolis and London: University of Minnesota Press.

Mohanty, C.T., Russo, A. and Torres, L. eds. 1991. *Third World Women and the Politics of Feminism*. Bloomington and Indianapolis: Indiana University Press.

Moorti, S. 2002. *Color of Rape: Gender and Race in Television's Public Spheres*. Albany, NY: State University of New York Press.

Moreton-Robinson, A. 2003. I still call Australia home: Indigenous belonging and place in a White postcolonising society. In Ahmed, S. ed. *Uprootings/Regroundings: Questions of Home and Migration*. Oxford: Berg Publishers.

——— 2000. *Talkin' up to the White Woman: Indigenous Women and Feminism*. St Lucia, QLD: University of Queensland Press.

Morgan, G. and Poynting, S. 2012. Introduction: The transnational folk devil. In Morgan, G. and Poynting, S. eds. *Global Islamophobia: Muslims and Moral Panic in the West*. Farnham, Surrey and Burlington, VT: Ashgate.

Motta, P. 2001. Violences. Sept jeunes jugés à Versailles pour des abus sexuels perpétrés en groupe sur une adolescente: Les cités ne sont pas seules concernées. *Le Figaro*, 2 May 2001.

Moyon, R. 2002. Tournantes, je vous hais! *Mouvements*, 20, pp. 66–69.

Mucchielli, L. 2005. *Le scandale des 'tournantes': dérives médiatiques, contre-enquête sociologique*. Paris: La Découverte.

Murphy, D. 2005. Thugs ruled the streets, and the mob sang Waltzing Matilda. *Sydney Morning Herald*, 12 December 2005.

Bibliography 209

Naffine, N. 1994. A struggle over meaning: A feminist commentary on rape law reform. *Australian and New Zealand Journal of Criminology*, 2(1), pp. 100–103.

Nagel, J. 2003. *Race, Ethnicity and Sexuality: Intimate Intersections, Forbidden Frontiers*. New York: Oxford University Press.

Narayan, U. 1997. *Dislocating Cultures: Identities, Traditions and Third-World Feminism*, New York: Routledge

Nasta, S. 1991. *Motherlands: Women's Writing from Africa, the Caribbean and South Asia*. London: Women's Press Ltd.

Ni Putes Ni Soumises (NPNS). 2004. Manifesto. Available at: www.niputesnisoumises. com/mouvement.php?section=historique_2004 [Accessed 12 May 2007].

Noble, G. and Tabar, P. 2002. On being Lebanese-Australian: Hybridity, essentialism and strategy among Arabic-speaking youth. In Hage, G. ed. *Arab-Australians Today: Citizenship and Belonging*. Carlton South, VIC: Melbourne University Press.

O'Dwyer, E. 2007. Post-traumatic strength. *The Sun-Herald*, 28 October 2007.

Okin, S.M. 1999. Is multiculturalism bad for women? In Okin, S.M. et al. *Is Multiculturalism Bad for Women?* Princeton, NJ: Princeton University Press.

Orlando, V. 2003. From rap to raï in the mixing bowl: Beur hip-hop culture and banlieue cinema in urban France. *Journal of Popular Culture*, 36(3), pp. 395–415.

O'Shaughnessey, M. 2007. *The New Face of Political Cinema: Commitment in French Film since 1995*. Oxford and New York: Berghahn Books.

Ozouf, M. 2003. Counting the Days. In Célestin, R., DalMolin, E. and de Courtivron, I. eds. *Beyond French Feminisms: Debates on Women, Politics, and Culture in France, 1981–2001*. New York and Basingstoke: Palgrave MacMillan.

——— 1995. *Les mots de femmes: essais sur la singularité française*. Paris: Fayard.

Parker, A., Russo, M., Sommer, D. and Yaeger, P. eds. 1992. *Nationalisms and Sexualities*. New York and London: Routledge.

Patai, R. 1973. *The Arab Mind*. Tucson, AZ: Recovery Resources Press.

Paydar, P. 1995. *Women and the Political Process in Twentieth Century Iran*. Cambridge, UK: Cambridge University Press.

Pech, M.E. 2002a. Tournantes: de l'injure sexiste au viol collectif, jamais les rapports entre garçons et filles n'ont été aussi agressif: La grande misère sexuelle des adolescents des cites. *Le Figaro*, 21 June 2002.

——— 2002b. Ils ont leurs codes et font souvent preuve d'une anachronique pudeur, source des pires dérapages: 'Une fille en jupe, c'est une taspé, une fille facile. *Le Figaro*, 21 June 2002.

——— 2002c. Les désolants enseignements d'une tournante ordinaire. *Le Figaro*, 27 May 2002.

Peralva, A. and Macé, É. 2002. *Médias et violences urbaines: Débats politiques et constructions journalistiques*. Paris: La Documentation française.

Peterson, V.S. 2000. Sexing political identities/nationalism as heterosexism. In Ranchod-Nilsson, S. and Tétreault, M.A. eds. *Women, States and Nationalism: At Home in the Nation?* London and New York: Routledge.

Pettman, J.J. 1995. Race, ethnicity and gender in Australia. In Stasiulis, D. and Yuval-Davis, N. eds. *Unsettling Settler Societies: Articulations of Gender, Race, Ethnicity and Class*. London, Thousand Oaks, CA and New Delhi: SAGE.

Philadelphoff-Puren, N. 2005. Contextualising consent: The problem of rape and romance. *Australian Feminist Studies*, 20(46), pp. 31–42.

——— 2004. Dereliction: Women, rape and football. *Australian Feminist Law Journal*, 21, pp. 35–51.

210   *Bibliography*

———— 2003. The right language for rape. *Hecate*, 29(1), pp. 47–58.

Phillips, A. 2003. When culture means gender: Issues of cultural defence in the English courts. *The Modern Law Review*, 66(4), pp. 510–531.

Pileggi, M. and Patton, C. 2003. Introduction: Bourdieu and cultural studies. *Cultural Studies*, 17(3), pp. 313–325.

Poussaint, A.F. 1972. *Why Blacks Kill Blacks*. New York: Emerson Hall Publishers.

Povinelli, E. 1998. The state of shame: Australian multiculturalism and the crisis of indigenous citizenship. *Critical Inquiry*, 24(2), pp. 575–610.

Poynting, S. 2006. What caused the Cronulla riot? *Race and Class*, 48(1), pp. 85–92.

Poynting, S. and Mason, V. 2007. The resistible rise of Islamophobia: Anti-Muslim racism in the UK and Australia before 9/11. *Journal of Sociology*, 43(1), pp. 61–86.

Poynting, S., Noble, G., Tabar, P. and Collins, J. 2004. *Bin Laden in the Suburbs: Criminalising the Arab Other*. Sydney, NSW: Sydney Institute of Criminology Series.

Priest, T. 2004. Don't turn a blind eye to terror in our midst. *The Australian*, 12 January 2004.

Puar, J. 2005. On torture: Abu Ghraib. *Radical History Review*, 93, pp. 13–38.

Racioppi, L. and O'Sullivan See, K. 2000. Engendering nation and national identity. In Ranchod-Nilsson, S. and Tétreault, M.A. eds. *Women, States and Nationalism: At Home in the Nation?* London and New York: Routledge.

Rackley, E. 2007. Judicial diversity, the woman judge and fairy tale endings. *Legal Studies*, 27(1), pp. 74–94.

Radford, J. and Stanko, E. 1996. Violence against women and children: The contradictions of crime control under patriarchy. In Hester, M., Kelly, L. and Radford, J. eds. *Women, Violence, and Male Power: Feminist Activism, Research, and Practice*. Buckingham, UK and Philadelphia, PA: Open University Press.

Raissiguier, C. 2002. The sexual and racial politics of civil unions in France. *Radical History Review*, 83, pp. 73–93.

———— 1999. Gender, race and exclusion: A new look at the French republican tradition. *International Feminist Journal of Politics*, 1(3), pp. 435–457.

Ramet, Sabrina P. ed. 1999. *Gender and Politics in the Western Balkans: Women and Society in Yugoslavia and the Yugoslav Successor States.* Pennsylvania: Pennsylvania State University Press.

Ranchod-Nilsson, S. and Tétreault, M.A. eds. 2000. *Women, States and Nationalism: At Home in the Nation?* London and New York: Routledge.

Razack, S.H. 2008. *Casting Out: The Eviction of Muslims from Western Law and Politics*. Toronto, Buffalo and London: University of Toronto.

———— 2004. Imperilled Muslim women, dangerous Muslim men and civilised Europeans: Legal and social responses to forced marriages. *Feminist Legal Studies*, 12, pp. 129–174.

———— 1998. *Looking White People in the Eye: Gender, Race and Culture in the Courtrooms and Classrooms*. Toronto: University of Toronto Press.

Rey, H. 1996. *La Peur des Banlieues, La Bibliothèque du Citoyen*. Paris: Presses de la Fondation Nationale des Sciences Politiques.

Richards, V. 2016. Cologne attacks: What happened after 1,000 women were sexually assaulted? *The Independent*, 12 February 2016. Available at: www.independent.co.uk/news/world/europe/cologne-attacks-what-happened-after-1000-women-were-sexually-assaulted-a6867071.html [Accessed 8 June 2016].

Rinaudo, C. 1999. *L'Ethnicite dans la Cite: Jeux et enjeux de la categorisation ethnique*. Paris and Montreal: L'Harmattan.

Robert-Diard, P. 2002. Les auteurs du viol collectif d'Argenteuil condamnés à des peines allant de 5 à 12 ans de prison. *Le Monde*, 29–30 September 2002.

Rosello, M. 2003. New gendered mosaics: Their mothers, the gauls. In Célestin et al. eds. *Beyond French Feminisms: Debates on Women, Politics, and Culture in France, 1981–2001*. New York and Basingstoke: Palgrave Macmillan.

——— 1997. North African women and the ideology of modernization: From *bidonvilles* to *cités de transit* and *HLM*. In Hargreaves A.G. and McKinney, M. eds. *Post-Colonial Cultures in France*. London & New York: Routledge.

Rotman, C. 2003. La longue marche des femmes des cites. *Libération*, 31 January 2003.

Roux, P., Gianettoni, L. and Perrin, C. 2007. L'instrumentalisation du genre: une nouvelle forme de racisme et sexism. *Nouvelles Questions Féministes*, 26(2), pp. 92–108.

Rubin, G. 1975. The traffic in women: Notes on the 'political economy' of sex. In Reiter, R.R. ed. *Toward an Anthropology of Women*. New York and London: Monthly Review Press.

Rutherford, J. 2000. *The Gauche Intruder: Freud, Lacan and the White Australian Fantasy*. Carlton, VIC: Melbourne University Press.

Saadaoui, L. Autour des 'Tournantes': Traitement journalistique du fait divers sur le viol collectif en France. Des représentations européennes d'une immigration. Seminar paper presented at *1er séminaire transfrontalier de l'Association des Jeunes Chercheurs*, Centre de Recherche sur les Médiations (CREM), Metz, France, 29 May 2007. Available at: http://ajc-crem.univ- metz.fr/upload/publi/Article_seminaire_Saadaoui.doc [Accessed 29 February 2008].

Said, E.W. 1995. *Orientalism*. London: Penguin.

Salhi, A.I. 2002. Sale temps pour les Arabes en France. *Libération*, 23 October 2002.

Sanday, P.R. 1990. *Fraternity Gang Rape: Sex, Brotherhood and Privilege on Campus*. New York: New York University Press.

Santucci, F.M. 2001a. Dans les cités, les clichés ont la dure. *Libération*, 9 March 2001.

——— 2001b. Viols: la spirale infernale de la 'tournante'. *Libération*, 9 March 2001.

Schneidermann, D. 2003. *Le Cauchemar Médiatique*. Paris: Éditions Denöel.

Schomburg, W. and Peterson, I. 2007. Genuine consent to sexual violence under international criminal law. *American Journal of International Law*, 101(1), pp. 121–140.

Scott, J.W. 2007. *The Politics of the Veil*. Princeton, NJ: Princeton University Press.

——— 2005. *Parité!: Sexual Equality and the Crisis of French Universalism*. Chicago and London: University of Chicago Press.

——— 2003. Vive la difference! In Célestin et al. eds. *Beyond French Feminisms: Debates on Women, Politics, and Culture in France, 1981–2001*. New York and Basingstoke: Palgrave Macmillan.

——— 1992. Experience. In Butler, J. and Scott, J.W. eds. 1992. *Feminists Theorize the Political*. New York and London: Routledge.

——— 1991. The evidence of experience. *Critical Inquiry*, 17(4), pp. 773–797.

Seifert, R. 1996. The second front: The logic of sexual violence in wars. *Women's Studies International Forum*, 19(1/2), pp. 35–43.

Sexton, J. 2003. Race, sexuality and political struggle: Reading *Soul on Ice*. *Social Justice*, 30(2), pp. 28–41.

Sharp, J.P. 1996. Gendering nationhood: A feminist engagement with national identity. In Duncan, N. ed. *Bodyspace: Destabilizing Geographies of Gender and Sexuality*. London and New York: Routledge.

Sheehan, P. 2006a. *Girls like You*. Sydney: Macmillan.

——— 2006b. Sheik's views show up the wider problem with Muslim men. *Sydney Morning Herald*, 27 October 2006.

——— 2006c. Rough, slow justice for rape victims. *Sydney Morning Herald*, 10 April 2006.

212 Bibliography

———— 2006d. Dad dies, but sons' evils go on. Sheehan, P. *Sydney Morning Herald*, 4 December 2006.

———— 2005. Cold-blooded law heats up cultural war. *Sydney Morning Herald*, 7 February 2005.

———— 2004. Ass of a law means the rights of rapists override those of their victims. *Sydney Morning Herald*, 6 September 2004.

———— 2001. Tolerant, multicultural Sydney can face this difficult truth. *Sydney Morning Herald*, 29 August 2001.

Silverman, M. 1999. *Facing Postmodernity: Contemporary French thought on Culture and Society*. New York and London: Routledge.

Silverstein, P.A. 2005. Immigrant racialization and the new savage slot: Race, migration, and immigration in the new Europe. *Annual Review of Anthropology*, 34, pp. 363–384.

Simons, J. and Fullbrook, K. eds. 1998. *Writing: A Woman's Business – Women, Writing and the Marketplace*. Manchester and New York: Manchester University Press.

Smart, C. 1989. *Feminism and the Power of Law*. London: Routledge.

Smith, S. and Watson, J. 2001. *Reading Autobiography: A Guide for Interpreting Life Narratives*. Minneapolis: Minneapolis University Press.

Special Broadcasting Service (SBS). 2006. True colours: Middle Eastern youths in Sydney. *Insight*, 15 August 2006.

Spivak, G.C. 1988. Can the Subaltern speak? In Nelson, C. and Grossberg, L. eds. *Marxism and the Interpretation of Culture*. Basingstoke, UK: Macmillan Education.

Steyn, M. 2002. Beware multicultural madness. *Chicago Sun-Times*, 25 August 2002. Available at: www.atrueword.com/index.php/article/articleprint/13/-1/7/ [Accessed 28 August 2003].

Stoler, A.L. 2002. *Carnal Knowledge and Imperial Power: Race and the Intimate in Colonial Rule*. Berkeley, CA: University of California Press.

———— 1995. *Race and the Education of Desire: Foucault's History of Sexuality and the Colonial Order of Things*. Durham, NC: Duke University Press.

Stora, B. 1999. *Le transfert d'une mémoire: De l''Algérie française'au racisme anti-arabe*. Paris: La Découverte.

Stratton, J. 1998. *Race Daze: Australia in Identity Crisis*. Annandale, NSW: Pluto Press.

Stubbs, J. 2003. Sexual assault, criminal justice and 'law and order'. *Women Against Violence*, 14, pp. 14–26.

Suleri, S. 1992. Woman skin deep: Feminism and the postcolonial condition. *Critical Inquiry*, 18(4), pp. 756–769.

Sutton, C. and Duff, E. 2002. Rapist's loving family: Where did we fail our son? *Sydney Morning Herald*, 8 September 2002.

Sykes, R. 1991. Identities – Who am I? *Hecate*, 17(2), pp. 32–35.

Taylor, C. 2011. *Dilemmas and Connections: Selected Essays*. Cambridge, MA and London: Harvard University Press.

Temkin, J. 2002. *Rape and the Legal Process* (2nd edition). Oxford, UK: Oxford University Press.

Ticktin, M. 2008. Sexual violence as the language of border control: Where French feminist and anti-immigrant rhetoric meet. *Signs: Journal of Women in Culture and Society*, 33(4), pp. 863–889.

Tohidi, N. 1991. Gender and Islamic fundamentalism: Feminist politics in Iran. In Mohanty et al. eds. *Third World Women and the Politics of Feminism*. Bloomington and Indianapolis: Indiana University Press.

Bibliography 213

Torres, L. 1991. The construction of the self in US Latina autobiographies. In Mohanty et al. eds. *Third World Women and the Politics of Feminism.* Bloomington and Indianapolis: Indiana University Press.

Tourancheau, P. 2002a. Seule face à se dix-huit violeurs et ses deux entremetteuses: Victime de 'tournantes' à Argenteuil, la jeune fille était manipulée par deux 'copines'. Procès à Pontoise. *Libération,* 23 September 2002.

——— 2002b. Un long calvaire et le deni des violeurs: Procès après un hiver de 'tournantes' à Argenteuil. *Libération,* 17 September 2002.

Toy, N. and Knowles, L. 2001. Pack rapists' racial taunts. *Sydney Morning Herald,* 24 August 2001.

Tribalat, M. 1995. *Faire France: Une grande enquête sur les immigrés et leurs enfants.* Paris: La Découverte.

Tribalat, M., Simon, P. and Riandey, B. eds. 1996. *De l'immigration à l'assimilation: enquête sur les populations d'origine étrangère en France.* Paris: La Découverte/INED.

Tshimanga, C., Gondola, D. and Bloom, P.J. eds. 2009. *Frenchness and the African Diaspora.* Bloomington and Indianapolis: Indiana University Press.

Tufail, W. 2015. Rotherham, Rochdale, and the racialised threat of the 'Muslim Grooming Gang'. *International Journal for Crime, Justice and Social Democracy,* 4(3), pp. 30–43.

Valverde, M. 2003, *Law's Dream of a Common Knowledge.* Princeton, NJ: Princeton University Press.

Vance, C. ed. 1984. *Pleasure and Danger: Exploring Female Sexuality.* Boston, London, Melbourne and Henley: Routledge and Kegan Paul.

Van der Veer, P. 2006. Pim Fortuyn, Theo van Gogh, and the politics of tolerance in the Netherlands. *Public Culture,* 18(1), pp. 111–124.

Van Dijk, T.A. 1992. Discourse and the denial of racism. *Discourse and Society,* 3(1), pp. 87–1180.

——— 1991. *Racism and the Press.* London: Routledge.

Vasta, E. and Castles, S. eds. 1996. *The Teeth Are Smiling: The Persistence of Racism in Multicultural Australia.* St Leonards, NSW: Allen and Unwin.

Veracini, L. 2010. *Settler Colonialism: A Theoretical Overview.* Cambridge, UK: Cambridge University Press.

Villechaise-Dupont, A. 2000. *Amère Banlieue: Les gens des grands ensembles.* Paris: Éditions Grasset.

Volpp, L. 2007. The culture of citizenship. *Theoretical Inquiries in Law,* 8(2), pp. 571–601.

——— 1994. (M)isidentifying culture: Asian women and the 'cultural defence'. *Harvard Women's Law Journal,* 17, pp. 57–101.

Wagner, D.A. 2006. 'La squale' et 'Samia': une rencontre de cultures de choc. *Lianes,* 1. Available at: www.lianes.org/-La- squale-et-Samia-une-rencontre-de-cultures-de-choc_a72.html [Accessed 10 December 2008].

Wagner, T. 2007. *The Making of Me: Finding My Future after Assault.* Sydney: Pan Macmillan Australia.

Wakim, J. 2004. Gang rape, sport, power – And prejudice. *The Age,* 9 March 2004.

——— 2002. The media's obsession with race sheds no light on crime. *The Age,* 24 July 2002.

Wallace, N. 2004a. Gang rapists told age, culture no defence. *Sydney Morning Herald,* 2 March 2004.

———2004b. A daughter's agony, her family's suffering. *Sydney Morning Herald,* 29 July 2004.

Ware, V. 2015. *Beyond the Pale: White Women, Racism and History.* London: Verso Books.

Warner, K. 2004. Gang rape in Sydney: Crimes, the media, politics, race and sentencing. *Australian and New Zealand Journal of Criminology,* 37(3), pp. 344–362.

214 *Bibliography*

Waters, M.C. 1990. *Ethnic Options: Choosing Identities in America.* Berkeley, CA: University of California Press.

Weber, E. 1976. *Peasants to Frenchman: The Modernization of Rural France, 1870–1914.* Stanford, CA: Stanford University Press.

Weil, P. 2003. Le statut des musulmans en Algérie coloniale: une nationalité française dénaturée. *EUI Working Paper* HEC No. 2003/3, European University Institute Florence. Available at: www.iue.it/PUB/HEC03–03.pdf [Accessed 13 December 2008].

Weiss, G. and Wodak, R. 2003. *Critical Discourse Analysis: Theory and Interdisciplinarity.* Basingstoke, Hampshire and New York: Palgrave Macmillan.

White, R. 1981. *Inventing Australia: Images and Identity 1688–1980.* Sydney: George Allen and Unwin.

Wihtol de Wenden, C. 1991. North African immigration and the French political imaginary (translated by Clare Hughes). In Silverman, M. ed. *Race, Discourse and Power in France.* Aldershot, Brookfield, WI, Hong Kong, Singapore and Sydney: Avebury.

Wihtol de Wenden, C. and Daoud, Z. eds. 1993. *Banlieues: Intégration ou explosion?* Paris: Panoramiques-Corlet, Diffusion Le Seuil.

Willis, K. 2006. The legal system's response to sexual assault. Presentation to the Institute of Criminology, University of Sydney, 5 September 2006. Available at: www.nswrapecrisis.com.au/ . . . /KarenWillisSpeech-5.9.06.pdf [Accessed 13 December 2008].

Winter, B. 1995. Women, the law, and cultural relativism in France: The case of excision. In Laslett, B., Brenner, J. and Arart, Y. eds. *Rethinking the Political: Gender, Resistance and the State.* Chicago: Chicago University Press.

Wockner, C. 2002. Bad behaviour not suited to a court of law. *The Daily Telegraph,* 17 July 2002.

Wodak, R. and Meyer, M. eds. 2001. *Methods of Critical Discourse Analysis.* London, Thousand Oaks and New Delhi: SAGE Publications.

Wolfe, P. 1999. *Settler Colonialism and the Transformation of Anthropology: The Politics and Poetics of an Ethnographic Event.* London and New York: Cassell.

Wood, L.A. and Rennie, H. 1994. Formulating rape: The discursive construction of victims and villains. *Discourse and Society,* 5(1), pp. 125–148.

Yegenoglu, M. 1998. *Colonial Fantasies: Towards a Feminist Reading of Orientalism.* Cambridge: Cambridge University Press.

Yúdice, G. 1991. Testimonio and postmodernism. *Latin American Perspectives,* 18(3), pp. 15–31.

Yuval-Davis, N. 1997. *Gender and Nation.* London: SAGE Publishers.

Index

Abood, Paula 78
Aboriginal women, sexuality/availability (racist constructions) 47
AEM *see R v AEM Snr, AEM Jnr and KEM*
affaires des foulards (headscarf affairs) 120, 142, 145
affective deficit 117; description 123
Africa, France (colonial engagement) 124
Agacinski, Sylvaine 170–1, 178
agency: absence 178; source 166
agency/dignity, regaining (feeling) 40–1
aggravated sexual assault in company (crimes amendment bill) 62–5
aggressive masculinity 117–18
Albrechtsen, Janet 72, 76–7; French context 117–18
Algeria: criminal conduct 132; struggle 148; women, plight 143
'Algeria Unveiled' 172
al Hilaly, Sheikh Taj el-din 80
Ali, Ayaan Hirsi 157, 176
Allan, Pamela 62; intervention 63; Dowling attack 63; support statement 63
Amara, Fadela 8, 149, 163, 171
anti-Arab racism, reinforcement/ legitimisation 131–2
anti-colonial nationalism, articulation 152
Anti-Discrimination Board: document 70; intention 73
anti-Muslim conspiracy 50–4; assertions 51; competitive racisms, relationship 96–101; victims, Skaf assertion 13
anti-Muslim defence 91
anti-racism, feminism (contrast) 187–8
anti-racist struggles (France) 169–70
anti-Semitic violence 181
anti-sexist trends 66
anti-social behaviour, descriptions/images 51–2

anti-sociality 117
ANZAC 188
Arab Mind, The (Patai) 88
Argenteuil, Parisian *banlieue* 119
Asad, Talal 30
Ashton, Alan 64–5
Aussie pigs, naming 50, 66
Australia: identity, Anglo-Celtic origins 5; identity, dominant hegemonic conceptions 72–3; multicultural politics 30; nationalist imagery 94–5; public discourse 71; state machinery 91; values 118; whiteness 5
authenticity: emphasis 156–7; recognition 155
authentic narrative 164–5
Awkward, Michael 16

backward immigrant, enlightened France (contrast) 119–24
'backward Third World Woman' 167–8
Badinter, Elizabeth 178
Balding, Janine (gang rape/murder) 70
Ball, Ian 60
banlieue (working-class suburb) 1, 8; binary understanding 128–9; cinema 111; communicative deficit 16; context 174; dangers 114–15; discourses 128–9; feminisation 105; feminist perspective 112–15; genre, claim 5–6; habitus 130–2; homosociality 132–4; immigrant/Islam/ violence, link (reinforcement) 182–3; juvenile delinquency, association 106; masculinity, problem 115; men 120–3; men, homosocial bonds 113; possession 123; presentation 105; public/private divide, reinforcement 111–12; racism/ sexism, site 128–9; sexism 147; sexually lost *banlieues* (Republic) 117; sexual

216 Index

violence, problem 124; society, traits 125; tribal practices 124; *les violences urbaines* 106–7; voice 163; women, manifesto 163–7; young *banlieue* residents, conformity 130–1
Bass Hill Boyz 65, 81–2
Battle of Algiers, The 172
behaviour models 151
being, liberating 142–4
Bellil, Samira 33, 34, 128, 137–41, 143, 164, 171; narrative, demonstration 146; positioning 139; role rejection 149; television reporter, encounter 144
Benguigui, Yamina 152
beur (identity) 145
beur (label) 144–5
beur (rapist description) 120
beurette (Republic) 137, 174; liberating 142–4; *Dans l'enfer des tournantes* 137–40; experience, authority (problematising) 154–9; gender consciousness 149–51; 'ma propre verité,' truth (self-narrative) 137–40; 'la petite beurette' 144–51; postcolonial, feminist (reconciliation) 151–4; race consciousness 146–9; survivor, testimony 137–40; testimony, collaborator role 140–4
'Beurette' identity, stereotypical traits 110
Beurettes, Des 145
Beyond Paranoid Nationalism (Hage) 101
Black Boy (American Hunger) 154
Black-on-Black violence 132
Black Power movement 169
Blacks: characters, presentation 109; female bodies, abuse 47; hyper-sexual violent Blacks, colonial sexual stereotypes (reinforcement) 109–11; male patriarchy, assertion 169
Bone, Pamela 69
Boulé, Jean-Pierre 155
Bourdieu, Pierre 3, 56; field, rules 57
Bowden, Tracey 67
Brearley, David 73
Brush, Paula Stewart 146–7
Butler, Judith 177–8

cailleras, les 109
Carr, Bob 60–1, 67
censorship 21
Ce que parler veut dire (Bourdieu) 3
cité 175; patriarchialisation 169; *see also banlieue*
civilising mission 143, 158

Clark, Anna 24
'Clash of Civilisations,' reinforcement 94
Cobby, Anita (gang rape/murder) 70
collaborator, role 140–4
collective identity 165
colonial habitus 57
colonial sexual stereotypes, reinforcement 109–11
colonisation, product 132
communitarianism 174
competing racisms, anti-Muslim conspiracy (relationship) 49–50, 96–101
Conklin, Alice 174
consciousness: gender consciousness 149–51; race consciousness 146–9
conspiracy theory *see* Sheehan, Paul
Cossins, Anne 18
Costello, Peter 76, 80
Cowdery, Nicholas 18–19
Crémieux Decree 172
Crichton, Sarah 26, 66
crime: ethnicising 67–8; ethnicity, linkage 64
Crimes Act (NSW) 1900 62
crimes amendment (aggravated sexual assault in company) bill (NSW; 2001) 62–5
criminal behaviour, inter-communal/inter-societal form (creation) 132
Criminal Procedure Amendment (NSW) 84
criminal trials, court appearance 39
critical discourse analysis (CDA), usage 3
Cronin, Ciaran 56
Cronulla: events 79, 101; riots 46, 79–80, 94, 102
Cronulla (2005), women (protection) 78–80
cross-examination 40; ordeal 55
cultural capital 3
cultural context 90
cultural defence, presentation 98
cultural dimension 28–31
cultural diversity, discourses (analysis) 97
'Cultural Identity and Diaspora' (Hall) 55
cultural timebomb 28–31; defence 99; threat 101
cultural tolerance, discourse 187–8
culture, term (usage) 91
Cunneen, Margaret 68, 91; Australian nationalist imagery, usage 94–5; police favourite 95
Cut Killer 111–12
Cuttoli, Paul 172

Index   217

Dadoo (rapper) 127
Dans l'enfer des tournantes (*In the Hell of the Tournantes*) 137–40, 142
de Brito, Kate 74
Debus, Bob 62
decolonialisation, ongoing project 190–1
dehumanising description 86–7
Delany, Samuel 164
Delphy, Christine 176
Department of Public Prosecutions (DPP), Goodwin description 94
Desirée (story) 108–14; abortion, discussion 115
deviance, level (demonstration) 15–16
Devine, Miranda 76, 80
difference, tolerance 69
discourse: media discourses 65–72; term, usage 3–4
disenfranchisement 128–9
disrespect 51–2
District Court of New South Wales, unreported judgment (Justice Finnane) 25–6
Durand, Jacky 121–2

educational initiative, Sully suggestion 16–17
embodied history 3
embodied social structure 3
empathy, limitation 36–7
Enlightenment principles 180
equality, principle 173
Estrich, Susan 44
ethnic identity, loyalty 156
ethnicity: crime, linkage 64; misogyny, merger 81–6
experience: authority, problematising 154–9

Fali, Linda 182
Fanon, Frantz 56, 77, 132, 153
Fassin, Éric 173
Fathia (case) 124
Fédération Nationale de la Maison des Potes 165
female sexuality, dominant construction (incorporation) 19
female socialisation, problematisation 42
feminism: analysis 20; anti-racism, contrast 187–8; critiques 44; enlightenment 82; framework 176–7; heterosexist feminism 176–9; left-wing feminist responses 74–6; multiculturalism, dichotomy

(identification) 98–9; normative feminine identity, reinforcement 176–9; politics, possibility 188–90; postcolonial (reconciliation) 151–4; right-wing feminist responses 76–8
feminist
féministes indigènes de la République, les 152, 172, 194
feminist struggles (France) 169–70
Figaro, Le (print media) 105, 122, 125
Finnane, Justice 22; conclusion 27; language, selection 25–6; sentencing judgment 26; unreported judgment, District Court of New South Wales 25–6
foulard, le 171; *see also hijab*
Four Corners 79; retrospective 64–5
France: Arabs, external violence 131–2; civilised French 109–11; colonialism, positive aspects 190–1; complementarity of the sexes 170; enlightened France, backward immigrant (contrast) 119–24; *l'exception française* 171; freedom, absence 168–9; Frenchness, assertion 179; heterosexual relations, exceptional nature 125–7; immigration/citizenship, political debate 107; integration policy, failure 123; Republican values, paradoxes 169–76; Republic, loyalty 152; Republican mythology 178; Republican values/nationalist myths, reclamation 180–1; society, gender equality 4; women, immigrant women (contrast) 167–9; Women's Suffrage movement 142–3
Fraser, Andrew 63–4

Galbraith, Janet 35–6, 44, 47, 48
gang rape 18, 61, 78, 33; condemnation 147; fraternal bond 133; homosociality 132–4; inter-ethnic conflict/conquest, logic 58; left wing anti-racist responses 72–4; Muslim gang rapes 75; New Bedford gang rape trial 38; 'new phenomenon,' perspective 42; organization 27; *see also* Sydney gang rapes
gang rapist 49; discourses, analysis 158
garçon arabe, le 145, 174
gender: consciousness 149–51; equality 4; heteronormative gender identity, reinforcement 186–7; identity construction, critique 42; identity, loyalty 156; normative gender identity, reinforcement 14–18; relations 121

218 *Index*

Génestal, Fabrice 107, 111; assertion 118
Gillard, Julia 194
Gilliam, Angela 182
Girls Like You (Sheehan) 13, 79, 84;
 rape, cultural context 89–96; rapists,
 description 86–9; victims 85–9; villains,
 creation 85–9
Giroux, Henry 108
Gleeson, Kate 78
Glendinning, Lee 93
global Islamophobia 191–2
Good Nation fantasy, reinforcement 102
goodness, fantasy 191
good White nation 187
good White nation, myth (reinforcement) 97
Goodwin, Sheridan 91–2, 94
Griffin, Susan 23
Gros, Marie-Joëlle 129
Guenifi, Asma 182
Guénif-Souilamas, Nacira 146, 152, 182;
 identification 155
guilt, admission (refusal) 52

habitus: Bourdieusian language, usage 53;
 colonial habitus 57; concept (Bourdieu)
 157; practices 56
Hage, Ghassan 73–4, 101
Haine, La 111, 181–2
Hall, Stuart 55
Hamel, Christelle 127, 132–3, 178
Hartcher, Chris 84
headscarf affairs 120
heteronormative gender identity,
 reinforcement 186–7
heterosexist feminism 176–9
heterosexuality: centrality 178;
 France, heterosexual relations
 (exceptional nature) 125–7; normative
 heterosexuality/rape continuum 18–19
heterosexual masculinity, Latham
 perspective 14–15
Hidden, Justice (decisions) 28–31
hijab 4; condemnation 176–7; discourse
 175; issue 121, 174; symbol 171–2;
 wearing 102; *see also foulard*
Hill, Anita 153
Howard, John 76, 78
Humphrey, Michael 28–9, 122
hyper-sexual Black man/woman, image 109
hyper-sexual violent Blacks 109–11

identity, problem (absence) 179
ideological systems, contestation 167

immigrants: *banlieue* (reinforcement)
 182–3; communities 117–18;
 communities, social/economic mobility
 181; groups, un-integratability 106;
 Lebanese backgrounds, stigmatisation/
 discrimination 81; 'Maghrébin' 8;
 nasty immigrant, impact 191; 'nasty
 migrants,' impact 101–3
immigrant woman, French woman
 (contrast) 167–9
in-depth comparative study, value 4–6
institutional racism, impact 111
instrumental rationality 166
inter-racial/stranger rape, problem
 (exaggeration) 45
Intifada 101–3
ISIS, rise of 6–7
Islam: *banlieue* (reinforcement)
 182–3; global Islamophobia 191–2;
 identification 121
Islamic terrorism 6–7

Jakubowicz, Andrew 73
Jones, Alan 79
'Journal de Mohamed' 140
judgments, social texts 13–14
Juppé, Alain 111
justice system, Wagner assessment 34
juvenile delinquency, *banlieue*
 (association) 106

Kablye society, characterisation 168
Kada, Saida 175–6
Kanneh, Kadiatu 155
Kaur, Raminder 77–8
K brothers 13; accused men, assertions
 51; behaviour, Sheehan depiction 89;
 case 29; case, conceptualisation 97;
 characterisation 94; cultural aspect
 98; description 92; dismissal 97; legal
 disadvantage 52–3; Sheehan discussion 48
KEM *see R v. AEM Snr, AEM Jnr and
 KEM*
Kennedy, Michael 102–3
Kids Help Line 37
knowledge production, centrality 30
Kremmer, Christopher 91
K sister, description 93

laïcité (secularism) 4, 172–3
Lakemba police station, shooting attack 68
Latham, Megan 10, 14; leniency,
 perception 60; submission dismissal 50

Lattas, Andrew 72
law: constitutive power 22; legal process, resistance space 43–5; legal system, inadequacies 100
law and order rhetoric 61; resistance 45–6
Laws, John 71
Leila 110–14; gang rape 18
L'Humanité interview 107
Liberté, égalité, laïcité! 169–76
'lived experience' 154
Lynch, Paul 64

Macé, Eric 106, 182
MacKinnon, Catharine 21, 26, 45
Maghrebi women, testimonies 140, 145
majority outrage/condemnation, mobilisation 45–6
Making of Me, The (Wagner) 13
male rape, possibility (exclusion) 17
male sexuality: dominant construction, incorporation 19; reproduction 127
'ma propre verité,' truth (self-narrative) 137–40
Marcus, Sharon 19, 42
Marin, Lynda 164–5
masculine displays 58
masculinity: ace 55; marginal model 58–9; problem 115; protest masculinity 49–54
Mazzocchi, Jo 67–8
McKay, Ken 92
McKay, Kim 67
media discourses 65–72; initial reporting 66–72
media responses: analysis 65–6; sexually lost *banlieues* 117
Mélanie, Loubna 182
Memmi, Albert 55
Menchú, Rigoberta 165
Middle East: extraction, rapes 66; identification 102; women, retaliatory rapes 77
migrants, impact 101–3
Minguettes 106; *see also banlieue*
Minh-Ha, Trinh 156
misère sexuelle, la 117, 125–7; *see also banlieue*
misogyny 51–2; ethnicity, merger 91–6; racism, contrast 78
Mohammad, Feiz 80, 99
Mohanty, Chandra 139, 142, 156
Monde, Le (print media) 105, 167
Motta, Philippe 118

mouvement des indigènes 170
mouvement des indigènes de la Republique (MIR) 152
Moyon, Richard 128
Mucchielli, Laurent 117, 128, 155–6; structural accounts 129
multiculturalism 70; discourses 90; feminism, dichotomy (identification) 98–9; language/policy, adoption 4–5; policies, critique 29
Muslims: Algerians, citizenship rights (extension) 172; anti-Muslim conspiracy 50–4; anti-Muslim conspiracy, competitive racisms (relationship) 96–101; backgrounds, stigmatisation/discrimination 81; *banlieue* (problem) 175; community, condemnation 80; culture, rape (linking) 97–8; defendants, case involvement 90; identification 102; identity 6; man, problem 6–7; masculinity, representation 82; misogynists 33; 'Muslim Other' 191–2; non-Muslim complainants, case involvement 90; population, focus 62; rapes 66; repressive sexuality 121–2; society, responsibility 58; terrorist hegemonic categorisation 53; womanhood, Western trope 93; women, deveiling (symbolism) 77; young Lebanese Muslim man, postcolonial habitus 55–7; young Muslim man 187; young Muslim man, responses 80–2

Naffine, Ngaire 19
narrative, truth 139
'nasty immigrant,' impact 191
'nasty migrants,' impact 101–3
national goodness 92
national identity, loyalty 156
nationalism: feminist perspective 95; rape, relationship 64–5
nation, rapes (attacks) 64–5
native informant: problem 141; role 6
New Bedford gang rape trial 38
New South Wales (NSW): Bureau of Crime Statistics and Research, press release 74; jails, security (tightening) 12; Rape Crisis Centre 76, 85, 100; Rape Crisis Centre, right-wing perspective 74–5
Ni Proxo Ni Macho 194
Ni Putes Ni Soumises (NPNS) 1, 129, 137, 145, 153, 163; *banlieue* (women,

220 *Index*

manifesto) 163–7; demonstration 173; feminist politics, possibility 188–90; heterosexist feminism 176–9; immigrant women, French women (contrast) 167–9; normative feminine identity, reinforcement 176–9; personal experience, politicisation 164–7; public reception 182–3; Republican integrationism, revisiting 179–82

NiqaBitch, performance art 194

Nique Ta Mère (NTM) 131

non-White men 126

non-White women, feminist position 190

normative female sexuality, reproduction 127

normative feminine identity, reinforcement 176–9

normative gender identity: articulation 178; reinforcement 14–18

normative heterosexuality/rape continuum 18–19

normative sexuality 20; understanding 27

North African characters 109–10

North African immigrants: sexual repression 122; testimonies 140

Notes of a Native Son 154

NSW Parliamentary Library briefing party, AEM/KEM response examination 11

objectification, pleasure 21

objective truth, concept 139–40

Odger, Stephen 98–9

Okin, Susan Moller 29

orientalism: generalised tropes 119; representations 192

'out-of-control ethnic gangs,' usage 72–3

Ozouf, Mona 171, 178

PaCS movement 171

Parité movement 170, 173

Pashtun tribal code, journalistic account 91

Patai, Raphael 88

pathological deviant, stereotypical image 52

patriarchy, re-affirmation 168

Pech, Marie-Estelle 122, 124–5, 129

Peralva, Angelina 106

'performing the victim' 35–8

perpetrators, determination 13–14

personal experience, politicisation 164–7

personal identity, facets (inscription) 55–6

personal motivations, irrelevance 58–9

personal vindication 153–4

perverted Arab, representation 125

'petite beurette, la' 142, 144–51

petite caïd 143–4, 149

phallocentric Black masculinity, glorification 81–2

Philadelphoff-Puren, Nina 78

Philippe, Gérard 179

plea-bargaining arrangement 10

police, complaint 147

politicality marginality 165

politically sympathetic editor/collaborator, role (celebration) 166–7

political trial 96

politicisation, removal 96

politics: anti-racist-feminist politics 193–4; feminist politics, possibility 188–90; judicialization 5

Ponchelet, Sophie 145

pornographic heterosexual script, usage 26

pornographic vignettes 24–6

postcolonial, feminist (reconciliation) 151–4

post-colonial, woman (coupling) 156

postcolonial Australian state 5

postcolonial feminism 154

postcolonial habitus 55–7, 164, 192; interrogations 157–8

postcolonial/subaltern women, voice (over-privileging) 157

postcolonial theory 157

post-Enlightenment theory, examination 139

power: effect 55–6; gendered structures, re-interrogation 87

Poynting, Scott 73–4

Priest, Tim 70–1

Prince Charming, fantasy 124, 127

protest masculinity 49–56; demonstrations 74

prudish patriarchal Arabs 109–11

public discourses, analysis 3–4

race: acts, boredom (impact) 14; consciousness 146–9; informative categories 44; language 7; left wing anti-racist responses 72–4; left wing feminist responses 74–6; race/gender consciousness 154; right-wing feminist responses 76–8; talking 60; young Muslim man, responses 80–2

racial hierarchy 133–4; external discourses 57

racial imperative, rapist awareness 52

racialised rapes 7

racial issue, discussion 68

racial marker, absence 74

racial stereotyping 70

racism: acts 57–8; anti-racism, feminism (contrast) 187–8; binary 129;

Index 221

competition 49–50; competitive racism 96–101; institutional racism, impact 111; issues, confrontation 108; left wing anti-racist responses 72–4; left wing feminist responses 74–6; misogyny, contrast 78; responsibility, transfer 71; right wing feminist responses 76–8; sexisms, intersection 57–9; site 128–9; talking 60; young Muslim man, responses 80–2
racist abuse (letters) 64
rape: appeal court 24–8; attacks 64–5; condemnation 80; convictions, duration 75–6; crime, cultural specificity 69; cultural context 89–96; debate, culture (examination) 68; description, language selection 25–6; discourses (Sheehan) 87–8; education 16–18; eroticism, reinforcement 24; feminisation process 20; gang rape 18; gangs, attack 1; graphic description 22; impasse 2; initial political responses 60–2; inter-racial/ stranger rape, problem (exaggeration) 45; language, intervention (framing) 65; legal treatment 44; legislation, introduction 62–5; male rape, possibility (exclusion) 17; miscommunication/ deviance 15–16; mis-education 126; nationalism, relationship 64–5; normative heterosexuality/rape continuum 18–19; opportunistic encounter 14–15; public responses 60; race, significance (analysis) 69; racialised rape 7; real rape 150, 186–7; real rape, appearance 19–22; reporting, rates (increase) 75; reprehensible realm 16; retaliatory rapes 77; second rape 34–5; significance, conceptualisation (Sheehan) 95; telephone counseling service, usage 37; trivialisation, accusations 14; war weapon 2, 26–7; *see also* gang rape; Sydney gang rapes
'Rape: The All-American Crime' (Griffin) 23
rape trials: feminist critiques 41; pornographic vignettes 24–6; process, victim (experience) 36
rape victims: Australian court treatment 85; creation 22–4; dominant constructions 44; dressing, provocation 99–100; 'fallen angel' 38–42; handling 85; identity, strategic performances 43; judicial treatment 90; normative categorisations 36

rapists: account 138; crimes 96; description 86–9; deviant creation 87; discourses 33–4, 49–54; masculinity, ace 55; racism 73; racist remarks, reporting 71; sexism 73; villain, identification 109
Razack, Sherene 30, 46, 61
real rape 150, 186–7; appearance 19–22
Reid, Campbell 70
re-membering/re-telling, struggle 47
Republic: *beurette* 137; (sexually) lost *banlieues* 117; *see also* France
Republican feminist discourse 148
Republican integrationism, revisiting 179–82
Republican values, paradigm 182
resistance, space 43–5
Richards, Bertrand 23
right-wing discourses, persuasiveness 71
risk taking 22–3
Robert-Dinard, Pascale 119–21, 124
romance, stereotypes 151
Rosello, Mireille 106
'Roxanne's Crucifix' 100
Rutherford, Jennifer 102
R v AEM (NSWCCA 58) 24–5; Latham categorisation 27; rape case, racial/ ethnic acknowledgment (Latham refusal) 69; victims, interviews 46–7
R v AEM Snr, AEM Jnr and KEM (2001) 10–11; appeal court judgment (2002) 15–16
R v Chami, M. Skaf, Ghanem, B. Skaf (unreported judgment; District Court of New South Wales) 25–6
R v KEM (NSWCCA 58) 24–6; rape case, racial/ethnic acknowledgment (Latham refusal) 69; rape, Lathan categorisation 27; victims, interviews 46–7
R v MAK: Justice Hidden decision (NSWSC 237) 28–31; Justice Sully decision 16–18
R v MM (NSWCCA 58) 24–6
R v MSK (Justice Hidden decision; NSWSC 237) 28–31
R v MSK (NSWSC 319) 16–17
Ryan, Peter 67–8

Said, Edward: orientalist imagery 6, 88–9
Salhi, Abdel-Illah 131
Sanoussi, Mahmoud 75
Santucci, Françoise-Marie 118
Scott, Joan 157, 163–4, 167
second rape 34–5
secularism *see laïcité*

222 *Index*

self-defeating notions, rejection 42
self-discovery 138
self-narrative (truth) 137–40
self-presentation 138
self-representation, conformity 127
Servan-Schreiber, Claude 170
sex: identification (exemplification) 113;
luring (script) 86
sexism: acts 57–8; binary 129; issues,
confrontation 108; racism, intersection
57–9; site 128–9
sexist violence, ethnicisation/racialisation 178
sexual acts 15
sexual deprivation 127
sexuality: normative view 134; repression
122–3
sexually lost *banlieues* (Republic) 117;
media responses 117
sexual offence, category 10–11
sexual sameness, disavowal 177–8
sexual violence: ethnicisation/racialisation
178; hidden truth 107; responses,
channeling 189; situating 117–19;
symbolic communal dimension 26–7
Sheehan, Paul 8, 13, 20, 46, 82, 84; anti-
Muslim conspiracy claim 54; brothers,
behaviour 88–9; French context 117–18;
K brother discussion 48; link, proposal
141; proceedings reporting 51; right-
wing commentary 74–5
signes religieux ostensibles, les 171
Skaf, Bilal 12, 49; actions, horror 12–13;
engagement, cessation 49–50; prison
sentence 75; rapes 66; rapes, reporting
70; sentence, reduction 75–6; young
men representation 82
Skaf, Mohammed 12
Skaf trials 11–13
slut, trapping 143
Smart, Carol 23
Smith, Sidonie 154
social causation, question 21
social rejects, culture (masculine culture)
73–4
socio-political feminist response 63
'Soldiers of Granville Boys' 65, 81–2
SOS Racisme 181–2
Souleymane 113–14
soumises, les 177
Spivak, Gayatri 139; argument 151–2;
questions 155
Squale, La (The Tearaway) 8, 18, 105;
female follow-up, presentation 112;
story 108–9

Stevenson, Andrew 26, 66
Stoquart, Josée 137, 140–1; collaboration
141; Third World Woman characterising/
stereotyping 148–9
Stubbs, Julie 45
Suleri, Sara 154, 156
Sully, Justice: decision 16–18; logical
conclusion 18
survivor: discourses 33; testimony 137–40
Sydney gang rapes 126; analysis
176; context 123, 131; non-White
male actors, discourses 158; riots,
connections 78–9; *see also* gang rape
Sydney gang rape trials 8, 45; conflict,
points 73; context 72; first trials 10–11;
judges, reasoning 20–1; K brothers 13;
media coverage 77; media/political
discourses 49; media reporting 65–6;
notoriety 13; public discourses,
emergence 118–19; *R v. AEM Snr, AEM
Jnr and KEM* (2001) 10–11; *R v. AEM
Snr, AEM Jnr and KEM* (2001), appeal
court judgment (2002) 15–16; *R v MAK*
16–18; *R v MSK* 16–18; Skaf trials
12–13; treatment 72–3
Sykes, Roberta 47–8
sympathy 38–9; limitation 36–7

Tabar, Paul 73
terminology, examination 7–8
testimony, collaborator role 140–4
Third Republic, Enlightenment
principles 180
Third World Woman: 'backward Third
World Woman' 167–8; characterising/
stereotyping 148–9; dominant stereotype
142; figure, construction 155–6;
freedom 143; juxtaposition 167–8; right,
promotion 157; voice, liberation 156
Thomas, Clarence 153
Tourancheau, Patricia 122–3, 125
tournantes, les 1, 8, 84, 98, 105, 128;
acceptance 118; affective deficit 117;
characterisation 120; *Dans l'enfer des
tournantes* 137–40; gang rapist 49; male
responses 42; phenomenon 69, 118;
term, usage 117–19; tribal practices 124
Toussaint (gang leader) 108–10;
interactions, reversal 114–15
trial, 'playing the game' 43
tribal imagery, discovery 124
tribal practices 124
'true' Western Pakistani culture, reading
29–30

truth: discovery 35–6; self-narrative
137–40
Tyson, Mike (rape trial) 16

unFrench, extrapolation 126

vaginal injuries: medical evidence, Court
rejection 100; representation 100–1
Vaissiére, Caroline 124
Vichy regime, realities 181
victims: actions, imprudence 23;
creation 85–9; cross-examination,
right 16–17; damage, articulation 22;
description 85–6; determination 13–14;
identification 46; interviews 46–7;
number, involvement 67; performing
35–8; playing, need 38; support/
sympathy, mobilisation 47; sympathy
38–9; targets, ease 58; treatment 147;
virgin victim, image 86
villains: creation 85–9; ideal villain 88
viol collectif 117
violence: absence 177; *banlieue*
(reinforcement) 182–3; male perspective
42–3
'violence against women' 77
violences urbaines, les 106; *banlieue*
(relationship) 106–7; manifestation 117
viol en réunion 117
Virgin Mary, images 39
virgin victim, image 86
voileurs et violeurs 120–3
Volpp, Leti 97

Wagner, Tegan 13, 33, 88, 137; emotive
impression (Sheehan) 85; experience,
documentation 72; gang rape, linkage
58; right-wing perspective 74–5; role,
identification 35; text, framing 139; trial
34–8; trial description 53
Walker, Alice 155
Wallace, Natasha 51
War on Terror, context 88, 89

Washington, Desiree (rape trial) 16
Watson, Julia 154
Welzer-Lang, Daniel 128–9
Western liberalism, framework 188
Western superiority, discourse 193
White: assertion 48; characters,
presentation 110–11; society,
responsibility 58; virtue 47
white angels 33
White/Australian, reading 48
White Australian society, Arabic-speaking
community (division) 68
White *banlieue* residents, inclusion 110
whiteness 5; invisible marker 46–9;
processes 47; valuable property 47
Willis, Karen 188; insistence 78;
perspective 100; right-wing perspective
74–5
Wockner, Cindy 68
women: division 113–14; manifesto
163–7; marginalisation 129; normative
categorisations 36; over-essentialising
21–2; post-colonial, coupling 156;
presence, sexual provocation 28;
protection 133; protection (Cronulla
2005) 78–80; respect 110; rights 158;
risk taking behaviour 22–3; thing,
representation 133; violence 42–3
Woodham, Ron 53; Skaf letter 12
Wretched of the Earth (Fanon) 132
Wright, Richard 154–5

Yasmine, rebellious act 112–13
young *banlieue* residents, conformity
130–1
young Lebanese Muslim man: postcolonial
habitus 55–7
young Muslim man 187; construction 6;
responses 80–2
Yúdice, George 164, 166

Zappi, Sylvia 163, 166
Zoulous 124